THE
CHINESE
ECONOMY

THE CHINESE ECONOMY

GREGORY C. CHOW
Princeton University

HARPER & ROW, PUBLISHERS, New York

Cambridge, Hagerstown, Philadelphia, San Francisco,
London, Mexico City, São Paulo, Singapore, Sydney

1817

To my father
Tin-Pong Chow
and the memory of my mother
Pauline Law Chow
(1893–1963)
who contributed to improving the welfare
of the Chinese people

Sponsoring Editor: David Forgione
Project Editor: Ronni Strell
Text Design: Betty Sokol
Cover Design: Wanda Lubelska
Text Art: Fine Line Inc.
Production: Debi Forrest-Bochner
Compositor: ComCom Division of Haddon Craftsmen, Inc.
Printer and Binder: R.R. Donnelley & Sons Company

The Chinese Economy

Library of Congress Cataloging in Publication Data

84 85 86 87 88 9 8 7 6 5 4 3 2 1

Contents

Starred sections are more technical and may be omitted without loss of continuity.

chapter **3** _____

Agriculture   77

chapter **4** _____

Industry   119

chapter **5** _____

Consumption   157

Preface

The main purpose of this book is to apply the basic tools of economic analysis to the economy of the People's Republic of China. Since many readers may not be familiar with the tools required for such an analysis, I explain these tools as I apply them to the study of China. This book is therefore as much about economic analysis as about the Chinese economy. It is written for students of economics who would like to understand China, for students of China who would like to understand economics, and for professional economists and lay readers who would like to understand the Chinese economy.

Economics is a difficult subject. To master it one has to learn how it can be applied to explain actual economic phenomena. In the undergraduate economics curriculum of Princeton University, for example, after a student takes courses on the basic tools of economic analysis, including econometric methods and macro- and microeconomic theory, he or she selects from subjects that are "extensions and applications of economic theory," including managerial economics, industrial organization, labor economics, urban economics, corporate finance, economic growth in less developed countries, international trade and finance, income distribution, public finance, money and banking, Soviet-type economies, American economic history, and population problems, among others. The study of the Chinese economy can be considered one of these applied subjects.

The study of the Chinese economy is interesting to economists for a number of reasons. First, China has a different cultural background and a different set of social and political institutions from the Western countries, in which most of the tools of economic analysis have been developed. It is therefore interesting to see how these tools can be applied to China and how they ought to be further developed or modified in the Chinese context. Second, since the People's Republic of China was founded, many drastic changes in economic policy and in economic institutions have taken place. Economists often envy the ability of natural scientists to conduct controlled experiments, which are rare in economics. The Chinese government has in fact performed important experiments in economics, and we should not lose the opportunity to study their results. Third, since the late 1970s much more information on the Chinese economy has become available. It is time for us to digest, to scrutinize, and possibly to help improve the economic data on China.

The prerequisite for reading this book is a solid introductory course in economics. For lay readers who are interested in understanding the Chinese economy such a course is also necessary. Although I have tried to explain all the necessary economic tools in the book itself, certain sections of the book, indicated by an asterisk in the table of contents and in the text, are more technical and may be difficult for readers whose preparation in economics includes no more than an introductory course. Such readers should skip the technical material in these sections and go on to study the less technical material, which forms about seven-eighths of this book. They should first glance through the theoretical sections of Chapter 1 and return to them only after studying Chapters 3 and 4.

One characteristic of this book is that it is brief on institutional details. Yet it probably has more institutional material than a text entitled *The American Economy* or *The World Economy.* To include more institutional material would be to make the book too lengthy. Readers wishing to learn about Chinese economic institutions can refer to the *Almanac of China's Economy 1981; 1982* and to other sources cited in the text. This book was written with the main purpose of teaching the student how to think about and how to analyze economic problems. Once the analytical skills are acquired and their application to the Chinese economy fully appreciated, the student can easily read up on additional institutional material and will understand its relevance.

Having grown up in China and completed my freshman year at a Chinese university, I have always had an interest in the Chinese economy. Since the 1960s I have served as economics consultant to the government in Taiwan on numerous occasions and learned how economics is applicable to a Chinese society. In 1980 I became Chairman of the American Economic Association's Committee on United States–China Exchanges in Economics. While lecturing in China in 1980 and 1982, I became keenly aware of the need expressed by my Chinese colleagues for modernization of the economics curriculum in their universities. In 1984, I organized an Economics Symposium to teach modern economics in China on behalf of the Chinese Ministry of Education and the material in this book was used in the symposium. Students of economics in China and in the United States have much to learn from one another. It is my hope that this book will contribute to the exchange of economic ideas and possibly to the development of economics on both sides of the Pacific.

While I am solely responsible for the contents of this book, I have been fortunate enough to receive helpful comments from Wang Chuan-Lun of the People's University, Nicholas Lardy of the University of Washington, and Yang Xaokai of Princeton and Wuhan Universities, who read drafts of the entire manuscript; from Robert Dernberger of the University of Michigan, Thomas Rawski of the University of Toronto, James Tsao of the U.S. International Trade Commission, and Wang Chi-tsu of Nankai University, who read Chapters 1 to 4; from T. W. Schultz of the University of Chicago and Anthony Tang of Vanderbilt University, who read Chapter 3; from Marc Nerlove of the University of Pennsylvania, who read Chapters 3 and 7; from Ding Shi-chang of the Chinese Academy of Social Sciences, who read Chapter 5; from John Taylor and Kenneth West of Princeton University, who read Chapter 6; from Gary Becker of the University of Chicago and Ansley Coale of Princeton University, who read Chapter 7; from Avinash Dixit of Princeton University, who read Chapter 8; and from K. C. Yeh of the Rand Corporation, who gave general advice and suggestions on the project. To all of them I express my sincere thanks. Some of these individuals may disagree with me on specific aspects of the book, and they should not be held responsible for its shortcomings. I would also like to thank Pia Ellen for typing the manuscript with efficiency and good spirit. The research on Chapter 6 was supported by a grant from the National Science Foundation.

GREGORY C. CHOW

chapter *1*

How a Market Economy Works

1.1 SOME IMPORTANT QUESTIONS IN ECONOMICS

In order to determine what phenomena to describe so that we can understand the Chinese economy, we need to know what the science of economics studies. We will therefore begin by discussing the subject matter of economics and the important questions one should ask about any economy.

According to the *Statistical Yearbook of China, 1981* (Chinese State Statistics Bureau, 1982, p. 20), the national income of the People's Republic of China was 388.7 billion yuan (RMB—People's currency in China) in 1981. With a population of about 1 billion, this amounted to about 390 yuan per person. At the official exchange rate of 1.9 yuan to $1, the per capita national income would have been $205 in 1981. This figure is only a very rough indicator of the output per person in China for a number of reasons: the concepts of national income are different; the exchange rate may not accurately reflect the ratio of the purchasing powers of the currencies in the two countries; and, more important, in a less developed country, a larger fraction of consumption is derived from home production, which is not recorded in the national income statistics. Be that as it may, national income per capita in the United States in 1981 was $10,237, about 50 times the corresponding Chinese figure. Our first question is, "What explains the quantity of output per person in a country—why is one country rich and another country poor?"

The output of a country depends on the natural resources, accumulated physical resources (stock of physical capital goods), and human resources (stock of human capital) available. In most cases, the endowment of natural resources is the least important. One can think of countries, such as Japan today and England before World War II, that have limited natural resources but are very rich. Today, a small country

1

can be rich simply by having a large deposit of oil, but many rich countries still do not have abundant natural resources. Even the quantity of agricultural output alone, not to speak of the entire output of an economy, does not depend mainly on the amount of land available. For example, mainland China has .27 acre of cultivated cropland per capita, while Taiwan has .12 acre, and yet agricultural output per capita in Taiwan is greater than in China—Taiwan is more than self-sufficient in agriculture, while China is not. Perhaps the most important factor in a country's output is the quality and quantity of human resources available. At the end of World War II, much of the physical capital of West Germany and Japan was destroyed, but these two countries have succeeded in rebuilding their economies until they are now among the most productive in the world. An important reason for their success is the human capital available in these two countries, in terms of managerial, scientific, and technical personnel as well as skilled and hardworking labor forces. Another is the way their economic institutions are organized.

Besides the three factors of production just mentioned, the output of a country depends on how these factors are put together in production. The type of technology used to combine these factors into products is important. Having an abundance of land and other natural resources, of machinery and buildings, and of skilled labor and technical personnel is not sufficient for a high level of output if outmoded technology is employed. Of course, if skilled labor and good technical personnel are present, outmoded technology is not likely to be found being employed in production. But even with sufficient qualified personnel and physical resources, it takes time to organize and to adopt a suitable kind of technology. One could not build another IBM in China by simply duplicating the corporation's physical plants and qualified personnel. An entire economy, with many and diverse economic enterprises, is that much harder to reproduce merely by having the required resources.

As important as technology, if not more so, is the kind of economic institutions that a country adopts to produce its products. The economic institutions determine how different productive units will coordinate in producing the goods that a country needs. A market economy represents one type of organization of economic institutions, and a centrally planned economy represents another. These two types of economic organizations have two different sets of rules in determining what kinds of goods to produce, how people are organized to produce them, and who will get to use the products. What and how to produce and how to distribute—in other words, *production* and *distribution*—are among the important questions in economics.

The ultimate aim of production is consumption, either by individuals or by the government. Some of the output produced during a given period is for consumption during the same period, while the remainder is for future consumption. The latter may be either durable consumer goods or capital goods that can be used to produce more consumption or capital goods. How a society decides on the percentages of output devoted to consumption and to capital accumulation is another important question. A country that devotes a larger percentage of current output to capital accumulation can be expected to grow more rapidly. Part of the process of economic development takes the form of capital accumulation. Another part, let us not forget, takes the form of the accumulation of human capital. Still other parts are the adoption of more advanced technology and the improvement of economic organizations.

Chapters 1 and 2 of this book are devoted to theoretical discussions of how a market economy and the Chinese planned economy, respectively, are organized to answer the above important economic questions. All economies in the world have certain elements that function like a market economy and other elements that are determined by government planning. The extent to which market forces and government planning affect an economy differs among countries. The Chinese economy relies on central planning to a large extent, but the market is used to solve some economic problems. Therefore, it is essential to understand how both types of economic organizations work. We discuss the functioning of a market economy first because more is known about the subject. Not only do we have good theoretical works on the market economy, accumulated for over two centuries, but we have also observed the functioning of market economies for centuries. We know less about centrally planned economies, because central planning of complicated economic activities has a much shorter history, beginning seriously in the Soviet Union only in the late 1920s, and because most qualified economists in the latter half of this century have done their research on market economies.

1.2   THE EFFICIENCY OF AN EXCHANGE ECONOMY

A market is where individuals can exchange or trade the goods they own. An economy consists of economic units that produce, consume, and trade. To begin our discussion of a market economy, let us leave out production for the moment and consider the trading activity alone, assuming that somehow goods have already been produced. To simplify the discussion even further, consider two individuals, a farmer and a textile worker, trading in the economy, with the farmer owning 100 kilograms of rice and the worker owning 20 meters of cotton cloth. The quantities of the two commodities will be denoted by x_1 and x_2, respectively. Since the farmer needs cloth and the worker needs food, they may go to the market to trade. Let us suppose that the farmer agrees to exchange 50 kilograms of rice for 10 meters of the worker's cloth, and the worker consents. After the trade the farmer has 50 kilograms of rice and 10 meters of cloth; the worker has 50 kilograms of rice and 10 meters of cloth. Both are better off, or at least neither person is worse off, because otherwise they would not have traded voluntarily.

An important point can be made concerning free trade among individuals. If we assume (and some people may not want to assume) that individuals can decide for themselves which bundles of goods are better than other bundles, allowing free trade can only increase the economic welfare of the individuals engaged in the exchange. In the above example, the farmer starts with a bundle consisting of 100 units of rice and 0 unit of cloth, and ends up with 50 units and 10 units, respectively. That is, he starts with the bundle $(x_1, x_2) = (100,0)$ and ends up with the bundle $(x_1, x_2) = (50,10)$. We assume that he prefers the bundle (50,10) to (100,0); otherwise he would not have traded. Similarly, the worker must prefer (50,10) to (0,20). The welfare of both is increased.

The second point to stress is that when voluntary trading ceases, no individual can improve his welfare by trade without decreasing the welfare of some other individual. When an economy is in such a situation, it is said to be *Pareto optimal*. The term is named after the economist Vilfredo Pareto (1848–1923), who taught economics and sociology at the University of Lausanne in Switzerland. In an economy where people can trade, free exchanges will yield a *Pareto-optimal solution.* If a farmer wishes to trade with a worker to improve his welfare without decreasing the worker's, but is prevented from doing so, the economy fails to be *Pareto optimal,* or *Pareto efficient.* An economy certainly cannot be called efficient if there is any way to improve the welfare of one of its members without decreasing the welfare of somebody else. (An underlying assumption is that the worker does not feel worse off because he is jealous of the farmer becoming better off. In such a case, the gain of the farmer through trade should be partly distributed to the worker to compensate for his psychic loss, but this point complicates our present discussion.)

Let us examine a Pareto-optimal solution more closely. When we claim that the solution (50,10) for the farmer and (50,10) for the textile worker is efficient, we mean that, starting from this solution, the two parties will not agree to trade anymore. For example, the farmer may offer 1 more kilogram of rice to the worker in exchange for .204 meter of cloth, but the worker refuses and is willing to give the farmer only .196 meter. The farmer may offer to buy back 1 kilogram of rice for .196 meter of cloth, but the worker again refuses and demands .204 meter of cloth back for her rice. Trade will not take place, and the solution (50,10) and (50,10) is thus a Pareto-optimal solution. Note that there are usually many Pareto-optimal solutions. When the farmer and the worker started with the bundles (100,0) and (0,20), respectively, the farmer might have bargained harder, trading 40 kilograms of rice for 12 meters of cloth. The worker might have agreed, and the solution would have been (60,12) and (40,8). If this solution were reached, and if they could not agree on further trade, it would be another pareto-optimal solution.

This discussion can be presented in an Edgeworth diagram, named after the British economist Francis Y. Edgeworth (1891–1926), who invented it (see Figure 1.1). Along the horizontal axis is measured the quantity x_1 of rice that the farmer possesses, and along the vertical axis is measured the quantity x_2 of his cloth. The bundle $(x_1, x_2) = (50,10)$ is represented by the point in the middle of the diagram.

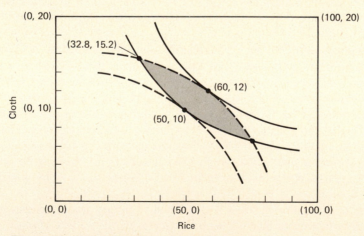

Figure 1.1 Pareto optimality and the Edgeworth diagram.

The bundle (60,12) is represented by another point northeast of it. The farmer certainly prefers the bundle (60,12) to the bundle (50,10) because he has more of both commodities. Once we know the farmer's bundle, we can easily determine the worker's bundle because the total quantity of rice is 100 and the total quantity of cloth is 20. Thus, if the farmer has (60,12) the worker must have (40,8). We will present our discussion mainly in terms of the farmer's bundles. If the reader wishes to find out what is happening to the worker, he can do the subtractions to get the worker's bundles, or he can turn Figure 1.1 upside down, using the point (100,20), now located at the southwestern corner rather than the northeastern, as the point (0,0) from the worker's viewpoint. We have shown two Pareto-optimal solutions (50,10) and (60,12), measured from the viewpoint of the farmer.

Consider the point (50,10). We have stated that if the farmer is asked to give up 1 unit of rice, he needs to be paid .204 unit of cloth. However, if he is asked to trade back cloth for rice, he is willing to pay only .196 unit of cloth for an additional unit of rice. The reason behind these numbers is that the more rice a person has, relative to cloth, the less he will care for having an additional unit of rice. In our example, the farmer is equally satisfied with the bundles (50,10), (49, 10.204), and (51, 9.804). In Figure 1.1, we represent all such points by the solid curve passing through (50,10). This curve is an *indifference curve* representing the preference of the farmer, who is indifferent among all bundles or points on this curve. The worker's indifference curve passing through the same point is represented by the broken curve, but you have to turn Figure 1.1 upside down and relabel all the points [changing (100,20) to (0,0), and so on] to read it. At the point (50,10), the two parties cannot agree to trade further because all the solution points that the worker is willing to accept, as represented by the broken indifference curve, are not acceptable to the farmer since they lie below the farmer's (solid) indifference curve. The only acceptable solution to both is (50,10). The point (60,12) in the diagram represents another Pareto-optimal solution. Starting from this point, the two parties cannot improve themselves by further trade.

Could it happen that, after the initial trade, the farmer ends up with (32.81, 15.24) and the worker with (67.19, 4.76) according to Figure 1.1? This point is where the farmer's indifference curve passing through (50,10) intersects the worker's indifference curve passing through (60,12). This point is not a Pareto-optimal solution because the parties will decide to trade further. By going down in the southeastern direction to any point in the shaded area, both parties will benefit. The farmer prefers the points inside the shaded area because they are northeast of his indifference curve passing through (32.81, 15.24). Similarly, the worker prefers these points because, after the figure is turned upside down, they are northeast of her indifference curve passing through the same point, which reads (67.19, 4.76) in her scale. Thus as long as the indifference curves of the two parties intersect at a certain point, they can improve themselves by trading from that point. That point is not Pareto optimal.

There are other Pareto-optimal points between the points (50,10) and (60,12). If the farmer is a good bargainer, starting from (32.81, 15.24), he will end up very close to (60,12), leaving the worker with a small gain from the trade. If the worker is a good bargainer, she will make the farmer take a point close to (50,10), leaving most of the gain for herself. There is a curve passing the points (50,10) and (60,12) representing all the Pareto-optimal points. It is called a *contract curve*. From any point on the contract curve, the two parties cannot improve themselves by further trading. At each point on the contract curve the indifference curves of the parties must be tangential to each other, as shown in Figure 1.1 for the two points (50,10) and (60,12). We have pointed out that if their indifference curves intersect, the two parties can improve themselves by trade. The contract curve, not drawn on the diagram, is a curve going from southwest to northeast passing through the points (50,10) and (60,12).

1.3 THE DEMAND FUNCTION

We would like to understand: (1) how prices affect the quantities of goods traded in the market, and (2) how prices are determined in the market. In the preceding section, we did not discuss prices explicitly, but the tools introduced here can be used to answer these two related questions about prices. Concerning the first question, common sense tells us that if the price of cloth is high, relative to the price of rice, the farmer having 100 kilograms of rice will buy a small quantity of cloth by trading his rice. If the price of cloth is low, he will buy more cloth. Let us find out why by using the farmer's *indifference curves.*

   Suppose that in a market many farmers and textile workers trade. Somehow the prices of rice and cloth are determined; how the prices are determined will be discussed in Section 1.4. We now ask how the prices affect the quantity of cloth that a farmer will buy and the quantity of rice that he will sell. Assume the price of rice is $.40 per kilogram and the price of cloth is $2.00 per meter. The farmer having 100 kilograms of rice can get .20 meter of cloth by trading 1 kilogram of rice. The bundles of goods available to him by trading different quantities of rice are points on a straight line joining the points (100,0) and (0,20), as shown in the line *AB* in Figure 1.2. *AB* is called the farmer's *budget line.* It shows the different bundles of goods that he can buy with his budget when he has 100 units of rice and the prices are $.40 and $2.00. Since the price of rice is $.40 per unit, the farmer's income from selling all his rice is $40. He can use this income to buy any combination of rice and cloth as long as the total cost

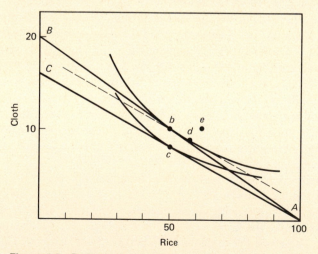

Figure 1.2 Deriving demand from indifference curves.

is $40. Let (x_1, x_2) denote the quantities of rice and cloth, respectively. The possible bundles (x_1, x_2) are given by equation 1.1, which is the equation for budget line AB shown in Figure 1.2:

$$\$.40\ x_1 + \$2.00\ x_2 = \$40 \tag{1.1}$$

Which point on the budget line will the farmer choose? It will be a point tangential to an indifference curve. If an indifference curve crosses the budget line at that point, the farmer can move along the budget line to get to a point on a higher indifference curve (on the northeast of the former indifference curve). Only when the budget line is tangential to an indifference curve at that point will the farmer be unable to move to a higher indifference curve. Given budget line AB, the farmer will settle on the point $(50, 10)$, or point b in Figure 1.2.

What if the unit price of cloth were to increase from $2.00 to $2.50 while the price of rice remained the same? If the farmer were to spend all his income of $40 on buying cloth, he would get only $40/$2.50, or 16 meters of cloth rather than 20. His budget line is given by the line AC in Figure 1.2 or by the equation

$$\$.40\ x_1 + \$2.50\ x_2 = \$40 \tag{1.2}$$

Again, along this new budget line, the farmer would find a point c touching the highest indifference curve. The new point c shows that he will buy less cloth—say, 8 units instead of the 10 units mentioned earlier. This example shows that as the price of cloth increases, the farmer will buy less of it.

According to point c in Figure 1.2, when the price of cloth increases from $2.00 to $2.50, the farmer uses about the same amount of rice. The reason for not buying more rice when it is cheap relative to cloth is that, with the same money income of $40, but with the new prices of $2.50 for cloth and $.40 for rice, the farmer is poorer than before in real terms. There is inflation as compared with the former prices of $2.00 for cloth and $.40 for rice. Although the farmer's money income is the same, his *real income* is less. He can no longer afford the old bundle of $(50, 10)$. This bundle would now cost him $\$.40 \times 50 + \$2.50 \times 10 = \$45$, which is more than his income of $40. There is an inflation rate of $45/$40, or 1.125. What used to cost $1.00 now costs $1.125, or 12.5 percent more. The farmer's real income is less than before. To keep his real income constant, he would need to have $45 at the new prices, as compared with $40 at the old prices. He does not consume more rice now because his real income has decreased.

In the above discussion, we have touched upon two related important problems in economics, the measurement of inflation and of real income. Starting with a given bundle of goods $(x_1, x_2, \ldots, x_n)$ that the consumer wants at the prices $(p_1, p_2, \ldots, p_n)$, let the prices change to $(p_1^*, p_2^*, \ldots, p_n^*)$. The total value of the bundle at the old prices is

$$p_1 x_1 + p_2 x_2 + \ldots + p_n x_n = \sum_{i=1}^{n} p_i x_i$$

The total value at the new prices is $\sum_{i=1}^{n} p_i^* x_i$. If the latter value is higher, there is inflation. We measure inflation by the ratio

$$p^* = \sum_{i=1}^{n} p_i^* x_i \; / \; \sum_{i=1}^{n} p_i x_i \qquad\qquad (1.3)$$

which is called a *price index*. If the price index for the initial prices is set equal to 1, the price index for the new prices is given by the above number p^*. If money income is \$40 at the initial prices, and is \$45 at the new prices, we can measure real income at the new prices in units of the old dollars (dollars that have the same purchasing power as before) by dividing \$45 by the price index p^*, or \$45/p^*.

Two things are happening when the price of cloth increases from \$2.00 to \$2.50. One is inflation, which is reflected in the price index p^* and in a reduction in the real income of the farmer if his money income remains at \$40. The second is an increase in the price of cloth relative to rice. The *ratio* of the price of cloth to the price of rice increases from \$2.00/.40 to \$2.50/.40, or from 5 to 6.25. It will now cost the farmer 6.25 kilograms of rice for a meter of cloth. We say that the *relative price,* or price ratio, of cloth to rice has increased. When this happens, the farmer will substitute rice for cloth. These two effects of the change in the price of cloth from \$2.00 to \$2.50 are respectively called the *income effect* and the *substitution effect.* The former is due to the reduction of the real income of the farmer as a result of inflation. The second is due to the change in the relative price of cloth to rice, making cloth more expensive as compared with rice.

The income and substitution (or relative-price) effects of the change in the price of cloth (moving the budget line from *AB* to *AC*) can be represented in Figure 1.2 by using the broken budget line in the diagram. This broken line passes the old equilibrium point *b* but is parallel to the new budget line *AC*. It is represented by the equation

$$\$.40 \; x_1 + \$2.50 \; x_2 = \$45 \qquad\qquad (1.4)$$

Since the bundle $(x_1, x_2) = (50,10)$ satisfies this equation, it passes through the point $(50,10)$, or point *b* in Figure 1.2. The coefficients of this equation are .40 and 2.50, the same as the coefficients of equation 1.2 or the budget line *AC*. Therefore the broken budget line represented by equation 1.4 is parallel to the budget line *AC*. Let the broken budget line be tangential to another indifference curve (not shown in Figure 1.2) at the point *d*, which the farmer would choose if his budget line were the broken line. The change from point *b* to point *c* resulting from the increase in the price of cloth can be broken down into the change from *b* to *d* and the change from *d* to *c*. The change from *b* to *d* shows the *substitution effect.* If the real income of the farmer were to remain the same as before, or if his money income were to increase from \$40 to \$45, so that he could buy bundle *b* if he chose, he would prefer to have more rice and less cloth, as indicated by point *d*, because the relative price of cloth has increased. From Figure 1.2, we see that when the price of cloth changes from \$2.00 to \$2.50, and if the farmer has the same *real* income (or \$45 money income), the demand for cloth decreases from 10 units to about 9 units, while the demand for rice increases from 50 to about 56.25 units. In general, when the relative price of one commodity increases, with real income held constant, the consumer will buy less of it. This is the substitution effect. The change from point *d* to point *c* shows the *income effect.* The farmer actually does not have an income of \$45 as we assume hypothetically in drawing the broken budget line; his income is only \$40. Because his real income is lower than the broken budget line indicates, he chooses bundle c rather than d, implying less of both rice and cloth in this example.

Thus, by assuming different prices of cloth and using the farmer's indifference curves, we can determine the corresponding quantities of cloth that the farmer will buy by using the techniques of Figure 1.2. (See Problem 2 at the end of this chapter.) In general, if the real income of the farmer remains the same, and the relative price of cloth increases, the farmer will buy less cloth. This is the substitution effect. If the relative prices are fixed, and the farmer's real income increases, he will buy more of most goods. Some goods are called *inferior goods* if a person buys less of them when he gets richer. Thus the amount of each commodity that a consumer will buy depends on the relative prices of all commodities and the consumer's real income. This demand relationship can be represented by an equation.

Let $x_1, x_2, \ldots, x_n$ represent the quantities of the n commodities that a consumer will choose and $p_1, p_2, \ldots, p_n$ be their respective prices. Let I be the consumer's income. The *demand function* for the first good is

$$x_1 = f_1(p_1, p_2, \ldots, p_n, I) \tag{1.5}$$

showing that the quantity demanded by the consumer is a function both of the prices of all commodities and of the consumer's income. In our example, there are only two goods, rice and cloth, and we are discussing the demand function for the second good,

$$x_2 = f_2(p_1, p_2, I) \tag{1.6}$$

We know that when

$$(p_1, p_2, I) = (.40, 2.00, 40)$$

the demand for cloth is 10, implying

$$10 = f_2(.40, 2.00, 40)$$

We also know the demand when $p_2 = 2.50$, with either money income or real income held constant:

$$8.0 = f_2(.40, 2.50, 40), \text{ money income constant} \tag{1.7}$$

$$9.0 = f_2(.40, 2.50, 45), \text{ real income constant} \tag{1.8}$$

Observe that if all prices are 10 times as before and the farmer's money income is also 10 times as before, the demands for all commodities will be unchanged, implying

$$10 = f_2(4.00, 20.00, 400)$$

This is so because the budget line drawn by using the new prices and income remains AB in Figure 1.2. The equation

$$\$4.00\, x_1 + \$20.00\, x_2 = \$400$$

is simply equation 1.1 multiplied by 10. The most important point to remember about a demand function is that with real income kept constant, the demand for a commodity decreases as its relative price increases.

The relation between the quantity of a commodity that a consumer buys and the prices of *all* commodities and his income is the *demand function.* The relation between the demand for a commodity and its price, holding all other prices and money (or real) income fixed, is called a *demand curve.* The demand curve of the farmer for cloth is drawn in Figure 1.3, showing the different quantities of cloth that the farmer is willing to buy at different prices. We know $x_2 = 10$ when $p_2 = 2.00$, and $x_2 = 8.0$ when $p_2 = 2.50$, if money income is held constant. (For some purpose, we may want to define a demand curve holding real income constant. In this case, $x_2 = 9.0$ when $p_2 = 2.50$.) If there are many individuals buying cloth in the market, the *market demand curve* will show the *total* quantity of cloth that all individuals will buy at each hypothetical price. It is obtained by adding up the demands of all individuals (horizontally in Figure 1.3). It has the same shape as an individual demand curve, except that the quantity is larger corresponding to each price.

Using demand functions, we have answered the first question posed at the beginning of this section: How do prices affect the quantities that people will buy? We now consider the second question: How are prices determined in an exchange economy?

1.4 DETERMINATION OF MARKET PRICES

To understand how prices are determined, consider an economy consisting of 100 farmers, each owning 100 units of rice, and 100 textile workers, each owning 20 units of cloth. To keep the arithmetic simple, let the indifference curves of each person, farmer or worker, be the same as depicted in Figure 1.2. Let the 100 farmers and the 100 workers trade in the market. Only one price for rice and one price for cloth will prevail in the market if the farmers and workers know what prices others are paying and are not willing to accept a worse deal than the others; if a farmer sees that one worker is offering a lower price for his rice than a second worker, he will try to sell to the second worker. What are the prices of rice and cloth that will clear the market, and what are the total quantities of rice and cloth that will be purchased?

We have constructed the numerical example of Figure 1.2 to answer these questions easily. Try the prices $.40 for rice and $2.00 for cloth and see what happens. At

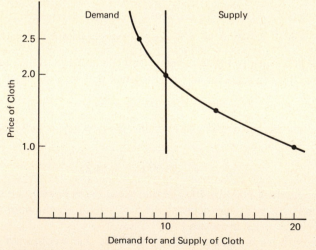

Figure 1.3 Demand and supply curves for cloth.

these prices, each farmer's budget line is AB in Figure 1.2 and his demand for cloth is 10 units, for which he will sell 50 units of rice. Since there are 100 identical farmers, together they will offer to buy 1,000 meters of cloth for 5,000 kilograms of rice. Each worker's budget line is also AB, because each owns 20 units of cloth at $2.00 per unit, thus having an income of $40 also. Each worker will also choose point b in Figure 1.2, which she can achieve by selling 10 units of cloth for 50 units of rice. The 100 workers will offer to sell a total of 1,000 units of cloth and offer to buy a total of 5,000 units of rice. Thus the workers offer to sell exactly the quantity of cloth that the farmers want to buy; they offer to buy exactly the quantity of rice that the farmers want to sell. The market is cleared at the prices $.40 and $2.00.

What would happen if the prices were $.40 and $2.50 instead? From Figure 1.2, we learn that each farmer wishes to buy 8 units of cloth and sell 50 units of rice, given his budget line AC. Each worker's budget line is parallel to AC because she faces the same prices as the farmer. It will pass point B because she owns 20 units of cloth. The reader should draw this budget line and mark a point e tangential to an indifference curve, somewhere northeast of point d, showing that the worker wishes to buy about 62.5 units of rice by selling 10 units of cloth. At the prices $(.40, 2.50)$, the 100 farmers will wish to buy 800 units of cloth and the 100 workers will offer to sell 1,000 units. When the supply of cloth exceeds the demand for cloth at the price of $2.50 per unit, the price will fall. The workers will lower the price to induce more farmers to buy more than 800 units of cloth, until the price reaches $2.00 per unit, at which both demand and supply equal 1,000 units. Similarly, if the price of cloth were set lower than $2.00, demand for cloth by the farmers would exceed the supply of cloth by the workers, and the price would increase to $2.00 when demand equaled supply. (See Problem 3.)

In Figure 1.3 we have also drawn a supply curve of cloth, which indicates that at the price of $2.00 each worker is willing to sell 10 units, and at the price of $2.50 each worker is also willing to sell 10 units in this example. Figure 1.3 can also be interpreted as showing the market demand curve for cloth of the 100 farmers and the market supply curve of cloth of the 100 workers. All we need to do is relabel the horizontal axis by making the quantities 100 times as large as before. Given $p_1 = .40$, the market price p_2 is determined by the intersection of the market demand curve and the market supply curve.

As we pointed out when we discussed the demand function in Section 1.3, the quantity demanded will not change if all prices and money income double. For example, if (p_1, p_2) becomes $(.80, 4.00)$ instead of $(.40, 2.00)$ and the farmer owning 100 units of rice has $80 in income instead of $40, the demand for rice and for cloth will remain the same as before. At the new prices, the worker owning 20 units of cloth will also have $80 in income instead of $40, and her demand for rice and for cloth will remain the same as before. Thus the reader can double all the prices in this discussion and arrive at the same results as before. In other words, only the *relative* price of cloth to rice is determined in Figure 1.3. In Figure 1.3 we have assumed $p_1 = .40$; but if we assume $p_1 = .80$, p_2 will be twice as large as indicated in the figure. Only relative prices are determined by the intersection of demand and supply in a market economy. (See Problems 4 and 5.) The determination of absolute prices depends mainly on the quantity of money as compared with the flow of goods in the economy; this subject is discussed in Chapter 6.

The process by which market prices are determined by demand and supply deserves closer examination. Referring to Figure 1.3, if the price of cloth happens to be $2.50, the price of rice being $.40, how does it get lowered to $2.00? Some farmers may already be buying 8 units of cloth at $2.50 per unit by selling 10 units of rice. Of course, eventually at this high price of cloth, some textile workers will want to sell cloth but will not be able to find farmers to buy, and the price of cloth will have to be reduced. However, before that time comes, some farmers and workers will have traded at the prices (.40, 2.50), and the *market* demand and supply curves for cloth by the *remaining* farmers and workers will no longer be as given in Figure 1.3 (with the quantities of cloth multiplied by 100). For these remaining traders the prices may not settle at (.40, 2.00). There are at least two ways to describe the process of price formation. One is an artificial device used by the French economist Léon Walras (1834–1910). An auctioneer is assumed to announce a price for cloth and to collect the orders to buy cloth from all farmers and the orders to sell cloth from all workers at this price. If total demand exceeds total supply, the auctioneer will raise the price. If total supply exceeds total demand, the auctioneer will lower the price, until supply equals demand. This device is quite artificial.

A more realistic view of the situation is to imagine that each farmer produces 100 units of rice *per month* and each worker produces 20 units of cloth *per month,* so that the quantities in the demand–supply diagram refer to *flows* of commodities *per unit time.* Twenty units of cloth per month means about $\frac{20}{30}$ unit of cloth per day. If we measure the demand and supply by the numbers of units per day, rather than per month, we divide the quantities along the horizontal axis of the demand–supply diagram by 30. The point of using this flow concept to define the quantities in the demand and supply curves is that the farmers and workers are assumed to trade continuously. On the first day, if the price of cloth starts at $2.50 in the morning instead of $2.00, some farmer may buy some of it, but later in the day it will be lowered, for reasons which we have discussed, though not necessarily lowered to $2.00. On the second day the starting price will be closer to $2.00. If the diagram depicts the demand and supply of commodities per day, after several days the price of cloth will reach its equilibrium level at $2.00 because, from past experience, traders will start with a price closer to $2.00 every day. Besides helping to describe the process by which market prices reach their equilibrium levels, the definition of demand and supply in terms of quantities *per unit time* is more descriptive of economic behavior. Consumption and production take place continuously in time and are not one-time transactions. They should thus be measured by *quantities per unit time.*

In the science of modern economics, an important question is what determines market prices—the prices at which people actually buy and sell goods. A more important question is how market prices affect the consumption and the production of goods. Well-known economists, including the English economist David Ricardo (1772–1823) and the German economist Karl Marx (1818–1883), used to discuss the "value" and not the market price of a commodity. Modern economists are more concerned with the market price of a commodity than with its "value," because the former is an observable quantity that affects the consumption and production decisions in an economy, whereas the latter is an abstract notion that is difficult to observe and measure. Marx had the conception that the value of a commodity is an intrinsic quantity dependent on its labor content and believed that the market price would tend toward this value. In the century since Marx wrote, however, economists have discovered a more direct approach to determine market prices by demand and supply.

First, factors affecting the demand for a commodity help to explain its market price. For example, even if much labor has been used to build a beautiful house in the middle of a desert, the house may have a very low market price because there is no demand for it. To cite a more realistic example, in 1983 the world price of crude oil declined not because it took less labor to produce oil, but partly because the demand for oil had declined as people learned to economize on oil (by driving new gasoline-saving cars, by driving less, and so on) and as many countries remained in recession (income effect).

Second, factors of production other than labor have been incorporated in the supply side for the determination of market prices. The next section shows how costs of production affect the supply curve of a commodity. Labor cost is only one of these costs. It may be argued that costs of capital goods and raw materials are dependent on their values, which are in turn determined by their labor contents. However, this argument does not easily explain the fact that different quantities of an agricultural product will be produced with the same quantities of labor and land but with different conditions of climate and rainfall. Nor can it explain why the price of a commodity will fall when there is a technological improvement. For example, the price of corn decreased when hybrid seeds were introduced that yielded several times as much corn as before for the same amounts of land and labor. Labor is only one factor on the supply side and both supply and demand determine market prices. Some economists today still adhere to the labor theory of value, but most have found demand and supply to be more appropriate and convenient tools for explaining market prices.

1.5 PRODUCTION DECISIONS OF A PRIVATE ENTERPRISE WITH MANY COMPETITORS

The market price of a commodity is determined by the intersection of the demand curve and the supply curve of the commodity. The demand curve is determined by the preferences of the consumers. Although we have defined a supply curve of cloth as showing the different quantities of cloth that textile workers are willing to supply at different prices, we have assumed that each worker owns a fixed quantity of cloth and we have not yet explained how the price of cloth affects the amount of cloth produced. In this section we discuss the production of cloth by a private enterprise operating in a market with many competitors.

Assume that someone owns an enterprise to produce cloth for profit. Cotton cloth can be produced by using the labor of workers, services from machines, and materials including cotton yarns. Let x_2 be the quantity of cloth that can be produced per day by using x_3 units of labor, x_4 units of machines, and x_5 units of materials. The relation between the output x_2 and the inputs x_3, x_4, and x_5 is called a *production function,*

$$x_2 = g(x_3, x_4, x_5) \tag{1.9}$$

Let p_2, p_3, p_4, and p_5 denote the prices of cloth and the three inputs, respectively. Given the *technology* as summarized by the production function, and given the prices of output and inputs, how much output should the enterprise produce per day, and how much of each input should it employ to maximize its profits? To simplify our discussion we will consider only two inputs, labor x_3 and machine services x_4. To illustrate the main points we will use a very special production function.

Let the production function be

$$x_2 = \sqrt{x_3 x_4} \tag{1.10}$$

This function implies that if quantities x_3 and x_4 of inputs are both doubled, the quantity x_2 of output will also be doubled. If the function were $x_2 = x_3 x_4$, doubling the inputs would quadruple the output, which is an unreasonable assumption. The total cost of using the quantities (x_3, x_4) of the inputs is

$$C = p_3 x_3 + p_4 x_4 \tag{1.11}$$

In order for the enterprise to make the most profit, it must be *efficient* in the sense that, given the total cost C, it should produce as much output as possible by a suitable combination of the two inputs. Efficiency is described in Figure 1.4, with x_3 and x_4 measured along the horizontal and vertical axes. A *production indifference curve* shows the various combinations of (x_3, x_4) that can be employed to yield the same quantity of output according to equation 1.10. For example, the combinations (1,16), (2,8), (4,4), (8,2), and (16,1) will each yield 4 units of output. We assume that the enterprise can employ fractions of a machine, either by renting a machine on a part-time basis or by using a machine of a lower or higher quality than a "standard" machine that counts as 1 unit of machines. All combinations (x_3, x_4) that have total cost C are given by equation 1.11. For example, if $p_3 = 2$, $p_4 = 1$ and $C = 11.3$, the combinations are given by the straight line in Figure 1.4. The enterprise should find that combination of inputs that will produce the most output. It will be a point on the straight line tangential to a production difference curve. In our example the point is (2.8, 5.7) on the production

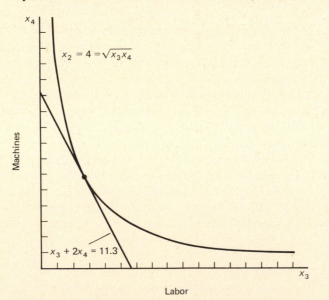

Figure 1.4   Efficiency in production—maximizing output given cost.

indifference curve shown in Figure 1.4. We can see from the diagram that *if the price of labor p_3 decreases* relative to p_4, the straight line with constant total cost will be rotated counterclockwise and *more labor will be used relative to machines.*

The above solution can be obtained mathematically. The problem is: Given p_3, p_4, and C, find the maximum output x_1 satisfying the production function (equation 1.10). Using equation 1.11, we know x_4 once x_3 is known:

$$x_4 = (C - p_3 x_3)/p_4 \tag{1.12}$$

The output that can be produced by using x_3 units of labor (and the corresponding x_4 units of machine services indicated by equation 1.12) is given by the production function

$$x_2 = \sqrt{x_3 x_4} = \sqrt{x_3 (C - p_3 x_3)/p_4} \tag{1.13}$$

We want to find x_3 that will maximize x_2. This problem can be solved by using elementary calculus. A reader lacking this background can appreciate the solution by assuming $C = 9.8, p_3 = 1.2$, and $p_4 = .7$ and by using equation 1.13 to plot x_2 against x_3 (on the horizontal axis); then find that value of x_3 that corresponds to the largest value of x_2. (Some concepts of calculus will be explained later on.) Using calculus, we set the derivative of x_2 given by equation 1.13 with respect to x_3 equal to zero:

$$\frac{dx_2}{dx_3} = \frac{1}{2} [x_3 (C - p_3 x_3)/p_4]^{-1/2}[(C - 2p_3 x_3)/p_4] = 0 \tag{1.14}$$

Equation 1.14 will be satisfied if $C - 2p_3 x_3 = 0$, or

$$x_3 = C/2p_3 \tag{1.15}$$

The value of x_3 given by equation 1.15 should be checked with the value given by your graph. Equation 1.15 shows that, given the same total cost C, the higher its price p_3, the smaller the quantity x_3 of labor that the enterprise will employ. When equation 1.15 is substituted into equation 1.12, we find

$$x_4 = (C - \frac{C}{2})/p_4 = C/2p_4 \tag{1.16}$$

which shows that, given the total cost C, the higher its price p_4, the smaller the quantity x_4 of machines the enterprise will employ.

What is the maximum quantity x_2 of cloth that the enterprise can produce with total cost C? Substituting equation 1.15 and equation 1.16 respectively for x_3 and x_4 in the production function equation 1.10, we find

$$x_2 = \sqrt{x_3 x_4} = C/2\sqrt{p_3 p_4} \tag{1.17}$$

By solving equation 1.17 for C,

$$C = 2\sqrt{p_3 p_4}(x_2) \tag{1.18}$$

we also answer the question, "What is the minimum total cost C required to produce x_2 units of cloth?" The relation (equation 1.18) between total cost C and the quantity x_2 of output is called the *total cost curve.* In this example when x_2 doubles, the total cost will double.

Consider the situation when the quantity of one input cannot be changed. (For example, in China, as a rule, workers cannot be dismissed and the hiring of new workers depends on the approval of personnel bureaus.) For our purpose assume that it takes a long time to order and receive additional machines. Within a short period of time, called the *short run* in economics, assume that the enterprise cannot change the quantity x_4 of machines. The enterprise may have a long-term contract to rent these machines at p_4 per unit per month. In this case $p_4 x_4$ is called a *fixed cost,* referring to the fact that the quantity x_4 is fixed in the short run. (What is fixed in the short run may not be fixed in the long run.) Assume that the enterprise can hire additional workers or dismiss existing workers in the short run, so that x_3 is not fixed. The labor cost $p_3 x_3$ is thus a *variable cost.* Assuming x_4 to be fixed and x_3 to be variable, what is the total cost curve for this enterprise?

If x_4 is fixed, according to the production function, to produce x_2 units of output requires

$$x_3 = x_2^2 / x_4$$

units of labor. Since labor costs p_3 per unit, the variable cost is

$$p_3 x_3 = p_3 x_2^2 / x_4$$

Total cost for the enterprise equals fixed cost plus variable cost, or

$$C = p_4 x_4 + p_3 x_3 = (p_4 x_4) + \frac{p_3}{x_4} x_2^2 \tag{1.19}$$

For $(p_3, p_4) = (1.2, .7)$ and $x_4 = 6$, the total cost curve is

$$C = 4.2 + .2 x_2^2 \tag{1.20}$$

which is graphed in Figure 1.5.

If the enterprise can sell the cloth it produces at \$2.00 per unit, how much cloth should it produce (per unit time)? Its profit (per unit time) is

$$\pi = p_2 x_2 - C = 2x_2 - (4.2 + .2 x_2^2) \tag{1.21}$$

Profit is the difference between the *total revenue* $p_2 x_2$, which the enterprise receives by selling x_2 units of its product, and the total cost C required to produce x_2 units of product. For $p_2 = 2$, the total revenue $p_2 x_2 = 2x_2$ is also graphed in Figure 1.5. Profit is at its maximum when the difference between total revenue $p_2 x_2$ and total cost 4.2 $+ .2 x_2^2$ is the largest. From Figure 1.5, we see that the maximum profit occurs when the quantity of output x_2 equals 5 units. When $x_2 = 5$, total revenue is 10 and total cost is 9.2, yielding a profit of .8 dollar.

We have found the quantity of output that maximizes profit by calculating (and graphing) the total revenues and total costs for different levels of output, and finding that level of output that corresponds to the largest difference between total revenue and total cost. A different, and very useful, method to obtain the same result is to compare the extra revenue and the extra cost of producing an additional unit. If the extra revenue is larger than the extra cost, the additional unit is worth producing. If the extra revenue is smaller, the additional unit is not worth producing. The enterprise should continue to

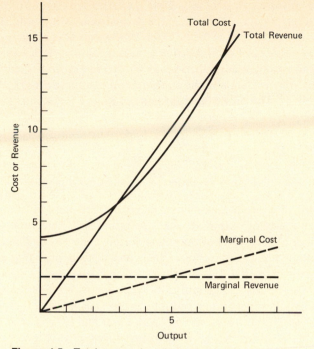

Figure 1.5 Total cost and total revenue curves.

produce units until, for the last unit, its extra revenue just covers or equals its extra cost. In our example the extra revenue from selling one additional unit is $p_2 = 2$ no matter how many units it sells. The extra cost of producing one additional unit depends on how many units it is producing. For example, the total cost of producing 3 units is $4.2 + .2(3)^2 = 6.0$; the total cost of producing 4 units is $4.2 + .2(4)^2 = 7.4$. Therefore, the extra cost of producing the fourth unit is $7.4 - 6.0 = 1.4$. Since that extra cost is smaller than the extra revenue of 2, the fourth unit is worth producing. The total cost of producing 5 units is $4.2 + .2(5)^2 = 9.2$; the extra cost of producing the fifth unit is $9.2 - 7.4 = 1.8$, making the fifth unit also worth producing.

Assuming that the product can be produced in a fraction of a unit (like .01 meter of cloth), we may ask whether it is worthwhile to increase the output in our example from 5 to 5.01 units. The total cost of producing 5.01 units is $4.2 + .2(5.01)^2 = 9.22002$. The extra cost of producing the .01 unit is .02002 as compared with its extra revenue of $2(.01) = .02000$. Therefore, the extra .01 unit is not worth producing once 5 units are being produced. In economics, the extra cost is called the *marginal cost* and the extra revenue is called the *marginal revenue*. At the output of 5 units, the marginal cost of an additional .01 unit is \$.02, or the marginal cost is \$2.00 *per unit*. The marginal revenue is also \$2.00 per unit. *A profit-maximizing enterprise will produce that quantity of output at which marginal cost equals marginal revenue.*

Marginal cost is the change in total cost per unit of output. It is the rate of change in total cost with respect to output or, in mathematical terms, the *derivative* of total cost with respect to output. Marginal revenue is the *derivative* of total revenue with respect to output. If total cost is $C = 4.2 + .2x_2^2$, the derivative dC/dx_2 of C with respect to x_2 is $2(.2)x_2$, or $.4x_2$. At $x_2 = 5$, the derivative is $.4 \times 5 = 2$. The derivative is smaller than 2 for $x_2 < 5$; it is larger than 2 for $x_2 > 5$. If total revenue is $R = 2x_2$, the derivative dR/dx_2 of total revenue with respect to x_2 is 2. Corresponding to these total-cost and total-revenue functions as plotted in Figure 1.5, we plot the marginal cost curve $dC/dx_2 = .4x_2$ and the marginal revenue curve $dR/dx_2 = 2$ in Figure 1.5 using broken lines. The profit function is $\pi = R - C$. π is maximized when its derivative with respect to x_2 is zero, or

$$\frac{d\pi}{dx_2} = \frac{dR}{dx_2} - \frac{dC}{dx_2} = 0 \qquad (1.22)$$

This will happen when marginal revenue $\dfrac{dR}{dx_2}$ equals marginal cost $\dfrac{dC}{dx_2}$.

The behavior of a profit-maximizing enterprise can now be summarized. The enterprise will set a level of output at which marginal cost equals marginal revenue. In order to produce a given level of output, it will find the most efficient or cheapest combination of inputs when such a choice is available. This implies that when the price of a variable input is increased, the enterprise will use less of it by substituting other inputs in production. When the quantities of some inputs are fixed in the short run, marginal cost usually increases when output increases, as in our example. Therefore, when the price of output increases, the enterprise will find it profitable to increase its output to make marginal cost equal to marginal revenue. In Figure 1.5, if $p_2 = 3$ instead of 2, the marginal revenue curve will move up to 3; marginal cost $.4x_2$ will equal 3 when the output x_2 is increased to $3/.4$ or 7.5 units. Referring to equation 1.19 for total cost, we know that marginal cost is

$$\frac{dC}{dx_2} = 2\left(\frac{p_3}{x_4}\right)x_2 \qquad (1.23)$$

In general, as in equation 1.23, marginal cost for any level x_2 of output increases as the price p_3 of a variable input increases. If $p_3 = 1.4$ instead of 1.2, with $x_4 = 6$, marginal cost will be $.467x_2$ instead of $.4x_2$. Given a marginal revenue of 2 as depicted in Figure 1.5, to equate its marginal cost $.467x_2$ to its marginal revenue, the enterprise will reduce its production to $x_2 = 2/.467$ or 4.29 units.

The marginal cost curve of an enterprise is also its *supply curve,* for it shows the amounts that the enterprise will supply at different prices of the product. As the price of the product increases, the enterprise will produce more of it. If there are 30 enterprises producing the same product in an industry, the *supply curve of the industry* shows the total amount that all the enterprises in the industry will supply at each price. This supply curve is obtained by adding all the quantities x_2 that the 30 enterprises will produce according to their individual supply curves. If the enterprises are identical and each has a supply curve (or marginal cost curve) as given by Figure 1.5, which is $p_2 = .4x_2$ or $x_2 = 2.5p_2$, the industry supply curve is $x_2 = 30(2.5p_2)$, or $x_2 = 75p_2$. This calculation assumes that when the enterprises try to expand their production as the price rises, the conditions defining the marginal cost of each enterprise do not change. For example, if many enterprises compete for the same input in the market, the price p_3 of the input may rise, raising the marginal cost of each firm. As another example, expanding the output of an industry may affect the environment adversely (polluting the air or the water), possibly also increasing the marginal cost (which is required to clean up the air or the water). The effects of the expansion of production by one enterprise on the economic conditions of other enterprises or economic units in the economy are called the *external effects*. Allowing for these external effects on marginal costs, we can derive the supply curve of an industry by summing the supply curves of the individual enterprises. The price of the product of the industry is determined by the intersection of this supply curve and the demand curve derived in Section 1.4.

Our analysis of the behavior of a private enterprise explains not only the supply curve for its output but the demand curve for an input that it employs. In our example, the *supply curve* is obtained by setting the marginal cost given by equation 1.23 equal to the marginal revenue (or the price p_2 of the product), yielding

$$x_2 = .5 \frac{p_2}{p_3} x_4 \tag{1.24}$$

When x_4 is fixed, to produce x_2 units of output requires $x_3 = x_2^2/x_4$ units of labor input, on account of the production function $x_2 = \sqrt{x_3 x_4}$. The quantity of labor input that the enterprise will employ is therefore

$$x_3 = \frac{x_2^2}{x_4} = .25 \left(\frac{p_2}{p_3}\right)^2 x_4 \tag{1.25}$$

Equation 1.25 is the *demand function for labor input* by the enterprise. It shows that as the price p_3 of labor increases, the demand will decrease; as the price p_2 of the output increases, the demand will increase (in order to produce more output).

The demand function for labor has another interpretation. The enterprise uses labor because labor helps to increase the enterprise's output, given the quantity x_4 of its other input. According to the production function $x_2 = \sqrt{x_3 x_4}$, if labor input is increased from x_3 units to $x_3 + .001$ units, the output will be increased by the amount

$$\sqrt{(x_3 + .001)x_4} - \sqrt{x_3 x_4} = \sqrt{x_4}[\sqrt{x_3 + .001} - \sqrt{x_3}]$$

$$= \sqrt{x_4}\left[\frac{\sqrt{x_3^2 + .001x_3} - x_3}{\sqrt{x_3}}\right] \simeq \sqrt{x_4}\left[\frac{\sqrt{x_3^2 + .001x_3 + (.0005)^2} - x_3}{\sqrt{x_3}}\right]$$

$$= \sqrt{x_4}\left[\frac{(x_3 + .0005) - x_3}{\sqrt{x_3}}\right] = .0005 \sqrt{\frac{x_4}{x_3}} \tag{1.26}$$

The increase in output is due to an increase in labor input by .001 unit. Therefore, the increase in output per unit increase in labor input is the above amount divided by .001, or $.5\sqrt{x_4/x_3}$. This is the *derivative* of $x_2 = \sqrt{x_3 x_4}$ with respect to x_3, *holding x_4 fixed,* or the *partial derivative* of x_2 with respect to x_3. In economic terms, it is the *marginal product of labor.* The enterprise should *employ labor up to the point where the value of its marginal product* $p_2(.5\sqrt{x_4/x_3})$ *is just equal to the price p_3 of labor.* This rule results from balancing the gain $p_2(.5\sqrt{x_4/x_3})$ in additional revenue due to the additional labor with the cost p_3 of having the additional labor. As long as the former exceeds the latter, it is worthwhile to hire more. Setting $p_2(.5\sqrt{x_4/x_3}) = p_3$, and solving for x_3, we get the same demand function for labor as given by equation 1.25.

In this section, we have assumed that there are many enterprises or business firms producing the same product. When one firm increases its output, the price of the output will not be reduced appreciably. If the firm is a *monopoly,* the demand curve for its product is identical with the demand curve for the industry. It has to charge a lower price when it wants to sell more. The price p_2 is no longer treated as a constant by the firm, but as a function of the amount x_2 of its output. Similarly, if the firm is one of the very few buying labor services, the price p_3 of labor services will increase as it wants more labor, and p_3 is no longer a constant but a function of x_2.

*1.6 DETERMINATION OF OUTPUTS AND PRICES IN A COMPETITIVE ECONOMY

By studying the behavior of consumers and private enterprises competing in the marketplace, we can answer some of the important questions mentioned in Section 1.1: what to produce, how much to produce, how to distribute the products, and how prices are determined. This section is devoted to answering these questions, using the tools developed in Sections 1.2 to 1.5.

In a market economy with many competing enterprises, which products to produce and how much to produce are determined by the demand for and the supply of the products. The demand function for each consumer good is derived from the preferences of the consumers, as summarized by the indifference curves. The supply function of each consumer good produced by private enterprises is derived from the production function, given the prices of the inputs. The demand function for each input is also derived from the behavior of the private enterprises that employ it. Some inputs, like machines, are produced by other enterprises, and the supply functions of these inputs are derived in the same way as described in Section 1.5.

The supply of labor input can be derived from the preferences of the consumer-worker who can choose different quantities of goods to consume *and* the amount of labor to supply or the number of hours to work. For example, in Figure 1.2, instead of choosing between rice and cloth, the consumer could be choosing between leisure time and cloth (and other goods). Instead of having 100 units of rice to trade, the consumer-worker may have a maximum of 100 hours (per week) to sell, excluding time to sleep and to take care of the necessities of life. He could choose to have 100 hours of leisure time for himself and consume nothing else, or sell some of it for $.40 per hour to buy cloth (and other goods). An analysis like the one we performed in Section 1.3 will explain the amount of labor that the consumer-worker will supply as a function of the price (or wage rate) for his labor relative to the price of cloth (and other goods). For example, the demand function of a worker for leisure time may be $I/2p_3$, where I is his income and p_3 is his wage per hour. Each extra hour of leisure time (or time spent not working) will cost him p_3 dollars, because he could be earning that amount by working. The higher the price of leisure time, the smaller will be his demand.

---

*Sections marked by an asterisk contain technical material. Readers with a minimal background in economics may skim over these sections and go on to the next unstarred section.

Assuming that the worker has 15 hours of possible working time (per day), the supply function of his labor is 15 minus his demand for leisure time.

$$x_3 = 15 - \frac{I}{2p_3} \qquad (1.27)$$

Let us see how the prices and quantities of the products of a market economy are determined by their demand functions and supply functions. We will consider an economy that has two consumer goods, or *final products*—rice and cloth—and four inputs, or *factors of production*—labor of industrial workers, machines, labor of farmers, and land. Rice is produced by using the labor of farmers and land. Cloth is produced by using the labor of workers and machines. (Of course, material must also be used in production, but here we will keep the illustration simple.) Let $p_1, p_2, \ldots,$ p_6 denote respectively the price of rice, cloth, workers' labor, machines' services, farmers' labor, and land's use. Their quantities are respectively $x_1, x_2, \ldots, x_6$. We want to construct demand functions and supply functions for these products to determine their prices and quantities. We assume that the supply of machines in the economy is fixed at $x_4 = 1000$ units (because, in the short run, there is not enough time to produce new machines) and the supply of land is fixed at 2000 units. Hence, the working of the market economy will determine only six prices and four quantities. Furthermore, from the theories of consumer's demand and enterprise's production we know that only the relative prices of the products are determined. Therefore, we can choose $p_1 = 1$, and measure the other five prices relative to p_1. Let there be 200 farmers and 100 workers. There are also owners of farmland and of the machines; some or all of them may be farmers or workers also. There are factories to produce cloth and farms to produce rice.

Specific demand and supply functions will be assumed to permit the reader to follow the algebra involved. Using equation 1.24, we let the supply of cloth by the ith factory be

$$x_{2i} = .5\frac{p_2}{p_3}x_{4i}$$

where x_{4i} denotes the quantity of machines used by the ith factory. The total supply of cloth is obtained by summing the supplies of all factories:

$$x_2 = \sum_i x_{2i} = .5\frac{p_2}{p_3}\sum_i x_{4i} = .5\frac{p_2}{p_3}x_4 \qquad (1.28)$$

where $x_4 = \sum_i x_{4i}$ denotes the quantity of machines used by all factories and is assumed to be equal to 1000 units. Let the demand for cloth by the jth consumer (farmer, worker, or owner of some farmland or machines) be

$$x_{2,j} = \frac{I_j}{2p_2}$$

where I_j is the income of the jth consumer. The total demand for cloth is obtained by summing the demands of all consumers.

$$x_2 = \sum_j x_{2j} = \frac{\sum_j I_j}{2p_2} = \frac{I}{2p_2} \tag{1.29}$$

where $I = \sum_j I_j$ denotes the total income of all consumers.

We next consider the demand for and supply of workers' labor. The demand for labor by each factory is assumed to be given by equation 1.25. Summing equation 1.25 over all factories, we find

$$x_3 = \sum_i x_{3i} = .25\left(\frac{p_2}{p_3}\right)^2 \sum_i x_{4i} = .25\left(\frac{p_2}{p_3}\right)^2 x_4 \tag{1.30}$$

where x_4 now denotes the quantity of machines used by all factories. If the supply function of labor by the jth worker is as given by equation 1.27, with the subscript j added to x_3 and I, the supply of labor by all 100 workers is

$$x_3 = \sum_j x_{3j} = 1500 - \frac{\sum_j I_j}{2p_3} = 1500 - \frac{I_w}{2p_3} \tag{1.31}$$

where I_w denotes the total income of the 100 workers.

Assume that rice is produced by private farms in a way similar to the production of cloth by factories, except that the inputs are farm labor and land. The supply and demand for rice, corresponding to equations 1.28 and 1.29, are given respectively by

$$x_1 = .5\frac{p_1}{p_5}x_6 \tag{1.32}$$

$$x_1 = \frac{I}{2p_1} \tag{1.33}$$

Note that p_5 is the price of farm labor and x_6 is the quantity of land used in farming, corresponding to p_3 and x_4 in the case of cloth production. Similarly, the demand and supply of farm labor, corresponding to equations 1.30 and 1.31, are given respectively by

$$x_5 = .25\left(\frac{p_1}{p_6}\right)^2 x_6 \tag{1.34}$$

$$x_5 = 3000 - \frac{I_f}{2p_5} \tag{1.35}$$

where I_f denotes the total income of the 200 farmers.

We now have four pairs of demand and supply equations, and we need two more for machines and for land. By applying the theory of marginal product to the demand for machines, as we have applied it to the demand for labor, we can write the demand function for machines by the ith cloth factory as

$$x_{4i} = .25 \left(\frac{p_2}{p_4}\right)^2 x_{3i}$$

This equation is analogous to equation 1.25. It is obtained by equating the value of the marginal product of machines $p_2(.5\sqrt{x_3/x_4})$ to the price p_4 of machines. Although we assume that the supply of machines is fixed, the demand for machines shows the quantity of machines that the factory *would like* to buy if it is using x_{3i} units of labor to produce cloth to sell at a price p_2 and if the price of machine services is p_4 per unit. Again, summing over all factories, we get the market demand function for machines:

$$x_4 = .25 \left(\frac{p_2}{p_4}\right)^2 x_3 \tag{1.36}$$

The supply of machines is assumed to be fixed at $x_4 = 1000$ units. Similarly, the demand for land by all farms is

$$x_6 = .25 \left(\frac{p_1}{p_6}\right)^2 x_5 \tag{1.37}$$

The supply of land is assumed to be fixed at $x_6 = 2000$ units.

The quantities and prices of all six commodities are determined by the above six pairs of demand and supply equations. We will now solve these equations algebraically, given $p_1 = 1$. To simplify our algebra, we assume that the workers do not own any land or machines, so that their total income consists entirely of wages. In other words, $I_w = p_3 x_3$. Using equation 1.31 for the supply of labor, we have

$$x_3 = 1500 - \frac{I_w}{2p_3} = 1500 - \frac{x_3}{2}$$

yielding $x_3 = 1000$. Without the above simplifying assumption, income of the workers would include rent from the land and machines that they own; in solving equation 1.31, we would have to know how much land and how many machines the workers own. Since all workers are identical, each of the 100 workers will work 10 hours per day. Also to simplify algebra, we assume that the farmers do not own any land or machines, or that the income variable I_f entering the farmers' supply function (equation 1.35) for their labor consists only of labor income $p_5 x_5$. Then equation 1.35 can be solved for x_5,

$$x_5 = 3000 - \frac{I_f}{2p_5} = 3000 - \frac{x_5}{2}$$

yielding $x_5 = 2000$. Each of the 200 workers will also work 10 hours per day in our economy.

Given the supply of farm labor to be $x_5 = 2000$, and given $p_1 = 1$ and $x_6 = 2000$, we can solve the supply equation 1.34 for p_5, yielding $p_5 = .50$. The price of farm labor is therefore \$.50 per hour. Given $p_1 = 1$, $x_6 = 2000$, and $p_5 = .50$, the supply function (equation 1.32) for rice can be used to obtain $x_1 = 2000$ as the output of rice. Given $x_3 = 1000$ and $x_4 = 1000$, equation 1.30 can be solved for the relative price $(p_2/p_3) = 2$. Given $x_1 = 2000$, the demand function (equation 1.33) for rice implies

$I = 4000$. Equating the supply (equation 1.28) and the demand (equation 1.29) for cloth, given (p_2/p_3), x_4 and I, we find the price of cloth $p_2 = 2$. Using either 1.28 or 1.29 and given $p_2 = 2$, we find $x_2 = 1000$. Since $(p_2/p_3) = 2$, we have $p_3 = 1$. Finally, given the supply of machines $x_4 = 1000$ and p_2 and x_3, the demand equation 1.36 for machines is solved to get $p_4 = 1$. Given the supply of land $x_6 = 2000$, p_1 and x_5, the demand equation 1.37 for land is solved to get $p_6 = .5$.

We have obtained the solution $I = 4000$ and

p_1	p_2	p_3	p_4	p_5	p_6
1	2	1	1	.5	.5

x_1	x_2	x_3	x_4	x_5	x_6
2000	1000	1000	1000	2000	2000

The reader can easily verify that if all prices and income I are doubled, all demand and supply equations will be satisfied. Thus the system of demand and supply equations determines only the relative prices and not the absolute prices of different commodities. In this economy calling one dollar two dollars will not affect any production and consumption decisions.

The use of demand and supply equations thus answers the questions as to how much of each commodity will be produced and what its price will be. Furthermore, it explains the distribution of income to different owners of productive factors. If we know the price of each factor or input, and the quantities of the factors each person owns, we can find out each person's income. In our example, total income I of all persons is found to be 4000 (dollars per day). This total income is called *national income*. National income I also equals the value of the final products, rice and cloth. The value of final products $p_1 x_1 + p_2 x_2$ is called *national product*.

$$I = p_1 x_1 + p_2 x_2 = 1(2000) + 2(1000) = 4000 \qquad (1.38)$$

Note that all the revenues $p_1 x_1 + p_2 x_2$ that the enterprises receive from selling their final products will be used to pay for the factors of production. Therefore, national income I and the value of national product $p_1 x_1 + p_2 x_2$ also equal the total payment to all factors of production.

$$I = p_3 x_3 + p_4 x_4 + p_5 x_5 + p_6 x_6 = 4000 \qquad (1.39)$$

In our example, the total wage bill to the factory workers is $p_3 x_3 = 1000$; the total wage to the farmers is $p_4 x_4 = 1000$; the total rent for all the machines is $p_5 x_5 = 1000$; and the total rent for all the land is also 1000. If one person happens to own a lot of land, she can be very rich.

*1.7 WELFARE PROPERTIES OF A COMPETITIVE ECONOMY

The most important point about the demand and supply equations in a competitive market economy is not that they can determine the (relative) prices and outputs in the economy. It is the way prices and outputs are determined. Underlying these demand and supply equations are the decisions of consumers to choose the products that they desire subject to the constraints of their budgets, and the decisions of the enterprises to find the right amounts to produce and to produce them most cheaply by using the right combinations of inputs, and to use the inputs efficiently so that each extra unit of input employed will contribute to an increase in output worthy of the cost of the input. The solution of prices and outputs by a competitive market economy is called a *competitive equilibrium.* In this section we will discuss the *efficiency* of a competitive equilibrium, using the term in the sense of Pareto. As we saw earlier in this chapter, an equilibrium solution is not Pareto efficient if there is a way to make someone in the economy better off without making anyone else worse off. An equilibrium is Pareto efficient if there is no way to make anyone better off without making someone else worse off.

Let us first illustrate how a competitive market economy will achieve efficiency by using the example of the last section. Recall that in our solution $p_3 = 1$ and $p_5 = .5$, or the wage rate of the factory worker is 1 and the wage rate of a farmer is .5. Implicitly we assumed that a factory worker cannot work in a farm and a farmer cannot work in a factory. One possible reason is that a factory worker does not know how to farm and a farmer does not know the factory's work. A second possiblity is that although each worker can do either type of work equally well, he or she is prevented from changing jobs by institutional barriers. For example, a farmer in China may not be allowed to move into the cities where some factories are located. Let us assume the second possibility to be true. The farmers know that the workers are earning more, but they are prevented from becoming factory workers. What will hapen to the economy of Section 1.6 if the farmers are allowed to work as factory workers, and vice versa?

We know that the solution with $p_3 = 1$ and $p_5 = .5$ cannot be a competitive equilibrium solution. Some farmers will want to work in the factories because they want to get a higher wage. The factory owners are willing to hire additional workers as long as the value of the marginal product of labor covers the wage cost. Beginning with the solution given in the last section, the first farmer seeking work in a factory will get a wage of approximately 1. As more and more farmers become factory workers, the wage rate of the factories will fall. According to the demand equation 1.30 for factory workers, the factories are willing to hire more workers (or to increase x_3) only if the wage p_3 is reduced, given the values of p_2 and x_4. In the meantime, as the laborers leave the farms, the wage p_5 of farm labor will increase. According to the demand equation 1.34 for farm workers, the farm owners are willing to raise the farm wage p_5 when there are fewer workers available because the value of the marginl product of labor increases as the quantity of labor employed is reduced. The movement of workers from farms to factories will cease when $p_3 = p_5$.

When the workers move from the farms to the factories to take advantage of the difference betwen p_3 and p_5, the value of national product must increase. Assuming $p_3 > p_5$, let 1 unit of labor be moved from a farm to a factory. Losing 1 unit of labor will reduce the value of the farm's product by p_5 because a profit-seeking farm owner will try to equate the value of the marginal product of labor to its wage p_5. For the same reason, gaining 1 unit of labor will increase the value of the factory's product by p_3. If $p_3 > p_5$, the gain in the value of the output of the factories is larger than the loss in the value of the output of the farms, yielding a net gain in the value of national product or national income.

To find the solution for prices and outputs in our illustrative economy when there is only one kind of labor, the system of equations 1.28 to 1.37 has to be modified. First,

p_3 stands for the wage of the only kind of labor, and p_5 becomes p_3. Second, the demand for labor is the sum of the demand by factories and by farms, or the sum of equations 1.30 and 1.34.

$$x_3 + x_5 = .25(p_2^2 x_4 + p_1^2 x_6)/p_3^2 \tag{1.40}$$

Third, the supply of labor is the sum of the supply by factory workers and by farmers, or the sum of equations 1.31 and 1.35:

$$x_3 + x_5 = 4500 - (I_w + I_f)/2p_3 \tag{1.41}$$

where $I_w = p_3 x_3$ denotes wage income of factory workers and $I_f = p_3 x_5$ denotes wage income of farmers, as before.

To solve the revised system of equations, substitute $p_3 x_3$ for I_w and $p_3 x_5$ for I_f in equation 1.41 to obtain

$$x_3 + x_5 = 4500 - (x_3 + x_5)/2$$

or $x_3 + x_5 = 3000$. Using this result and given $p_1 = 1$, $x_4 = 1000$, and $x_6 = 2000$, we can write equation 1.40 as

$$3000 = (250p_2^2 + 500)/p_3^2$$

implying

$$p_3^2 = (p_2^2 + 2)/12 \tag{1.42}$$

Equating 1.32 and 1.33 gives

$$x_1 = 1000/p_3 = I/2 \tag{1.43}$$

or $I = 2000/p_3$. Using this result for I and equating 1.28 and 1.29 yield

$$x_2 = 500\left(\frac{p_2}{p_3}\right) = \frac{1000}{p_2 p_3} \tag{1.44}$$

or $p_2^2 = 2$. We thus obtain $p_2 = \sqrt{2}$. From equation 1.42 we have $p_3^2 = \frac{4}{12}$, or $p_3 = \sqrt{\frac{1}{3}}$. Equation 1.43 now implies $x_1 = 1000\sqrt{3}$ and $I = 2000\sqrt{3}$. From equation 1.44 we get $x_2 = 500\sqrt{6}$. Using equation 1.30, we have $x_3 = 1500$. Using equation 1.34, we have $x_5 = 1500$. The sum $x_3 + x_5$ is 3000, which checks with our previous result. Given x_3, x_4, x_5, x_6, p_1, and p_2, equations 1.36 and 1.37 can be solved for $p_4 = \sqrt{.75}$ and $p_6 = \sqrt{.1875}$.

The equilibrium of the illustrative competitive market economy, or the solution of the revised set of demand and supply equations, is displayed below. The numbers in parentheses are the solutions found in the last section, provided here for comparison.

p_1	p_2	p_3	p_4	p_5	p_6
1	1.4142	.5774	.8660	.5774	.4330
(1)	(2.0000)	(1.0000)	(1.0000)	(.5000)	(.5000)

x_1	x_2	x_3	x_4	x_5	x_6	
1732	1225	1500	1000	1500	2000	
(2000)	(1000)	(1000)	(1000)	(2000)	(2000)	(1.45)

The solution can be checked by computing national income in two different ways, as the value of the final product and as the total payment to all factors.

$$I = 3464 = p_1 x_1 + p_2 x_2 = p_3 x_3 + p_4 x_4 + p_5 x_5 + p_6 x_6$$

The total wage payment to all 300 workers is $p_3 x_3 + p_5 x_5$, or 1732, with each person getting 5.773.

In our previous solution, the output of rice was 2000 units. It is now reduced to 1732 as farmers have moved to become factory workers. The output of cloth is increased from 1000 to 1225 units. Is the economy better off? Consider first the farmers. Previously there were 200 farmers with a total wage income of $p_5 x_5 = 1000$, or with each having an income of 5. Given his demand functions and the prices

$$x_1 = \frac{I}{2p_1}, \; x_2 = \frac{I}{2p_2}, \; p_1 = 1, \; p_2 = 2$$

each farmer was consuming $x_1 = 2.5$ units of rice and $x_2 = 1.25$ units of cloth. Now each worker earns a wage-income of 5.773. Given the same demand functions and $p_1 = 1$ and $p_2 = 1.4142$, each will consume $x_1 = 2.89$ units of rice and $x_2 = 2.04$ units of cloth. Thus each farmer now consumes more rice and cloth than before.

How about the factory workers who were already working in the factory? The total wage payment to the 100 workers was 1000, with each worker getting 10. Given her demand functions and the old prices $p_1 = 1$ and $p_2 = 2$, each worker was consuming $x_1 = 5$ units of rice and $x_2 = 2.5$ units of cloth, more than each worker is consuming now. The owners of machines as a group had an income of $p_4 x_4 = 1000$, as compared with 866 after the change. Their consumptions of rice and cloth were 500 and 250, respectively, as compared with 433 and 306 at present. Finally, the owners of land had a total income of $p_6 x_6 = 1000$, as compared with 866 after the change. Their consumptions of rice and cloth were and are the same as the machine owners'.

Is the society better off consuming 1732 units of rice and 1225 units of cloth than consuming 2000 units of rice and 1000 units of cloth? The 200 former farmers are consuming more of both goods than before, but the 100 workers are consuming less. If the 200 farmers can share their gains with the 100 workers, will everyone be better off? The gain of each farmer consists of $2.89 - 2.50 = .39$ unit of rice and $2.04 - 1.25 = .79$ unit of cloth. If the total gain of the 200 farmers were distributed evenly to the 100 workers, each worker would receive an additional .78 unit of rice and 1.58 unit of cloth. Each worker would then have $2.89 + .78 = 3.67$ units of rice and $2.04 + 1.58 = 3.62$ units of cloth, as compared with $x_1 = 5$ and $x_2 = 2.5$ before. Is the bundle (3.67, 3.62) better than the bundle (5, 2.5)? At the current prices $(p_1, p_2) = (1, 1.4142)$ the first bundle is worth 8.79 and the second 8.54. Therefore each worker could always trade the first bundle to get more of both rice and cloth than the second bundle, making herself better off than before.

Finally, consider the machine owners and the landowners. Each group is now consuming a bundle $(x_1, x_2) = (433, 306)$, as compared with (500, 250) before. Can we say that (433, 306) is a better bundle than (500, 250)? The following test can be used to answer this question. Each group has an income of 866. Given this income and $(p_1, p_2) = (1, 1.4142)$, the group chooses to consume the bundle (433, 306) according to its demand functions. If, using the same income, the group could afford to buy (500,

250) and yet it chooses to buy (433, 306), we say that (433, 306) is *revealed* to be better than (500, 250). In the present case, the bundle (500, 250) would cost $854 at the prices $(p_1, p_2) = (1, 1.4142)$. Since 854 is less than 866, the group could afford the bundle (500, 250) but it has chosen (433, 306). Therefore, the latter bundle is revealed to be better than the former. The property owners are better off now than before. We have thus found that the solution obtained when the farmers are prevented from working in the factories is socially less desirable than the competitive market solution in the sense that, in the latter solution, some people in the society can be made better off and no one is worse off than in the former solution.

    Can we still improve on the competitive-market solution displayed in equation 1.45? The answer is no, because a competitive-market solution is Pareto optimal, or Pareto efficient. A Pareto-optimal solution is characterized by three conditions. We will show that each of the three conditions is satisfied by the competitive-market solution.

Condition 1   For any pair of final products 1 and 2 and any pair of consumers A and B, there is no way for A and B to trade to improve the welfare of either person without decreasing the welfare of the other person. In terms of Figure 1.1 the solution must be on the contract curve. To show that a competitive equilibrium solution satisfies this condition, observe that for any consumer A or B, the quantity x_2 of commodity 2 that he will require to trade an extremely small unit of commodity 1 (as depicted by the slope of his indifference curve in Figure 1.2) must equal the ratio p_1/p_2 of the prices of commodity 1 to commodity 2 (as depicted by the slope of his budget line). The budget line is

$$p_1 x_1 + p_2 x_2 = I$$

or

$$x_2 = \frac{I}{p_2} - \frac{p_1}{p_2} x_1$$

The slope of the budget line is $-p_1/p_2$, which, according to Figure 1.2, must equal the slope of the indifference curve, or the rate x_2 must increase per unit reduction in x_1 to keep the consumer equally well off when the reduction of x_1 is extremely small. Because the prices p_1 and p_2 are the same for each consumer, each must be willing to trade x_1 for x_2 at the same rate. Each person's indifference curve must have the same slope $-p_1/p_2$ at a competitive equilibrium. No one could improve himself by trading because each would ask for a slightly larger quantity of x_2 per unit of x_1 than p_1/p_2 when trading commodity 1 for commodity 2.

Condition 2   For any pair of inputs 3 and 4 and any pair of enterprises A and B, there is no way for A and B to exchange the inputs to increase the product of either enterprise without decreasing the product of the other enterprise. Figure 1.4 can be used to show that a competitive equilibrium satisfies this condition in the same way that Figure 1.2 was used to show that Condition 1 is satisfied. Assume that both A and B use both inputs 3 and 4. At a competitive equilibrium, each enterprise will face a diagram like Figure 1.4, with its production indifference curve tangential to its budget line of given total cost, both having a slope of $-p_3/p_4$. To give up a small unit of input 3, each enterprise would want slightly more than p_3/p_4 units of input 4 in return in order to keep its output level constant. Therefore, when inputs are reallocated in two different enterprises (which may be producing two different products), there is no way to increase the output of one without decreasing the output of the other.

Condition 3 For any pair of final products 1 and 2, there is no way to reallocate the inputs to increase the value of one product by more than the reduction in the value of the other product from which inputs are taken. In a competitive equilibrium, let a small unit of one input, say labor, be taken from the production of good 1 in order to increase the production of good 2. The reduction in the value of good 1 is slightly larger than the cost of the input, which is p_3 per unit, because a profit-maximizing enterprise equates the price of an input to the value of its marginal product. The increase in the value of good 2 is slightly smaller than the cost of the input, which is also p_3 per unit for the second enterprise. Therefore Condition 3 follows.

Let each consumer be in equilibrium, so that the ratio $-p_1/p_2$ of the prices of any two products equals the slope of his indifference curve. Then Condition 3 is equivalent to Condition 3a.

Condition 3a The extra quantity of any product 2 that the economy *can produce* by sacrificing a very small unit of product 1 must equal the extra quantity of product 2 for which each consumer is *willing to trade* by sacrificing a very small unit of product 1. For example, let a small amount of labor be shifted from the production of product 1 to the production of product 2, so that .707 extra unit of product 2 and 1 less unit of product 1 result. By Condition 3, the value of .707 unit of product 2 should be just equal to the value of 1 unit of product 1; that is,

$$p_2 \times .707 = p_1 \times 1 \text{ or } \frac{p_1}{p_2} = .707 \tag{1.46}$$

Since we assume that each consumer in equilibrium is willing to trade for (p_1/p_2) units of product 2 per unit of x_1, Condition 3a follows. Conversely, if Condition 3a holds and if each consumer is in equilibrium, equation 1.46 follows. The value of the increase in product 2 can be just equal to the reduction in the value of product 1, satisfying Condition 3.

If Condition 3a is not satisfied, society should reallocate resources to increase the production of one good at the expense of another and make people better off. For example, if .708 unit of product 2 can be produced by reducing 1 unit of product 1, and the slope of the indifference curve of each consumer using goods 1 and 2 is $-.707$, the society should produce .708 extra unit of product 2 and 1 less unit of product 1. We have shown that a competitive market solution satisfies Condition 3. Since the solution implies the equality of the price ratio $(-p_1/p_2)$ to the slope of each consumer's indifference curve, it also satisfies Condition 3a.

Condition 3a is sometimes shown graphically as in Figure 1.6. The curve *ab* shows the different combinations of the two products, rice and cloth, which can be produced by the economy. Two points on this *production-transformation curve* were

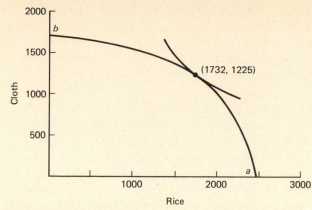

Figure 1.6 Equality between rates of substitution in production and consumption.

given in equation 1.45, namely (1732, 1225) and (2000, 1000). By the production functions $x_1 = \sqrt{x_5 x_6}$ and $x_2 = \sqrt{x_3 x_4}$, if all labor were devoted to farming, the outputs would be (2449, 0); if all labor were devoted to cloth manufacturing, the outputs would be (0, 1732). At competitive-market solution (1732, 1225), the slope of the production-transformation curve is equal to the slope of the indifference curve for each member of the society, both being equal to $-p_1/p_2$, or $-.707$. In other words, the rate at which product 2 can be exchanged for product 1 in production equals the rate at which product 2 can be substituted for product 1 in consumption by each consumer. When any consumer has 1 less unit of product 1, he can be equally well off by getting .707 extra unit of product 2 according to *his* indifference curve. If we draw an indifference curve for the *society* near the equilibrium point (1732, 1225), as we do in Figure 1.6, we are assuming that when the society takes away 1 unit of product 1 from *some-one* and gives .707 unit of product 2 to *anyone* else, the society is equally well off. This is a fairly strong assumption, stronger than necessary to state Condition 3a. Condition 3a says that the amount of product 2 that can be produced by sacrificing 1 unit of product 1 should be the same as the amount that will just compensate *any* consumer for losing 1 unit of product 1. It does not say that society is equally well off if one person loses 1 unit of product 1 and a second person gains .707 unit of product 2. It would imply the latter statement if we can redistribute the gain of the second person to the first person.

1.8 MONOPOLY AND MONOPOLY POWER

A condition for a competitive-market economy to be Pareto efficient is that no enterprise can monopolize the market. Let us consider the solution to the cloth industry if there is only one enterprise producing cloth. Assume that this enterprise owns all 1000 units of the machines for cloth production and hires labor at p_3 per unit. (Actually, a monopolist may bid up the price of labor when he hires more labor, but we ignore this possibility.) The total cost of the monopoly producing x_2 units of cloth is given by

$$C = p_4 x_4 + p_3 x_3 = (p_4 x_4) + \frac{p_3}{x_4} x_2^2 \qquad [1.19]$$

where $x_4 = 1000$. Its marginal cost is

$$\frac{dC}{dx_2} = 2\left(\frac{p_3}{x_4}\right)x_2 \qquad\qquad [1.23]$$

As we have pointed out in Section 1.5, an enterprise will maximize its profit by setting marginal cost equal to marginal revenue.

Total revenue is $p_2 x_2$, but p_2 is now dependent on the quantity x_2 that it sells. If demand increases only when price falls, the more the monopoly wants to sell, the lower the price it can charge. If the demand function were as in equation 1.29, $p_2 x_2 = I/2$, or half of national income, would be spent on cloth no matter what price the monopoly charged. In this case, the monopoly would produce a very small, or literally zero, quantity of cloth and let the price rise to a very high level, or literally infinity, in order to make the most profit. A better approximation to the market demand function than equation 1.29 for the purpose of studying monopoly behavior is

$$x_2 = 1225 + .3536I - 866p_2 \qquad\qquad (1.47)$$

which implies

$$p_2 = 1.4142 + .0004083I - .001155x_2 \qquad\qquad (1.47a)$$

Total revenue for the monopolist is therefore

$$R = p_2 x_2 = (1.4142 + .0004083I)x_2 - .001155x_2^2 \qquad\qquad (1.48)$$

Marginal revenue is the derivative of R with respect to x, or

$$\frac{dR}{dx_2} = (1.4142 + .0004083I) - .00231x_2 \qquad\qquad (1.49)$$

At $p_3 = .5774$, $x_4 = 1000$, $I = 3464$, equating marginal cost (equation 1.23) and marginal revenue (equation 1.49) gives

$$.0011548x_2 = 2.8284 - .00231x_2$$

or $x_2 = 816$. The monopoly output 816 is smaller than the output 1225 of a competitive cloth industry. In a competitive industry each enterprise considers p_2 as given, not to be influenced by its output. Marginal revenue of each enterprise equals p_2. If all enterprises in the industry produce 1225 units of output and $I = 3464$, p_2 will be 1.4142 according to equation 1.47a. Each enterprise j owning x_{4j} units of machines will set its output x_{2j} to equate its marginal cost with 1.4142, so that

$$2\,\frac{.5774}{x_{4j}}\,x_{2j} = 1.4142$$

or

$$x_{2j} = 1.225x_{4j}$$

The total supply of all enterprises will be

$$x_2 = \sum_j x_{2j} = 1.225\sum_j x_{4j} = 1.225(1000) = 1225$$

which is the output of a competitive market. As the output of the monopolist is smaller, the price is raised above the competitive level 1.4142. By the demand function 1.47a, if $I = 3464$ (which will change when the cloth industry is monopolized) and $x_2 = 816$, the price p_2 will be 1.8859 instead of 1.4142.

Figure 1.7 depicts the determination of output and price by a monopolist. For $I = 3464$, $p_3 = .5774$, and $x_4 = 1000$, the demand curve (equation 1.47a), the marginal revenue curve (equation 1.49), and the marginal cost curve (equation 1.23) are plotted. The marginal revenue (MR) curve intersects the marginal cost (MC) curve at the output level $x_2 = 816$. At this output, the price that the consumers are willing to pay, according to the demand curve, is 1.8859. If the industry consists of many small enterprises, the supply curve of the industry is the MC curve. At any price p_2, the supply curve shows the quantity that all enterprises in the industry together are willing to supply. If $p_2 = 1.4142$, supply will be 1225. At this price, demand is also 1225 and demand equals supply. Thus, in a competitive market, output and price are determined by the intersection of the demand and supply curves. In an industry with a monopoly, output is determined by the intersection of the MR and MC curves, while price is given by the demand curve for this quantity of output. As long as demand decreases with price, the monopoly solution gives a smaller output and a higher price than the competitive solution.

In a market economy, if there are opportunities for some enterprises to monopolize, they will try to do so in order to make larger profits. If they succeed in doing so, the conditions for Pareto optimality will no longer hold. For example, when a monopolist balances the cost and benefit of hiring 1 additional unit of labor, the cost is p_3 per unit and the benefit is the marginal product times marginal revenue (and not times price, as in the case of a competitive enterprise). The extra revenue that a monopolist obtains by selling the marginal product is less than the price p_2 of the product times the marginal product because the price has to be reduced when a larger quantity is sold. The extra revenue per unit of output is precisely the marginal revenue. Therefore, the benefit to a monopolist is marginal revenue times the marginal product of labor. Since

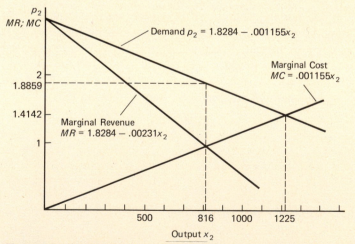

Figure 1.7 Determination of output and price by a monopolist.

MR is lower than price, the benefit is smaller than $p_2 \times$ marginal product. For an economy to be Pareto optimal, according to Condition 3 or Condition 3a of Section 1.7, when a unit of labor is transferred to produce more of product 2, the value of the extra product, or $p_2 \times$ marginal product, must be just equal to the price p_3 of labor. In the case of a monopoly, the value of the extra product is larger than p_3 because p_3 is set equal to $MR \times$ marginal product. From the viewpoint of social welfare the monopolist should be hiring more labor (and producing more output) to make $p_2 \times$ marginal product equal p_2, but it does not. Thus Pareto optimality is violated.

Economists have suggested means to prevent firms from becoming monopolies and to foster competition. They have also suggested ways to regulate monopolies in industries where one or two firms seem to be economically efficient, for example one supplier of electricity and natural gas to a city or one railway between two locations. Others have pointed out that apparent monopolists often do not have much monopoly power to reduce output and increase price because other firms can potentially enter the industry to compete or because firms in related industries can act as competitors (airlines and buses competing with railroads, for example). Still others, notably Joseph Schumpeter (1883–1950), believe that allowing for some monopoly power is good for society because by having such power the large firms can develop new technology and new products to promote economic growth and development. We will turn to the subject of growth and development in the next section.

1.9 INVESTMENT AND NEW TECHNOLOGY

The first question raised in this book was, Why have some countries become rich while others remain poor? The main answer is that some have more physical and human capital that they have accumulated through time. Our analysis of a market economy so far has been confined to the way consumers and private enterprises interact to determine the prices and quantities of final products and inputs and how inputs will be used efficiently to produce different products. We now come to the question, How is capital accumulated in a market economy?

Assume first that technology is known to members of the society. An economy accumulates physical capital when enterprises decide to expand their productive capacity by investment in buildings, machines, equipment, and other capital goods. An enterprise will invest if the additional revenues to be derived from the investment are more than the cost of the investment. The term *investment* means the increase in the stock of capital goods. If the stock of capital goods, or *capital stock* for short, could be changed by small units, the expansion of capital stock would stop when the additional revenues to be derived from one extra unit would just cover the cost of that unit. This is the same principle as hiring an input up to a point where the value of its marginal product (or MR times the marginal product in the case of a monopoly) just equals its marginal cost. The only complication in the present case is that the additional revenues will come in different times in the future, and a revenue of $1 next year does not have the same worth as $1 today.

In order to add up the revenues that are forthcoming in future periods, we have to *discount* each future revenue to find its value in today's dollars, or its *present value*. If the rate of interest is .05 per year, $1 today will be worth $1.05 a year from now; $1 a year from now will be equivalent to $1/1.05 today; $1 two years from now will be equivalent to $1/1.05 one year from now, or to $1/(1.05)^2$ today. Let the additional revenues from an extra unit of capital stock be v_1 one year from now, v_2 two years from now, and so forth up to v_k k years from now. If the rate of interest is r, the *present value* of these additional revenues is

$$V = \frac{v_1}{1+r} + \frac{v_2}{(1+r)^2} + \ldots + \frac{v_k}{(1+r)^k} \tag{1.50}$$

If the additional revenues v_i to arrive i years from now were all equal to $1 and if they would continue forever, as one would get by lending $20 out forever at 5 percent interest per year, the present value of these revenues is

$$V = \frac{1}{1+r} + \frac{1}{(1+r)^2} + \frac{1}{(1+r)^3} + \ldots \equiv \Theta + \Theta^2 + \Theta^3 + \ldots$$

$$= \frac{\Theta}{1-\Theta} = \frac{1}{r} \tag{1.51}$$

Thus the present value of $1 every year forever discounted at an interest rate of 5 percent is 1/.05, or $20. The higher the interest rate, the smaller is the present value of a given stream of future revenues.

To decide whether to acquire an extra unit of capital stock, a profit-maximizing enterprise calculates the *present value* of the additional revenues net of the additional costs (that is, the *additional profits*) in the future due to the extra unit of capital stock. It then compares the present value with the cost of this unit of capital stock. As long as the present value of additional future profits covers the cost, the investment is worth making. Since the present value will be lower the higher the rate of interest, a profitable investment will become unprofitable when the rate of interest is increased. Thus, raising the rate of interest will lower the amount of investment undertaken by enterprises.

When a certain investment is found to be profitable, where does a firm find money to finance it? One source of funds is the profits earned in previous years. Another source is borrowing from outside. Let us consider how consumers determine to lend money to enterprises for investment purposes. For an economy to grow, consumers cannot consume all the national income, because that would leave nothing for capital accumulation. Consumers must save some of their income. The analysis of the saving behavior of a consumer can be carried out in the same way as in Figure 1.2. Instead of choosing between rice and cloth, the consumer would be choosing between total consumption in year 1 and total consumption in year 2. When the rate of interest increases, sacrificing $1 of consumption in year 1 will yield a larger amount of consumption in year 2, thus encouraging the consumer to consume more in year 2, which can be achieved by saving more in year 1. The price of consumption in year 2 relative to the price of consumption in year 1 is $1/(1+r)$. This relative price decreases as the rate of interest increases, encouraging more saving in year 1 and more consumption in year 2. Thus, when the rate of interest increases, more funds will be available from the savings of consumers (see Problem 14).

Consumers through their savings are the suppliers of funds for investment. The demand for funds comes from the enterprises wishing to invest. The rate of interest serves as a price to equate demand and supply. If at a given rate of interest the demand for funds is smaller than the supply of funds, the rate of interest will fall, so as to encourage enterprises to invest more and consumers to save less until demand equals supply. At equilibrium the additional benefit from an extra unit of investment just equals the cost of the investment. By investing, the enterprises take away resources from present consumption to increase future consumption. The rate of interest governs the rate of exchange between the production of present goods and future goods. In equilibrium the rate of exchange in production is equal to the rate at which each consumer is willing to trade present consumption for future consumption. Without this equality the economy will not be Pareto optimal. If by investing $1 today an enterprise can get $1.05 next year, but a consumer is asking for $1.06 more consumption next year to give up $1 of consumption now, the investment should not be carried out and the $1 should be used for current consumption. If a consumer is indifferent between consuming $1 today and $1.04 next year, the investment should be carried out to obtain $1.06 next year, which will more than compensate the consumer's loss of present consumption.

In practice, consumers seldom deal with the investing enterprises directly. *Banks* are instituted to channel consumers' savings for use in investments by enterprises. In any case, the rate of interest and the quantity of total saving or investment are determined by the demand for and supply of funds. This is the mechanism by which a market economy determines how much to invest or whether to accumulate the stock of capital.

A similar analysis applies to the investment in the stock of capital embedded in human beings in the form of their skills and knowledge, called *human capital.* A person decides on how much to invest in himself or his children by balancing the future returns to an extra unit of investment with its cost. Education and training (on the job or otherwise) are the forms of investment. The cost includes tuition and the earnings that the individual forgoes while receiving the education or training. The benefits include extra money and psychic incomes that will be received after the investment. This is how human capital is accumulated in a market economy (see Chapter 7).

Investment in both physical and human capital can take the form of employing new technology. An enterprise can acquire new technology by investing in new types of machinery and training its workers or hiring qualified workers to operate them. Often such an investment is risky. New technology may result from the enterprise's own innovations (in its own laboratories) or from adoption and development of the technology of others. Whenever an enterprise tries something new, there is a risk involved. Schumpeter (1942) has argued that certain monopolistic practices of large enterprises are good for the society because such practices are part of the process of innovation —inventing, developing, and marketing new products, and inventing and adopting new methods of production. These innovations contribute significantly to economic development.

1.10 THE ROLE AND BEHAVIOR OF GOVERNMENT

The description of how a market economy, or any economy, works is incomplete without a discussion of the role of the government. Two different questions can be asked: How should the government behave? How does the government actually behave?

The first is a question in *normative economics,* which deals with issues of good and bad. The second is a question of *positive economics,* which is concerned with the explanation and prediction of economic behavior by individual economic units and by groups of economic units. Our main concern in this chapter, and in this book, is with positive economics. We have explained how prices and outputs are determined in a competitive market economy, how they are modified by behaviors of monopolists, and how savings and investments are determined so that a market economy can accumulate physical and human capital to become more productive. We have not entirely neglected normative economics, pointing out that the working of a competitive market economy will produce results that are desirable (efficient and optimal in a certain sense).

Let us first answer the normative question: What should a government do in a market economy?

A. Since a competitive market economy will function efficiently if the conditions for its proper functioning prevail, the government ought to foster these required conditions.

1. As we pointed out, the operation of private enterprises may have *external effects* on the society that are not included in their cost and benefit calculations. For example, if the cost to society of the waste generated by an enterprise is not paid by the enterprise, it will produce extra units of output at a cost to society higher than the value of the product. The government should find some way to charge the enterprise for the social cost of environmental deterioration that results from the disposal of its waste material. In general, the government should help make the private costs and benefits of enterprises equal to the social costs and benefits.

2. To the extent that monopolistic practices are undesirable, the government should promote competition or regulate monopolists, or both. The issues here are not clearcut if monopolistic practices are part of the process of innovation.

B. Certain commodities cannot be produced efficiently by private enterprises because they benefit many people and individuals cannot be charged separately for using them. These commodities can be provided for by the government.

1. There are *public goods* that individuals jointly consume. National defense is an example. Highways and public parks are other examples, although one can debate whether these should be private, with appropriate tolls charged for their use.

2. A related category is sometimes referred to as the *infrastructure* of the economy, which includes harbors, railroads and highways, and other facilities necessary to the production process. Private enterprises may not be able to supply them because of insufficient capital or because of their inability to collect all the benefits from the investment. If the development of a harbor or a railroad benefits the residents in nearby communities who do not directly use them, it is difficult for a private enterprise to collect the right taxes from these residents.

C. Especially in a less developed economy, the educational level of certain members of the population may be low. Members of the society may not know how to adopt a new technology. The government has a role in educating these people. For example, the Joint Commission on Rural Reconstruction in Taiwan sponsored programs to teach farmers better methods of farming and marketing their products. The Taiwan government has also conducted programs to train skilled workers to produce integrated circuits and other products related to the computer or information industry. Governments in both developed and less developed countries have established educational institutions to supplement private educational institutions. Some people have argued that the social benefit of getting a person educated is more than the benefit to the individual alone and that therefore education should be subsidized by the government. People may disagree on whether the government should merely subsidize private educational institutions or should itself operate some or all educational institutions. In China, the view of many is that the government should operate most educational institutions, for political or other reasons.

D. A related point to the above is that in a less developed economy, managerial talents may be limited. If some farmers do not know how to farm well, perhaps some business managers do not know how to improve the technology and products of their enterprises. Whether because of a lack of technical knowledge, of managerial talent, or of capital from existing enterprises, certain potentially profitable industries may not get developed without government intervention. The government may decide to operate an enterprise in a potentially profitable industry, sometimes as a joint venture with a foreign corporation, in order to lead the development of this industry. In a small economy like that of Taiwan, an able minister of economic affairs can run the government enterprises in the same way that an able chairman of a large conglomerate runs its many operating divisions and subsidiaries. The minister or chairman decides what new enterprises to develop and whom to appoint to run them. In 1982, Taiwan's minister of economic affairs, Chao Yao-Tung, while actively developing new enterprises, decided to transfer a large number of unprofitable government enterprises to private ownership.

E. The government has been called on to redistribute income and wealth among members of a society. In the illustrative economy of Section 1.6, as in many actual economies, some people may own large amounts of land and capital. It is often felt that rich people should not be allowed to leave all their wealth to whomever they please; instead, inheritance taxes should be levied. Similarly, progressive income taxes have been instituted to tax the people with high income proportionally more than people with low income. Also welfare programs are instituted to make sure that certain basic needs of the poor members of the community are satisfied. Beyond the scope of our inquiry are questions of how progressive the income tax should be or whether there should be an income tax at all (rather than a tax on consumption alone, which would encourage people to save more and to work more), and what kinds of welfare programs are desirable. Most people agree, however, that some form of income redistribution by the government is desirable.

F. The above discussion deals mainly with the government's role in the allocation and distribution of resources that, in a market economy, are the result of decisions of many individual economic units—consumers and enterprises. This is the branch of economics known as *microeconomics,* to be distinguished from *macroeconomics,* which deals with economic aggregates or averages, such as the national income, total employment, the price level as measured by some price index, and the changes in these aggregates. There are many explanations of business fluctuations. For example, rapid rise in production in certain years may result from the introduction of new products, from the increase in the supply of money (as through the discovery of gold), from a very good harvest, and from other causes. Slowdown in production may be caused by a lack of investment opportunities, by slow growth in the purchase of durable goods after large purchases in the recent past, by a drop in the money supply because some people withdraw their money from the banks after hearing of a few bank failures, and by other factors. We cannot go into these explanations here. The government has a role in promoting price stability, full employment, and reasonable growth in the economy by adjusting government expenditures and taxation (*fiscal* policies) and by adjusting the supply of money and the availability of credit (*monetary* policies).

G. The government has a role in influencing the flow of foreign trade by setting tariffs, import quotas, subsidies to export industries, and the exchange rate of its currency. Some economists are in favor of free trade—that is, no tariffs, import quotas, or subsidies—because such measures only improve the welfare of certain members of the community at the expense of others. Some are in favor of having a flexible exchange rate as determined by the forces of demand for and supply of its currency. In any case, many countries are not practicing free trade. The government of each country has to make decisions concerning foreign trade policy.

H. Finally, in describing a market economy we have assumed implicitly that there is law and order in the economy that government is helping to provide. In some developing countries such an assumption cannot be made. For example, in China, the political instability that existed at least since the Opium War of 1839–1842 became more acute during and after the war with Japan of 1894–1895, and intensified again with the Boxer Rebellion of 1900. In 1911, the Ching Dynasty was overthrown and the Republic of China was established, but the country was divided by warlords and by the influence of foreign powers, and later by the civil war and the war with Japan of 1937–1945. Not until the establishment of the People's Republic of China in 1949 was political stability restored. With continuing political conflicts and wars, and with warlords extracting levies on if not stopping the transportation of goods passing through their territories, one cannot say that a market economy was functioning properly. The importance of political factors in economic development should not be overlooked.

It is one thing to discuss what the government ought to do. It is another to explain what it actually does. Examples can be found in different countries where government officials fail to perform their duties faithfully and diligently, some showing incompetence, corruption, or bureaucratic rigidity. The science of economics has not explained the actual economic behavior of government very satisfactorily, although good research results on certain aspects of this topic are available. Not infrequently, government officials have sided with particular economically influential groups in the society to promote their own interests at the expense of the rest of society. One hypothesis that economists have advanced to explain the behavior of government officials is that they look after their self-interest in the same way as other individuals competing in the marketplace. Often economists take the behavior of government as given and go on to explain the economic consequences of given government policies or actions. In the Chinese economy, the government plays such an important role that one cannot fully understand the working of the Chinese economy without considering the behavior of the government. In the next chapter, more attention will be devoted to explaining the behavior of the Chinese government. A distinction will be made between the top government leaders who direct economic planning and the government officials at lower levels whose interests and objectives are different.

PROBLEMS

1. Label Figure 1.1 from the viewpoint of the textile worker and discuss the two Pareto-optimal points in this figure in terms of the worker.

2. In the example of Figure 1.2, let the price of cloth decrease from \$2.00 to \$1.60. Draw a new budget line AC' and write the new budget equation. Break down the effect of this price change into an income effect and a substitution effect, using a diagram and another budget equation with constant real income. What is the new money income that keeps the farmer's real income constant?

3. Using Figure 1.2, explain the total demand and total supply of cloth by the 100 farmers and the 100 workers if the price of cloth were \$1.60 per unit. Why will the price increase to \$2.00?

4. Using the information in Figures 1.2 and 1.3, draw a market demand curve for and a market supply curve of rice. Determine the market-clearing relative price of rice.

5. You may reproduce Figures 1.2 and 1.3 by assuming that the indifference curves are given by $x_1 x_2 = u$. Given the value of u, all points (x_1, x_2) on the same indifference curve satisfy $x_1 x_2 = u$. Thus $u = x_1 x_2$ can be considered the utility level of the bundle of goods (x_1, x_2). Using different values of u, one can draw different indifference curves in a diagram like Figure 1.2. To derive the demand functions from the *utility function* $u = x_1 x_2$, we maximize $x_1 x_2$ subject to the constraint $p_1 x_1 + p_2 x_2 = I$, where I denotes the money income of the consumer. Differentiating the Lagrangian expression

$$x_1 x_2 + \lambda(I - p_1 x_1 - p_2 x_2)$$

with respect to x_1, x_2 and the Lagrange multiplier λ and set the partial derivatives equal to zero, we can solve for the unknowns x_1, x_2 and λ. The results are the demand functions for x_1 and x_2,

$$x_1 = I/2p_1$$
$$x_2 = I/2p_2$$

The farmer's money income is $I = 100p_1$; the worker's income is $I = 20p_2$.

Write out the market demand function for and the supply function of cloth. Explain how they determine the price of cloth relative to the price of rice.

6. Compare the production function (equation 1.10) with the production function

$$x_2 = \alpha x_3^\beta x_4^{(1-\beta)}$$

where α and β are constants. This production function is called a *Cobb-Douglas* production function. Equation 1.10 is a special case with $\alpha = 1$ and $\beta = .5$. Interpret the constants α and β.

7. Rework the example of Figure 1.5 by changing the price p_4 of the fixed input from $p_4 = .7$ to $p_4 = .5$, and to $p_4 = 1.0$. What would happen to the output x_2, to the use of input x_3, and to profits π in each case? How would the total cost and the marginal cost change?

8. Revise Figure 1.2 to show the choice between the consumption of leisure time and cloth (and all other consumer goods), instead of rice and cloth. Let the consumer have a maximum of 100 hours (per week) to sell. Show how the price of cloth (and all other consumer goods) and the wage of labor affect his choice. Discuss the income effect and the substitution effect of an increase in the wage rate. Derive the supply curve of labor by this worker-consumer.

9. In the solution of the competitive economy described in Section 1.6, we do not discuss the profits of the cloth factories. How many units of machines x_4 does a cloth factory need to operate in order not to incur a loss?

10. What will happen to the economy of Section 1.6 if there are 2000 units of machines instead of 1000? Discuss the new solution by explaining why each price and quantity changes from the old solution value in the way it does.

11. What will happen to the economy of Section 1.6 if there are 200 workers instead of 100? Discuss the new solution by explaining why each price and quantity changes from the old solution value in the way it does.

12. What will happen to the economy of Section 1.7 if the demand function (equation 1.29) is replaced by the demand function (equation 1.47) but the cloth industry remains competitive?

13. What will happen to the economy of Section 1.7 if cloth is produced by a monopoly with a demand function given by equation 1.47?

14. Analogous to Figure 1.2, draw a diagram with the two axes measuring the total values of consumption in year 1 and year 2. Let the consumer have $100 now for use in consumption in both years. Draw her budget constraints when the rate of interest is 5 percent and 10 percent. Discuss the changes in her consumption in the two years when the interest rate is raised from 5 percent to 10 percent. Explain the income effect and the substitution effect. How is the consumer's saving affected by the rise in the interest rate?

REFERENCES

Baumol, William J. 1961. *Economic theory and operations analysis.* Englewood Cliffs, N.J.: Prentice-Hall.

———— and Alan Blinder. 1982. *Economics: Principles and policy.* 2d ed. New York: Harcourt Brace Jovanovich.

Chao, Yao-Tung. 1982. *Concepts and methods for industrial development.* Taipei: Ministry of Economic Affairs.

Chinese State Statistics Bureau. 1982. *Statistical yearbook of China, 1981.* Hong Kong: Hong Kong Economic Review Publishing House.

Fischer, Stanley, and Rudiger Dornsbusch. 1983. *Economics.* New York: McGraw-Hill.

Friedman, Milton. 1962. *Price theory: A provisional text.* Chicago: Aldine.

Henderson, James M., and Richard E. Quandt. 1980. *Microeconomic theory: A mathematical approach.* 3d ed. New York: McGraw-Hill.

Hirschleifer, Jack. 1980. *Price theory and applications.* 2d ed. Englewood Cliffs, N.J.: Prentice-Hall.

Mansfield, Edwin. 1980. *Economics: Principles, problems, decisions.* New York: Norton.

Samuelson, Paul A. 1980. *Economics.* 11th ed. New York: McGraw-Hill.

Schumpeter, Joseph A. 1942. *Capitalism, socialism and democracy.* New York: Harper & Row.

chapter *2*

How the Chinese Economy Works

2.1 MODEL OF A CENTRALLY PLANNED ECONOMY

This chapter describes and explains the working of the Chinese economy in the 1980s. In China major economic decisions are made by the central economic planners, while market forces also play their part. To understand the Chinese economy, one needs to know how a centrally planned economy works. In Sections 2.1 and 2.2 we will discuss an abstract model of a centrally planned economy. This model serves as a blueprint to explain the Chinese planned economy from the 1950s to 1977. Economic institutions in China have changed rapidly since 1978 and are still changing. In Section 2.3 we will discuss a second model, which modifies the first by introducing certain elements of a market economy. This second model can help to explain the present working of the Chinese economy.

Before we proceed, a word about economic theory is in order. In the preceding paragraph we refer to a "first model" and a "second model." A *model* is an abstract construct that incorporates certain important elements from reality. The economic reality of any country is very complicated. To understand it we select certain important features from it and use them to construct a hypothetical economy, which is our model. The model is good if its behavior corresponds closely to the behavior of the actual economy that it is constructed to explain. It is impossible and wasteful to include in a model *all* the elements of a complicated reality. To understand the Chinese economy, for example, it is impossible and unnecessary to describe China's every farm, factory, restaurant, farmer, worker, factory manager, economic planning bureau, economic planner, and so on. Such information would take billions of pages to describe—China has more than a billion people (all consumers, each having certain special economic characteristics), millions of farms, and so on—and most of it is not essential for understanding the Chinese economy.

In Chapter 1 we describe a model of a highly competitive market economy, in which the consumers decide what to buy in the market and a large number of enterprises in each industry compete in their production of outputs and employment of inputs. In such a world, the government should provide law and order but need not participate in any economic activities; it has to collect some taxes to pay for police services. We modified this model by introducing monopolistic practices, external effects of private production on the society, lack of knowledge, public goods, and other areas toward which government economic activities can be directed. In this chapter we start from the other extreme by constructing a model in which central economic planners make almost all decisions concerning consumption, production of outputs, employment of inputs, distribution of income, and investment. Note that in a centrally planned economy these same economic problems have to be solved as in a market economy, but the methods for solving them are different.

In our model of a centrally planned economy, let there be a *planning authority* consisting of a group of economic planners. We will not specify the political structure of this group, whether one member has more authority than the others, or in what fashion the group works. The planning authority has control over all physical productive resources, including land, buildings, machinery, and other capital goods, including taxicabs and automobiles. Directly or indirectly, it controls all enterprises, farms, and factories. It can assign a production target to each farm and each factory to tell it how much of each good to produce. It controls all sources of supply of inputs. In assigning an output quota to a farm or a factory, it also supplies the inputs required for production, such as fertilizer and tractors for farming and materials for industrial production. In addition, it assigns workers to different factories. It can direct a person from a city to work in a particular farm. It can direct a farmer to work in a different farm or to work in the city (although the latter seldom actually happens in China). Thus, the production of final outputs and the allocation of inputs for production are controlled by the planning authority.

As far as the consumption of final products is concerned, the supplies of all consumer goods are under the control of the planning authority. There are two kinds of consumer goods, rationed goods and nonrationed goods. The former include food grain, vegetable oil, meat, sugar, and cotton cloth. They are distributed to consumers through a rationing system. Every month each consumer is given a fixed number of ration coupons, which have to be used, in addition to money, to pay for the rationed goods. The nonrationed goods are sold through stores operated by the authority, but the consumer can decide what and how much to buy.

The income of a factory worker depends on the wage rate that the authority determines. Workers have job security in the sense that they cannot be dismissed; rarely is a worker reassigned to another job. A farmer gets a fraction of the income of the farm on which he or she works: Each farmer accumulates work points throughout the year; at the end of the year the work points of all farm members are added together, and the fraction attributed to each person is calculated, which determines what share of the farm income he or she gets. The total income of the farm is the difference between its revenue and its cost. The revenue is the money value of the products of the farm.

A part of the products must be sold to the planning authority (through an agent), and the remainder is left in the farm for distribution to its members. The planning authority decides on the amount and price of each product it will purchase from each farm. By changing the purchase prices and purchase quotas of farm products, the authority controls the incomes of the farmers.

Figure 2.1 compares the functioning of our hypothetical centrally planned economy with that of a market economy. In each economy there are consumers and enterprises (including farms and factories). Each arrow indicates a flow of goods or services. Consumer goods flow from producers to consumers. Labor services flow from consumers to producers. Material inputs and capital goods flow from producers to producers. In a market economy all flows go through markets. In a centrally planned economy all flows are controlled by the planning authority. It orders the producers to produce certain consumer goods and distribute them to the consumers. It assigns laborers to work in various production units. It orders producers to produce material inputs and distribute them to other producers. It also directs the production of capital goods and the construction of investment projects.

When goods and services flow in one direction, money payments for these goods flow in the opposite direction. Consumers pay for the goods they buy. Producers also pay for the inputs and capital goods that they use. In a market economy the buyers and sellers can settle the exchanges directly in a market or through intermediaries who perform the services of commerce and trade. The prices are determined by the forces of demand and supply, as we discuss in Chapter 1. In a centrally planned economy the users and the producers have to go through the planning authority or distributors who work under the direction of the planning authority. All prices (including wages for labor services) are determined by the planning authority.

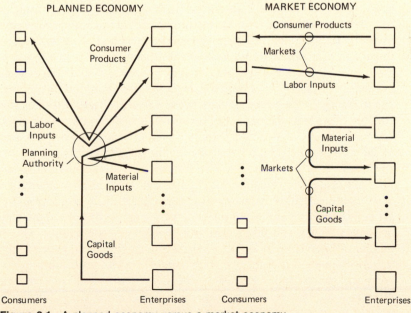

Figure 2.1 A planned economy versus a market economy.

In any economy, goods have to be produced for consumption and for capital accumulation. Consumer goods are produced mainly for present consumption, and capital goods are produced in order to expand the future productive capacity of the economy. In a centrally planned economy the planning authority has the responsibility to decide the total amount of each consumer good and capital good to be produced, the specific quantities of each good to be produced by the enterprises under its control, the supplies of each important input to be allotted to these enterprises, and the amounts of capital investment to be allotted to the enterprises. It then decides how the consumer goods are to be distributed to consumers. Works get done by central command as in an army. The commander of an army directs all activities of the soldiers and determines their food rations. Great projects have been completed by central command all through history, including the Great Wall of China and the pyramids of Egypt. However, only recently has a central government authority attempted to direct all the complicated tasks connected with the production of thousands of goods by millions of enterprises and their distribution to millions of people in a modern economy. In the remainder of this section we examine these major tasks of a central planning authority.

Referring back to Figure 2.1, we find that in the case of a centrally planned economy, the production and distribution decisions are made by the planning authority. In the case of a market economy they are made by individual consumers and producers trading in the market. As we explain in Chapter 1, no central direction is involved in the latter case. Given his or her income and the prices of different products, each consumer decides what to buy from the market. When the price of a good goes up, the consumer will consume less of it. Given its production function and the prices of outputs and inputs, each enterprise decides how much output to produce and how much of each input to use in production. Prices will adjust so that the quantities produced will equal the quantities demanded by the users. Each enterprise only needs to know its own economic conditions (including its method of production or technology, the productivity of its workers, the capacity of its capital equipment, and the kinds of inputs required) and the prices of its products and of its inputs. It will then know the quantity of output to produce and the quantities of inputs to use for producing it most economically. For a central planning authority to assign production quotas to millions of productive units and to supply them with appropriate inputs, it has to know the economic conditions of all these units. The central authority therefore needs a large staff to collect information and to supervise these enterprises. In a market economy no one needs to have all this information. As far as each enterprise is concerned, the prices of the outputs and inputs constitute all the outside information it needs to produce efficiently.

Besides the information requirement, the central planning authority has to find ways to ensure that the enterprises produce efficiently, by employing the most economical combination of inputs for any output, by employing the right kind and the right quantity of labor, and by producing a product of good quality. This boils down to a problem of providing *incentives* to management. In a market economy, incentives are largely material: profits for owners of enterprises and profit sharing for managers who are part owners. In a centrally planned economy, both material and nonmaterial incentives can be used to encourage managers of enterprises to operate efficiently. The central authority may allow them to share profits, or it may appeal to their sense of patriotism and reward the successful ones with honors. The Chinese have accumulated valuable experience concerning the use of nonmaterial incentives.

To carry out investment projects the central planning authority has the option of instructing enterprises to invest according to its directives or allowing enterprises to retain a part of their profits for investment at their discretion. In the latter case, it is difficult for the central planning authority to provide sufficient incentives for the enterprises to undertake an investment project when the success of the project is uncertain. In a market economy the owner-manager is willing to undertake a risky project because when it succeeds the reward is great. For example, suppose that a risky project costing $200,000 has a 40 percent chance of being successful; if it is successful, the enterprise will make $1,000,000, but if it fails, the enterprise will make nothing. An owner of the enterprise will probably decide to take the risk, hoping to get the $1,000,000. A manager of a private corporation will probably not undertake such a risky project if he owns only a small share of the corporation and receives only a small share of its profits. Likewise, a manager of a government enterprise who will receive no portion of the profit will probably not take the risk because if the project succeeds he may get some reward (though nothing like $1,000,000), but if it fails he will be blamed. Conversely, if an investment project is safe but not very profitable, it is difficult for a central planning authority to discourage a manager from undertaking it. The high cost of the project, relative to its future benefits, is not borne by the manager, so he or she has no incentive to save the government money.

The last task of the planning authority to be discussed here is the setting of prices. In a market economy, prices affect the consumption, production, and distribution of goods. In a centrally planned economy, prices can affect consumption but cannot encourage or discourage production if the enterprises do not operate to make profits. Prices perform an important function in the distribution of consumer goods to consumers and of producer goods and materials to producers. In the case of consumers, purchase prices of agricultural products and wage rates affect the income of farmers and workers, respectively. Prices of consumer goods affect the quantities of these goods that they demand. Prices of producer goods and materials affect the revenues of those enterprises producing them and the costs of those enterprises employing them. In setting these prices, the central planning authority has to consider three sets of balances.

First, the total value of all consumer goods produced should be equal to the total value of the quantities that consumers want to buy, given the total value of their incomes. Since the supplies of all consumer goods as well as their prices are set by the planning authority, the total value of all consumer goods is determined. In the meantime wage rates and purchase prices of farm products help determine the incomes of consumers. Consumers decide how much of their incomes to spend on consumer goods and how much to save. If the total value of consumer goods that consumers decide to purchase, given their incomes, is larger than the total value of the goods available, there will be hidden inflation, or open inflation if the prices of some goods are not controlled. In fact, at any price that the planning authority happens to set for a particular nonrationed good, the supply of that good may not be sufficient to satisfy the demand. In that case there will be shortages, with consumers waiting for more supplies to come.

Second, the planning authority has to set prices so as to balance the books for all the enterprises under its control. The total revenue of each enterprise is determined by the production quota and the price of the output. Its total expenditure is determined by the quantities and prices of the inputs that it employs and the capital goods that it needs for the targeted expansion. If an enterprise's total revenue exceeds its total expenditures, it has a surplus that belongs to the planning authority. If total revenue is less than total expenditures, the enterprise needs a subsidy from the planning authority to balance its books. The planning authority cannot let the total revenues from all enterprises be less than their total expenditures, unless it has other sources of revenues to be used as subsidies.

Third, the planning authority has to balance its budget or find ways to finance its deficits. Deficits can be financed in two ways, by issuing new money and by borrowing, either from the public through government bonds or from other countries and international organizations in the form of foreign debts. Issuing too much new money will cause inflation, open or hidden. Since prices will affect the balancing of the government's budget, the central authority has to take this factor into account in setting prices.

2.2   BEHAVIOR OF ECONOMIC UNITS IN A PLANNED ECONOMY

We have described the basic organizational arrangement of a centrally planned economy and the functions of the planning authority. How the economy works and how well it works depend on how, and how well, the planning authority performs its functions and how the economy's other units respond to its directions. Therefore, the description of a centrally planned economy is incomplete without a discussion of the behavior of all the component economic units, including consumers, farmers, workers, farms, industrial enterprises, as well as the central planning authority itself. In this chapter the description of the economic behavior of each type of economic unit is simplified and brief, leaving out details that are discussed in later chapters. Our present purpose is to gain a broad picture of how the Chinese economy functions.

As far as the behavior of consumers in a centrally planned economy is concerned, the basic theory presented in Section 1.3 is essentially valid if the rationing of consumer goods is taken into account. If there is no rationing, the theory of Section 1.3 is applicable to a consumer or consumer unit not only in China but in any part of the world. A consumer is assumed to be able to rank different bundles of consumer goods according to his or her preferences. Graphically, bundles of goods equally preferred are points on an indifference curve. Given his income and the prices of all goods, the consumer is assumed to choose that bundle on the highest-ranked indifference curve that he or she can afford. The most important implication of this theory is that when the relative price of a commodity goes up, the consumer will buy less of it. A demand function for each commodity is derived by the consumer's search for the highest-ranked indifference curve, subject to the constraints of his or her budget. The demand for any commodity is thus a function of consumers' incomes and the prices of all commodities.

When *rationing* is present, the consumer not only has to pay the price of a rationed good, but also has to surrender a ration coupon for one unit of that commodity. The rationing of a particular commodity is said to be *effective* if all rationed coupons for that commodity are used up. If they are not used up, the ration coupons are not serving to restrict the consumption of that commodity and the demand for that commodity is just like the demand for a nonrationed commodity. If there are several commodities for which rationing is effective, the theory of consumer behavior can be developed in the following way. The quantities and prices of these commodities are given, the former equal to the numbers of coupons issued. Subtract the value of these commodities from the consumer's income. The consumer now has a smaller income to spend on the remaining commodities. Given this smaller income (net of the spending on the rationed commodities) and given the prices of the remaining commodities, the consumer now chooses a bundle of the remaining commodities that he or she prefers, subject to budget constraints on purchases of the remaining commodities. The demand for each commodity is a function of the net income and the prices of the remaining commodities. When the relative price of a remaining commodity goes up, its consumption will go down, as usual.

For the purpose of studying the demand for nonrationed commodities by a Chinese consumer, a first approximation is to treat as given his income (net of the necessary expenditures on the rationed commodities) and the prices of all nonrationed commodities, and to apply the standard theory of demand to these commodities, as presented in Section 1.3. However, the theory of consumer behavior under rationing is complicated by the fact that the consumption of rationed commodities is related to that of nonrationed commodities. If cotton cloth is rationed effectively, for example, the demand for buttons and for tailors' services will be affected. So will the demand for cloth made of artificial fibers (see Problem 1). There is a well-developed theory of consumer behavior under rationing, which we present in Sections 5.4 and 5.5.

Next, we consider the behavior of a Chinese farmer, which depends on his working arrangement. In the planned economy studied in this section and the preceding section, the arrangement is a simplified version of the Chinese reality of 1959 to 1977. The farms are organized as *communes,* which serve as both political-administrative and economic units of the government. Each commune is divided into *brigades,* and each brigade is divided into *work teams.* According to the *Almanac of China's Economy, 1981* (p. 965), the total population of the communes in 1979 was 807.4 million. There were 174.9 million families organized into 53,348 communes, 699,000 brigades, and 5,154,000 teams. On the average, these statistics imply 13.1 brigades per commune, 7.4 teams per brigade, and 157 persons per team. The central planning authority directs each commune to grow particular kinds of crops, assigns production quotas for the products and the amounts to be delivered to the government purchasing agency at given prices, and provides the necessary supplies of farm inputs to each commune. The communes also engage in large projects, such as road construction and irrigation, that require the work of an entire brigade, as well as sideline nonfarm activities such as factories to produce light-industrial products. Each farmer is paid a fraction of the income of the team to which he belongs. The fraction is the ratio of the number of work points the farmer earns to the total number earned by all team members. An incentive problem arises because the farmer is not paid according to the marginal product of his labor: If he works harder to increase output, he gets very little of the additional output because that, too, is shared by all members of the team. Chinese planners have indeed found little incentive among farmers to work hard.

The behavior of a Chinese industrial worker likewise depends on her working arrangement. In the first place, the worker's job is assigned to her by a labor bureau, which tries to match jobs with workers. As compared with a market system, in which workers find jobs for themselves and enterprises decide for themselves which workers to hire and discharge, this system is likely to lead to the mismatching of jobs and workers. Furthermore, the government's labor bureau is less qualified than an enterprise's personnel manager to decide whether a particular worker is suitable for a certain job. The labor bureau staff will often assign the more desirable jobs as compensation for favors. In addition, once assigned a job, the worker cannot be discharged, and she gets the same pay whether she works harder or not. (From 1960 to 1977 the wages of most workers were not changed at all, although some received bonuses or awards of one kind or another. Different wage rates apply to different jobs.) Under these conditions, one can expect to find a lack of incentive and low productivity among the workers, as the Chinese planners have found.

We next consider the behavior of Chinese farms as economic units. First, each commune is directed by the planning authority to produce particular kinds of products and sometimes to use certain acreage allotments and farming techniques, such as multiple cropping. The lack of expertise on the part of the central planning authority and its staff can lead to, and has led to, the misuse of farmland and low productivity. Second, when the planning authority assigns production targets to each commune, the latter in turn assigns production targets to the brigades and the production teams. The production teams have difficulty in getting the farmers to work hard because, as we have pointed out, the farmers do not receive the value of the marginal product of their labor under the payment system. In other words, by commanding farmers to produce as teams and not paying them according to their individual productivity, the commune cannot effectively manage the production of farm products.

As for a Chinese factory, inefficiencies can come from three sources. First, with jobs guaranteed and wages independent of productivity, the management has difficulty in motivating workers to work harder, as we have pointed out. Second, a main goal of the management is not to maximize profits, but to meet the production targets set by the planning authority; there is a lack of incentive for the management to increase outputs beyond the targeted amounts. Since the management can influence the setting of production targets by providing the planning authority with estimates of the productive capacity of the enterprise, it has an incentive to lower the production targets in order to make them easier to meet. Third, because the management receives materials and other required inputs from the planning authority, it has little incentive to economize on the use of the inputs. Nor does it have much incentive to keep its input estimates low, because the management does not bear the cost of additional inputs but it is penalized if inputs are insufficient to meet the production targets. Waste of material and other inputs will result, leading to the accumulation of large inventories.

Finally, we come to the behavior of the planning authority itself. It has the responsibility for solving all the economic problems related to the production and distribution of goods and to the accumulation of capital. It has to rely on the above-mentioned individual economic units to carry out all the tasks of production, distribution, and capital accumulation. How and how well the tasks are accomplished depends on the rules set by the planning authority. We have discussed the behavior of each type of economic unit under one set of rules that approximates the actual conditions in China from 1959 to 1977. At present we will not explain why the planning authority might want to increase the production of one kind of product relative to another, such as more consumption goods and fewer investment goods, or more agricultural products and fewer products of heavy industry. We can say, however, that in trying to achieve its objectives, the planning authority has to face the constraints of its economic environment: the physical and human resources available, the way productive economic units are organized, the technology they use, and the rules they have to follow. When the planning authority attempts to increase the outputs of certain products relative to other products, it will try to increase the production targets of the former products relative to the latter products. How much of one product can be increased when another product is reduced depends on the economy's *production transformation curve* (also called the *production possibility frontier*), such as the one depicted in Figure 1.6. The production transformation curve in Figure 1.6 was constructed under the assumption that production is organized by a set of competitive enterprises in a market economy. However, in a centrally planned economy, given its resources and organizational arrangements, there is a limit to the increase in the output of one product by the reduction in the output of another product. The planning authority will select a point on the production transformation curve that is most preferred. If the preferences of the planning authority are summarized by sets of indifference curves, the combination of outputs will be a point at which the production transformation curve is tangential to an indifference curve, as depicted in Figure 1.6 (see Problem 2).

To look behind the production transformation curve of a centrally planned economy, we need to describe how resources are transferred from the production of one commodity to the production of another commodity. When the planning authority desires an increase of one product, it must ensure that sufficient resources will be made available from somewhere else. In other words, if a central planner wishes to produce x_1 units of good 1, x_2 units of good 2, and so on, it must make available the inputs required to produce them. The *balancing of inputs* is an essential task for a central planning authority that sets production targets for its production units.

The process of balancing the total requirement and total supply of each input consists of the following steps. First, on the basis of its knowledge of each productive unit (industrial enterprise or farm), including its inputs and outputs of the last period, the central planning authority, through its staff and lower-level administrators, sets preliminary production targets for each enterprise and obtains requests from it concerning the amount of each important input required. Second, the planning authority adds up the quantities of each input required by all production units and compares the total with the total produced by all enterprises. If the two sums are the same, the requirement and the supply of this input are in balance. Otherwise, as a third step, the central planning authority advises some production units to reduce their input requirements, instructs some units to raise their production of the required inputs, and reduces the output targets of enterprises producing less essential products. After some negotiations, the planning authority goes back to the first step by issuing a revised set of production targets for each enterprise and a revised set of inputs to be made available to each enterprise. An annual plan is created based on the output targets so obtained. Often the balance between the production and the use of each product is achieved only on paper. When actual production takes place, some materials may be in short supply, creating bottlenecks in production, while other materialss may be in excess supply, creating large inventories. Excess of inventories held by one enterprise may not be made available to another enterprise that needs it; there is no incentive and no mechanism to transfer the excess material from one enterprise to another. The problem of balancing the demand for and supply of each input is solved in a market economy. When demand exceeds supply, the price of that item will rise to discourage its use and encourage its production. When the consumers as a group decide to have more of product 2 relative to product 1, the relative price of product 1 goes up relative to the price of product 2, and production of product 2 increases while production of product 1 decreases. Producers of product 2 demand more inputs and obtain them from the other producers through the market. All balancing is achieved by the price mechanism, without the interference of a central planning authority.

Li (1982) describes the management of supplies in China. Between 1949 and 1952 supply management was controlled by the Financial and Economic Commission of the Administrative Council. In 1950 eight major materials, including rolled steel, timber, coal, and cement, were allocated directly by the central government or administrative regions, each consisting of several provinces. The number of major materials under state control was increased to 55 in 1952. In the first Five-Year Plan of 1953–1957, the State Planning Commission increased the number further. Producer goods allocated by government units were classified into three categories: those under unified state allocation, those allocated by different industrial ministries, and those allocated by local authorities. By 1957 the number of products in the first and second categories had increased to 532. These were mainly products of enterprises run by the state at a level not lower than the provincial government or some large-scale state-private joint enterprises and products of private enterprises entirely purchased and marketed by the state. They were not allowed to be marketed by the enterprises themselves, but were to be supplied by a combination of direct planning through central allocation and indirect planning through the market. They accounted for 70 percent to 90 percent of all producer goods in the country. The rest was allocated by provincial, municipal, and autonomous regional authorities; they were distributed through market channels.

Li (1982, pp. 613–614) writes:

> Between 1958 and 1960, there was a serious shortage of materials, chaotic management and frightening waste, all of which caused great difficulties for major production units and construction projects directly under the control of the central authority. This predicament came about because the production targets of industry—heavy industry in particular—were set so high as to be beyond the capability of the country's economy. To make matters worse, control over allocation and distribution of many kinds of materials in the first and second categories were given over to the local authorities. In 1961, the Party Central Committee and the State Council decided to adopt policies of readjustment, consolidation, expansion and raising standards for the national economy. While reducing the scope of capital construction and readjusting industrial production, the state strengthened its unified control of materials. The number of materials in the first and second categories increased to about 500. . . .

> Between 1962 and 1965, the question of controlling the supply of materials was discussed on many occasions by the Party Central Committee and the State Council; decisions for work improvement were made. . . .

On controlling the circulation of goods, Comrade Liu Shaoqi's concept of setting up a system of "second commerce" was put into practice. This included establishment of institutions in charge of materials management, i.e., specialized material supply corporations and stations; organizing service teams to keep regular contacts with user enterprises at the grassroots level; setting up many factories and shops for processing materials according to fixed models. . . . As a result, there was a marked improvement in the supply of materials. . . .

During the ten years of turmoil between 1966 and 1976, however, the supply of producer goods was seriously disrupted. The ministry in charge of that supply was "smashed." Such state institutions in 24 provinces and autonomous regions were suspended and most of the special goods supply companies, service companies and supply stations were either dissolved or merged. . . . Consequently, state control of the allocation and distribution of producer goods was greatly weakened. . . .

The institutions in charge of material supply gradually resumed work and some regulations for the management of goods which had proved effective during the 1960's were reinstated. There has been a strengthening of state control for the allocation and distribution of producer goods. Most of the goods in the first category have been placed once again under control of the state organizations in charge of material supplies. . . . Meanwhile, local authorities have been enjoying greater power in the control of goods. The goods in the first category under the control of local authorities in 1978 accounted for the following percentages of the national total: coal, 46%, rolled steel, 42%, copper, aluminum, lead and zinc, 36%, timber, 18%, and cement, 71%.

This quotation suggests that the central direction of a planned economy, including the supply and allocation of materials, does not cover all goods and services, but only the most important ones. In China the coverage and the effectiveness of control varied from time to time according to political conditions. This fact has to be borne in mind when discussing a model of the Chinese planned economy up to the late 1970s.

Side by side with the balancing of materials in a centrally planned economy, there is a need to balance the flow of money that accompanies the flow of materials. Each enterprise obtains revenues from the goods that it delivers to the central authority or, at the direction of the central authority, to other enterprises. It incurs expenses for the materials it receives for production. It may have a surplus or a deficit as total revenue exceeds or falls short of total costs. In the event of a deficit, a subsidy from the planning authority is required. In order to have a net transfer of resources to all enterprises for the purpose of capital formation, the planning authority may have to run a deficit in its operation of all enterprises. This deficit can be financed by borrowing from or taxing the public, or by borrowing from abroad. In any case, a government budget has to be prepared in connection with the balancing of the materials to summarize the flows of money. (Accordingly, in September 1980 officials of the State Council of China presented for approval to the National People's Congress the National Economic Plans summarizing the production targets for major products for 1980 and 1981, the Final State Budget for 1979, the Draft State Budget for 1980, and the Projected State Budget for 1981.)

Intimately related to the material and financial flows are the prices of various outputs and inputs controlled by the planning authority. A deficit can become a surplus after certain price changes. Prices in a free market are not controlled, but a central planning authority has many options in setting prices, including the use of market signals, as is discussed in Section 2.4. In China the prices of important consumer and producer goods that are distributed through the central planning system are centrally controlled. Prices of products distributed locally are controlled by the local economic administrators. The central planning authority can set prices to control consumption, the distribution of income, the finances of government enterprises, and the rate of inflation. Prices of certain consumer products are set very low to guarantee that each family can afford to purchase some preassigned quantities. Rent for urban housing is extremely low; prices of food grain are also low, requiring government subsidies. Prices of other consumer goods, such as television sets, are set very high to discourage consumption. In order to prevent inflation, prices of certain materials are not allowed to change. Prices of certain supplies to farmers are set high as a tax on farmers to support the process of capital formation. At this point of our discussion we only indicate the motivations of the Chinese planning authority for the setting of certain prices, without implying that such practices are either good or bad. In any case, the planning authority regards the setting of prices as a means to control the economy in the process of economic planning.

A description of the behavior of the planning authority would be incomplete without a mention of the administrative and political problems of the planning organization itself. First, the leadership of the planning authority may fail to perceive all the economic constraints that limit its economic choices. Grossly unrealistic economic plans that cannot be implemented are not unusual, especially if the person or persons in power do not have the required knowledge of or professional advice on economic matters. The two "great leaps" in China in 1958 and 1978 were illustrations of this problem. Second, even with a trained, professional planning staff, the problems of economic planning and balancing of resources for the entire country are extremely difficult, as we have discussed. A reader who has read Sections 1.6 and 1.7 and solved Problems 10, 11, and 12 of Chapter 1 can begin to appreciate the difficult mathematical and informational problems of central economic planning when there are thousands of products and perhaps millions of production units involved, and when the production functions of the production units are not completely known by the economic planners. Third, assuming that a sound and detailed economic plan has been made, the planning authority still faces the problem of supervising its administrative staff, which will carry out its orders all the way down to the individual economic units. There are incentive problems associated with the large bureaucracy required for central planning. False reporting and receiving bribes for doing favors for the enterprises are not uncommon practices. Often the appointment of the staff is influenced by political considerations and not by the candidates' professional qualifications. Once on the staff, a person may use his administrative and economic powers to further his own interests, which may differ from the interests of the central planning authority. Fourth, an additional complication on the Chinese scene is that administrative units of different provinces have their own economic and political objectives. Local powers have persisted through history, and the central planning authority has the problem of getting the provincial and local units to work for its economic goals. The self-interests of lower-level economic administrators often do not coincide with the interest of the top planning authority and create serious problems in China and elsewhere in the world.

We can briefly summarize the behavior of different economic units in our model of a centrally planned economy. The planning authority has certain objectives, which can be summarized by a set of indifference curves showing which combinations of products are equally preferred. If the planning authority is assumed to function intelligently, it tries to find the most preferred combination subject to the restriction of the production-transformation relation among the different products. In the case of two commodities the problem is depicted in Figure 1.6. An unqualified planner will not know the production-transformation curve and may seek a point beyond the productive capabilities of the economy. In the process of mobilizing the different economic units to produce and distributing the products for consumption and for capital accumulation, the central planning authority sets production targets, supplies materials necessary for production, balances the supplies of materials with their requirements, balances the financial flows, sets the wage rates and prices, rations the consumption of certain consumer goods, and assigns jobs to the workers. Given the wage system, the employment system, the rationing system, and the setting of prices and production targets by the planning authority, the other economic units—consumers, farmers, workers, farms, and industrial enterprises—respond accordingly, in ways that we have previously analyzed. This is essentially how a centrally planned economy with features abstracted from the Chinese conditions of 1957–1977 works.

In reality, the effectiveness of planning and the degree of central control vary according to political conditions. In China the above model approximates fairly well the situation in the period of the first Five-Year Plan (1953–1957). After 1958 the process of planning was often interrupted, and annual plans were sometimes announced after the fact. Even during the period of the first Five-Year Plan, central control of the economy did not cover all economic resources and activities. Provincial and municipal authorities and local markets remained to assert influences on the working of the economy. Furthermore, the central planning units, instead of giving directions, often relied on the autonomous working of the bureaus and enterprises under their control to solve the production and distribution problems through barters and other arrangements. As we have pointed out, the control of supply of materials was partial and incomplete, leaving much discretion to local authorities and allowing exchanges by barter between enterprises in certain instances. Concerning the control of prices, before 1966 deviations from the centrally determined prices were permitted within certain ranges in order to meet local demand and supply conditions. After 1966, because of the need to control the political and economic disorder resulting from the Cultural Revolution, the centrally administered prices became more rigid and deviations were not permitted until 1983.

2.3   A MODEL OF THE CHINESE ECONOMY IN THE 1980s

Just as the model of a competitive market economy presented in Chapter 1 fails to represent accurately any actual market economy unless monopolistic elements and elements of government intervention and planning are added, the model of Sections 2.1 and 2.2 is not an accurate representation of the Chinese economy in the 1980s unless we incorporate certain elements of a market economy. Since 1978 there have been important economic reforms in China that have brought the forces of the market into play to a significant extent. We will incorporate the essential features of these reforms into our model of the Chinese economy as of 1984. Some readers may wonder whether, if the reforms continue, an entirely new book on the Chinese economy will be needed by 1994. Certainly, a new book to study the effects of the new reforms would be desirable, but the present discussion will still be useful for an understanding of the reforms yet to take place. The main purpose of this book is to apply economic analysis to understand the Chinese economy. As economic institutions change, the responses of the economic units will also change. The usefulness of economic analysis lies in its ability to predict what the responses will be under different sets of institutional arrangements. We will now analyze the institutional reforms that have taken place up to 1984. Similar methods can be used to analyze any future reforms. It is unlikely that the Chinese planning authority will introduce institutional arrangements that have never been tried elsewhere in the world. Therefore, to analyze the economic effects of future reforms, we can rely not only on the power of economic theory but also on actual experiences accumulated elsewhere in the world. To the extent that some reforms will consist of the adoption of elements from a competitive market economy, we will understand them in light of the analysis presented in Chapter 1 and later in this section.

To understand the Chinese economy in 1983, we must modify the model of Sections 2.1 and 2.2 in two respects. First, a *private sector* has to be introduced in which market forces are at work. Second, different institutional arrangements for the economic administration of the communes, the industrial enterprises, and the distributional units of the *public sector* have been introduced, which affect the behavior of the corresponding productive units.

Even before the economic reforms that began in 1978, there was a small private sector in the Chinese economy. For example, small private plots consisting of some 5 to 7 percent of the cultivated land were allowed in certain times and in certain areas. Since 1978 the private sector has expanded. Private plots have become more common and accounted for larger fractions of the total cultivated land—as much as 10 to 15 percent in some areas. In addition, small private businesses operating for profit have been permitted. They include farm families engaged in productive sidelines such as handicrafts, transportation of farm products to the cities, pushcarts, food stands, restaurants, tailor shops, small stores, repair shops, and carpenters, among others. Free markets for farm produce and handicrafts produced in the communes but not distributed through government agencies have greatly expanded. Private suppliers in the free markets compete with government distributors of agricultural products for customers. While the prices in government retail stores are set by the government, prices in the free markets are determined by the demand and supply conditions. Often when the supplies are plentiful, prices of vegetables, meats, and fruits in the free markets are not much higher than in government stores, but the quality is better.

In a small sector of the Chinese economy, private enterprises coexist with government enterprises, as in the economies of the United States and Taiwan. For example, in the United States, postal services are available from the government's Post Office and from private enterprises. The U.S. government sets the prices not only for products and services of government enterprises, such as postal rates, but for products available in the private sector, notably prices of farm products through the federal farm price support program (which is also the case in Taiwan). Of course, the relative sizes of the public and private sectors in these economies are very different, with the United States being mainly a market economy, China mainly a planned economy, and Taiwan somewhere in between. The trend in China in the 1980s is that the private sector, though small, is expanding.

Perhaps more important than the expansion of the private sector are the institutional reforms of the way in which the public sector is administered. We will discuss in turn certain important elements of the reforms in agriculture and in industry. While the reforms in agriculture are studied in greater detail in Chapter 3, we will incorporate here two important features in our model of the Chinese economy, the first concerning the relation between the planning authority and the work teams, and the second concerning the relation between the teams and their member families. We are leaving out noninstitutional reforms, which include raising the government purchase prices of farm products and increasing government expenditures on the agricultural sector. See Wiens (1983) for a discussion of these reforms.

A team is often a traditional village that has been organized into a production unit in a commune. The planning authority, through the communes, gives directions to the teams. The nature of the directions has been changed since reforms were instituted in many provinces in 1980. Previously, the commands given to the teams included the kinds of products to produce, the quantities of these products, the acreage allotted to each product, and sometimes even the method of farming. Since the reforms, only the quantities of certain essential products are specified by the planning authority, and not the acreage or farming methods. Furthermore, the teams are allowed to participate in the decisions on what to produce with the land under their control, and the administrators of the communes are asked to consider their suggestions seriously. This procedure brings the knowledge of the teams to bear on the selection of crops to suit the local conditions.

More important is the change in the way each team accomplishes its production goals. Previously the team leader would assign tasks to the workers in different farm families and would give them work points for the work done, which determine each worker's share of the income of the team. Now, however, the team assigns to each *farm family* the necessary inputs—including land, cattle, farm equipment, and machinery—in return for which each family is required to deliver a fixed amount of its produce to the team as its contribution to the team's production quota. Any amount produced in excess of this fixed quantity belongs to the farm family, to consume or to sell in the free market. (See Economic Research Center, *Almanac of China's Economy, 1981,* pp. 396–397, for a description of this system, which was originally instituted in local villages and later approved by the State Council. There are different versions of this "responsibility system," but we will simplify it for our model.) A model of the production decisions of a farm family under this system is similar to that of a private enterprise, described in Section 1.5 with differences to be pointed out below.

Assume tentatively that the quantity x_4 of land made available to a farm family is fixed, that the family pays a rent of p_4 per unit of land, that it can purchase all equipment and other necessary inputs in the free market, and that it can sell its output in the free market. In this case the farm family would behave like a competitive private enterprise. In trying to maximize its profit, it would produce at a point where price equals marginal cost. It would employ inputs efficiently so that the value of the marginal product of each input equals its price. Now assume that instead of paying a rent of $p_4 x_4$ for the use of its land, a farm family has to give up a quantity x_2^0 of its output to the work team for delivery to the central planning authority. If the price p_2 of its output is assumed to be known, the farm family under the second assumption would behave in exactly the same way as under the first assumption when $p_4 x_4 = p_2 x_2^0$. Under the first assumption, $p_4 x_4$ is a *fixed cost* to the enterprise. Referring to equations 1.19 and 1.20 for total cost and equation 1.23 and Figure 1.5 for marginal cost, one realizes that the fixed cost $(p_4 x_4)$ has no effect on the marginal cost and therefore does not affect the quantity of output, which is determined by equating marginal cost and price. Under the second assumption, the value $(p_2 x_2^0)$ of the output to be surrendered to the leadership of the team is also a *fixed cost* to the enterprise. It does not affect the quantity of output, and the farm family would behave like a profit-maximizing enterprise in a competitive industry as described in Section 1.5. In general, a levy of a fixed value by the government is a *lump-sum tax*. Since a lump-sum tax is a fixed cost, it has no effect on the decisions of the enterprise regarding the production of outputs and the efficient use of inputs.

The above conclusion about the effect of a fixed cost or a lump-sum tax on the behavior of a private enterprise is valid provided that the management is not allowed to close down the enterprise. Of course, increasing the lump-sum tax or any other fixed cost will lower the profit of the enterprise according to equation 1.21. However, if the farm family has no choice but to work on the farm, it will still try its best to maximize profit, however small, or to make the best of the situation—provided, of course, that it can earn enough to subsist. A fixed cost is a cost that does not vary with the quantity of output. The main characteristic of a lump-sum tax is that it does not vary with the quantity of output. By contrast, if the team were to extract a certain *percentage* of the output from the farm family, the family would produce less. Let 10 percent of the output be taxed. If the market price of the output is p_2, the extra cost, including the tax, of producing one more unit of output is $.1p_2$. The marginal cost curve in Figure 1.5 would be raised by $.1p_2$, leading to a reduction in the quantity of output, which equates price with marginal cost (see Problem 2).

Requiring each farm family to surrender to the work team a fixed quantity of its output is like a lump-sum tax on the farm and does not affect its production decisions. Now we replace the assumption that the farm family can buy all its other inputs in the free market by the assumption that these inputs are assigned to it by the team leadership. To the extent that the farm family cannot alter the quantities of some of these inputs, production will be less efficient. In general, if an enterprise tries to maximize its profit by using the most economical combination of inputs to produce a given quantity of output, and if there are some restrictions on its choice of inputs, it will be producing less efficiently than otherwise. In the case of Chinese agricultural production, how serious this possible source of inefficiency is depends on how well the team's leadership assigns and makes available the required inputs to the farm families, and on whether the families can influence the assignment of the inputs or acquire them from the market. If this possible source of inefficiency is minor, the Chinese farms will produce as efficiently as a private enterprise in a competitive industry. There have been numerous reports on the favorable effects of this institutional reform on agricultural productivity in China. Note that the institutions differ to some extent from province to province, depending on the percentage of the total targeted output of the team that is allocated to production by individual farm families rather than by the entire team, on the way expenses for the use of farm inputs are paid by the farm families, and on other characteristics of the arrangement. Nevertheless, this description brings out the essence of the agricultural reform in China. The economic effects of the reform were striking.

In 1980, while much of the agricultural reform was going on in various provinces, the central government was also instituting reforms in the management of a large number of enterprises. Some 6,000 enterprises were affected among the 84,000 state enterprises in China, excluding Tibet. These enterprises accounted for about 60 percent of the value of total output. Under the rubric of "autonomy for industrial enterprises," the government allowed the enterprises a certain discretion in their production decisions. The new institutional reforms have three important elements. First, the enterprises were allowed to retain about 10 percent of their profits. Second, they were given some voice in the selection of products and some freedom in the production of new products and in the production and marketing of products after fulfillment of their assigned production quotas. Third, they were given some freedom in the acquisition of inputs and in personnel policy. We will compare the behavior of an enterprise under these institutional rules with that of a private enterprise in a market economy.

First, retention of 10 percent of the profit is equivalent to a 90 percent profit tax. What are the economic effects of such a profit tax? If the enterprise is not allowed to contract or expand its capital stock, then, given its fixed costs in the short run, the 90 percent profit tax will not affect its production behavior. The choice of the quantity of its output and the combination of its inputs would be unaffected because the optimal choice for maximizing 90 percent of profit, or $.9\pi$ given by equation 1.21, is the same as the optimal choice for maximizing π (see Problem 5). However, *if* the enterprise is allowed to expand or contract its capital stock, a profit tax will discourage it from expansion. Recall our discussion in Section 1.9 concerning the enterprise's decision to invest. Capital investment is worthwhile if the present value of the additional future profits generated by the investment can cover the cost of the investment. When a profit tax is introduced, the additional future profits will decrease. An investment that was worthwhile before the tax will no longer cover its cost and therefore will not be undertaken. Hence, by taking away 90 percent of the enterprise's profit, the planning authority will discourage the enterprise from its investment activities. More important, the 10 percent of the profit retained is given to the managers not for their personal use, but only for use in the operation of the enterprise, including restricted distribution to its workers. Therefore this situation contrasts sharply with the arrangement available to the farm families described earlier. A farm family is subject not to a profit tax, but to a lump-sum tax, which has different effects on investment incentives (see Problems 6 and 7). The most significant difference is that a farm family keeps its profits after paying out all the expenses and the lump-sum tax. In contrast, an enterpriser's retention of 10 percent of profit that managers cannot use personally provides only a small incentive for the management to produce an optimum quantity of output efficiently.

Second, when the enterprises were allowed some freedom in the selection, production, and marketing of their products, the economic effects were positive, but they could not compensate for the weaknesses of the profit scheme described in the preceding paragraph. Furthermore, the freedom to sell their products in a free market, while varying in extent from enterprise to enterprise and from product to product, was in general more limited for the enterprises than for a farm family. Free markets for producer goods were also more limited, as enterprises did not have complete freedom to trade with other enterprises directly, though that situation was changing.

Third, concerning the freedom to employ inputs, we have already mentioned that the direct purchases and sales of producer goods were not completely free. The central planning authority still allocated the supplies of producer goods to a substantial degree. A very serious problem, as pointed out earlier, was the lack of freedom to hire and discharge workers. The labor problem is much less serious in a farm family. Although it is hard to imagine that the leader of a farm family would disown a family member for not working hard, the leader certainly can discipline a family member and change that member's reward (the wage). Also, a family being much smaller than an industrial enterprise, each member gets a significant fraction of the profit of the family farm and thus has an incentive to work harder. When output was shared by all members of a team before the agricultural reform of 1980, the individual farm workers did not try to work very hard either, as is the case with workers in an industrial enterprise after the reform of industry under discussion.

Analyzing the economic effects of the above three aspects of the reforms for industrial enterprises introduced in 1980, one can conclude that they would not serve to raise incentives and productivity in the same way as the reforms introduced for agriculture. The performance of Chinese industries from 1980 to 1984 confirmed this expectation. Efficiency in a market economy depends on the ability of the enterprises to earn profits and to determine freely the quantities of their outputs and inputs. The Chinese industrial enterprises, after the reform of 1980, were still handicapped in these three respects. Furthermore, efficiency in an economy depends not only on the freedom and incentive of the enterprises to optimize but also on the prices they use to carry out their profit calculations. If each enterprise tries its best but is given the wrong information through the prices arbitrarily set by the planning authority, it is not producing most efficiently for the economy.

If the price of a certain input, such as electricity, is arbitrarily set low, a profit-maximizing enterprise will use a great deal of it in production. The value of the marginal product of electricity is set just to cover the price of electricity, but the price does not measure accurately the cost of the electricity to society. When the price of electricity is determined by the free market, it will measure the value of the other things that must be given up to produce one more unit of electricity. Recall the production transformation curve of Figure 1.6, showing that the ratio of the price of electricity to the price of another product equals the quantity of the latter that could be produced by sacrificing one unit of electricity. For example, if the price ratio is 3, by producing one unit of electricity the economy gives up producing three units of the other commodity. The value of the quantity of the other commodity that could be produced instead of one unit of electricity is the *social cost* (or cost to society) of one unit of electricity. In a competitive market economy this social cost equals the price of electricity. If, for some reason, the planning authority sets the price of electricity below its social cost, it would induce a profit-maximizing enterprise to waste electricity. Similarly, if the price of electricity is set too high, the enterprise should produce a larger quantity of output by using more electricity, but it will not do so, leading to underutilization of capacity (see Problem 8). Thus, even if all enterprises were allowed to retain all their profits and to choose their outputs and inputs freely, the arbitrary setting of input prices would lead to inefficient production (see Problem 9).

We can now summarize the way the Chinese economy functions as of 1984. It is mainly a centrally planned economy, but it contains important elements of a market economy. It can therefore be considered a mixed economy with emphasis on central planning. The central planning authority controls most productive resources, including land and capital goods in the farms and factories. It assigns production targets to the production units in agriculture and in industry, supplies inputs to them, controls the prices of most products, and regulates the incomes and consumption of the population through the setting of purchase prices of farm products and wage rates for workers and through the operation of a rationing system. We present a model of the working of such a centrally planned economy in Sections 2.1 and 2.2. The elements of a market economy introduced since 1978 include a small private sector, in which small private enterprises sell their products and services in free markets, and a set of institutional reforms in agriculture and industry, which make the government production unit behave more like enterprises in a market economy. The reforms introduced in agriculture have made farm families behave much like private farms, but industrial enterprises after the reform do not behave like private enterprises in a market economy. Improvements in productivity since 1980 have apparently been much greater in agriculture than in industry. Further economic reforms are being introduced, as we will discuss in the next section. As of today the Chinese economy is a mixed economy with a large element of central planning, but with an expanding private sector and continuing intitutional reforms for government enterprises, which may further incorporate elements of enterprise management of a market economy.

2.4 POSSIBLE DIRECTIONS OF ECONOMIC REFORMS

As of 1984, economic reforms in China were continuing. What directions can these reforms take? What directions are likely to be taken? The first question is easier, for answering it amounts to examining the possible economic institutions that might be introduced. The second question is more difficult because to answer it, we have to predict the future actions of the Chinese political leaders.

Let us take up the easier question first. The possible directions of economic reforms can be conveniently viewed as leaning either toward more central command or toward more decentralized decision making and the use of market forces. The Chinese themselves have viewed the central issue of economic reform in this way. Volumes have been written in China since 1979 that discuss the issues of whether the economy should be regulated by central planning or by market forces, what should be regulated by central planning and what by the market, and so on. In Chapters 1 and 2 of this book, we examine how a completely centrally planned economy and a competitive market economy solve the important economic problems of production, distribution, and capital formation. The reader will also appreciate that in any actual economy both government planning and free markets are used to solve the basic economic problems. In the case of China, since we have already examined a model of an almost completely centrally planned economy in Sections 2.1 and 2.2, we will now discuss the possible directions toward a market economy.

The starting point of our discussion is the contrast between the institutional reforms in agriculture and in industry presented in Section 2.3. To the extent that the reforms in industry deviate from the institutions in a market economy, can these differences be eliminated? Let us consider the four elements of the differences discussed in the preceding section, three concerning the management of a government industrial enterprise and the fourth concerning the setting of prices by the central planning authority. We will then consider a fifth element—reforms of the market sector.

The first issue is the retention of profits versus a fixed charge to an industrial enterprise. The Chinese government is currently trying to institute the system of charging an industrial enterprise a fixed amount, in terms of a fixed quantity of its output or a fixed rental, in a larger segment of the Chinese industry. We studied the economic effect of such a system for farm families in the preceding section. The arrangement is essentially a *lease,* whereby the government leases an enterprise to its management and workers for a fixed rental. Any profits after payment of the rental and other costs belong to the enterprise. In late 1982 and early 1983 such a leasing arrangement was first introduced to small government retail shops in certain urban areas and later to certain small industrial enterprises. One important aspect is the freedom that the management has in using the retained profits of the enterprise: whether managers can use a large fraction of the total profit personally and how much of it goes to the workers and to required reinvestment in the enterprise itself.

Depending on what fraction of total profit has to be shared with the workers, the management of an enterprise will behave differently. The analysis of production decisions of an enterprise in Section 1.5 assumes that the management gets all the profit after paying out all costs, including wages to the workers. In such an arrangement the management will try to maximize its profit by hiring inputs (including services of the workers) in such a way that the value of the marginal product of the last unit of each input just covers the price (or cost) of that unit. If the profits are shared with the workers, who also participate in the management of the enterprise, the behavior of the enterprise will be different. The enterprise discussed in Section 1.5 is assumed to maximize profit given by Equations 1.21 and 1.19, namely,

$$\pi = p_2 x_2 - C = p_2 x_2 - (p_4 x_4 + p_3 x_3) \tag{2.1}$$

where x_2 is the quantity of the output, x_4 is the quantity of a fixed input such as capital equipment or land, x_3 is the quantity of labor input, and $p_2, p_4,$ and p_3 are the respective unit prices. If, instead of maximizing π, the worker-management is assumed to maximize profit *per worker,* namely,

$$\frac{\pi}{x_3} = (p_2 x_2 - p_4 x_4 - p_3 x_3)/x_3 \tag{2.2}$$

where, for simplicity, we have assumed that each worker works the same number of hours per period so that the quantity x_3 of labor input is proportional to the number of workers. Without analyzing the behavior of an enterprise that maximizes 2.2 instead of 2.1, one notes immediately that the use of labor input will not be as efficient because labor has become a fixed input.

Alternatively, let us assume that the workers share the profit but do not participate in the management, so that the management can fire and hire workers, but each worker is entitled to share the profit of the enterprise. Compared with the model of Section 1.5, this arrangement would have the effect of decreasing the incentive for the management to invest optimally, as we have discussed in Section 2.3. To what extent it would induce the workers to work hard depends on how much of the profit attributable to their hard work will accrue to the workers. If all workers share equally a certain fraction of the profit of the enterprise and there are many workers in the enterprise, the inducement to work hard is small. If the management can identify the contributions made by individual workers to the output of the enterprise and uses the retained profits as bonuses to augment the wages to the workers according to their individual contributions, the workers can be induced to work harder. The problem of providing the right incentives to the management and to the workers in a large enterprise in a market economy are similar: To the extent that the managers share only a small fraction of the profit of the enterprise, most of which goes to a large number of stockholders, they do not have the same incentive to invest optimally as the owner-manager of a small private enterprise. The management also has the problem of identifying the marginal product of each worker and compensating him or her accordingly.

The second issue in discussing possible economic reforms is the degree of freedom a Chinese industrial enterprise may have in choosing its products and in marketing them. In the early 1980s more freedom was given to enterprises in designing their products. Increasing fractions of their products could be sold directly in the market to consumers and to other producers. Some government retail outlets were allowed to purchase directly from their suppliers. Users of producer goods as inputs were beginning to find direct sources of supply from the producers.

As a third important direction that economic reforms in China could take, the freedom of enterprises to use inputs could be expanded. If enterprises can deal with one another directly in a market for producer goods or materials, the choice of inputs can become less restricted and more efficient. Most important is the freedom to change the quantity of labor inputs. In 1983 the system of job assignment by government labor bureaus was in the process of change. Enterprises were beginning to hire some of their workers directly. They were given limited freedom to discipline and even to discharge workers. One can imagine the government labor bureaus allocating labor side by side with a free market. Workers and other people might be allowed to find their jobs freely, and enterprises might be allowed to choose their employees freely. The government bureaus might simply provide employment services to workers and potential employers, helping the former to find jobs and the latter to locate suitable workers.

Fourth is the issue of the control of prices by the government planning authority. At one extreme the government planning authority would not control prices at all, instead letting prices be determined by the forces of demand and supply in the market. The rationing of consumer goods might be gradually abolished. Even when rationing of a particular commodity is in effect, the demand for this commodity is restricted by the number of ration coupons issued by the government, and the planning authority might decide not to control the price of such an item, instead letting it be determined in the market. Similarly, determination of the prices of all producer goods and materials used in production could be left to buyers and sellers trading in the market. The same would apply to rents for apartments in urban areas, which are now set very low. To decontrol rents, the units that control the existing apartments might be allowed to operate for profit, paying a fixed tax to the central planning authority. Urban families could be allowed to find their own apartment spaces at rentals determined by demand and supply. Given these reforms, rents will probably increase, but the increase will be limited by two factors. First, the incomes of urban families are limited and will restrict demand. Second, there will be many government suppliers of housing spaces competing against one another for customers, and they will build more apartments for profit when the rents are high. The present shortage of apartments in urban areas is due mainly to the arbitrarily low rents. When rents increase, demand will decrease and supply will increase. Higher rents will also discourage people from migrating from rural to urban areas even when migration is free. Eventually, prices of products and services, including rents for housing spaces, will be determined by the forces of demand and supply. If the market is competitive, prices will measure the social costs of the products, and these social costs should be taken into account by the users of different products for the economy to operate efficiently, as we have discussed.

The above four aspects of possible economic reforms are concerned with ways in which the government can control the activities of government enterprises. A fifth aspect has to do with the private sector itself. Since all land in the cities belongs to the national government (is "state owned") and all land in the rural areas is either "state owned" or "collectively owned" (by the communes) according to the Chinese Constitution of 1982, no private enterprise or individual owns any land. The private sector consists of private enterprises that use publicly or collectively owned land to conduct business. It includes private plots and small handicraft enterprises run by farm families, repair shops, restaurants, tailor shops, carpentry shops, and small retail stores or stands in urban areas. Actually, the functioning of an enterprise in what we call the private sector and in the public sector can be identical if the institutional arrangements are identical. For example, a farm family will behave the same way concerning its management of the private plot and land assigned to it to grow a particular crop after the agricultural reform of 1980, if the family decides that the land is most suitable for the crop it is assigned to grow. The family has to pay a fixed quantity of the crop to the team as a lump-sum tax, but this does not affect its economic behavior. Therefore, by appropriate institutional arrangements, the government can make enterprises in the public sector behave like enterprises in the private sector. Nevertheless, there is room for the private sector itself to grow if the government allows more and larger enterprises to operate privately. For example, in the early 1980s a private enterprise was allowed to have a maximum of only five employees. The scale of operations could be increased. More kinds of private enterprises could be allowed.

2.5 LIKELY OUTCOMES OF ECONOMIC REFORMS

Now we come to the more difficult of our two questions: In what directions and how far are the economic reforms in China likely to go? We will try to answer this question in the same way that economists answer questions about the behavior of economic agents. In the present case we are trying to predict the actions of the Chinese political leaders. Our question can be broken down into two parts: What do the Chinese leaders want to accomplish, and what are the constraints that limit their actions? We have studied the behavior of a consumer unit by postulating that it wants to seek a commodity bundle with the highest ranking according to its preferences and subject to a budget constraint. We have studied the behavior of a business enterprise in a competitive industry by assuming that it tries to maximize profits subject to the constraint of a production function and given the prices of its output and inputs. In studying the economic planning behavior of a central authority concerning what goods to produce and what resources to use in producing them, we also assume that the authority has a set of preferences and that it is subject to the restriction of a production possibility frontier, or a production-transformation relationship among all products. In the last case we have assumed that the *economic institutions are fixed* and the planning authority merely sets production targets, prices, wages, and other instruments at its disposal to achieve its objectives. Now we are approaching a broader question: What economic reforms or institutional changes will the Chinese leaders introduce in the next decade to accomplish their objectives? The way we approach this question is the same. We ask: What do they want to accomplish, and how far will they go given the environment in which they operate?

The objective of the Chinese leadership, within the realm of our discourse on economic reform, is to design a set of economic institutions to help them *plan effectively* in the process of modernizing the Chinese economy. The Chinese leadership is committed to econoimc planning that will make the Chinese economy different from a competitive market economy in its ways of solving the major economic problems. While a free market economy leaves it to the price mechanism and decentralized decision making to solve the problems of investment, consumption, and distribution, the Chinese leadership intends to direct these three important economic activities. Like the leadership of any organization, the Chinese leadership needs to find a way to reach an agreement among its members, but we will not be concerned with internal disputes, instead discussing the actions of the Chinese political leadership or government as a unit.

First, to develop the Chinese economy the government intends to build up the infrastructure and direct investments in the industries and projects of its own choice. We have pointed out that even in a market economy the government provides public goods and an infrastructure. The Chinese government cannot be expected to do less. In a market economy, as we pointed out in Section 1.9, private enterprises will find their own investment projects and will invest to the point where the present value of future profits will just cover the cost of the investment. In a developing economy like Taiwan, government planning officials not only help private enterprises develop new products but also set up government enterprises to produce industrial and consumer products, like steel and automobiles, that have to be produced in large scale to be economical. In the areas of building an infrastructure, setting up industrial enterprises, and directing the investment activities of new and existing enterprises, the Chinese government will continue to play a major role and a more important role than in an essentially market economy.

Second, the Chinese leadership wants to plan the kinds and the quantities of consumer goods to be made available to consumers. While in a market economy the consumers themselves choose what they would like to consume by their purchases in the market, in China the government often decides what goods should be made available, and in what quantities. There are certain basic necessities that the government feels responsible for providing to the consumers, including housing for the urban population and certain basic items of food and clothing, which are rationed. The supplies of many durable goods are also determined by the government according to what, in its judgment, the consumers need and to the productive capacity of and the resources available to the industries producing them.

Third, in the area of distribution the Chinese leadership wants to manage the incomes of farmers and workers by controlling the purchase price of farm products and the wages of the workers. The wage rates and other compensations to professionals can also be used to reward those professions which the government considers important. The distribution of certain important materials to industrial users will be made according to the priorities set by the government, going first to those enterprises producing goods considered most essential by the government.

Therefore, in the areas of investment, consumption, and distribution, the Chinese government will continue to plan. Our major question is how the Chinese government will reform the economic institutions to carry out economic planning in these areas more effectively. There is a choice of greater or less reliance on the forces of the market. At one extreme, all consumer goods can be rationed. All investment projects have to be directed by the planning authority. The output targets of all productive units have to be assigned, and all the required inputs and capital equipment have to be distributed by the government. All wages, incomes, and prices are fixed by the government.

At the other extreme, no consumer goods are rationed. The government directs only the large projects for building the infrastructure of the economy, and provides capital and know-how to set up certain new industrial enterprises to produce certain goods not currently produced. Once this is done, if the government wants to encourage further investment by a certain enterprise, it may pay the enterprise an extra amount for each unit of its output that is *sold in the market* in a specified period of time. This will increase the present value of the expected profits of the enterprise and encourage more investment. (This scheme is better than giving the enterprise a direct subsidy, because it is difficult to ensure the use of the subsidy for investment purposes.) No production targets need be set. The government enterprises will be allowed to retain all profits after paying specified lump-sum taxes. They will produce to satisfy the demand by consumers or other enterprises willing to pay for their products in the market. Consumer and producer goods will be freely traded in the market, and there is no need to allocate inputs to the government enterprises. All prices and wages are determined in the market by demand and supply.

In the area of distribution, if the government wants the farmers to be richer, it can provide a subsidy to each farm family. If it wants the workers to be richer, it can provide a subsidy to each working family. There is a difference between providing a fixed subsidy to a person or a family and changing the price of a farm product or the wage rate. The latter schemes affect the efficient allocation of resources. Setting a price above the market price encourages some people to produce more than is needed and encourages others to consume less than can be produced. The government would have to take care of the surplus. Setting a wage above the market wage rate will discourage enterprises from hiring workers if the enterprises are to produce efficiently to maximize profits. In summary, the government's only instruments for economic planning are financial, consisting of taxes and subsidies, in areas other than the building of the economic infrastructure and the setting up of enterprises to produce new products. In addition, the government can encourage the expansion of private enterprises, besides altering the ways it exercises control over the investment, production, and distribution of goods by government enterprises.

Given these two extremes of possible economic reforms, which way is the Chinese leadership likely to go and how far? The tendency in the 1980s is that reforms will continue toward the use of more market forces and less central command, but there are limits to such reforms. This statement is based on the fact that the Chinese leadership has discovered the shortcomings of overcentralized economic planning and the effectiveness of using market forces, and is in the process of extending the use of markets. At the same time, there are several reasons why the expansion of the market economy will be limited.

First, the tasks of building an infrastructure and developing new industries occupy a large part of the economic planning activities of the government, and central direction is significantly involved in these activities.

Second, the central planning authority desires to have direct control over certain important resources for the purpose of performing its tasks of capital construction and expansion rather than having to compete for these resources with government enterprises or with the private sector through the market. Also, the government wants to exercise control over the kinds of consumer goods to be made available in the market, rather than letting the government and private enterprises produce what the consumers want to buy. Hence it is unlikely that the government will rely on financial means alone to allocate the scarce resources for producing capital and consumer goods. It is more convenient to exercise power directly than to give up power and use indirect financial methods.

Third, the control of prices and wages is also a means for the government to influence directly the distribution of income. Although subsidies are economically more efficient than the setting of prices and wages, the persons receiving them prefer to keep their pride and to have their products or their labor services command a higher price. The planning authority often does not wish to give up its power to set prices when it can use this power to gain control over economic resources and their distribution. For example, by keeping the wage of an artist at a very low level, the government can sell his paintings to earn valuable foreign exchange for its own use.

Fourth, partly to limit the economic power of the private sector and partly for ideological reasons, the government will restrict the expansion of enterprises in the private sector and limit the distribution of large profits to managers of enterprises in the public sector.

Fifth and finally, there is inertia to any institutional reforms. There is resistance from the middle management and bureaucracy, which would lose their powers if market forces were allowed to replace their discretionary authority in the allocation of scarce resources. It is always difficult for any government leadership to dismantle or reduce the size of a large bureaucracy. The first three reasons explain why the Chinese leadership would not wish to give up too much of its direct control over economic activities. The last two reasons are due to restrictions from the environment in which it has to conduct its affairs.

With this perspective on the likely direction and extent of future economic reforms in China, we will review the five elements of economic reform discussed in the preceding section and comment on the prospects for each. First, how far will the responsibility system with a lump-sum tax go, and to what extent will profits of industrial enterprises be used at the discretion of their management? The answer is, not very far for large enterprises. The reason for our answer also explains why the lease system, with each farm family reaping all the profits after paying a lump-sum tax, was not introduced in industry in the first place. The reason is that industrial enterprises are much larger than family farms. It is one thing to let the head of a farm family take all the profits after delivering the production quota and paying all necessary expenses for the use of the inputs. It is another matter to let the managers of a large industrial enterprise in a socialist economy take all the profits for themselves. Furthermore, many of the enterprises have monopoly power in China, partly because the government has designated them to produce certain goods and has provided them with the supplies of the necessary inputs that are not available in the market. In any case, there is no competition from potential enterprises entering the market because no one is allowed to or able to set up a new enterprise to compete with the government industrial enterprises. It would be unwise to let the managers of these monopolistic enterprises reap the profits without providing them with sufficient competition from other enterprises that produce the same and similar products and without requiring all enterprises to compete for inputs in the marketplace (see Problem 10).

One issue concerning the retention of profits that are partly shared by the management is the ultimate use of the money earned. Profits and other forms of income will provide an incentive to manage efficiently only if the earners can make good use of them. This point applies to the profits now earned by the successful farmers. Where do the incomes go if the earners are now allowed to buy land, housing, and other expensive durable goods such as automobiles? If the profit incentive is to be effective, the government may have to institute changes to allow the private ownership of automobiles and other expensive durable goods and of better-quality housing than is now available. In the case of housing, renting a good-quality apartment may be a substitute for owning it. When the apartment unit or house is owned by an individual consumer, the government may still own the land, as the Constitution of 1982 stipulates that no land can be privately owned. (Many university professors in the United States own their houses built on land belonging to the university. Condominium owners in the United States often do not own the land either.)

The leasing arrangement that became successful in agriculture and was being considered for more widespread adoption in other areas in 1984 may suffer a setback in the future precisely because profits are too high. It must be remembered that political forces are at work to limit the high earnings of the people. Government economic administrators may feel that when the economic units are earning a lot, it is time to tax them. There are numerous instances in the Chinese economy when the administrators, seeing the economic success of certain economic units, decided to increase the taxes on them to absorb their economic gains. This may occur even in family farms when the rich farmers, after the agricultural reform, may be subject to a higher taxation or production quota. Often administrators do not realize that when taxes are increased, the farmers learn that the so-called fixed tax is not really fixed—the more they produce, the more they get taxed, eventually. The farmers will then cease to produce more than they did before the reform. A fixed tax has no harmful effect on incentives because the economic unit gets all the gains resulting from its extra effort. When the so-called fixed tax keeps on increasing to tax away all the fruits of extra effort, the economic unit will get the same profit no matter how hard it works, and it will have no incentive to work hard. In any case, bureaucratic and ideological forces might turn the clock backward from the widespread use of the leasing arrangement in agriculture and in industry that allows large profits to be retained by managers or owners of enterprises.

Concerning the second element of economic reform, the freedom of enterprises to choose what kind of products to produce and how to market their products, perhaps the political forces opposing it are not as strong as in the case of the retention and private use of profits. If profits are shared by workers or go to the central planning authority, what is wrong in giving the enterprises some freedom in the production and distribution of their products? The fact that some such freedom was instituted in 1980 shows that the political forces opposing it might not be very strong. However, some limits to this kind of freedom will be imposed by the apparatus of central planning itself. Many of the products produced by the industrial enterprises were distributed by the central planning authority as a part of its economic planning, including consumer goods as well as industrial products and materials required by other enterprises as inputs. The government wants to ensure that all the required products are produced and its method is to instruct the enterprises to produce them, in the same way that it instructs the communes to produce the required agricultural products. Since for reasons discussed earlier in this section the government may not be willing to give up its direct control over the production and distribution of some important products and over the supply of the required inputs through a system of materials balancing, it might not be willing to give the enterprises complete freedom to produce and distribute their products as enterprises in a market economy.

Third, concerning free markets for material inputs and for labor, progress might be easier to achieve toward the former than toward the latter. The management of labor is influenced by the political ideas that the government should put the population under its control and should provide jobs for them. The first idea is partly a remnant of the Chinese political tradition when the people were ruled by emperors. At present, though not in the past, movements of people from commune to commune, from city to city, and from rural to urban areas are restricted. However, as economic conditions improve, the government might be willing to loosen its control over the Chinese population. The recent policy of allowing some people to seek their own jobs and enterprises to select some of their workers indicates that the practice of having the labor bureaus assign all jobs is not as rigid as it might have appeared in 1980. However, the policy of allowing wages to be freely negotiated by the workers and management may encounter political resistance.

Fourth, concerning the setting of prices in free markets, we have pointed out that the central planners may not be willing to give up the power to use prices and wages as instruments for the distribution of income and for the balancing of materials. Furthermore, there may be resistance from the administrative bureaucracy at the middle level. Once prices are set free in the marketplace, where purchasers can acquire the necessary products directly from the producers, the administrators distributing the products under a system of materials balancing for producer goods and government distribution of consumer goods will lose their economic power—and will lose the kickbacks and other favors they may be getting from the purchasers who depend on them for their supplies. Political pressures aside, the Chinese economic planners are concerned that if many prices are set free during a short period, there would be undesirable economic consequences, including inflation, large losses for some enterprises, very high profits for others, and the associated dislocation and possible unem-ployment of labor in the nonprofitable enterprises. Although such concerns may be unjustified because the market can adjust more rapidly and in a more orderly fashion than they expect and because there are ways to lessen the pains of economic adjust-ments, such concerns do partially explain why the prices of many goods are still controlled by the government planning authority in China.

Fifth and finally, the private sector may expand to some extent. The Chinese leadership realizes that small private enterprises serve the useful functions of supplying goods and services to consumers and of employing workers who might otherwise be unemployed and hence burdensome to the government labor bureaus. Some of them, including private peddlers transporting agricultural products from rural to urban areas and private restaurants in the cities, compete with government units performing similar functions and may help increase the efficiency of the government enterprises if the latter are required to operate at a profit. To the extent that private enterprises are useful for the economy, do not interfere with central planning, and do not create large private wealth for a small group of individuals, they will be allowed to expand.

In summary, the tendency in China is for the government enterprises to be allowed to operate more like profit-maximizing enterprises in a market economy and for the private sector to expand. However, the desire on the part of the planning authority to exercise direct control rather than to use only financial means for economic planning, the resistance of a middle-level administrative bureaucracy, and the inertia in the economic and political system will limit the expansion of market forces. Precisely how far the reforms toward adopting features of a market economy will go in the next decade is difficult to predict. However, it appears safe to say that in absolute terms the market elements will be much more important in 1994 than in 1984, but will still fall short of being the major means used by the Chinese government to achieve its planning objectives. In the meantime, we may observe oscillations in the trend toward a market-oriented economy, because the Chinese leaders are in the process of experimenting with and learning about the working of a market economy.

In this section we have discussed the question, How far in the direction of a market economy will the economic reforms in China go? A related question is, How far *should* the reforms go? There have been extensive discussions among economists in China concerning which areas of the economy should be directed by central planning and which by the private sector or government enterprises operating through the market. [See the two volumes of essays edited by the Institute of Economics of the Chinese Academy of Social Science (1980).] To approach this question from a theoreti-cal point of view would require a lengthy discussion. For a basically market economy, the role of government intervention was discussed in Section 1.10. For the Chinese economy, which is committed to central planning, the discussion of Section 1.10, though relevant, has to be modfied. Rather than trying to answer the above question theoretically, the Chinese economic planners can find an answer in a pragmatic way by letting private enterprises and certain government enterprises operate freely in the market to fulfill their economic functions. If they can do a better job than the enterprises operating under the direct command of the central planning authority, they should be allowed to function and expand. If they fail in certain areas, the central planning authority should continue to direct the activities of the government enterprises in these areas, always allowing the competition of private and autonomous enterprises to ensure the efficiency of the directly controlled operations. If the Chinese central planners have a better way to direct certain areas of their economy, they can at least allow the private and autonomous government enterprises to enter the market to compete. Not only in the production of consumer goods and producer goods but in the construction of large projects, if conditions allow, several government enterprises can be established and allowed to compete for the contract. A large project may consist of many parts that might be undertaken separately by different enterprises, each having to compete for its part of the contract. Before economists have settled the question theoretically, the Chinese economic planners will probably have found out much of the answer through practical experience in the next decade.

2.6 ORGANIZATION AND ADMINISTRATION OF ECONOMIC PLANNING

As is generally known, the political power in China resides in the Chinese Communist party. The Communist party exercises power partly by placing its members in key positions in the government. The executive branch of the Chinese government is headed by the State Council. The State Council, through its various ministries, directs the economic activities of the country. To appreciate the comprehensiveness of central economic planning, let us examine the organization of the State Council. The State Council is responsible to the National People's Congress. It is headed by the premier and, as of 1984, two vice premiers. A list of the commissions and ministries of the State Council as of April 30, 1981, can be found in the *Almanac of China's Economy, 1981* (pp. 57–58). Some consolidations took place in the spring of 1982. The following list applies to the summer of 1982 and contains supplementary material found in Fu (1982, pp. 53–54).

Two commissions are in charge of coordinating the activities of the ministries concerned with economics. The State Planning Commission has overall responsibility for economic planning, including the drafting of five-year and other medium-term economic plans. The Economics Commission reviews the fulfillment of the annual economic plans and institutes economic reforms. There are 27 ministries dealing with different segments of the economy. They are:

Agriculture and Fisheries
Forestry
Coal Industry
Petroleum Industry
Chemical Industry
Metallurgical Industry
Light Industry
Textile Industry
Machine-Building Industry
Electronics Industry
Nuclear Energy Industry
Aircraft Industry
Ammunitions Industry
Space Industry
Geology and Mineral Resources

Water Resources and Electric Power
State Bureau of Labor
Railroads
Transportation and Communications
Posts and Telecommunications
Urban and Rural Construction and Environmental Protection
Finance
Commerce
Foreign Trade
People's Bank of China
Family Planning Office
State Scientific and Technological Commission

The following 14 bureaus are also concerned with the management of economic activities:

Bank of China
People's Construction Bank
Agricultural Bank of China
General Administration of Customs
Civil Aviation Administration
State Statistics Bureau
State Administration of Standards
Industrial and Commercial
  Administration Bureau
Administration Bureau for
  Commodity Prices

State Bureau of Supplies
General Administration of Travel
  and Tourism
Bureau of Drug Administration
Bureau of Import-Export Control
  (under Ministry of Foreign Trade)
State General Administration of
  Exchange Control (under
  People's Bank of China since
  1982)

The ministries and bureaus in charge of economic affairs greatly outnumber the remaining 11 ministries of the State Council:

Foreign Affairs
National Defense
State Nationalities Affairs
  Commission
Public Security
Civil Affairs
Justice

Culture
Education
Public Health
State Physical Culture and Sports
Cultural Relations with Foreign
  Countries

The classification of the Family Planning Office and the State Scientific and Technological Commission as economic and of the ministries of Education and Public Health as noneconomic is arbitrary. I have divided these four ministry-level organizations equally between the two groups for the purpose of counting the ministries to indicate the importance of economic administration in the affairs of the State Council. Note that among the economic ministries, those concerned with different industries outnumber the two concerned with agriculture and forestry. In part, this reflects the complexity of central economic planning for industry as compared with agriculture.

Generally speaking, directions from the central government to the individual economic units go through three intermediate levels of the Chinese government. The first level consists of 21 provinces, 5 autonomous regions, and 3 municipalities directly under the central government. The 21 provinces are Anhui, Fujian, Ganzu, Qinghai, Guangdong, Guizhou, Hebei, Heilongjiang, Henan, Hubei, Hunan, Jiangsu, Jiangxi, Jilin, Liaoning, Shaanxi, Shandong, Shanxi, Sichuan, Yunnan, and Zhejiang. The 5 autonomous regions are Guangxi, Inner Mongolia, Ningxia, Tibet, and Xinjiang. The 3 municipalities are Beijing (Peking), Shanghai, and Tianjin. On the second level and under each province or autonomous region are large cities and prefectures. On the third level and under each prefecture are counties and small cities. The communes are administrative units under the counties. There are over 2,000 counties and over 50,000 communes (a list of counties is found in the *Almanac of China's Economy, 1981,* pp.

59–71.) Also on the third level and under each large city are neighborhoods (which are further subdivided into streets and courtyards). Factories are frequently controlled by units of the government at the level of counties and cities, but smaller production and distribution units (like restaurants and retail shops) are frequently controlled at the level of neighborhoods. Some large industrial enterprises are under the direct control of the corresponding industrial ministries or are controlled by corporations directly under the ministries. Some enterprises are under the control of provincial governments.

Through the administrative units at different levels the central government prepares and executes its economic plans. The production and distribution of important consumer and producer goods are centrally planned. These goods include food grains, vegetable oils, pork, beef, lamb, eggs, consumer durable goods, industrial raw materials, and capital goods. To achieve materials balancing in its annual plan, the demand and supplies of the centrally planned commodities from each province are reviewed by the State Planning Commission; deficits from some provinces will be balanced by surpluses from other provinces or by imports. The provincial plans are assembled from economic units within the respective provinces through the administrative units at the county or city level. To execute its plan, the State Planning Commission gives directions through the ministries. In the areas of agriculture-fishery, forestry, commerce, and light industries under the control of the communes, directions from the corresponding ministries pass through the provincial and county administrative units to the communes. In the area of urban industry, directions from the corresponding ministries pass through the provincial and city-county administrative units to the factories or enterprises. The exceptions are large enterprises directly controlled by the ministries and enterprises under the control of provincial governments. Also, very small enterprises like restaurants and retail shops are controlled by units below the level of cities, such as neighborhoods or even streets.

An organization chart or a summary of organizational structure does not fully describe how much authority the administrators at each level have in the preparation and execution of economic plans. It is possible, though not true, that the State Planning Commission simply assembles the production targets submitted by the individual communes or enterprises through the county-city and provincial levels of the administration. It is also possible that the State Planning Commission is very powerful in ordering the individual communes and enterprises to change their production targets. The truth is somewhere in between, depending on the particular people in command of the commission and on the particular provinces and/or enterprises involved. Many industrial and commercial enterprises receive directions from two sources, the ministry of the State Council and the administrative unit of the provincial government (see Gao et al., 1980, p. 47). Interesting questions have arisen concerning the authority of the ministries and of the provincial governments. In general, provincial governments have more authority over the production and distribution of commodities for local consumption, but this general rule does not describe the influence of the provincial government in any particular situation. In any large organization, not to speak of a country as large as China, it is always difficult to specify precisely how administrators at different levels exercise their authority, but this is not a topic that we need to go into. In China the discussion of political control is complicated by the committees of the Communist party, which are parallel to the organizations at the different levels of the Chinese government. How the Chinese Communist party exercises its control through these committees is a subject for a political scientist to ponder.

2.7 MAJOR HISTORICAL PERIODS IN THE DEVELOPMENT OF THE CHINESE ECONOMIC SYSTEM

In Section 2.3 we outlined a model of the Chinese economic system as of 1984. Here we will indicate briefly the important periods of the development of this system.

1949–1952   This was a period of recovery from the Civil War, after the Chinese Communist party took over China in 1949 and founded the People's Republic of China. In a land reform, land was redistributed from the richer landowners to the farmers. Industrialists were allowed to maintain their enterprises. The economic system did not change drastically.

1953–1957   Period of the first Five-Year Plan. Institutions for central planning were established, mainly following the model of the Soviet Union. The plan raised the proportion of national income for investment to about 20 percent by taxing agriculture and industry and by using the profits from state-owned industries. In 1955 cooperatives were organized in agriculture, making possible direct planning based on output targets and acreage allotment. By 1956 over 90 percent of the Chinese peasants belonged to cooperatives. Private industrial enterprises also came under government control by nationalization, leaving the former owners nominal shares of the profits. To transfer farm products to the urban areas for rapid industrialization, compulsory government purchases of grain and cotton from the farmers and rationing of certain consumer goods in the cities were instituted.

1958–1961   In 1958 Chairman Mao Zedong launched the Great Leap Forward to accelerate Chinese economic growth to a rate that proved unattainable and transformed the agricultural cooperatives into communes within a year. In technical terms, Mao tried to reach a combination of outputs beyond the production possibility frontier of the Chinese economy. The result was a great economic failure. The *Almanac of China's Economy, 1981* (pp. 966 and 971) provides the "value" of gross outputs of agriculture, light industry, and heavy industry with 1952 = 100, as shown in the accompanying table. More recent publications from China indicate that during this

| Year | Gross output value of | | |
	Agriculture	Light industry	Heavy industry
1958	127.8	245.0	555.5
1959	110.4	299.0	822.7
1960	96.4	269.5	1,035.5
1961	94.0	211.1	553.6
1962	100.0	193.5	428.4
1963	111.6	198.1	487.8
1964	126.7	233.4	590.3
1965	137.1	344.5	650.6

period economic administrators at lower levels were under political pressure to over-estimate the outputs of their units. Therefore the figures in the table for 1960–1961 probably overestimate output values and underestimate the economic failure. These value figures have been calculated at constant 1952 prices to reflect the quantities of output in real terms. The reduction of the index of gross output value of agriculture from 100 in 1952 to 94 in 1961 should be adjusted for the increase in population to arrive at figures for per-capita consumption of agricultural products. (From the *Almanac of China's Economy, 1981,* p. 959; population was 574,820,000 in 1965 and 725,380,000 in 1982.)

The significance of the period of the Great Leap Forward for a student of the Chinese economic system is twofold. First, this period saw the establishment of a system of communes that placed the economic activities of the Chinese rural population under direct government control. In China the assets of government industrial enter-prises are "state owned," whereas the assets of the communes are said to be "collec-tively owned" because the communes were transformed from the cooperatives. This distinction has no economic significance, since it has no effect on the behaviors of the enterprises and the communes. Second, the events of this period illustrate the possibility that mistakes by one single political leader in a centrally planned economy can lead to national economic disaster.

1962–1965   Period of economic readjustment after the Great Leap Forward. More liberal economic policies were introduced, including private plots for farmers. In fact, the lease or contract system introduced in the agricultural reform of 1980 saw its origin in this period (see *Almanac of China's Economy, 1981,* p. 396). Economic recovery was rapid, according to the values of agricultural and industrial outputs shown above. In December 1964 Premier Chou En-lai addressed the Third National People's Congress and suggested that China pursue the "Four Modernizations" of industry, agriculture, defense, and science and technology. The significance of this period is that it illustrates how rapidly China's economic units can respond to more liberal economic policies of the central planners.

1965–1975   Period of the Cultural Revolution. The Chinese administrative and eco-nomic system was under attack by the millions of Red Guards, who transferred political power from the pragmatic economic planners to the radical elements of the Communist party in the name of destroying the old cultural tradition, which was said to hinder social revolution. The effects of the Cultural Revolution on the Chinese education system are discussed in Section 7.6. The ensuing political turmoil, including the de-mand for higher wages by workers, led to a resolution to freeze all prices at the end of 1966, which lasted for over a decade and prevented the proper functioning of China's price system.

1976–1979   After Chairman Mao died in September 1976, political power was soon transferred from the radical and irrational elements of the Communist party to the more pragmatic planners who would like to see China modernized. Four radical leaders, Mao's widow Jiang Qing, Zhang Chunqiao, Wang Hongwen, and Yao Weny-uan, were vilified as the "Gang of Four" and stripped of political power. A political and economic system somewhat resembling the one existing in the early 1960s was restored. In 1978 the "Four Modernizations" originally suggested by Chou En-lai in 1964 were put forth as a program for modernizing China. During 1977–1978 ambitious economic plans were formulated, also beyond the production possibility frontier, but such plans were soon abandoned and the targets for economic growth were revised downward. The period of 1976–1979 witnessed the reestablishment of political and economic order after the Cultural Revolution. In 1979 the People's Republic of China established formal diplomatic relations with the United States. Foreign trade and investment, together with cultural exchanges with foreign countries, rapidly expanded. During the three years from 1977 to 1979 the total value of Chinese imports and exports almost doubled, representing an average annual growth rate of 17 percent in real terms (*Almanac of China's Economy, 1981,* p. 621). The expansion of foreign investment and trade was another significant development during this period.

1980–Present Following the resolution of the Third Plenary Session of the 11th Central Committee of the Chinese Communist party, the second annual session of the Fifth National People's Congress in June 1979 adopted a policy for the modernization of China. In August 1980 the third annual session of the Fifth Congress adopted major economic reforms, although certain reforms actually originated before 1980. We have incorporated some of the important reforms in our model of the Chinese economic system in Section 2.3 and discussed the possible and likely directions of future reforms in Sections 2.4 and 2.5, respectively. The effects of economic reforms on the agricultural and industrial sectors will be discussed in Chapters 3 and 4, respectively.

Five-Year Plans In discussing the different periods of the Chinese economy since 1949, it is useful to record the periods of the various five-year plans, although economic planning was often interrupted. The first Five-Year Plan lasted from 1953 to 1957. The second was scheduled for 1958–1962 but was interrupted by the Great Leap Forward movement beginning in 1958. After a period of adjustment following the economic collapse of the Great Leap, a third Five-Year Plan was put into effect in 1966–1970, followed by a fourth in 1971–1975 and a fifth in 1976–1980. The third and fourth plans coincided with the period of the Cultural Revolution, with its political, administrative, and economic disruptions. The sixth Five-Year Plan started in 1981. For a discussion of the Chinese economic system, including the institutions of economic planning and the institutional settings of various sectors prior to 1966, the reader is referred to Donnithorne (1967).

In later chapters we will analyze the working of the individual sectors and units (microeconomics) and the working of the entire system using aggregate data (macroeconomics) in more detail. More economic tools will be introduced and applied to analyze the facts about the Chinese economy.

PROBLEMS

1. If cotton cloth is rationed, discuss how the demand for buttons, for tailors' services, and for cloth made of artificial fibers (which are not rationed) will be affected.

2. Assume that there are three kinds of final products instead of two, with respective quantities denoted by x_1, x_2, and x_3. Draw a three-dimensional diagram showing the production transformation relation among the three commodities as a generalization of Figure 1.6, using three axes to measure x_1, x_2, and x_3. Using your diagram, explain how a combination (x_1, x_2, x_3) is chosen by a planning authority that can rank different combinations according to its preferences.

3. For a private enterprise as described in Section 1.5, assume that 10 percent of the output is taxed by the government. How will its total cost and marginal cost be affected? Give your answer both algebraically and graphically. Show in a diagram how the output of a competitive industry consisting of many such firms will be affected. How will the price of the product be affected?

4. For a private enterprise as described in Section 1.5, assume that some fixed amount, say \$.50, is charged by the government on *each* unit of output it sells. Answer the same questions given in Problem 3 above.

5. Using the information for Figure 1.5, draw a curve for profit as a function of output. Draw a curve for the *net* profit of the enterprise after the government levies a tax of 90 percent of its profit. Explain why the quantities of the output produced and all inputs employed by the firm will not be affected by the tax.

6. Compare the effects of a lump-sum tax and a profit tax (on a fixed percentage of profit) on the short-run production decisions and on the investment decisions of a private enterprise in a competitive industry.

7. Compare the effects of a lump-sum tax and a profit tax (on a fixed percentage of profit) on the short-run production decisions and on the investment decisions of a monopolistic enterprise.

8. State why, from the social point of view, a profit-maximizing enterprise should produce more than it does when the price of an input, say electricity, is arbitrarily set higher than its free-market price.

9. Discuss the statement: "Even if all enterprises were allowed to retain all their profits and to choose their outputs and inputs freely, the arbitrary setting of *output* prices would lead to inefficient production." What is the meaning of the word "inefficient"? In what sense is this statement true, and why?

10. When the government supplies industrial enterprises with certain necessary inputs that are not available in the market and when there are very few enterprises producing the same product, discuss why it is unwise to allow the managers of the enterprises to reap all the profits after paying the government a certain fixed charge. (Review Sections 1.5, 1.7, and 1.8.)

11. For each of the five areas of economic reforms discussed in Section 2.4, present your view on the likely direction of change up to 1994, indicating how drastic the change will be, and why.

12. Specify one important area of economic reforms in China not included among the areas discussed in Section 2.4. Explain why it is important. In which direction will reform in this area be likely to go?

13. After the reforms of 1980, a farm family fulfills a fixed production quota and keeps the rest of the output, which it can sell in the market. In analyzing the behavior of the farm family, we have stated that given the price of the output, surrendering a fixed quantity of output to the team is equivalent to payment of a fixed charge or a lump-sum tax. Since the price of the product is unknown to the farm family when it starts planting the crop, in what way should our analysis be modified? For example, can we redefine the production function by subtracting the production quota before counting the "net output" that can be produced by using a certain combination of inputs?

14. From the viewpoint of the central planning authority, is there a difference between collecting a fixed quantity of a specified product from a team consisting of farm families and collecting a fixed amount (so many yuan) in taxes? If you were a central planner, which would you prefer, and why? Consider what you would do with either the product or the tax money.

15. Name three important economic activities that should be centrally controlled directly rather than indirectly by the use of financial means through the market. State your reasons. Assume that the Chinese government is committed to planning and directing economic activities as we have described in this chapter.

REFERENCES

Economic Research Center, State Council of the People's Republic of China. 1982. *Almanac of China's economy, 1981.* Hong Kong: Modern Cultural Company Limited.

Byrd, W. 1983. Enterprise-level reforms in Chinese state-owned industry. *American Economic Review* 73:329–332.

Cheng, C.-Y. 1982. *China's economic development: Growth and structural change.* Boulder, Colo.: Westview Press.

Deaton, A., and J. Muellbauer. 1981. *Economics and consumer behavior.* New York: Cambridge University Press.

Donnithorne, A. 1967. *China's economic system.* New York: Praeger.

Fu, F.-C. 1982. The evolution and operation of central economic organization in mainland China. *Economic Papers No. 19.* Taipei: Chung-hua Institution for Economic Research.

Gao Guangli, Che Li, and Wang Yang. 1980. *Zhongquo shangye jingji guanlixue* [Chinese business economic administration]. Beijing: People's University Publishing House.

Howe, C. 1978. *China's economy: A basic guide.* New York: Basic Books.

Institute of Economics, Chinese Academy of Social Sciences, ed. 1980. *Shehuizhuyi jingji jinua yu shichang de guanxi* [Relations between planning and the market in a socialist economy]. 2 vols. Beijing: Chinese Social Science Publishing House.

Johnson, D. G. 1982. Progress of economic reform in the People's Republic of China. Paper No. 82:7. Chicago: University of Chicago, Office of Agricultural Economic Research.

Li Kaixin 1982. How China Manages its Supplies, in *Almanac of China's Economy,* 613–620.

Ma Hong and Sun Shangqing, eds. 1982. *Zhongquo jingji jiegou wenti yanjou* [Studies of the problems of China's economic structure]. 2 vols. Beijing: People's Publishing Society.

Tobin, J. 1952. A survey of the theory of rationing. *Econometrica* 20:521–553.

Wiens, T. B. 1983. Price adjustment, the responsibility system and agricultural productivity. *American Economic Review* 73:319–324.

Xue Muqiao 1981. *China's socialist economy.* Beijing: Foreign Language Press.

Therefore, for the new output $y*$ to be three times the former output y, a necessary and sufficient condition is

$$\beta_1 + \beta_2 + \ldots + \beta_k = \sum_{i=1}^{k} \beta_i = 1 \qquad (3.5)$$

Referring to the general production function (equation 3.2), this property means that, for any positive constant c,

$$f(cx_1, cx_2, \ldots, cx_k) = cf(x_1, x_2, \ldots, x_k) \qquad (3.6)$$

A function f having the property indicated in equation 3.6 is said to be *homogenous of degree one.* A demand function $f(p_1, \ldots, p_n, I)$ showing the quantity demanded as a function of the prices $p_1, \ldots, p_n$ and income I has the property that, if all prices and income are multiplied by a positive constant c, the quantity demanded will be *unchanged,* that is,

$$f(cp_1, cp_2, \ldots, cp_n, cI) = c^0 f(p_1, p_2, \ldots, p_n, I) \qquad (3.7)$$

Here the resulting quantity is multiplied by $c^0 = 1$. A function f having the property indicated in equation 3.7 is said to be *homogenous of degree zero.*

Why do we wish to specify a production function to be homogenous of degree one? Do we not observe empirically that when the quantities of inputs double, the output sometimes is less than doubled and sometimes is more than doubled? Our answer is that a homogenous production function of degree one is a convenient analytical device for helping us to understand the relationships in production. It is a convenient way to conceptualize the factors entering into the production relation. For example, if we observe that when the inputs double, the output is less than doubled, we will realize, using such a production function, that *some inputs* that we overlook are *not* actually *doubled.* Referring to equation 3.4, if we forget to include the input x_1 and triple only the other $k - 1$ inputs, the new output $y*$ will be

$$y* = (3)^{\beta_2 + \ldots + \beta_k} y < 3y \qquad (3.8)$$

because $\beta_2 + \ldots + \beta_k < 1$. Thus, seeing that the output fails to increase proportionally with the inputs, we should start looking for the missing inputs that have prevented the proportional increase in output. In the opposite case, when we conceive that output may increase more than proportionally to the inputs, we are saying that a production process of a given large scale cannot be reduced in size by proportional reduction in all inputs and output. For example, a large farm with 10 hectares of land and 10 laborers may yield more than 10 times the output of a small farm with 1 hectare of land and 1 laborer because the larger farm can use a tractor efficiently. Here again there is an input, namely the use of a tractor, the quantity of which cannot be changed proportionally. We cannot reduce a tractor used for a 10-hectare farm to one-tenth of a tractor for operation in a 1-hectare farm. The *indivisibility* of certain inputs makes production in a large scale more efficient because proportional reduction of all inputs is impossible.

The production function can be used to describe the relation between output and the inputs in an enterprise, as was done in Section 1.5, in an industry or in an economic sector. When we say that the output of the agricultural sector depends on the natural resources, physical capital, human capital, technology, and economic institutions, we have in mind a production function summarizing the relation between the aggregate output of the agricultural sector and the inputs including land, physical capital, and labor. The aggregate output and inputs are obtained by adding together the outputs and the corresponding inputs of all the farms. If the farms are efficient, in the sense of producing a large quantity of output for given amounts of the inputs, the aggregate production function for the agricultural sector will show a large aggregate output for given quantities of aggregate inputs. Economic institutions and policies will affect the efficiencies of the individual farms and thus the aggregate production relationship as summarized by the production function for the agricultural sector.

One immediate lesson to be learned from the concept of a production function is that several factors determine the quantity of output, and therefore no single factor tells the entire story about the level of output. In particular, the importance of land as a limiting factor of agricultural output has been overemphasized. For example, the total area of cultivated land in mainland China in 1979 is reported in the *Almanac of China's Economy, 1981* (Economic Research Center, 1982, p. VI-9), to be 99.5 million hectares; the total area of cultivated land in Taiwan in 1979 is reported in the *Statistical Yearbook of the Republic of China, 1982* (p. 113), to be 915,000 hectares. Divided by the corresponding population figures of 971 million and 17.5 million, these figures yield per-capita cultivated land of .102 and .052 hectares, respectively. Thus China has about twice as much cultivated land per person as Taiwan, and yet China is a net importer of food whereas Taiwan is a net exporter of food. [For the major imports and exports of China and of Taiwan, see respectively *Statistical Yearbook of China, 1981* (Chinese State Statistics Bureau, 1982, pp. 372 and 388), and *Statistical Yearbook of the Republic of China, 1982* (pp. 430–431).]

The reason output per unit of land can vary a great deal from country to country and from region to region is that it depends on the quantities and qualities of the other inputs used in conjunction with land, on the technology adopted, and on the economic institutions and policies. The effects of fertilizers and irrigation on output are obvious. T. W. Schultz (1980) has emphasized the importance of human capital, meaning the education and the health of the farmers. As far as the impact of technology as an input is concerned, the classic example is the tripling of the output of corn per acre in the United States by the late 1950s after hybrid strains of corn were introduced in the 1930s.

Using a Cobb-Douglas production function of two inputs

$$y = \alpha x_1^{\beta_1} x_2^{\beta_2} = \alpha x_1^{\beta} x_2^{(1-\beta)} \tag{3.9}$$

we can demonstrate how the output per unit of one input, or the *average product* of that input, depends on the quantity of the other input (or on the quantities of the other inputs in the case of three or more inputs). The average product of the first input, say land, is

$$y/x_1 = \alpha x_1^{\beta} x_2^{(1-\beta)}/x_1 = \alpha x_1^{\beta-1} x_2^{(1-\beta)} = \alpha \left(\frac{x_2}{x_1} \right)^{1-\beta} \tag{3.10}$$

Thus the larger the quantity x_2 of the other input, given the quantity x_1, the larger will be the average product y/x_1 of the first input. Also, the larger the quantity x_1, the smaller is the average product—when $\beta - 1$ is negative, $x_1^{\beta-1}$ decreases with x_1.

An important concept is the *marginal product,* which is the change in output per unit change in an input when the change in input is very small. The marginal product of x_1 is the *derivative* of y with respect to x_1 *holding x_2 fixed;* that is, it is the *partial derivative* of y with respect to x_1. The concept of a derivative was used and explained in Section 1.5. Given the production function in equation 3.9, the marginal product of x_1 is the partial derivative

$$\frac{\partial y}{\partial x_1} = \alpha\beta x_1^{\beta-1} x_2^{(1-\beta)} \tag{3.11}$$

The marginal product of the first input thus decreases as its quantity x_1 increases. This phenomenon is known as *diminishing returns.* If the first input is labor and the second input is land, given the quantity of land, then the more labor is used, the smaller the extra output that can be produced by using an additional unit of labor. This is also true for the marginal product of land. Given the same quantity of labor, the extra output that can be produced by having an additional unit of land decreases as more land is used. The laborers cannot attend to the extra land when a lot of land is available. Equation 3.11 also shows that the marginal product of the first input will increase when the quantity of the other input is increased. It is a characteristic of the Cobb-Douglas production function that the marginal product of an input is a fraction of the average product; equation 3.11 is a fraction β of equation 3.10.

If we take the logarithms of both sides of equation 3.9, we get

$$\log y = \log \alpha + \beta_1 \log x_1 + \beta_2 \log x_2 \tag{3.12}$$

The logarithm of output is a linear function of the logarithms of the inputs. When $\log x_1$ increases by 1, $\log y$ will increase by β_1 units. β_1 is the derivative of $\log y$ with respect to $\log x_1$, holding $\log x_2$ fixed. Taking the partial derivative of equation 3.12 with respect to $\log x_1$ yields

$$\frac{\partial \log y}{\partial \log x_1} = \beta_1 \tag{3.13}$$

Since the change in $\log y$ is the proportional change in y, that is,

$$\Delta \log y = \frac{\Delta y}{y}$$

where Δy denotes the change in y and $\Delta \log y$ denotes the change in $\log y$, we have, for very small changes in $\log y$ and in $\log x_1$ and holding $\log x_2$ fixed,

$$\beta_1 = \frac{\partial \log y}{\partial \log x_1} = \frac{\Delta \log y}{\Delta \log x_1} = \frac{\Delta y/y}{\Delta x_1/x_1} \tag{3.14}$$

In economics the proportional change in one variable y with respect to a small proportional change in another variable x_1 is called the *elasticity* of y with respect to x_1. If the elasticity is 1.5, we know that when x_1 changes by 1 percent, y will change by 1.5 percent. β_1 is the elasticity of output with respect to the first input according to the production function in equation 3.9. $\beta_1 = .5$ means that when the first input increases by 1 percent, output will increase by half of 1 percent. A similar interpretation applies to β_2. With these basic concepts, we can examine the aggregate production relations in Chinese agriculture.

3.3 AGGREGATE PRODUCTION RELATIONS IN CHINESE AGRICULTURE

According to the *Almanac of China's Economy, 1981* (pp. 959 and 965), total population in mainland China increased from 575 million at the end of 1952 to 971 million at the end of 1979. During the same period the area of cultivated land changed from 107.9 million hectares to 99.5 million hectares, with a footnote in the above source stating, "The figures of cultivated land are underestimated and remain to be verified." In any case the cultivated-land area probably did not increase by much in percentage terms. In the meantime, the index of "gross agricultural output value" found in the *Statistical Yearbook of China, 1981* (p. 18), increased from 100.0 in 1952 as the base year to 249.4 in 1979, 256.1 in 1980, and 270.7 in 1981. This index is supposed to measure the value of the total gross output of the agricultural sector by multiplying the physical outputs of different products by their prices at the base years 1952, 1957, and 1970. The change of the output index from 100.0 in 1952 to 256.1 in 1980 while the cultivated-land area remained constant illustrates that output per unit of land can be increased significantly. The fact that agricultural output per unit of land in 1980 was much larger in Taiwan than in mainland China, as we pointed out in Section 3.2, further indicates that agricultural output in China can be further increased. The main purpose of this section is to explain the increase in agricultural output in China from 1952 to 1980.

Anthony Tang (1981) has studied the change in agricultural output in China in relation to the various inputs. He has constructed an index of gross value of agricultural output, which is exhibited in column 1 of Table 3.1. This index increases from 100 in the base year 1952 to 237 in 1980. The State Statistical Bureau of the People's Republic of China has also published an index of gross agricultural output value in the *Almanac of China's Economy, 1981* (p. 966), which is exhibited in column 2 of Table 3.1. This official index increases from 100.0 in 1952 to 256.1 in 1980. From 1975 on, this index is somewhat higher than Tang's index, being 3.1 percent higher in 1975 and 8.1 percent higher in 1980. Tang (1981, p. 12) has attempted to reconcile the two figures for 1980 by subtracting the component due to "production-brigade-run industrial enterprises," which has been included in the Chinese official index since 1977. According to the *Statistical Yearbook of China, 1981* (p. 136), gross agricultural output value in 1980 at 1970-constant prices is 162.72 billion yuan, of which 19.44 billion (or 11.9 percent) is from production-brigade-run industrial enterprises and 4.21 billion (or 2.6 percent) is from production-team-run industrial enterprises. The combined brigade and team-run industrial enterprises thus account for 14.5 percent of the gross agricultural output value in 1980. The brigade-run component alone is more than sufficient to explain the 8.1 percent discrepancy between the Chinese official figure and Tang's figure. Subtracting both components would make the adjusted Chinese official figure 7.6 percent lower

Table 3.1   INDICES OF AGGREGATE PRODUCTION RELATIONS IN CHINESE AGRICULTURE

Year	1 Gross output (Tang)	2 Gross output (official)	3 Effective sown area	4 Sown area (official)	5 Labor in agriculture	6 Capital stock	7 Current inputs	8 Input	9 Total factor productivity
1952	100	100.0	100.0	100.0	100.0	100.0	100	100	100
1953	103	103.1	101.5	102.0	100.7	106.5	107	102	101
1954	106	106.6	103.7	104.7	101.7	107.7	118	105	101
1955	115	114.8	105.5	107.0	103.2	105.3	128	108	106
1956	120	120.4	111.0	112.7	104.6	110.1	161	115	104
1957	125	124.8	110.9	111.3	105.1	115.9	164	116	108
1958	139	127.8	109.2	107.6	105.6	137.5	204	124	112
1959	112	110.4	106.7	100.8	106.5	124.1	220	125	90
1960	95	96.4	104.6	106.6	107.3	110.3	235	126	75
1961	100	94.0	102.5	101.4	108.2	105.3	186	118	85
1962	111	100.0	104.1	99.3	109.7	111.6	198	122	91
1963	122	111.6	105.8	99.3	111.5	125.1	220	128	95
1964	132	126.7	107.0	101.6	113.8	151.3	244	134	99
1965	141	137.1	108.8	101.4	116.5	151.3	271	141	100
1966	150	148.9	109.2	103.9	119.3	160.3	290	146	103
1967	159	151.3	109.5	102.6	121.8	164.2	306	151	105
1968	149	147.5	109.8	99.0	124.5	162.9	321	154	97
1969	152	149.2	110.2	99.8	127.4	164.0	341	159	95
1970	168	166.4	110.7	101.6	130.8	176.2	367	166	101
1971	171	171.4	111.8	103.1	134.3	190.3	400	174	98
1972	179	171.1	112.4	104.7	137.8	209.9	435	183	98
1973	189	185.5	113.5	105.2	141.3	206.2	464	189	100
1974	192	193.2	114.6	105.2	144.7	210.5	503	198	97
1975	196	202.1	115.4	105.9	148.2	230.8	547	208	94
1976	196	207.1	115.6	106.0	151.7	240.8	587	217	90
1977	199	210.6	115.8	105.7	155.4	255.5	645	230	87
1978	213	229.6	115.7	106.3	157.5	266.5	712	243	88
1979	231	249.4	116.5	105.1	161.1	282.7	744	253	92
1980	237	256.1	117.1	103.6	165.0	281.9	797	260	91

Sources: All data, except columns 2 and 4, are from Table 1 of Tang (1981). Column 2 is from *Almanac of China's Economy, 1981,* p. 966, and column 4 is from *Statistical Yearbook of China, 1981,* pp. 136 and 140. The 1952 absolute values for columns 1, 3, 4, 5, and 6 are respectively 40.05 billion yuan, 130.7 million hectares of "effective" sown area, 141.3 million hectares (2,119 million mu) of total sown area, 168.677 million workers, and 11.292 billion (1952) yuan of capital.

than Tang's figure. For the following analysis, we can tolerate an error of 8 percent in either index.

Column 3 of Table 3.1 is an index of effective sown area, which has been adjusted for irrigation and for reduced yields on multicropped land as compared with single-crop yields. Column 4 is the Chinese official index of total sown area. For 1980 there is a discrepancy between 117.1 and 103.6 in the two indices. Column 5 is an index of the number of persons working in agriculture. Column 6 is an index of capital stock, including the value of livestock and farm machinery. Column 7 is an index of current agricultural inputs, including feed, seed, chemical and organic fertilizers, insecticides, fuel, and others. For an idea of some of the components of the indices of capital and current inputs, see Table 3.2. The large increases shown by Tang's indices of these two

Table 3.2 SELECTED COMPONENTS OF CAPITAL AND CURRENT INPUTS IN AGRICULTURE

Year	Draft animals (millions)	Agricultural machinery (million hp.)	Tractors of 20 hp. or over	Chemical fertilizer per hectare of cultivated land (kg.)	Electricity consumed per hectare of cultivated land (kwh.)
1952	76.46	.25	1,307	0.7	—
1957	83.82	1.65	14,674	3.3	1.3
1965	84.21	14.94	72,599	18.7	35.8
1975	96.86	101.68	344,518	53.8	183.6
1979	94.59	181.91	666,823	109.2	284.1

Source: *Almanac of China's Economy, 1981,* pp. 969–970.

inputs are consistent with Table 3.2. In fact, the data of Table 3.2 could be used to construct indices of capital and current inputs that would show larger increases than Tang's corresponding indices.

The data of Table 3.1 can be used to explain the increase in agricultural output in China from 1952 to 1980. We will first use Tang's data and then comment on the modifications that would result from using the Chinese official indices for output and land. Assume a Cobb-Douglas production function of the form shown in equation 3.3, explaining output y by the four inputs land, labor, capital, and current inputs, the quantities of which are denoted by x_1, x_2, x_3, and x_4, respectively. Taking natural logarithms, we have

$$\log y = \log \alpha + \beta_1 \log x_1 + \beta_2 \log x_2 + \beta_3 \log x_3 + \beta_4 \log x_4 \quad (3.15)$$

Taking derivatives with respect to time yields

$$\frac{d \log y}{dt} = \beta_1 \frac{d \log x_1}{dt} + \beta_2 \frac{d \log x_2}{dt} + \beta_3 \frac{d \log x_3}{dt} + \beta_4 \frac{d \log x_4}{dt} \quad (3.16)$$

Since

$$\frac{d \log y}{dt} = \frac{1}{y} \frac{dy}{dt}$$

is the proportional change in y per time period, equation 3.16 states that the proportional change in output per unit time (such as 3 percent per year) is a weighted sum of the proportional changes in the four inputs per unit time. The weights β_1, β_2, β_3, and β_4 are the elasticities of output with respect to the four inputs. If the production function is homogenous of degree one, these weights sum to one, or

$$\beta_1 + \beta_2 + \beta_3 + \beta_4 = 1$$

The proportional change in output per unit time is thus a weighted average of the proportional changes per unit time in the inputs.

In column 1 of Table 3.1 we find that gross output grew from 100 in 1952 to 237 in 1980. What would be the proportional change per year if output had the same proportional growth per year? Assuming y to grow by the same proportion per year, starting with the value 100 at year zero ($t = 0$), we have

$$y(t) = 100e^{\gamma t} \tag{3.17}$$

where $y(t)$ denotes the value of y at year t and e is the base of the natural logarithm. By equation 3.17, the ratio of output in year $t + 1$ to output in year t is $100e^{\gamma(t+1)}/100e^{\gamma t}$, or

$$e^{\gamma} = 1 + \gamma + \frac{1}{2}\gamma^2 + \frac{1}{3!}\gamma^3 + \cdots$$

If γ is small, e^{γ} is approximately $1 + \gamma$. Thus, output changes each year by a fraction slightly larger than γ. What is the value of γ if $y(t)$ grows from 100 at $t = 0$ to 237 at $t = 28$? Given y at year 28 to be 237, we apply equation 3.17 to obtain

$$y(28) = 100e^{\gamma(28)} = 237 \tag{3.18}$$

Taking natural logarithms of equation 3.18 gives

$$\log 100 + 28\gamma = \log 237$$

or

$$\gamma = \frac{\log 237 - \log 100}{28} = \frac{5.46806 - 4.60517}{28} = .03082 \tag{3.19}$$

Thus, gross agricultural output in China, according to Tang's index, grew about 3.1 percent per year from 1952 to 1980. If we use the Chinese official index in column 2 of Table 3.1 instead, we replace 237 in equation 3.19 by 256.1 and obtain

$$\gamma = \frac{\log 256.1 - \log 100}{28} = \frac{5.54557 - 4.60517}{28} = .03359$$

yielding an annual rate of growth of about 3.4 percent.

The four input indices grew from 100 in 1952 to 117.1, 165.0, 281.9, and 797, respectively, in 1980. Replacing 237 in equation 3.19 with these numbers, we find the exponential rates of growth γ for land, labor, capital, and current inputs to be .5638, 1.7885, 3.7014, and 7.4132 percent, respectively, per year. If we followed Tang (1981) by assuming the output elasticities with respect to these inputs to be .25, .50, .10, and .15, respectively, we could apply the formula in equation 3.16 to find the annual exponential rate of growth in output due to the growths in these inputs to be

$$.25(.5638) + .50(1.7885) + .10(3.7014) + .15(7.4132) = 2.517 \tag{3.20}$$

Thus, 2.5 percent out of the observed 3.1 percent (based on Tang's index) exponential rate of growth of agricultural output can be explained by the growths in inputs, leaving some .6 percent unexplained, according to the assumptions and data we are using.

Using the above data, Tang (1981) has performed a different calculation for the combined effect of the inputs. He weights the input indices by the above weights to form an aggregate input index. Thus, for 1980 his input index is

$$.25(117.1) + .50(165.0) + .10(281.9) + .15(797) = 260 \tag{3.21}$$

Comparing the value 260 with the output index of 237, Tang concludes that output has increased less than what the combined effect of all inputs would have yielded under the assumption of a constant relation between output and the inputs. This conclusion is just opposite to the conclusion reached in the preceding paragraph, where we pointed out that the combined effect of all inputs would have produced only 2.5 percent annual growth, as compared with an actual growth of 3.1 percent. The difference between these two conclusions is due to the methods of calculation.

Starting with the number 100 at the base year, if the output and input indices have increased by small percentages the two methods shown in equations 3.20 and 3.21 will yield similar results. For example, growing continuously at the exponential rates of .005638, .017855, .037014, and .074132, respectively, the four indices after one year will become 100 times e raised to the above powers, or 100.5654, 101.8015, 103.7708, and 107.6949, respectively. By the method of equation 3.21, the combined input index will be

$$.25(100.5654) + .50(101.8015) + .10(103.7708) + .15(107.6949) = 100 +$$
$$.25(.5654) + .50(1.8015) + .10(3.7798) + .15(7.6949) = 102.573 \quad (3.22)$$

which shows an increase of 2.573 percent, only slightly larger than the 2.517 figure of equation 3.20. However, when the input indices increase from 100 to 117.1, 165.0, 281.9, and 797, respectively, after growing continuously at the above exponential rates for 28 years, the two methods of 3.20 and 3.21 will yield very different results.

The two methods are different because 3.21 is a *weighted arithmetic mean* of the four input indices, whereas 3.20 is based on a *weighted geometric mean* of the four indices. A geometric mean of x_1, x_2, x_3, and x_4 is defined as

$$g = x_1^{.25} x_2^{.25} x_3^{.25} x_4^{.25} \quad (3.23)$$

A weighted geometric mean is

$$g = x_1^{\beta_1} x_2^{\beta_2} x_3^{\beta_3} x_4^{\beta_4} \quad (\beta_1 + \beta_2 + \beta_3 + \beta_4 = 1) \quad (3.24)$$

If the production function is Cobb-Douglas,

$$y = \alpha x_1^{\beta_1} x_2^{\beta_2} x_3^{\beta_3} x_4^{\beta_4} \quad (\beta_1 + \beta_2 + \beta_3 + \beta_4 = 1)$$

and the output index y and the four input indices are all set equal to 100 in the base year so that

$$100 = \alpha 100^{\beta_1 + \beta_2 + \beta_3 + \beta_4} = \alpha 100$$

implying $\alpha = 1$, the output index

$$y = x_1^{\beta_1} x_2^{\beta_2} x_3^{\beta_3} x_4^{\beta_4}$$

is a weighted geometric mean of the input indices.

In our example, the output index for 1980 constructed by the weighted geometric mean is

$$y = (117.1)^{.25}(165.0)^{.50}(281.9)^{.10}(797)^{.15} = 202.4 \quad (3.25)$$

The natural logarithm of the output index is

$$\log y = .25\log(117.1) + .50\log(165.0) + .10\log(281.9) + .15\log(797)$$
$$= 1.19076 + 2.55297 + .56416 + 1.00213 = 5.31002 \quad (3.26)$$

and the output index y is $e^{5.31002}$, or 202.354. Since

$$202.354 = 100e^{.02517(28)}$$

the value 202.354 would obtain if the output index were to grow continuously for 28 years at an exponential rate of .02517, which agrees with the result in equation 3.20. To see the agreement between the methods of 3.26 and 3.20, we observe that 3.20 is obtained by subtracting both sides of 3.26 by log 100 and dividing the result by 28:

$$(\log y - \log 100)/28 = .25(\log 117.1 - \log 100)/28 +$$

$$.50(\log 165.0 - \log 100)/28 + \ldots$$

or

$$.02517 = .25(.5638) + .50(1.7885) + .10(3.7014) + .15(7.4132) \qquad (3.27)$$

Tang (1981) uses a weighted arithmetic mean (equation 3.21) to form the aggregate input index 260 for 1980. A geometric mean (equation 3.25) of the same input indices based on a Cobb-Douglas production function would yield an aggregate input index 202.4 for 1980. In general, an arithmetic mean of several positive numbers is larger than the geometric mean because it is influenced more by the large values, 797 in our example. Using the geometric mean, one would conclude that actual output of agriculture 237 in 1980 is larger than the combined effect 202.4 of the four inputs.

Besides the choice of a geometric mean or an arithmetic mean, a second factor affecting the aggregate input index is the system of weights given to the four components. For example, if we were to give a weight of .15 to land and a weight of .25 to current inputs, the exponential rate of growth of the geometric aggregate input index according to 3.20 or 3.27 would become .03202 instead of .02517, slightly higher than the exponential rate .031 of the observed output growth. How can the coefficients β_1, β_2, β_3, and β_4 in the Cobb-Douglas production function be determined? There is a method in statistics known as *regression analysis,* which can be used to estimate these coefficients provided that good data on the output y and the four inputs x_1, $\ldots$,x_4 are available. We can postulate a relation between y and the x's as

$$y_t = \alpha x_{1t}^{\beta_1} x_{2t}^{\beta_2} x_{3t}^{\beta_3} x_{4t}^{\beta_4} e^{\gamma t} \qquad (3.28)$$

where y_t, $x_{1t}, \ldots, x_{4t}$ denote the values of y, $x_1, \ldots, x_4$ at year t, and γ is the exponential rate of change of y *after* the combined effects of all inputs have been netted out. If $\gamma = .006$, that means the observed growth rate of output is about .6 of 1 percent higher than the growth rate of the geometric aggregate input index. Using data on y_t, x_{1t}, $\ldots, x_{4t}$ such as given in Table 3.1, regression analysis can be applied to estimate the coefficients α, $\beta_1, \ldots, \beta_4$ and γ in equation 3.28. It is beyond the scope of our discussion to describe regression analysis in more detail here (see Section 4.2).

To conclude our discussion of the growth of agricultural output in China, we recall that according to Tang's index, the gross value of agricultural output grew at an exponential rate of 3.1 percent per year from 1952 to 1980. According to the Chinese official index, the exponential rate was 3.4 percent. The increase in output is explained mainly by increases in labor, capital, and current inputs, which have grown at exponential rates of 1.79, 3.70, and 7.41 percent, respectively, with land increasing at a very modest exponential rate of .56 percent. Whether the combined effect of the four inputs is larger than the observed output depends on whether an arithmetic mean or a geometric mean of the input indices is used, and on the weights $\beta_1, \ldots, \beta_4$ used to compute the means. Using an arithmetic mean makes the aggregate input index larger than using a geometric mean. Since the index of current inputs has grown very rapidly, giving it a larger weight β_4 in calculating the mean, whether geometric or arithmetic, will produce a larger aggregate input index. It is therefore difficult to decide whether output has grown more or less than the combined effect of all inputs, given technology. If output has grown more, one may conclude that there is a positive trend in technology; if less, a negative trend in technology. Regression analysis in principle can be used to settle this issue, but the data are probably too inaccurate for the results of such an analysis to be useful.

More accurate statistical data are needed for us to say more about the relation between agricultural output and the various inputs in China. For example, the Chinese official index of land shows an increase of only 3.6 percent from 1952 to 1980, whereas Tang's index shows an increase of 17.1 percent. The components of current inputs as given in Table 3.2 have shown such dramatic increases that they could be used to construct an index of current inputs rising much faster than the Tang index given in column 7 of Table 3.1. This would yield a larger value for the aggregate input index in 1980, possibly larger than the value of the output index. Without more accurate data, we can conclude from equation 3.20 that the increase in agricultural output in China is due mainly to the increases in current inputs (.15 $\times$ 7.41, or 1.11 percent) and labor (.50 $\times$ 1.79, or .89 percent), and only slightly to the increases in capital (.10 $\times$ 3.7, or .37 percent) and land (.25 $\times$ .56, or .14 percent). The percentages in parentheses, which are based on equation 3.20, are accurate enough to provide the relative orders of magnitude of the contributions made by the four inputs to the growth of agricultural output in China. The data do not allow us to decide whether there is a positive or negative technological change—that is, whether output has grown more or less than the combined effect of all inputs given a constant technology. Sufficient evidence does not exist of a substantial technological improvement in Chinese agriculture between 1952 and 1980.

Since World War II, very large increases in agricultural output in many countries have come about from three important sources, according to Schultz (1980). First, investment in human capital in the form of improvements in the education and health conditions of farmers has contributed greatly to agricultural output. If we measure labor input simply by the number of persons (or man-hours) working on the farms when the education and health conditions of the farmers have improved, we will find output to increase more than the combined effect of the inputs; that is, we will find a positive technological change in agricultural production. This observed technological change is due to the investment in human capital. A better way is to measure labor input by efficiency units, so that a farmer with more education and better health will count more units. Using such a measure of labor input (or of capital invested in the laborers), we should no longer find actual output to be larger than the combined effect of the inputs, since the quantity of labor inputs in efficiency units has increased more than the number of laborers. China has invested substantially in human capital in agriculture; farmers are more educated and have better health than in 1952. However, the increase in output made possible by this substantial investment has not manifested itself in the data of Table 3.1.

The second source of increase in agricultural output is investment in physical capital, which the farmers in market economies have been able to finance through their own earnings. Like other people, farmers respond to profit incentives. They also know their own business and will make the kinds of investments that will yield the greatest returns. In China, under the commune system and before the reforms in agriculture at the end of the 1970s, the farmers did not have substantial private earnings for investment. The investment in physical capital shown in Table 3.1 has been made mainly through government planning. As we point out in Chapter 2, it is difficult for economic planners to know the kinds of capital investment most suitable for individual farms. In any case, the Chinese government did not give Chinese farmers the opportunity to invest out of their own earnings, while such investments have contributed to substantial growth in agricultural outputs in other parts of the world.

The third important source of growth in agricultural output is the introduction of high-yield crops. We have mentioned the dramatic increase in the output of corn in the United States due to the introduction of hybrid strains. Schultz (1980) has also mentioned the growth in output that resulted from the introduction of Mexican strains of wheat to India. In order to introduce high-yield hybrid crops successfully, good research work by local scientists is essential. The scientists include geneticists and plant breeders who have to adapt the new crops to local conditions. After the Cultural Revolution, China has been very short of scientists in all areas. Agriculture remains one of the "Four Modernizations" that the Chinese government has set out to achieve.

These three important sources of growth of agricultural outputs in many other countries and their absence in China are mentioned here to explain why agricultural output in China has not grown more than the combined effect of the inputs. Agricultural output has grown in China mainly through the application of more current inputs (fertilizers) and labor, not through modernization. Modernization would mean a manifold increase in agricultural output through the planting of high-yield crops and the use of more fertilizer and irrigation but much less labor.

3.4 THE ROLE OF AGRICULTURE IN ECONOMIC DEVELOPMENT

The increase in agricultural output has just been explained. What is the role of the agricultural sector in the economic development of China?

Economic development is manifested in many ways. Consequently, there are many indices to measure the state of an economy. The most important index is the value of output, or income per capita. The total value of all outputs is obtained by weighting the different physical products by their prices. In a market economy prices reflect the rates of substitution of the different commodities in both production and consumption, as we point out in Chapter 1. If an apple is priced at 10¢ and an orange at 15¢, an orange should count as 1.5 apples because if we produce one fewer orange, we could produce 1.5 apple with the resources made available (substitution in production), and if we take away one orange from the consumer, we need to compensate him with 1.5 apple to keep him on the same indifference curve (substitution in consumption). Thus, we can add different commodities together by using their prices as weights. Without a market system, it is difficult to know the rates of substitution in production and in consumption for different commodities. In any case, to measure the value of total output produced in an economy, prices of different commodities are required. The value of the national product, or national income per capita, serves as an important index of the state of economic development. Economic development takes place by the increase in the value of the national product or income per capita.

In order for per-capita income to increase, an economy must save. That is, it must consume less than it produces, leaving part of the output for capital formation or investment. Savings can take place in the agricultural sector or in the industrial sector or other sectors. When savings are made available, they can be used for investment in the agricultural or the other sectors. Two crucial questions concerning the role of the agricultural sector in the process of capital formation are: How much saving is generated by the agricultural sector? and How much investment takes place in the agricultural sector? We will answer these questions by using the national income data made available by the State Statistical Bureau (SSB) of the Chinese government. Students of the Chinese economy have questioned the accuracy of these data. It is always healthy to question the accuracy of data used in economic analysis, and we have occasion to do so in this book. Sometimes the accuracy of data can be revealed by drawing implications from them and examining the reasonableness of the implications. In the present analysis, it is of interest to examine what the SSB data reveal concerning the role of the agricultural sector in the development of the Chinese economy.

Table 3.3 presents data on national income, in current values and in constant 1952 values, in total and in per-capita terms. Table 3.4 shows the large fraction of national income going into accumulation. Table 3.5 breaks down national income into its contributing sectors. After deflation by appropriate price indices, the figures of Table 3.5 would show the real outputs of different sectors. Table 3.6 provides gross output values of agriculture and industry. Given the output of the agricultural sector, saving generated by this sector can be deduced using the consumption data provided in Table 3.7, which makes it possible for us to examine the amount of investment going into the agricultural sector.

Table 3.3   NATIONAL INCOME OF CHINA

Year	1 National income (billions, current yuan)	2 National income index (1952 = 100)	3 National income (billions, 1952 yuan)	4 Population (millions at end of year)	5 National income (per capita, current yuan)	6 National income (per capita, 1952 yuan)
1952	58.9	100.0	58.9	574.82	102.5	102.5
1957	90.8	153.0	90.1	646.53	140.4	139.4
1962	92.4	130.9	77.1	674.3	137.0	114.3
1965	138.7	197.5	116.3	725.38	191.2	160.3
1978	301.0	453.2	266.9	958.09	314.2	278.6
1979	335.0	484.9	285.6	970.92	345.1	294.2
1980	366.7	510.1	300.4	982.55	373.2	305.7
1981	388.7	525.4	309.5	996.22	390.2	310.7

Sources: Columns 1 and 2 are from *Statistical Yearbook of China, 1981,* p. 20. Column 3 equals column 2 times .589. Column 4 is from *ibid.,* p. 89, and *Almanac of China's Economy, 1981,* pp. 959 and 996, except for the figure 674.3 for 1962, which equals the implicit mid-year population figure 666 used to derive per capita output figures of major agricultural products in *Statistical Yearbook, 1981,* p. 171, from the total output figures in ibid., pp. 145–146, multiplied by 1.0125, under the assumption of an annual growth of 2.5 percent in population in 1961 (see ibid., p. 89, for population growth rates). Columns 5 and 6 are respectively columns 1 and 3 divided by column 4.

Table 3.4 NATIONAL INCOME AVAILABLE AND ACCUMULATION RATE

Year	1 National income available (billions, current yuan)	2 Consumption (billions, current yuan)	3 Accumula- tion	4 Accumula- tion rate (percent)	5 Consumption per capita
1952	60.7	47.7	13.0	21.4	83.0
1957	93.5	70.2	23.3	24.9	108.6
1962	94.8	84.9	9.9	10.4	125.9
1965	134.7	98.2	36.5	27.1	135.4
1978	297.5	188.8	108.7	36.5	197.1
1979	335.6	219.5	116.1	34.6	226.1
1980	368.4	251.9	116.5	31.6	256.4
1981	384.9	275.9	109.0	28.3	276.9

Source: Columns 1, 2, 3, and 4 are from *Statistical Yearbook of China, 1981*, p. 21. Column 5 equals column 2 divided by the population figures in column 4 of Table 3.3. National income available is not equal to total national income because imports minus exports are included in the former and because of statistical discrepancy.

The *Statistical Yearbook of China, 1981* (pp. 509–510), gives the following definition of national income (italics added). It would be useful to review equations 1.38 and 1.39 on the two different ways of calculating national income that are described below.

The term *national income* used in this Yearbook refers to the sum total of net output, in value terms, created during a year in the following material production sectors: industry, agriculture, construction, transport and commerce (the catering trades and materials supply and marketing enterprises included). In China two methods are used in calculating the national income: (1) The production method: by this method, national income is taken to mean the sum total of *net output,* in value terms, of the material production sectors. National income is therefore obtained by subtracting the value of material consumption (for instance, the raw materials, seeds, fertilizer, fuel and power consumed in production and the depreciation of fixed assets used in production) from the *gross output value.* (2) The distribution method: by which national income, according to the concept of primary distribution, is equal to the sum of payments received by the labourers in the material production sectors plus profits, taxes and interest in these sectors.

Excluded are non-material production sectors such as the service trades, educational, scientific research, cultural, and public health departments, as well as military and government administrations. These sectors are an indispensable part of social development as a whole, because they, too, render services that are useful to the people's livelihood and society's material production. But since they are not directly involved in the material production of society, they are not taken into account in the calculation of the national income.

Through the process of distribution and redistribution, the available portion of the national income is further broken down into two parts: the *consumption fund* and the *accumulation fund.*

Consumption fund is that part of the national income represented by expenditure by individuals as private consumption and that by the public as public consumption. Its material formation is the total expenditure on consumer goods by individuals and the public plus the wear and tear of non-productive fixed assets, including residential houses, during a year.

Accumulation fund is that part of the national income which is used for expanded reproduction, non-productive construction and increase of productive and non-productive stock. Its material formation is the newly added fixed assets of material and non-material sectors (less depreciation of the total fixed assets) and the newly acquired circulating fund in kind by the material sectors during the year. Thus accumulation fund can be further divided, in accordance to purpose, into that of productive and non-productive; or that of accumulation of fixed assets and of circulating funds.

Accumulation rate is the proportion of accumulation fund, in percentage terms, over the available national income in the year.

Given these definitions, Tables 3.3 and 3.4 are self-explanatory. Note that national income per capita in 1952 yuan, as presented in column 6 of Table 3.3, grew from 102.5 in 1952 to 305.7 in 1980. The implied exponential rate of annual growth is 3.98 percent. Let us now consider the rate of growth of per-capita output contributed by the agricultural sector.

Table 3.5 reveals that, in terms of current values, net output of the agricultural sector grew more slowly than net output of the industrial sector. To obtain net outputs of these two sectors in constant prices, we need price indices for these two sectors. The values of these indices for 1957, 1970, and 1980, with 1952 = 100, are obtained as the ratios of the gross values at 1957 prices, at 1970 prices, and at 1980 prices respectively to the gross values at 1952 prices. The gross values are given in Table 3.6. The implicit price indices of agricultural output for 1957, 1970, and 1980 are obtained by dividing columns 2, 3, and 4 of Table 3.6 respectively by column 1, yielding 88.9, 131.3, and 176.5. The implicit price indices of industrial output for 1957, 1970, and 1980 are obtained by dividing columns 6, 7, and 8 respectively by column 5, yielding 89.8, 77.2, and 76.9. Using these indices for 1980 to deflate the values of net output given in Table 3.5, we find that net output from agriculture grew from 34.0 billion 1952 yuan in 1952 to 146.6/1.765, or 83.1 billion, in 1980, and that net output from industry grew from 11.5 billion in 1952 to 169.8/.769, or 220.8, in 1980. The increase in net output from

Table 3.5 **NATIONAL INCOME BY CONTRIBUTING SECTORS**
(Billions of Current Yuan)

Year	Agriculture		Industry		Construction	Transport	Commerce
	1 Billions	2 Percentage	3 Billions	4 Percentage	5 Billions	6 Billions	7 Billions
1952	34.0	57.7	11.5	19.5	2.1	2.5	8.8
1957	42.5	46.8	25.7	28.3	4.5	3.9	14.2
1962	44.4	48.0	30.3	32.8	3.2	3.8	10.7
1965	64.1	46.2	50.5	36.4	5.3	5.8	13.0
1978	106.5	35.4	140.8	46.8	12.5	11.8	29.4
1979	131.8	39.3	153.6	45.9	13.0	12.1	24.5
1980	146.6	40.0	169.8	46.3	15.0	11.1	24.2
1981	163.4	42.0	171.9	44.2	15.2	11.2	27.0

Source: Statistical Yearbook of China, 1981, p. 20. The sum of columns 1, 3, 5, 6, and 7 equals national income as given in column 1 of Table 3.3.

Table 3.6 GROSS OUTPUT VALUES OF AGRICULTURE AND INDUSTRY

	Gross agricultural output value (billions)				Gross industrial output value (billions)			
	1	2	3	4	5	6	7	8
	1952	1957	1970	1980	1952	1957	1970	1980
Year	Yuan	Yuan	Yuan	Yuan	Yuan	Yuan	Yuan	Yuan
1952	48.4				34.3			
1957	60.4	53.7			78.4	70.4		
1962	48.4	43.0			94.6	85.0		
1965	66.4	59.0			155.2	139.4		
1978	111.1		145.9		548.3		423.1	
1979	120.7		158.4		594.9		459.1	
1980	124.0		162.7		646.7		499.2	
1981	131.0		172.0	231.2	673.2		519.9	517.8

Sources: Columns 1 and 5 are, respectively, the indices of gross agricultural and industrial output values from *Statistical Yearbook of China, 1981,* p. 18, multiplied by the values 48.4 and 34.3 for 1952. The remaining columns are from ibid., p. 17.

agriculture is a factor of 83.1/34.0, or 2.44. The increase in net output from industry is a factor of 220.8/11.5, or 19.2. From Table 3.6, the corresponding increases in gross output are (124.0/48.4) = 2.56 and (646.7/34.3) = 18.9. Thus, the net and gross output figures give very similar pictures of the rates of growth of the two sectors. The industrial sector has grown much more rapidly than the agricultural sector.

We are now ready to examine the amount of savings generated by the agricultural sector. From 1952 to 1980, while net output from agriculture grew, population in the agricultural sector also grew. Data on population in the agricultural sector are given in column 3 of Table 3.7. We can divide column 1 of Table 3.5 by population to obtain per capita income in current yuan generated by the agricultural sector, as shown in column 1 of Table 3.7. Per capita saving is estimated subtracting per capita consumption from per-capita income (official figures given in column 2 of Table 3.7). The ratio of saving to income in the agricultural sector is found to be 13.0 percent in 1952, 3.7 percent in 1957, 7.7 percent in 1965, and 6.9 percent in 1979. The high ratio of saving to income in 1952 suggests that after the land reform and before collectivization, Chinese farmers were willing to devote large fractions of their low incomes to saving, testifying to the second important source of growth in agricultural output, according to Schultz (1980), mentioned at the end of Section 3.3.

For the years 1957, 1965, and 1979, the per capita saving figures (column 1 minus column 2 of Table 3.7), when multiplied by agricultural population (column 3 of Table 3.7), yield total savings from the agricultural sector of 1.56, 4.97, and 9.04 billion current yuan, respectively. If we compare these savings figures with the accumulated figures 23.3, 36.5, and 116.1 for the three years given in column 3 of Table 3.4, we find that agricultural savings account for 6.7 percent, 13.5 percent, and 7.8 percent of total accumulation in the years 1957, 1965, and 1979, respectively.

We should note that the small level of saving on the part of the agricultural sector may be partly the result of the pricing of agricultural and industrial products in China. Income is generated from the agricultural sector through the production of products that provide food for the urban population and raw materials for industry. Columns 3 and 5 of Table 3.7 show that in 1952 about 49 persons in the agricultural sector were

Table 3.7 AGRICULTURAL INCOME AND CONSUMPTION PER CAPITA

Year	1 Income from agriculture per cap. (current yuan)	2 Private consumption per cap. peasants (current yuan)	3 Agricultural population, year-end (millions)	4 Private consumption per cap. nonagric. (current yuan)	5 Nonagric. population, year-end (millions)	6 Private consumption expenditure per cap. (current yuan)	7 Private consumption per cap. (1952 = 100)	8 Private consumption per cap. peasants (1952 = 100)	9 Private consumption per cap. nonagric. (1952 = 100)
1952	71.3	62	477.02	148	97.80	76	100	100	100
1957	82.0	79	518.59	205	127.94	102	122.9	117.1	126.3
1965	108.4	100	591.22	237	134.16	125	126.4	116.0	136.5
1975		124	777.12	324	142.58	158	156.9	143.1	181.1
1979	163.2	152	807.39	406	163.53	197	184.9	165.2	214.5

Sources: Column 1 equals column 1 of Table 3.5 divided by column 3 of Table 3.7. Columns 2, 4, 6, 7, 8, and 9 are from *Almanac of China's Economy, 1981*, p. 985. Column 3 equals population in rural communes (ibid., p. 965, and *Statistical Yearbook of China, 1981*, p. 133) for 1965 and after; for 1952 and 1957 it equals rural population (*Almanac of China's Economy, 1981*, p. 959) times .9480, the ratio of commune to rural population in 1965. Column 5 equals column 4 of Table 3.3 minus column 3, the 1957 population figure being found on p. 959 of *Statistical Yearbook of China, 1981*. Column 6 is obtained by dividing private consumption expenditure (excluding services) from available national income by mean population of the year. It is smaller than column 5 of Table 3.4 presumably because it excludes government consumption. Because the population figures in columns 3 and 5 are year-end figures, the product of column 6 and total population (column 4 of Table 3.3) should not be exactly equal to the product of columns 2 and 3 plus the product of columns 4 and 5. The differences are small and reassuring.

94

providing food and materials for 10 persons in the nonagricultural sector, a ratio that changed to 41 for 10 in 1957, 44 for 10 in 1965, 55 for 10 in 1975, and 49 for 10 in 1979. The exports from the agricultural sector would constitute savings, except that they are cancelled by the imports of industrial goods consumed by the agricultural sector. The estimated saving from the agricultural sector depends on how the exports from the imports to the agricultural sector are priced. Even if the agricultural sector exports a great deal and consumes very little imported nonagricultural products, the prices of these imports could be set so high compared with the prices of the agricultural exports as to make their values equal, thus yielding no saving from the agricultural sector, according to the national income statistics. Pricing the imports to the agricultural sector high and the exports from the agricultural sector low will increase the consumption figures in column 2 and decrease the income figures in column 1 of Table 3.7, leading to small recorded savings. Lacking the prices generated by a free market for evaluating the exports and imports of the agricultural sector, it is difficult to measure accurately the savings generated by the agricultural sector.

Our second question—How much investment has gone into the agricultural sector?—is partially answered by the growth of capital stock in agriculture, as given in column 6 of Table 3.1. The index increases from 100.0 in 1952 to 281.9 in 1980, or from 11.292 billion 1952 yuan to 31.832 billion. From the *Almanac of China's Economy, 1981* (p. 964), we learn that fixed assets of state-owned enterprises in the industrial sector, expressed in billions of yuan at original value, are as follows:

1952	*1957*	*1965*	*1975*	*1979*
10.72	27.22	96.10	229.03	325.32

These figures are not in constant 1952 prices. Also, in 1952 many industrial enterprises were not yet state-owned. Bearing in mind these qualifications, we can still conclude that capital formation in agriculture is very much smaller than in industry. The result is a slower growth in income from agriculture than from industry and other sectors, as Table 3.5 shows.

The Chinese experience in economic development from 1952 to 1980 differs from the successful development experiences of other countries in two related respects. First, in most countries economic development takes the form of a drastic reduction in the proportion of population and labor force remaining in the agricultural sector. In China this did not happen, partly because of a government policy to restrict labor mobility in all directions—from commune to commune, from city to city, and from rural to urban areas—and partly because the industrial and other nonagricultural sectors were not able to absorb the large increase in population in the rural areas. Columns 3 and 5 of Table 3.7 show that the agricultural population remained 83 percent of the total population in 1979, as it had been in 1952. Some members of the rural population in rural communes were working in sideline industrial enterprises, which accounted for 12.5 percent of total gross agricultural output value in 1979 (see *Statistical Yearbook of China, 1981*, p. 137). However, economic development usually means a reduction of the labor force working in agriculture to about 20 to 30 percent. In Taiwan, for example, the number of persons employed in agriculture, forestry, and fishing decreased from 1.728 million in 1967 to 1.553 million in 1978, or from 43 to 25 percent of the total number of employed persons (see *Statistical Yearbook of the Republic of China, 1979,* p. 46).

Second, economic development usually means a large reduction in the percentage of national income or product contributed by agriculture, from about 60 to 15 percent. Table 3.5 shows that in China, this percentage only decreased from 58 percent in 1952 to 42 percent in 1981. In Taiwan, for example, the fraction of gross domestic product accounted for by agriculture, hunting, forestry, and fishing decreased from 29 percent in 1960 to 9 percent in 1979 (see *Statistical Yearbook of the Republic of China, 1980,* p. 463).

In Section 3.3 we concluded that Chinese agriculture was not yet modernized in 1980. In this section we have found that, although industrial output increased fairly rapidly (as seen in Table 3.5) and although much of capital formation took place in the industrial sector (as seen from the large increase in fixed assets of state-owned enterprises in that sector), population did not get transferred out of the agricultural sector, and agricultural production still accounted for a large fraction, some 42 percent, of national income. The process of economic development usually takes the form of a large reduction in the fraction of total labor force engaged in agricultural activities and in the fraction of national income contributed by the agricultural sector. Outmigration of labor from the agricultural sector accompanies, and is instrumental to, the development process.

It is easy to understand why labor should be transferred out of the agricultural sector to increase national income. If the value of the marginal product of labor is higher in industry than in agriculture, a transfer of labor from agriculture to industry will increase national income. Using a hypothetical economy, we showed in Section 1.7 how national income is increased by a transfer of labor from the production of rice to the production of cloth, where the value of the marginal product of labor is higher. In China, as in other less developed countries, the marginal product of labor in agriculture is low. The reason is that there is plenty of labor as compared with other factors of production, including land, capital, and current inputs. Equation 3.11 for the marginal product of an input x_1

$$\frac{\partial y}{\partial x_1} = \alpha \beta x_1^{\beta-1} x_2^{(1-\beta)} \qquad (1-\beta) > 0 \qquad (3.29)$$

shows that the marginal product of labor decreases as the quantity x_1 of labor increases and as the quantity x_2 of other inputs decreases. A large quantity of labor relative to the quantity of land and other inputs makes for low marginal productivity of labor. In a well-known paper, W. Arthur Lewis (1954) proposes the approximation that for many underdeveloped economies, the marginal product of labor in agriculture is practically zero. Therefore, when labor is transferred out of the agricultural sector, total agricultural output is practically unchanged and the average output per worker will increase. In the meantime, the laborers can be productive in the industrial and other sectors, helping to increase national income.

A centrally planned economy has to solve the problem of transferring labor to the area of economic activity where the value of its marginal product is the highest. When wages and prices are set by criteria other than the balancing of demand and supply, and when labor is made almost completely immobile and is prevented from seeking the best opportunity available, it is difficult to have an efficient allocation of labor to maximize national income. In China the economic planners were mainly concerned with mobilizing the labor force in agriculture to provide sufficient food for the rural and urban populations and to work in construction projects in the rural areas. Economic efficiency and economic incentives did not appear to be a main concern until the late 1970s, when economic reforms in agriculture were instituted and when efficiency and incentives were recognized to be important. Having examined Chinese agriculture in aggregate terms, we will now examine it at the microeconomic level by looking at the commune system under which Chinese agriculture was organized after 1958.

3.5 PRODUCTION AND DISTRIBUTION UNDER THE COMMUNE SYSTEM

At the time this chapter was being written, in April 1983, the Chinese government had already decided that the commune system as an economic organization for agriculture should be abolished. This section will soon be regarded as a piece of economic history. The Chinese economic planners have learned a valuable lesson in operating the communes, and this lesson should be recorded for students of economics and economic policy makers.

From 1952 to 1957, national income per capita in constant 1952 prices (Table 3.3, column 6) grew from 102.5 to 139.4, or at an exponential rate of 6.34 percent per year, while income from agriculture per capita in 1952 prices (Table 3.7, column 1, the implicit price index for 1957 being 88.9) increased from 67.6 to 87.4, or at an exponential rate of 5.27 percent per year. This was probably the golden period of the Chinese economy since 1949. In the agricultural sector the farmers were organized as cooperatives, but the commune system had not yet been introduced. Prices of agricultural products were determined mainly by the forces of demand and supply in the free market, although centralized procurement of agricultural products was instituted in 1953. The first Five-Year Plan was just completed in 1957, and the second Five-Year Plan was to begin in 1958. Suddenly, Chairman Mao Zedong decided to launch the Great Leap Forward in 1958 to speed up the industrialization process and to push China quickly into a communist system according to his definition. The introduction of the commune system was a key component of the Great Leap.

The transformation of Chinese agriculture through the land reform of 1949–1952, the formation of mutual aid teams and cooperatives in 1951–1957, and the introduction of the commune system in 1958 are a fascinating chapter of political, social, and economic history. Cheng (1982, Chapter 3), among others, has provided such a chapter. We will omit the details of this story because our primary concern is with economic analysis; we will concentrate on describing the functioning of the commune system from 1958 to 1979. It is a testament to the political power and organizational skill of the leadership of the Chinese Communist party that within about five months, between April and September 1958, 98.2 percent of the total number of peasant households had been organized into 26,425 communes (see Table 3.8 and Cheng, 1982, pp. 98–99).

As we point out in Chapter 2, a commune is both a political-administrative unit and an economic unit of production. In such a unit peasants, workers, students, and members of the army engage in agriculture, fishing, forestry, industrial sideline, and

Table 3.8 COMPOSITION OF RURAL PEOPLES' COMMUNES, 1958 TO 1981

Year	Number of peoples' communes	Production brigades (thousands)	Production teams (thousands)	Households in the communes (millions)	Persons in the communes (millions)	Average number of brigades per commune	Average number of teams per brigade	Average number of persons per team
1958	23,630	—	—	128.61	560.17	—	—	—
1962	74,771	703	5,580	134.10	—	9.4	7.9	109
1965	74,755	648	5,412	135.27	591.22	8.7	8.3	109
1979	53,348	699	5,154	174.91	807.39	13.1	7.4	157
1980	54,183	710	5,662	176.73	810.96	13.1	8.0	143
1981	54,371	718	6,004	180.16	818.81	13.2	8.4	136

Source: Statistical Yearbook of China, 1981, p. 133.

construction activities. Labor is mobilized to perform the important economic tasks of supplying food and materials for industrialization and building roads, bridges, irrigation systems, and other construction projects. If a command economy is to work, the labor force has to follow the directions of the central economic planners. Under the commune system, central directions can be disseminated through the communes. Each commune is headed by an administrative committee. Construction projects are carried out by brigades. Farming is done by the smaller teams. How much land to be devoted to each crop and the method of farming are subject to central directions. Each team is given production targets and is required to deliver specified quantities of the products at given purchase (or procurement) prices. Given the quantities of outputs, the incomes of the communes are affected by the procurement quantities and procurement prices set by the government. Thus, the production and distribution of agricultural products and the distribution of income to the farmers are controlled by the government. We will first examine some statistical facts concerning the production and distribution of agricultural products and the distribution of income in the agricultural sector. We will then discuss the efficiency of agricultural production as it is affected by the institutional arrangements under the commune system and by the pricing and output policies of the government.

One important fact concerning the composition of agricultural output is that the output of farming has declined while the output of sideline industrial products has increased in relative terms. As Table 3.9 shows, farming accounted for 83.1 percent of gross agricultural output value in 1952 and only 64.4 percent in 1981, while the percentage due to sideline production increased from 4.4 percent to 14.3 percent. In 1981, 11.9 of the 14.3 percentage points were from brigade- and team-run industrial enterprises. Thus an increasing, though still small, fraction of the product of the agricultural sector consisted of sideline industrial products. This indicates that industrialization was taking place to some extent in the rural areas of China.

Concerning government procurement of farm and sideline products, Table 3.10

Table 3.9   COMPOSITION OF GROSS AGRICULTURAL OUTPUT VALUE
(Percentages)

Year	Farming	Forestry	Animal husbandry	Fishing	Sideline total	Products of brigade- and team-run industrial enterprises
At 1957 constant prices						
1952	83.1	0.7	11.5	0.3	4.4	
1957	80.6	1.7	12.9	0.5	4.3	
1962	78.9	1.7	10.3	1.8	7.3	
1965	75.8	2.0	14.0	1.7	6.5	
At 1970 constant prices						
1979	66.9	2.8	14.0	1.2	15.1	12.5
1980	64.3	3.1	14.2	1.3	17.1	14.5
1981	64.1	3.0	14.3	1.3	17.3	15.0
At 1980 constant prices						
1981	64.4	4.1	15.4	1.8	14.3	11.9

Source: Statistical Yearbook of China, 1981, p. 137.

Table 3.10 PURCHASES OF FARM AND SIDELINE PRODUCTS

Year	1 Purchase of farm and sideline products (billion yuan)	2 Ratio of purchase to income from agriculture	3 Grain output (million metric tons)	4 Grain purchase (million metric tons)	5 Ratio of purchase to output of grain	6 Cotton output (million metric tons)	7 Cotton purchase (million metric tons)	8 Ratio of purchase to output of cotton
1952	14.08	.414	163.92	39.03	.238	1.304	1.087	.834
1957	21.75	.512	195.05	45.97	.236	1.640	1.412	.861
1962	21.10	.475	160.00	32.42	.203	.750	.632	.843
1965	30.71	.479	194.53	39.22	.202	2.098	1.956	.932
1978	55.79	.524	304.77	50.73	.166	2.167	2.096	.967
1979	71.36	.541	332.12	60.10	.181	2.207	2.081	.943
1980	84.22	.574	320.56	61.29	.191	2.707	2.610	.964
1981	95.50	.584	325.02	68.46	.211	2.968	2.872	.968

Sources: Columns 1, 4, and 7 are from *Statistical Yearbook of China, 1981,* p. 345. Columns 3 and 6 are from ibid., pp. 145 and 146. Column 2 is the ratio of column 1 to column 1 of Table 3.5. Column 5 is the ratio of column 4 to column 3. Nicholas Lardy has pointed out that the grain output figures in column 3 are measured in unhusked weight, whereas the grain purchase figures in column 4 refer to trade grain (mao-i-liang; see p. 341 of the Chinese edition of *Statistical Yearbook of China, 1981*). The ratio of trade grain to original grain varies from year to year; it was .837 in 1977, according to Lardy. Thus, column 4 should be increased somewhat. But since the purchase figures in column 4 include the direct agricultural tax and sales in rural periodic markets, those figures should be reduced to reflect government procurement. Neither adjustment has been made. Column 8 is the ratio of column 6 to column 7.

shows the fraction of total value of net agricultural income and the fractions of grain output and cotton output purchased by the government. Column 2 shows the ratio of total value of purchase of farm and sideline products to national income generated by the agricultural sector. The ratio increased somewhat over time, from .414 in 1952 to .584 in 1981. The ratio of total purchase to gross agricultural output value increased from 14.08/48.4, or .29, in 1952 to approximately 95.50/(231.2 × 1.059), or .39, in 1981 (see Table 3.6 for gross agricultural output values and *Statistical Yearbook of China, 1981,* p. 415, for the index 1.059 of purchase price of farm and sideline products). If we break down total purchase into its components and consider the purchases of grain and cotton in particular, we find in columns 5 and 8 that the government purchased about 20 percent of grain output and 95 percent of cotton output in 1980. Since about 86 percent of the Chinese population in 1980 was rural and most of the grain produced was consumed locally, the above purchase figures indicate that except for local consumption, the total outputs of grain and cotton were purchased by the government. The extent to which the government monopolized the distribution of farm and sideline products in China in 1981 is seen by the breakdown of the total purchase of 95.50 billion yuan into its components: 74.40 purchased by departments of domestic trade, 2.07 purchased by departments of foreign trade, 10.09 purchased by industrial and other departments, and only 8.94 purchased from peasants by nonagricultural residents (see *Statistical Yearbook of China, 1981,* p. 347).

As for the distribution of agricultural income, Table 3.11 shows how much gross income or revenue of the communes went to production cost and other expenditures, state taxes, accumulation and welfare funds, and finally to distribution to commune members. Total income, given in the first column, is a very large fraction of national income generated by the agricultural sector, as given in column 1 of Table 3.5. The

with the Ministries of Finance and Agriculture and Fisheries and subject to the approval of the State Council and the Central Committee of the Chinese Communist party. Agricultural products are divided into three categories. Category 1 products are subject to unified procurement and include food, grain, cotton, and vegetable oils. Category 2 products are subject to designated procurement and include pork, fresh eggs, tobacco, tea, silkworm cocoons, sugar cane, sugar beets, raw lacquer, hemp and flax, animal hides, wool, major aquatic products, fresh and dried fruits, and more than 100 other products. All remaining products belong to category 3 and are not subject to compulsory purchase or price control. As we pointed out in discussing Table 3.11, members of the communes may be paid any of four different prices for their products: list purchase price, above-quota purchase price, negotiated price, and market price. Not all category 1 and category 2 products are subject to these four prices. The above-quota price applies mainly to food grain. The government divides the compulsory grain purchase into two levels, the first having a lower purchase price and the second having a somewhat higher above-quota (meaning above-first-quota) purchase price. These two prices are often much lower than the negotiated price and the market price, the latter two being almost identical. However, some products, such as cotton, cannot be sold in the market, nor at a negotiated price. Essentially, there are the compulsory purchase price (which is further divided into two levels in the case of food grain) and the market price (which the government purchasing departments have to follow when buying more than the compulsory purchase quota).

The historical development of the purchase prices of farm products is shown in Table 3.13. Column 1 shows the general purchase price index of farm and sideline

Table 3.13   LIST PURCHASE PRICES OF AGRICULTURAL PRODUCTS
            (1950 = 100)

Year	1 General purchase price index of farm and sideline products	2 List purchase price index of farm and sideline products	3 List purchase price index of grain	4 List purchase price index of industrial crops	5 List purchase price index of cotton	6 List purchase price index of sugar crops	7 List purchase price index of oil-bearing crops
1952	121.6	121.6	121.4	113.0	113.3	87.2	108.2
1953	132.5						
1954	136.7						
1956	139.2						
1957	146.2	146.2	141.4	126.4	111.1	102.9	167.9
1958	149.4						
1960	157.4						
1961	201.4						
1965	187.9	185.1	190.9	152.8	122.9	135.3	246.7
1978	217.4	207.3	224.4	174.0	138.8	151.5	321.3
1979	265.5						
1980	284.4						
1981	301.2	257.2	283.5	215.0	179.0	197.1	398.9

Source: Statistical Yearbook of China, 1981, pp. 411–412 for column 1 and p. 414 for columns 2, 3, 4, 5, 6, and 7.

products, while column 2 gives their list purchase price index. The two indices differ in the years 1978 to 1981 because the general index is an average of list prices, above-quota purchase prices, and negotiated prices (which are close to market prices). Compulsory purchase was instituted in 1953 to obtain agricultural products for carrying out the first Five-Year Plan of 1953–1957. There were two large increases in purchase prices, one occurring in 1961 (to 201.4 from 157.4 in 1960) and the other occurring in 1979–1981 (see column 2). Both increases were motivated by the need to distribute more income to the farmers, the first after the economic disaster of the Great Leap Forward and the second after the Cultural Revolution and the elimination of the Gang of Four and the institution of a policy to place more emphasis on agricultural production. Here we see that even in a centrally planned economy, the two economic functions that prices serve in the distribution of income and the regulation of production cannot be entirely separated. In order to stimulate production, the government had to pay more to the farmers. The above two instances are crisis situations. In other periods the government often acted as if production could be increased by administrative orders alone, without the provision of material incentives through the price system.

After this brief look at the list prices of farm products through time, it is of interest to compare the four kinds of prices for wheat and paddy rice in 1980. Table 3.14 shows that the above-quota purchase prices are 50 percent higher than the list purchase prices, and that the negotiated purchase prices are the same as the rural market prices, both being much higher than the above-quota purchase prices, about 57 percent higher for rice and 20 percent higher for wheat. Besides these four prices, which apply to the sale of farm products in the communes, there are two prices for the urban population, one under rationing and the other in urban free markets, the latter being much higher than the former in 1980. Sometimes the government had to resell some of the agricultural products to certain segments of the rural population at prices not much higher than the list purchase prices in order to satisfy their needs. The internal accounting prices are used to evaluate the output distributed to members of the communes. They appear to be very low, and may be used to calculate the income figures of the communes as reported in Table 3.11.

To the extent that compulsory purchase prices (list or above-quota) are lower than the prices prevailing in rural markets, the procurement system represents a form of taxation of the rural population. From the viewpoint of the Chinese government, which intends to develop the Chinese economy, a tax burden on the rural population is deemed necessary to obtain resources for capital formation. However, one may

Table 3.14 VARIOUS PRICES OF WHEAT AND RICE, 1980
(Yuan per Kilogram)

	List purchase price	Above-quota purchase price	Nego-tiated purchase price	Rural market price	Urban market price	Urban ration price	State resale to rural	Accounting price distribution to commune members
Wheat	.3296	.4944	.5940	.5940	—	.333	.3560	.2722
Rice	.2312	.3468	.5460	.5460	.620	.2128	.2497	.1904

Source: Lardy (1983b), Table 1.1, p. 7.

question whether a system of compulsory purchases at below-market prices is an efficient system for extracting taxes from the rural population. In the next section we will present an economic analysis of this system and discuss its economic consequences.

3.7 AN ECONOMIC ANALYSIS OF COMPULSORY PURCHASE

To understand the economic effects of the system of compulsory purchases, it is useful to contrast it with a system of voluntary purchases at market prices. Such a system prevailed in the early 1950s, before compulsory purchases were instituted. We will apply the tools introduced in Chapter 1 to study the determination of price and output in Chinese agriculture in the early 1950s, when the system of free markets and privately owned farms prevailed. How the institution of compulsory purchases under the commune system affects agricultural output can then be understood by comparison with the results of a market system.

To begin our analysis, let us make some simplifying assumptions to bring out the most important aspects of the economic problem so that we can understand the essence of the situation without being confused by minor complications and details. First, let us deal with only one product. This product may be rice, wheat, or cotton, for example. It may be a group of products, such as food grains. Second, we consider only two prices, the procurement price (without making the distinction for an above-quota procurement price) and the market price. Third, we consider only one market by ignoring the transportation and distribution costs of bringing the product from the rural producers to the rural and urban consumers. (We can extend our analysis to deal with a rural and an urban market by using two demand curves for these markets; see Problem 14.) One market price is assumed to prevail in the market, and regional differences are ignored.

In the first instance, consider a market system where the farmer-producers can sell directly to the consumers without intervention by government procurement agencies. From the discussion of Chapter 1, we can use a supply curve to describe the quantities that the private farmers would supply at different prices and a demand curve to describe the quantities that the consumers would buy at different prices. When the price is higher, the farmers can supply more; they need a higher price to cover the higher marginal cost incurred when they produce a larger quantity of output. When the price is higher, the consumers will buy less; they will substitute other goods to maximize their well-being. The price of the product will be determined by the intersection of the supply curve S and the demand curve D, as shown by the value p in Figure 3.2, the quantity of output being q.

Before introducing government procurement, let us elaborate on certain aspects of the determination of price and output in Chinese agriculture under the market system when land is privately owned and when labor is freely mobile. Consider the economics of the individual farms. The aggregate supply curve S in Figure 3.2 is obtained by adding the quantities that all the farms will supply at any given price, or by adding horizontally the supply curves of the individual farms. The supply curve of each farm is its marginal cost curve. To give a numerical illustration, let the total cost of producing output x be

$$C = 5.0 + .2x^2 \qquad (3.30)$$

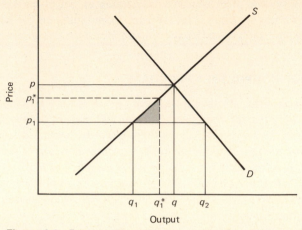

Figure 3.2 Determination of price and output in Chinese agriculture.

and let the marginal cost be

$$MC = .4x \tag{3.31}$$

The *average cost,* or cost per unit, is then

$$AC = C/x = 5.0/x + .2x \tag{3.32}$$

The marginal cost and average cost curves are drawn in Figure 3.3. If the market price is 2 per unit, the farm will supply 5 units to maximize its profit. This quantity is obtained by equating the marginal cost $.4x$ to 2, yielding $x = 5$. The total revenue of

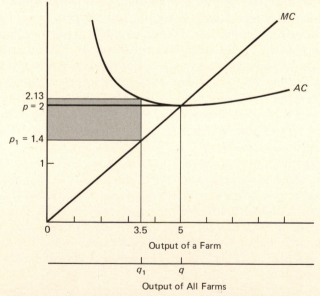

Figure 3.3 Marginal cost and average cost of an individual farm.

the farm is 10 and its total cost, according to the above formula, is also 10. The farm is making zero profit, but it earns enough to cover all costs, including costs of labor, land, equipment, and other inputs. If the market price is greater than 2, the farm will make a profit; if less than 2, the farm will incur a loss. For example, if price is 1.4, output will be 3.5. Average cost will be 2.13. The loss will be $(2.13 - 1.4)(3.5) = 2.55$, as given by the shaded area in Figure 3.3. Figure 3.3 explains what makes up the supply curve of Figure 3.2.

When there are many farms in competition with one another, the equilibrium market price p given by Figure 3.2 is such that the farms will be making no profits *if* all inputs are paid by their market prices. The economics of a typical farm is given in Figure 3.3, where, at $p = 2$, average cost equals price and profit is zero. The conclusion of zero profit might be puzzling to the reader at first glance. One would think that the profits would be higher for those farms with better land. A moment's reflection reveals that this is not the case *if* we include the higher rent of the land as part of the cost. If the farmer rents a better piece of land from a landowner, he will have to pay a higher rent. To the extent that the better piece of land enables the farm to earn more income, the landowner can demand a higher rent for it because some other farmers will be willing to pay a higher rent in order to produce more output. If the farmer owns this piece of land himself, he should consider the extra income of his farm not as profit, but as a higher rent paid to himself to be included in his cost. He should do so because he could rent out the land for which some other farmers would be willing to pay more in order to have a larger output. A system that prevents the payment of higher rent for better land through the market is economically inefficient, because it prevents the land from being transferred to its most productive use as measured by the willingness of people to pay for it.

Let the curves S and D of Figure 3.2 represent the supply and demand curves for an agricultural product in China under the market system prevailing in the early 1950s. The price p is an equilibrium price. In general, the farms do not make extra profits if the costs of all inputs are accounted for. Food is supplied to the urban population through the market. If the farms are adjacent to an urban area, perhaps the farmers can supply the nearby urban population directly. Otherwise, there are merchants who transport the food to the urban areas. Now suppose that the government wants to take over the distribution of food through a system of compulsory purchase. The purpose is to supply food more cheaply to the urban population. Consider two cases. In case A the government simply institutes compulsory purchase without changing the system of private ownership of individual farms. In case B the government reorganizes the farms into communes, directs the activities of the production units, and prevents the transfer of land and the mobility of labor among the production units. What are the economic consequences in the two cases? In both cases we assume that the government pays a compulsory purchase price below the price that would prevail in a free market. This is a main feature of compulsory purchase.

Consider case A. Let the compulsory purchase price be p_1 in Figure 3.2, which is below the market price p. If the farmers do not receive directions from the government and are autonomous in their decisions, as in the case of China in the early 1950s, they will supply a smaller quantity q_1. If the government sells the quantity q_1 to the urban population at the same price p_1 (ignoring transportation and distribution costs), there will be a quantity $q_2 - q_1$ of unsatisfied demand. The demand curve tells us that at the price p_1 the consumers will demand q_2, but the government has only the quantity q_1 available. This necessitates rationing. The government will issue a limited number of ration coupons, which must be used to purchase the available quantity q_1 of supplies. If the government sells q_1 to the consumers at a price even lower than p_1, the urban unsatisfied demand will be even larger, because at a lower price the consumers would desire even more. How will the unsatisfied demand be met? It will not be met at all if the farmers cannot sell directly to the urban consumers.

Still under case A, assume that the government pays a procurement price p_1 but orders the farmers to deliver a quantity q_1^* larger than q_1. From our discussion in Section 1.5, we know that the supply curve S shows the marginal costs that the farmers have to pay in producing different quantities of output. For example, when the farmers produce the quantity q_1, the marginal cost is p_1, or it costs p_1 to produce an extra unit. When the farmers are ordered to produce the quantity q_1^*, the marginal cost is p_1^*, which is higher than the purchase price p_1 paid by the government. The concepts of total cost and marginal cost are applicable no matter whether an enterprise is privately run or government directed. It will cost something to produce the outputs. (Of course, if the government arbitrarily raises or lowers the prices of the inputs to a producer, the cost from the producer's viewpoint will be affected, but there is still a marginal cost curve for the operation of the enterprise.) When output exceeds q_1, the marginal cost is higher than p_1. The more the farmers are asked to produce to sell at the price p_1, the more money they lose. The amount they lose by selling the extra quantity $q_1^* - q_1$ is given by the shaded area of Figure 3.2. This area equals the sum of the areas of the small rectangles. Each small rectangle shows the loss (the difference between the extra cost and the price) associated with a small amount of output. If we approximate the shaded area by a triangle, the total loss from producing the quantity $q_1^* - q_1$ is $\frac{1}{2}(q_1^* - q_1)(p_1^* - p_1)$. Thus, the government is directing the farmers to operate at a loss in producing the output $q_1^* - q_1$.

It is very difficult, if not impossible, for the government to direct the farmers to sell the quantity $q_1^* - q_1$ to its purchasing departments at a purchase price p_1 below the marginal cost. The farmers will resist because it is a losing proposition. The more they sell to the government, the more money they lose. As the quantity q_1^* is increased or the point q_1^* is moved to the right, the area of the shaded triangle—that is, the amount of the loss—will be larger. Therefore, it is difficult to force an increase in the supply of a product without increasing its price to pay for the marginal cost. The fact that the Chinese government found it necessary to raise its purchase prices, as shown in column 2 of Table 3.13, in order to increase agricultural outputs testifies to this basic *law of supply* in economics: in order to increase supply, it is necessary to raise the price. In terms of Figure 3.2, if the government insists on paying a procurement price of p_1 and wants to purchase q_1^*, it is unlikely to succeed and may end up obtaining a quantity smaller than q_1^*.

We have just explained why it is difficult to direct the farmers to sell at a price below marginal cost, or below the price given by the supply curve. It is even more difficult if the farmers are incurring a loss in the entire operation. We know that selling the extra quantity $q_1^* - q_1$ shown in Figure 3.2 is a losing proposition, but the farmers may make enough money in selling the quantity q_1 to make up for this loss. Whether the entire operation yields a profit or a loss depends on whether *total revenue* is larger or smaller than *total cost,* or whether purchase price is larger or smaller than *average cost.* In the early 1950s, Chinese farmers were in general not making extra profits if the costs of all inputs, including land, are properly included. In other words, at the level of output q determined by the market system, average costs for most farms equal market price p and profits are zero, as shown in Figure 3.3. To direct the farmers to sell at a price p_1 below the market price p will mean a net loss in the entire operation, where the costs are computed by using the market prices of all the inputs. The loss is the smallest when total output is q_1; any extra output will yield a greater loss.

How could the government direct the farmers to operate at a loss and to sell below marginal cost? By changing the prices of the inputs in the cost calculations. This leads to case B, where the government not only sets the quantity and price of compulsory purchase but also changes agricultural production from a system of private ownership to a commune system. Under the commune system, land is assigned and labor becomes immobile. From the viewpoint of the accounting of a production team, land has no cost because it cannot be rented out to other producers who would appraise its economic value in alternative use. Labor also has no cost because laborers are not allowed to go elsewhere to earn a competitive wage. Once it abolishes the markets for land and labor, the government has no way to evaluate their economic costs. Under a market system, the price of an input equals the amount other users are willing to pay, which is the value of its marginal product. By not being charged an appropiate rent for the land it uses, a production team under the commune system may be showing a positive income in its accounts even when it is actually operating at a loss if an appropriate rent were to be subtracted. Note that in the accounts of the production units under the commune system as shown in Table 3.11, the costs of using land and labor are not included as costs.

The economic consequences of not including the costs of land and labor in the economic calculations of a production unit under the commune system are serious. In Section 3.5 we pointed out that the immobility of labor or the absence of a market for labor services prevents laborers from moving to farms where their marginal products would be higher, which would increase national output. Similarly, if land cannot be transferred to alternative producers who are willing to pay a higher rent because they can find a more productive use for it, agricultural output will be reduced. A poorly managed production team having the good fortune of being assigned a fertile piece of land may still produce enough to earn an income according to the accounts of Table 3.11, but the land could be made more productive if a better-run team were allowed to use it. How can production units be economically efficient if they have no conception of, and are not required to pay for, the costs of some of its inputs? The government is able to direct the production units to produce at a loss in the true economic sense (defined by including the economic costs of all inputs) because the production units are not asked to account for the true costs of the inputs. The society cannot avoid paying for these costs in the form of lost outputs that could have been produced by the efficient use of these inputs.

One aspect of the misuse of farmland in China has been generally recognized. In the 1960s the Chinese government directed many communes to convert farmland producing commercial crops such as cotton, peanuts, and sugar to the production of food grain. There was a sizeable economic loss in this conversion because the land suitable for the production of commercial crops (as discovered by the farmers under a market system) was not suitable for producing grain. The output of grain per hectare turned out to be low in general after the conversion. The value of the commercial crops that were sacrificed was often much higher than the value of the grain produced, leading to large economic losses. The failure to allow specialization in agriculture and its economic consequences have been studied by Lardy (1983) and Lyons (1983). This mistake has been partly corrected, as evidenced by the increases in acreage allotments to and in the purchase prices of selected commercial crops (see columns 5, 6, and 7 of Table 3.13). This misdirected policy is mentioned to suggest that if the farmers had had to pay an appropriate rent for the land they used, they could not have afforded to, and the government would have had more difficulty in directing them to, convert high-valued commercial-crop land to the production of grain at a loss. In terms of Figure 3.3, if rent is excluded from the total cost, the average cost curve is lowered and the production unit might even show a profit. For example, the total cost of equation 3.30 may be changed to $2 + .2(x)^2$ and the average cost of equation 3.32 to $2/x + .2x$ (see Problem 12).

Even when some inputs are not appropriately priced under the commune system, each production unit still performs its cost calculations using the misguided data. It still has a marginal cost curve where the cost figures are calculated by using whatever prices of inputs it has to pay. Its marginal cost is still an increasing function of output. If the government pays a compulsory purchase price below the unit's marginal cost, the more it produces the more money it loses, or the less income it earns. As in case A, it is difficult for the government to direct the production units to increase output without paying a higher price for it, because no unit wants to produce more and get less. The economic law of supply remains valid in case B. Again, let S represent the supply curve of all producers under the commune system and ignore the possible effects of the misguided cost data in the calculation of marginal costs of the individual production units. If the compulsory purchase price p_1 is below the market price p, the government will find it difficult to direct the production units to produce the quantity q of output that would result if the producers could sell directly to consumers in free markets. Even in case B the production units will produce more if they can sell directly to the consumers at a higher price than under the system of compulsory purchase.

To summarize our findings concerning compulsory purchase under the commune system, let us refer to Figure 3.2. Under a market system, where producers can sell directly to consumers and where the prices of all inputs, including rents for land use and wages for labor services, are determined in the markets, the price p and the output q of an agricultural product available in the market are determined by the intersection of a supply curve S and a demand curve D. Such a system prevailed in China in the early 1950s. But then the Chinese government decided to take over the distribution of major agricultural products from the producers to the consumers by instituting a compulsory purchase system. At the same time, production was organized under the commune system and the markets for land and labor were abolished, so that there was no longer a market rent for land and a market wage for labor. A main objective of instituting such a system was to enable the government to deliver as much output to the urban consumers as before while paying a lower price for it. Assume that immediately after these institutional changes, the government directed the farmers to produce the same output q shown in Figure 3.2 and paid a compulsory purchase price p_1 (below the market price p) for it. If the farmers' previous incomes had just covered all costs, so that both the total revenue and the total cost of all farmers had equaled $p \times q$, the farmers as a group would now be operating at a loss equal to total cost $p \times q$ minus total revenue $p_1 \times q$, or $(p - p_1) \times q$.

However, under the new system the production units did not recognize the loss because they did not include rent as a part of the cost. The fixed cost in equation 3.30 might be reduced from 5 to 2 when rent is excluded, for example. Under the new accounting system, the production units as a group managed to earn a positive income, as shown in Table 3.11. When the use of land incurred no cost and when labor became immobile, these valuable resources could not be efficiently used and productivity was most likely reduced. In other words, to produce the same output q as before, more inputs were needed under the new system. In the meantime, the production units were directed to produce extra units below their marginal costs. They would resist because the more they produced, the smaller their income would be. (If the purchase price had been above marginal cost, the production teams would have volunteered to produce more in order to earn more income, and the purchase would not have been compulsory.) This analysis applies to the behavior of the production team as a unit, without considering the system of payment to the individual farmers by work points, which, as we have seen, adversely affected their incentives and further reduced productivity.

The economic consequences of introducing compulsory purchases under the commune system can be summarized as follows. First, output is less than the quantity q under the market system because it is difficult to force the production units to produce when the purchase price p_1 is below marginal cost. Second, whatever the level of output that is actually produced (which is somewhere between q_1 and q), the true economic cost is higher than before because of the inefficient use of land and labor. Third, even if the government were able to obtain the same output q under the new system, if this output is sold to urban consumers at the below-market price p_1, there will be a shortage of $q_2 - q$ units and a rationing system will be required. Therefore, this system of taxing the farmers has undesirable economic consequences.

Let us assume, somewhat unrealistically, that the government manages to obtain the same output q as under a market system. The tax obtained by compulsory purchase is $(p - p_1) \times q$. If the government wanted to extract this amount $(p - p_1) \times q$ from the farmers, a much better system would be to charge the farmers an appropriate rent for the use of the land. The appropriate rent could be decided by allowing a free market for land rentals—that is, by allowing different producers to compete to rent any piece of land. The government could collect rent for all the land in China instead of paying a lower compulsory price for the farm products. The market price and output under this system would be respectively p and q, the same as under a market system. The government could use the rent to finance economic development. This would avoid the first two undesirable economic effects of compulsory purchase under the commune system as stated in the preceding paragraph. If under the present accounting system, which excludes the cost of land, the production units have sufficient incomes to cover other costs, the average cost (excluding rent) of producing q units must be equal to or below p_1; otherwise, the production units would be operating at a loss. Let this average cost be $p_0 \leq p_1$. The rental value of all land used for producing q units is $(p - p_0) \times q$, where p is the average cost, including rent, of producing q units. With $p_0 \leq p_1$, this rental value must be at least $(p - p_1) \times q$, which is the amount of tax revenue under the compulsory procurement system.

3.8 AGRICULTURAL REFORMS AND THEIR EFFECTS

Changes in agricultural policies in China since 1978 consisted of institutional reforms as well as changes in the structure of prices. The major institutional reform in agriculture, as discussed in Chapter 2, amounts to converting the compulsory purchase from an item affecting the marginal cost to an item affecting the fixed cost of a producing unit. A producing unit will be reluctant to produce a quantity of output for sale at a price below its marginal cost. It will try to reduce output when the purchase price is below marginal cost. In contrast, if it is asked to surrender a fixed amount as a lump-sum tax *and* if it is allowed to sell additional units at a price above marginal cost, it will increase output until price equals marginal cost.

Again, Figure 3.2 can be used to depict the economics of compulsory purchase before the recent institutional reforms. Let S be the supply curve of all production units, calculated by using the input prices which they have to pay and which may be different from market prices. Assume that the compulsory purchase price is p_1 but the government somehow succeeds in procuring the quantity q_1^* from the producers, who are incurring a loss in producing the quantity $q_1^* - q_1$. The producers will try to reduce the purchase quota to q_1, but the government is persuasive. Now if the government does not monopolize the purchase of agricultural products and allows the producers to sell their products in rural markets, the producers will try to produce more than q_1^* units. In fact, they will produce q units where the supply curve S and the demand curve D intersect at output q and price p. (Here we ignore the shifts in the demand curve, which depend on the price that the government charges the consumers for the quantity q_1^*. There will be no shift if the government charges the market price p.) By producing the additional $q - q_1^*$ units, the producers will raise their income because price is above marginal cost. By allowing the sale of agricultural products in free markets, the government shifts the marginal calculation from the production of the quantity q_1^* for compulsory purchase to the quantity q that can be sold at price p. The marginal cost of producing the additional quantity $q - q_1^*$ will be compared with the price p, and the lower compulsory purchase price p_1 will be irrelevant in this calculation. As Figure 3.2 shows, production will increase to the quantity q.

As we discussed in Chapter 2, one important result of the institutional reforms is to shift the economic decisions from the production teams to the farm households. To fulfill its purchase quota, a production team assigns a fixed amount of output to be delivered by each farm household. As far as the farm household is concerned, this fixed amount of compulsory delivery is equivalent to a lump-sum tax. The relevant marginal cost calculation of the farm household applies to the extra output after the compulsory delivery is made. For this extra output, the price to be compared with the marginal cost is the market price *if* the extra output can be sold at a rural market.

Comparing this reform with the proposal made at the end of Section 3.7 to charge the farmers an appropriate rent for the use of land, one can see the following similarities and differences. First, both compulsory delivery and land rental are fixed costs that do not affect the willingness of the production units to increase output until marginal cost equals market price. Thus, both reforms will yield a larger output than the compulsory procurement system, under which the government acted as the only purchaser. Second, to the extent that the farmers can increase their incomes by working harder as members of a farm household and do not receive incomes by the number of work points they receive as members of a much larger production team, the reforms increase incentives to work. Third, land will be more efficiently utilized if a market rental is charged for its use. The system after the reform would do as well only if the value of the output subject to compulsory delivery by the farm household happened to be equal to the market value of the land rent it should pay. Fourth, immobility of labor is another source of economic inefficiency that remains after the reform. Fifth, this chapter is concerned with efficiency in agricultural production and not with the problem of distributing the quantity of output purchased by the government to the urban consumers. Neither of the systems compared deals with this problem, which is discussed in Chapter 5. The first two points above bring out the desirable characteristics of the institutional reform in agriculture, while the second two state the remaining problems.

Turning to the changes in the structure of purchase prices in agriculture, we have pointed out that since 1978 purchase prices of many farm products have been increased, as shown in Table 3.13. Even after the reforms, not all products can be sold in rural markets. For example, no free market for cotton is allowed. Also, the markets are limited in scope because of transportation costs and because private traders are not allowed to distribute agricultural products free. When the access to markets is limited, the above-quota purchase price and the negotiated price are often the prices relevant for the marginal calculation of the producers. Raising these prices will have the effect of increasing output. Another aspect of the price reform is the change in the structure of relative prices. Wiens (1983, pp. 319–324) compares the above-quota purchase prices of Chinese agricultural products with border prices of imports. He finds that the relative price structures of the two are very similar: "With the price of nitrogenous fertilizer as numeraire, the price relatives for wheat, rice, maize, soy, and cotton based on border prices are 0.85, 0.78, 0.62, 1.17, and 8.07, respectively. Taking above-quota prices as the closest approximation to a marginal domestic price, the corresponding relatives are very similar: 0.90, 0.74, 0.65, 1.25, and 8.15, respectively."

Is there any evidence that the reforms in agriculture brought an increase in agricultural output? We may first look at the growth in the gross output value index for agriculture for 1952 to 1978 and from 1978 to 1981 (see Table 3.1, column 2). In the first period the index increased from 100 to 229.6, or at an exponential rate of 3.25 percent per year. In the second period the index increased from 229.6 to 270.7, or at an exponential rate of 5.64 percent. The growth rate after the reforms is much larger. If we choose a later starting date for the first period to eliminate the decline in output during the Great Leap Forward and consider the growth from 126.7 in 1964 to 229.6 in 1978, the exponential growth rate becomes 4.34, still below the 5.64 figure. (It would be inappropriate to start from 1962 or 1963, when there was a rapid recovery from the lowest output level resulting from the Great Leap.) Thus, there is evidence from aggregate data that the reforms were successful.

Wiens (1983) supplies more detailed evidence of the positive effects of the agricultural reforms. The positive effects are the results of both institutional and price reforms. For instance, while the output of grain increased from 304.77 million metric tones in 1978 to 325.02 in 1981, the output of cotton increased from 2.167 million metric tons to 2.968, and the output of oil-bearing crops increased from 5.218 to 10.205 (*Statistical Yearbook of China, 1981,* pp. 146–147). In per capita terms, the output of grain increased from 320 kilograms in 1978 to 328 in 1981, while the output of cotton increased from 2.28 to 3.00, the output of oil-bearing crops increased from 5.48 to 10.32, and the output of pork, beef, and mutton increased from 9.0 to 12.8 (*Statistical Yearbook, 1981,* p. 171). Wiens points out that the increase in productivity takes the form not only of increased agricultural output but also of increased output of sideline activities such as house building and commerce. It is also reflected in the increase in the farmers' personal income, some 38 percent of which is derived from private household activities, mostly from animal raising and private plots. (For the increase in per capita consumption expenditure of farm households from 1978 to 1981, see Table 5.3.)

Although the agricultural reforms were successful, economic efficiency could be further improved by the appropriate pricing of the services of land and labor and of other inputs through the use of markets. Lardy (1982) suggests that further increases in purchase prices of farm products are difficult because of the already large deficit that the government incurs in selling the products at lower rationed prices to some 160 million urban consumers. Our analysis suggests that even without further increases in government purchase prices, agricultural output can be increased by extending the scope of the free market for agricultural products. As long as the market exists, the higher market price will be used for the producers' marginal calculations, and output can be stimulated in spite of the lower purchase price. An important aspect of extending the scope of free markets is to allow traders to participate in the distribution of farm products to the consumers. This would decrease the administrative burden of the government purchasing departments and improve their efficiency through competition. Finally, as we discussed in Section 3.3, Chinese agriculture is yet to be modernized. It will be interesting to observe future developments in these directions.

Before closing this chapter, we should note that Chinese agriculture is a broad subject and many interesting and important topics have not been touched upon here. For example, we have studied the trends of agricultural output without going into its fluctuations, which can partially be explained by political considerations; see Tang (1981) on cycles of agricultural production. We have been brief on institutional material, which is supplied in Cheng (1982). We have ignored the historical development before 1949; on this topic the reader should refer to Chao and Chen (1982), Perkins (1969), and Buck (1937). Our modest aim has been to study a few important aspects of the agricultural sector of the Chinese economy today by using the familiar tools of economic analysis.

PROBLEMS

1. Given a Cobb-Douglas production function of three inputs, find the average product of the first input and discuss its characteristics.
2. Given a Cobb-Douglas production function of three inputs, find the marginal product of the first input and discuss its characteristics.

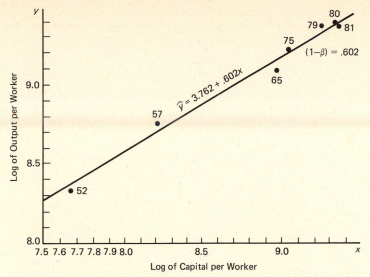

Figure 4.1 Regression of gross output per worker on capital per worker in state-owned industrial enterprises.

1979, 1980, and 1981. There is an *observation* (x_i, y_i), or *data point,* for each of these seven years $(i = 1, \ldots, 7)$, the first observation being $(x_1, y_1) = (7.651, 8.335)$, and so on. These observations, or data points, are plotted in Figure 4.1. They fall approximately along a straight line. If we draw a line to fit these points, we will find that the slope of the line is approximately .6. When $x = \log(X_2/X_1)$ increases by 1, $y = \log(Y/X_1)$ increases by .6. Thus, our estimate of $(1 - \beta)$ is .6.

It may be of interest to present an algebraic method for obtaining an estimate of the slope of a line or equation explaining a variable y by a variable x. Uninterested readers may skip the algebra and use the results. Suppose we wish to explain y_i by the equation

$$\hat{y}_i = a + bx_i \qquad (i = 1, \ldots, n) \qquad (4.6)$$

where n is the number of observations, or data points. To find the constants a and b in this equation, called the *regression equation,* we can apply the *method of least squares,* which makes the sum of squares S

$$S = \sum_{i=1}^{n} (y_i - \hat{y}_i)^2 = \sum_{i=1}^{n} (y_i - a - bx_i)^2 \qquad (4.7)$$

of the deviations $(y_i - \hat{y}_i)$ of y_i from the estimated equation $\hat{y}_i$ as small as possible. Differentiating equation 4.7 with respect to a and b yields

$$\frac{\partial S}{\partial a} = -2 \sum_{i=1}^{n} (y_i - a - bx_i) = 0 \qquad (4.8)$$

$$\frac{\partial S}{\partial b} = -2 \sum_{i=1}^{n} (y_i - a - bx_i)x_i = 0 \qquad (4.9)$$

To solve these two equations for the unknowns a and b, we divide equation 4.8 by $-2n$ and denote the averages $\frac{1}{n}\sum_{i=1}^{n} y_i$ and $\frac{1}{n}\sum_{i=1}^{n} x_i$ by $\bar{y}$ and $\bar{x}$, respectively, to obtain

$$\frac{1}{n}\sum_{i=1}^{n}(y_i - a - bx_i) = \frac{1}{n}\sum_{i=1}^{n} y_i - a - b\frac{1}{n}\sum_{i=1}^{n} x_i$$

$$= \bar{y} - a - b\bar{x} = 0 \qquad (4.10)$$

or

$$a = \bar{y} - b\bar{x} \qquad (4.11)$$

Substituting $\bar{y} - b\bar{x}$ for a in equation 4.9 gives

$$\sum_{i=1}^{n}(y_i - \bar{y} + b\bar{x} - bx_i) = \sum_{i=1}^{n}(y_i - \bar{y})x_i - b\sum_{i=1}^{n}(x_i - \bar{x})x_i = 0 \quad (4.12)$$

or

$$b = \left[\sum_{i=1}^{n}(x_i - \bar{x})x_i\right]^{-1}\sum_{i=1}^{n}(y_i - \bar{y})x_i = \left[\sum_{i=1}^{n}(x_i - \bar{x})^2\right]^{-1}\sum_{i=1}^{n}(y_i - \bar{y})(x_i - \bar{x})$$

$$(4.13)$$

where the second equality sign is due to the identities

$$\sum_{i=1}^{n}(y_i - \bar{y})\bar{x} = \bar{x}\sum_{i=1}^{n}(y_i - \bar{y}) = \bar{x}(n\bar{y} - n\bar{y}) = 0$$

$$\sum_{i=1}^{n}(x_i - \bar{x})\bar{x} = \bar{x}\sum_{i=1}^{n}(x_i - \bar{x}) = 0 \qquad (4.14)$$

Equation 4.13 is the formula for the slope b by the method of least squares.

Using the seven observations given in columns 7 and 8 of Table 4.1, we can compute

$$\bar{y} = 9.077857 \qquad\qquad \bar{x} = 8.834286$$

$$\sum_{i=1}^{n}(y_i - \bar{y})^2 = .9529888 \qquad\qquad \sum_{i=1}^{n}(x_i - \bar{x})^2 = 2.6044014$$

$$\sum_{i=1}^{n}(y_i - \bar{y})(x_i - \bar{x}) = 1.5672163 \qquad (4.15)$$

Therefore,

$$b = \frac{1.5672163}{2.6044014} = .601757$$

$$a = \bar{y} - b\bar{x} = 3.761765 \qquad (4.16)$$

The regression equation

$$\hat{y} = 3.762 + .602x \tag{4.17}$$

is drawn in Figure 4.1.

Besides the average or arithmetic mean $\bar{y}$ or $\bar{x}$ of a variable, there are two other kinds of averages often used in statistical analysis. One is the *variance*

$$\text{var } y = \frac{1}{n} \sum_{i=1}^{n} (y_i - \bar{y})^2 = \frac{.9529888}{7} = .136141 \tag{4.18}$$

which is an average of the squared deviations $(y_i - \bar{y})^2$ of a variable y from its arithmetic mean $\bar{y}$. It measures the extent to which different observations deviate from the mean. Its unit is the square of the unit for y_i; if y_i is in meters, the variance is in meters squared. The square root of the variance is the *standard deviation,* which has the same unit as the original variable. In our example, the standard deviation of y, denoted by s_y, is $\sqrt{.136141}$, or .369. The following interpretation of the standard deviation is worth noting. If the frequency distribution of the data y_i is *normal,* as shown in Figure 4.2, 68 percent of the data are within one standard deviation from the mean, 95.4 percent are within two standard deviations from the mean, and 99.7 percent are within three standard deviations from the mean. Refer to Figure 3.1 for the definition of a frequency distribution. Many types of data such as weights and heights of adult human populations of the same sex have frequency distributions very close to the normal shape.

The second average is the *covariance* of two variables y and x

$$\text{cov}(y,x) = \frac{1}{n} \sum_{i=1}^{n} (y_i - \bar{y})(x_i - \bar{x}) = \frac{1.5672163}{7} = .223888 \tag{4.19}$$

which is an average of the products $(y_i - \bar{y})(x_i - \bar{x})$ of the deviations of the two variables from their arithmetic means. If the two variables increase and decrease together, $(y_i - \bar{y})$ will be large and positive when $(x_i - \bar{x})$ is, and $(y_i - \bar{y})$ will be large and negative when $(x_i - \bar{x})$ is. The average of their products will be large and positive. If the two variables change in opposite directions, $(y_i - \bar{y})$ will be large and positive when $(x_i - \bar{x})$ is large and negative, and this average will be large and negative. If the two variables do not change together, this average will tend to be small. The covariance is a measure of the degree of covariation, or association, between two variables. It is affected by the change of unit in either variable; if y is measured in meters instead of kilometers, the covariance will be 1000 times as large. A measure of covariation unaffected by the changes in units is the *correlation coefficient:*

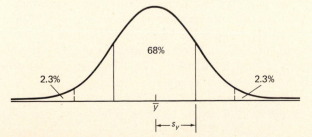

Figure 4.2 The normal frequency distribution.

$$r_{yx} = \frac{\text{cov}(y,x)}{s_y \; s_x} = \frac{.223888}{\sqrt{.136141 \times .372057}} = .9948 \tag{4.20}$$

In our example, the correlation coefficient between y and x is .9948. It is very high in view of the fact that the correlation coefficient is between -1 and $+1$. We can see from Figure 4.1 that the two variables are closely and positively associated.

Another measure of how well y is explained by x is the variance of the deviations $(y_i - \hat{y}_i)$. The regression equation $\hat{y}_i = a + bx_i$ does not explain y_i perfectly, leaving the deviations $(y_i - \hat{y}_i)$, which are called the *residuals* of the regression. The variance of the residuals is

$$s^2 = \frac{1}{n-2} \sum_{i=1}^{n} (y_i - \hat{y}_i)^2 = \frac{1}{5} (.0099057) = .00198114 \tag{4.21}$$

In computing the above average, we divide by $n - 2$ instead of n because if only two points were used to fit a straight line, both residuals $y_i - \hat{y}_i$ would be zero, and the number of residuals useful for computing the variance in equation 4.21 is in effect $n - 2$. The standard deviation of the regression residuals is the square root of equation 4.21, to be denoted by s and called the *standard error of the regression.* In our example, $s = .04451$ (see Problem 2).

Having obtained an estimate of .602 for b, or the elasticity of industrial output with respect to capital, we need a measure of its accuracy. One such measure is the variance of b. The idea is that, because the residuals of the regression are random, like the numbers resulting from throwing a die, the observations y_i for a fixed set of x_i are random and will vary from one set of data to another. We use only one set of data to estimate b. A different estimate of b would result if another set of data was used. The variance of b refers to the variance of different possible estimates of b resulting from different sets of data. This idea is difficult to grasp at first and will be further explained in Section 4.2. The variance of b is given by

$$s_b^2 = [\sum_{i=1}^{n} (x_i - \bar{x})^2]^{-1} s^2 = 2.60440^{-1} (.00198114) = .00076069 \tag{4.22}$$

Thus, the estimate .602 is subject to error. The standard deviation of this error is the square root of the quantity given in equation 4.22, to be denoted by s_b and called the *standard error of the regression coefficient.* In our example, $s_b = .02758$.

In this section we have found that if a Cobb-Douglas production function homogenous of degree one is postulated, and if the data for state-owned industrial enterprises are used, the elasticities of industrial output with respect to labor and capital are .40 and .60, respectively. Output has increased because of the increases in labor and capital. From column 3 of Table 4.1, we see that output per person increased from 4,167 1970 yuan in 1952 to 11,815 in 1981. This increase in productivity per person is explained by the amount of capital available per person, which increased from 2,102 yuan in original value in 1952 to 11,836 in 1981. It is found that for every 1 percent increase in the ratio of capital to labor, productivity per worker increases by .6 of 1 percent.

*4.2 REGRESSION ANALYSIS OF INDUSTRIAL OUTPUT RELATIONS

In the preceding section we estimated equation 4.4, which is derived by assuming that the elasticities of output with respect to labor and capital add up to 1. In this section we will use the same data to estimate a production function given by equation 4.2 without introducing the assumption that the two elasticities sum to 1. This analysis will help us decide whether the above assumption is supported by the data. Taking logarithms of equation 4.2 without this assumption gives

$$\log Y = \log \alpha + \beta_1 \log X_1 + \beta_2 \log X_2 \qquad (4.23)$$

Denoting $\log Y$, $\log X_1$, and $\log X_2$ by y, x_1, and x_2, respectively, we wish to estimate the constants a, b_1, and b_2 in the regression equation

$$\hat{y}_i = a + b_1 x_{1i} + b_2 x_{2i} \qquad (i = 1, \ldots, n) \qquad (4.24)$$

where the subscript i denotes the ith observation, as in equation 4.6. The data for output Y, labor X_1, and capital assets X_2 are given in columns 2, 4, and 5, respectively, of Table 4.1.

By the method of least squares we choose the constants a, b_1, and b_2 to minimize the sum of squares of the residuals of y_i from the regression $\hat{y}_i$.

$$S = \sum_{i=1}^{n} (y_i - \hat{y}_i)^2 = \sum_{i=1}^{n} (y_i - a - b_1 x_{1i} - b_2 x_{2i})^2 \qquad (4.25)$$

Setting the partial derivatives of S with respect to a, b_1, and b_2 equal to zero yields

$$\frac{\partial S}{\partial a} = -2 \sum_{i=1}^{n} (y_i - a - b_1 x_{1i} - b_2 x_{2i}) = 0$$

$$\frac{\partial S}{\partial b_1} = -2 \sum_{i=1}^{n} (y_i - a - b_1 x_{1i} - b_2 x_{2i}) x_{1i} = 0$$

$$\frac{\partial S}{\partial b_2} = -2 \sum_{i=1}^{n} (y_i - a - b_1 x_{1i} - b_2 x_{2i}) x_{2i} = 0 \qquad (4.26)$$

which is a set of three equations for the three unknowns a, b_1, and b_2. Dividing the first equation of 4.26 by $-2n$ and denoting the arithmetic means of y_i, x_{1i}, and x_{2i} by $\bar{y}$, $\bar{x}_1$, and $\bar{x}_2$, respectively, we find

$$\frac{1}{n} \sum_{i=1}^{n} (y_i - a - b_1 x_{1i} - b_2 x_{2i}) = \bar{y} - a - b_1 \bar{x}_1 - b_2 \bar{x}_2 = 0 \qquad (4.27)$$

Substituting $\bar{y} - b_1 \bar{x}_1 - b_2 \bar{x}_2$ for a in the second and third equation of 4.26, we have

$$\sum_{i=1}^{n} (y_i - \bar{y}) x_{1i} - b_1 \sum_{i=1}^{n} (x_{1i} - \bar{x}_1) x_{1i} - b_2 \sum_{i=1}^{n} (x_{2i} - \bar{x}_2) x_{1i} = 0$$

$$\sum_{i=1}^{n} (y_i - \bar{y}) x_{2i} - b_1 \sum_{i=1}^{n} (x_{1i} - \bar{x}_1) x_{2i} - b_2 \sum_{i=1}^{n} (x_{2i} - \bar{x}_2) x_{2i} = 0 \qquad (4.28)$$

which are two linear equations for the two unknowns b_1 and b_2. Equation 4.28 can easily be generalized to the case of three or more explanatory variables. It is reduced to equation 4.12 when there is only one explanatory variable instead of two.

Taking natural logarithms of columns 2, 4, and 5 of Table 4.1 provides the following observations:

	y	x_1	x_2
1952	4.605	1.629	2.372
1957	5.407	2.012	3.304
1965	6.256	2.516	4.565
1975	7.143	3.292	5.434
1979	7.453	3.437	5.785
1980	7.516	3.480	5.922
1981	7.546	3.528	6.000

$\bar{y} = 6.560857$
$\bar{x}_1 = 2.842000$
$\bar{x}_2 = 4.768857$

$$(4.29)$$

We use these data to compute the coefficients of b_1 and b_2 in equation 4.28 and write these equations as

$$3.70071\, b_1 + 6.67386\, b_2 = \sum_{i=1}^{n} (y_i - \bar{y})x_{1i} = 5.507518$$

$$6.67386\, b_1 + 12.25270\, b_2 = \sum_{i=1}^{n} (y_i - \bar{y})x_{2i} = 10.048314 \qquad (4.30)$$

Elementary algebra can be used to solve equation 4.30. However, it is useful to introduce the notation of *vectors* and *matrices* for solving a system of linear equations. A *row vector* is a row of several elements, which may be numbers or variables. For example, (3.464   6.325) and $(b_1 \quad b_2 \quad b_3)$ are row vectors. A *column vector* is a column of several elements. A vector is used to represent several variables. Two vectors are equal if their corresponding elements are equal. To add two vectors, we add the corresponding elements. We can *multiply* a row vector by a column vector on its right to obtain an *inner product,* which equals the sum of the products of the elements. For example,

$$[3.701 \quad 6.674] \begin{bmatrix} b_1 \\ b_2 \end{bmatrix} = 3.701\, b_1 + 6.674\, b_2$$

An n by m *matrix* is a rectangular array of elements having n rows and m columns. A row vector of m elements is a 1 by m matrix; a column vector of n elements is an n by 1 matrix. Two matrices are equal if their corresponding elements are equal. To add two matrices, we add the corresponding elements. We can *multiply* an n by m matrix by an m by p matrix on its right to obtain an n by p matrix as the product. The element in the ith row and the jth column of the product equals the inner product of the ith row of the first matrix and the jth column of the second matrix. For example,

$$\begin{bmatrix} a_{11} & a_{12} & a_{13} \\ a_{21} & a_{22} & a_{23} \end{bmatrix} \begin{bmatrix} b_{11} & b_{12} \\ b_{21} & b_{22} \\ b_{31} & b_{32} \end{bmatrix} = \begin{bmatrix} \sum_{i=1}^{3} a_{1i}b_{i1} & \sum_{i=1}^{3} a_{1i}b_{i2} \\ \sum_{i=1}^{3} a_{2i}b_{i1} & \sum_{i=1}^{3} a_{2i}b_{i2} \end{bmatrix} \tag{4.31}$$

Using the above definitions, we can write the two equations 4.30 as a matrix equation for the vector $(b_1 \quad b_2)$ of unknowns:

$$\begin{bmatrix} 3.70071 & 6.67386 \\ 6.67386 & 12.25270 \end{bmatrix} \begin{bmatrix} b_1 \\ b_2 \end{bmatrix} = \begin{bmatrix} 5.507518 \\ 10.048314 \end{bmatrix} \tag{4.32}$$

The solution of the matrix equation 4.32 can be expressed in terms of the *inverse* of the matrix on the left. The *inverse* of a square matrix A, denoted by A^{-1}, is a square matrix having the property

$$A^{-1}A = AA^{-1} = I \tag{4.33}$$

where I is an *identity matrix,* which consists of ones along the diagonal and zeros elsewhere. For example,

$$\begin{bmatrix} 3.70071 & 6.67386 \\ 6.67386 & 12.25270 \end{bmatrix}^{-1} = \begin{bmatrix} 15.253296 & -8.308239 \\ -8.308239 & 4.606987 \end{bmatrix} \tag{4.34}$$

which has the property

$$\begin{bmatrix} 15.253296 & -8.308239 \\ -8.308239 & 4.606987 \end{bmatrix} \begin{bmatrix} 3.70071 & 6.67386 \\ 6.67386 & 12.25270 \end{bmatrix} = \begin{bmatrix} 1 & 0 \\ 0 & 1 \end{bmatrix} \tag{4.35}$$

To solve equation 4.32, we can multiply both sides by the inverse (equation 4.34) on the left and use equation 4.35 to obtain

$$\begin{bmatrix} 1 & 0 \\ 0 & 1 \end{bmatrix} \begin{bmatrix} b_1 \\ b_2 \end{bmatrix} = \begin{bmatrix} b_1 \\ b_2 \end{bmatrix} = \begin{bmatrix} 15.253296 & -8.308239 \\ -8.308239 & 4.606987 \end{bmatrix} \begin{bmatrix} 5.507518 \\ 10.048314 \end{bmatrix} = \begin{bmatrix} .52401 \\ .53468 \end{bmatrix} \tag{4.36}$$

which is the solution for b_1 and b_2. The intercept a is found by equation 4.27, or

$$a = \bar{y} - b_1\bar{x}_1 - b_2\bar{x}_2 = 2.52183 \tag{4.37}$$

The coefficients b_1 and b_2 sum to 1.059, which is close to 1. The coefficient b_2 is not far from .6, which was our estimate using equation 4.4 in the preceding section.

As in the preceding section, we can find the variance of the regression residuals

$$s^2 = \frac{1}{n-3} \sum_{i=1}^{n} (y_i - \hat{y}_i)^2 = \frac{1}{4}(.0087377) = .0021844 \tag{4.38}$$

where $n - 3$ is used because if there were only three observations, the residuals $(y_i - \hat{y}_i)$ would all be zero, as the equation 4.24 would fit the three points perfectly. The standard error of the regression is $s = .04674$.

Our estimates b_1 and b_2 are subject to errors because different estimates would result if different sets of data were used. The variances of b_1 and b_2 equal the diagonal elements of the inverse matrix (equation 4.34) times the variance of the regression residuals.

$$s_{b_1}^2 = 15.25330 \cdot s^2 = .033319$$

$$s_{b_2}^2 = 4.60699 \cdot s^2 = .010064 \tag{4.39}$$

Equation 4.39 is a generalization of the formula in equation 4.22. When there is only one regression coefficient b, the inverse matrix (equation 4.34) is reduced to $[\sum_{i=1}^{n} (x_i - \bar{x})^2]^{-1}$. In fact, the estimates b_1 and b_2 have a covariance which equals the off-diagonal element of the inverse matrix (equation 4.34) times s^2.

$$\text{cov}(b_1, b_2) = -8.30824 s^2 = -.018149 \tag{4.40}$$

In this case the covariance is negative, suggesting that when b_1 is high, b_2 tends to be low. From equation 4.39 we find $s_{b_1} = .1825$ and $s_{b_2} = .1003$. Because we have only seven observations, the estimates b_1 and b_2 are inaccurate, the former having a standard error of .183 and the latter having a standard error of .100.

To understand the meaning of the variances of b_1 and b_2 and their covariance, imagine that we had 1000 sets of data on y, x_1, and x_2, each set having seven observations and having the same seven values for x_1 and for x_2 as given in equation 4.29. Because the regression residuals are random, each set of data would have seven *values for y* that were *different* from the values given in equation 4.29. Using these 1000 sets of data, we could compute the regression coefficients b_1 and b_2 1000 times. These coefficients would be different from the .52401 and .53468 found in equation 4.36. Call these coefficients $b_{11}, b_{12}, \ldots, b_{1,1000}$ and $b_{21}, b_{22}, \ldots, b_{2,1000}$. We could use them to compute

$$\text{var } b_1 = \frac{1}{1000} \sum_{i=1}^{1000} (b_{1i} - \bar{b}_1)^2$$

$$\text{var } b_2 = \frac{1}{1000} \sum_{i=1}^{1000} (b_{2i} - \bar{b}_2)^2$$

$$\text{cov}(b_1, b_2) = \frac{1}{1000} \sum_{i=1}^{1000} (b_{1i} - \bar{b}_1)(b_{2i} - \bar{b}_2) \tag{4.41}$$

which explain the meaning of $s_{b_1}^2$, $s_{b_2}^2$, and $\text{cov}(b_1, b_2)$.

Imagine that we form the sum $z_i = b_{1i} + b_{2i}$ $(i = 1, \ldots, 1000)$. What is the variance of $z = b_1 + b_2$? It is easy to show

$$\bar{z} = \frac{1}{1000} \sum_{i=1}^{1000} z_i = \frac{1}{1000} \sum_{i=1}^{1000} (b_{1i} + b_{2i}) = \bar{b}_1 + \bar{b}_2 \tag{4.42}$$

and

$$\text{var } z = \frac{1}{1000} \sum_{i=1}^{1000} (z_i - \bar{z})^2 = \frac{1}{1000} \sum_{i=1}^{1000} (b_{1i} + b_{2i} - \bar{b}_1 - \bar{b}_2)^2$$

$$= \frac{1}{1000} \sum_{i=1}^{n} [(b_{1i} - \bar{b}_1)^2 + (b_{2i} - \bar{b}_2)^2 + 2(b_{1i} - \bar{b}_1)(b_{2i} - \bar{b}_2)]$$

implying

$$\text{var}(b_1 + b_2) = \text{var } b_1 + \text{var } b_2 + 2\text{cov}(b_1, b_2) \tag{4.43}$$

In our example, the estimate for $b_1 + b_2$ is 1.059. The variance of this estimate is

$$\text{var}(b_1 + b_2) = .033319 + .010064 + 2(-.018149) = .007085$$

and the standard deviation of the sum $b_1 + b_2$ is $\sqrt{.007085} = .0842$. Note that this standard deviation is smaller than both $s_{b_1} = .1825$ and $s_{b_2} = .1003$ because of the large negative covariance. When the two variables move in opposite directions, their sum can be estimated more accurately than the individual variables.

The analysis in this section confirms the assumption of the preceding section that the elasticities of industrial output with respect to labor and capital sum to 1, and the result that the elasticity with respect to capital is approximately .6. Using a simple example, we have illustrated the method of regression analysis, which can be used to estimate the coefficients of regression equations as well as their standard errors. In our example, the number of observations is very small, leading to inaccuracy in the estimates. It is hoped that, as more data regarding industrial production in China become available, one can improve the accuracy of the estimates using regression analysis. Our limited data, as shown in Table 4.1 and Figure 4.1, suggest that industrial output increased in China mainly as a result of the increase in capital assets, rather than of improvement in technology, because a constant production function without incorporating technological change is capable of explaining aggregate output from 1952 to 1981. This conclusion can be further examined using more data (see Problem 6).

4.3 COMPOSITION OF INDUSTRIAL OUTPUT

Having presented a broad picture of the aggregate production relation in Chinese industry, we will examine the composition of industrial output. An important division of industry output is between heavy industry and light industry. According to Chinese official definition, as stated in the *Statistical Yearbook of China, 1981* (pp. 514–515), heavy industry usually produces capital goods and light industry usually produces consumer goods. Heavy industry consists of two branches: (1) mining and felling industry, including metallurgy, coal extraction, petroleum, and timber felling; (2) manufacturing industry, including smelting and processing of metals, power and fuel, petroleum and coal processing, machine building, and part of the chemical industry. Light industry also consists of two branches: (1) industries using farm products as raw materials, including food, textiles, clothing, leather, paper, and cultural and educational articles; (2) industries using nonagricultural products as raw materials, including the manufacturing of metal products for daily use, household machines, electronic and electrical apparatus, chemicals for daily use, chemical fibers and fabrics, glass for daily use, ceramics, and processing of fuel for daily use.

In 1981 gross industrial output values, in billions of 1970 yuan, by the various industries are provided by the *Statistical Yearbook of China, 1981* (pp. 212–213), as follows:

Heavy Industry	252.413	*Light Industry*	267.470
Metallurgical industry	41.540	Food industry	64.023
Power industry	19.409	Textile industry	86.825
Coal and coke industries	12.205	Clothing	15.343
Petroleum	24.537	Leather	5.779
Chemical industry	65.128	Paper, educational	
for daily use	(18.076)	articles	18.550
Machine building	122.617	Chemicals for daily use	18.076
for daily use	(32.706)	Machines for daily use	32.706
Building materials	18.087	Glass, ceramics, etc.	3.023
Glass, ceramics, etc.	(3.023)		
Forest industry	8.616		
Total	258.334	Total	244.325

In 1981 output in light industry was slightly larger than in heavy industry, whereas in 1980 it was smaller, being 234.364 billion 1970 yuan as compared with 264.879 billion. Note that the outputs from individual industries do not add up to the total for heavy and light industries. The individual industries are listed in the two columns according to the definitions given in the preceding paragraph because outputs from some industries are mixed, such as the power and forest industries.

From 1952 to 1981 heavy industry grew twice as rapidly as light industry, as indicated by the indices of gross industrial output values in constant prices (with 1952 = 100) given in Table 4.2. Note that in 1979 the index for heavy industry was 2,991.6, almost three times the figure 1,061.0 for light industry. There was a drastic change in policy to shift output from heavy to light industry in 1979. As a result, the index for heavy industry decreased to 2,890.9 in 1981, while the index for light industry increased to 1,433.3. This shift is also revealed in Table 4.3. Heavy industry accounted for 56.9 percent of gross industrial output value in 1979, but only 48.5 percent in 1981. During the period of the first Five-Year Plan (1953–1957), the output index of heavy industry grew from 100 in 1952 to 310.7 in 1957. As a percentage of total industrial output, it grew from 35.6 in 1952 to 48.3. Before 1979 the only period in which heavy industry grew less rapidly than light industry was from 1962 to 1965, when it grew from 428.4 to 650.6, less rapidly than the growth from 193.5 to 344.5 for light industry. That was

Table 4.2 INDICES OF GROSS INDUSTRIAL OUTPUT VALUE
(1952 = 100)

Year	Gross industrial output value		
	Total	Light industry	Heavy industry
1957	228.6	183.2	310.7
1962	275.9	193.5	428.4
1965	452.6	344.5	650.6
1978	1,598.6	968.1	2,777.7
1979	1,734.4	1,061.0	2,991.6
1980	1,885.3	1,256.2	3,033.5
1981	1,962.7	1,433.3	2,890.9

Source: Statistical Yearbook of China, 1981, p. 210.

Table 4.6 COST AND PROFITS OF FIRST LATHE FACTORY OF BEIJING

Year	Output (number of machine tools)	Total cost (10,000 yuan)	Profits (10,000 yuan)	Profits remitted to government (10,000 yuan)	%	Profits remitted to Machine-Electric Bureau, Beijing (10,000 yuan)	%	Profits retained by factory (10,000 yuan)	%
1957	615	718	426	393	92.3	6	1.4	27	6.3
1958	1159	1156	1139	901	79.1	35	3.1	202	17.7
1959	1461	1523	1321	1047	79.1	158	11.9	116	8.8
1960	2131	2001	2414	1911	79.1	302	12.5	201	8.3

Source: Survey of the First Factory of Beijing, 1980, pp. 63–65.

141

Table 4.7   COST BREAKDOWN FOR NO. 2 GENERAL PURPOSE LATHES

Year	Average cost (yuan per unit)	Materials as % of cost	Administrative expenses as % of cost	Wages as % of cost
1957	9819	49.1	44.6	6.3
1958	6919	56.1	37.6	6.3
1959	7171	53.2	42.3	4.5
1960	6164	56.4	38.9	5.7

Source: Survey of the First Lathe Factory of Beijing, 1961, p. 65.

would not be easy to find another country in which labor cost accounts for only 5 or 6 percent of the cost of manufacturing lathes. One reason is that the wage rates were low. A highly paid worker of this lathe factory, named Wang, earned 80 yuan a month in 1957 and 74.5 yuan a month in 1960; a lower-paid worker, Lin, earned 35.2 yuan a month in 1957 and 50.4 yuan in 1960; an even lower-paid worker, Zhang, earned 18.4 yuan per month in 1958 and 26.7 in 1960 (*Survey,* 1961, pp. 247–249).

4.6   INDUSTRIAL WAGE AND PRICE POLICIES

Let us turn from the case study of the First Lathe Factory to a general discussion of the economics of Chinese industry. The figures on wages just cited are illustrative. A comprehensive picture of wages in China can be obtained by examining the average wage rate through time (Table 4.8) and the structure of wage rates.

Table 4.8 shows the average annual wage (including bonuses) of staff and workers in state-owned units for all sectors (column 1) and for the industrial and agricultural-forestry sectors (columns 2 and 3). Before commenting on the figures, we note first that the total wage bill in state-owned units is much larger than in collectively owned units in cities and towns, being 66 billion yuan as compared with 16 billion in 1981, and that the average annual wage (including bonuses) is higher in state-owned units, being 812 yuan as compared with 642 yuan in 1981, with average annual wage of both types of units equal to 772 yuan in 1981 (*Statistical Yearbook of China, 1981,* p. 431). There were increases in wages from 1952 to 1957 and some reductions after 1957. Wages went up again in 1962 and 1963 after the economic collapse resulting from the Great Leap Forward, but were reduced again after 1964. Not until 1978 did the average nominal wage (644 yuan) of workers in all state-owned units exceed the figure (637 yuan) in 1957. If we allow for the increase in the general price index of living cost for staff and workers, which increased from 115.5 in 1952 to 144.7 in 1978, as shown in column 5 of Table 4.8, the real wage was actually lower in 1978 than in 1957. Only in 1981 did real wage catch up—barely—with the 1957 level, being 812/162.5, or 500 1950 yuan, as compared with 637/126.6, or 503. Therefore, we can conclude that wages were held down in China for some 25 years, with increases taking place in the early 1960s and the late 1970s, but not enough to raise the real wage above the 1957 level.

Concerning the structure of wage rates, industrial workers are classified into eight grades. Riskin (1975, pp. 216–217) reports that in 1972–1973 the basic wages of the eight grades in the First Lathe Factory of Beijing were 34.0, 40.1, 47.5, 55.0, 61.1, 77.1, 90.9, and 107.1 yuan per month, and that basic wages were similar in a rolling mill of

Table 4.8 WAGE RATES IN STATE–OWNED UNITS AND SELECTED PRICE INDICES

Year	1 Average wage of all state-owned units (yuan)	2 Average wage of state-owned industry (yuan)	3 Average wage of agri-culture, forestry, etc. (yuan)	4 General retail price index (1950 = 100)	5 Price index of living cost for staff and workers	6 General ex-factory price indices of industrial products (1950 = 100)	7 General purchasing price indices of farm and sideline products (1950 = 100)
1952	446	515	375	111.8	115.5	113.2	121.6
1953	496	576	433	115.6	121.4	109.5	132.5
1954	519	597	459	118.3	123.1	107.8	136.7
1955	534	600	461	119.5	123.5	106.4	135.1
1956	610	674	498	119.5	123.4	98.5	139.2
1957	637	690	501	121.3	126.6	98.7	146.2
1958	550	526	471	121.6	125.2	98.1	149.4
1959	524	514	411	122.7	125.6	98.7	152.1
1960	528	538	365	126.5	128.8	98.0	157.4
1961	537	560	362	147.0	149.6	102.9	201.4
1962	592	652	392	152.6	155.3	106.9	200.1
1963	641	720	421	143.6	146.1	106.3	194.4
1964	661	741	433	138.3	140.7	104.2	189.5
1965	652	729	433	134.6	139.0	99.3	187.9
1966	636	689	428	134.2	137.3	95.1	195.8
1967	630	701	426	133.2	136.4	93.9	195.5
1968	621	689	419	133.3	136.5	91.9	195.2
1969	618	683	418	131.8	137.8	88.8	194.9
1970	609	661	419	131.5	137.8	84.9	195.1
1971	597	635	426	130.5	137.7	84.4	198.3
1972	622	650	423	130.2	137.9	83.9	201.1
1973	614	640	436	131.0	138.0	83.5	202.8
1974	622	648	483	131.7	138.9	82.7	204.5
1975	613	644	460	131.9	139.5	82.4	208.7
1976	605	634	459	132.3	139.9	82.2	209.7
1977	602	632	459	135.0	143.7	81.4	209.2
1978	644	683	492	135.9	144.7	81.6	217.4
1979	705	758	548	138.6	147.4	82.9	265.5
1980	803	854	636	146.9	158.5	83.4	284.4
1981	812	852	654	150.4	162.5	83.6	301.2

Source: Statistical Yearbook of China, 1981, pp. 411–412, 435–436.

the Anshan Steel Factory and in the First Machine-Tool Factory of Shenyang. The wage in the highest grade was more than three times that of the lowest grade. Besides the basic wage, workers received bonuses and welfare benefits. The *Survey of the First Lathe Factory of Beijing* (1961, p. 73) reports that more than 90 percent of the workers received bonuses irrespective of the quality of their work, and that therefore the bonuses did not provide any significant incentive to work. This situation is similar to the practice of merit rating in the United States military services, where most people receive high ratings irrespective of performance.

A major goal of price policy in China has been to keep prices stable, except for unusual circumstances when prices had to be raised to increase production, as we discussed in Chapter 3. The prices of centrally distributed goods are set by the Administration Bureau of Commodity Prices of the State Council, which delegates the authority of price fixing for the regionally distributed commodities to its administrative units at the regional levels. Column 6 of Table 4.8 shows that the index of ex-factory prices (prices charged by the factories for their products) had a declining trend in the 1950s and 1960s, being 113.2 in 1952, 106.9 in 1962, and 83.9 in 1972, and remained roughly constant from 1972 to 1981. A reason for this decline is that the Chinese government realized that industrial products were overpriced in the 1950s. Cheng (1982, p. 228) quotes an article in the Chinese statistical journal *Tongji Gongzuo* (1957) as saying that, compared with 1936 = 100, the price index of industrial products in 1952 was about 250 and the price index of agricultural products was about 200. (The 250 figure is the average of an index of about 300 for producer goods and an index of 200 for consumer goods.) As China became more industrialized than in 1936 and as the supply of industrial products increased, the prices of industrial products relative to agricultural products should have declined. A comparison of columns 6 and 7 of Table 4.8 suggests that the setting of prices in China has reflected the increase in the relative supply of industrial products.

4.7   THE ECONOMICS OF INDUSTRIAL PRODUCTION

In the preceding three sections we have presented some facts concerning the operation of a Chinese industrial enterprise and the setting of wages and prices in Chinese industry. Is industrial production economically efficient? The *Survey of the First Lathe Factory of Beijing* highlights some problems in judging the economic efficiency of a Chinese industrial enterprise. Although the facts reported in the survey and cited in Sections 4.4 and 4.5 are reliable, we must be careful in generalizing from them. One reason for caution is that the period from 1958 to 1961 was a difficult one for Chinese economic planning and industrial production, with the Great Leap Forward asserting a disruptive influence. A second reason is that the survey team was given the mission to find problems and recommend improvement, so it was supposed to be critical. To balance these possible biases from the reported facts concerning the First Lathe Factory toward painting a dark picture of Chinese industry, one should note that this factory has been recognized to be a model factory. Furthermore, even though the period 1958 to 1961 was considered abnormal, it did demonstrate the possibility of political interference with and disruption of industrial production and economic activities in general. The longer period 1966 to 1976 of the Cultural Revolution provided another example. These two periods cannot be considered abnormal in the 28 years between 1952 and 1980 because they represent half of this time span. Nevertheless, in this section we will assume the absence of serious political interruptions in our discussion of the economics of industrial production in China.

In Chapter 1 we examined the concept of economic efficiency by studying a private enterprise operating in a market economy. The same concept can be used to study a Chinese industrial enterprise. There is a long history to document the fact that, by and large, enterprises in a market economy have performed well. They have contributed to rapid economic growth in many countries in the world since the nineteenth century, a fact recognized by Karl Marx and Friedrich Engels in their Communist

Manifesto (1848). If we replace the management of a private enterprise in a market economy with the management of a state-owned enterprise in a centrally planned economy, what are the differences as far as economic efficiency is concerned? This question can be separated into two parts. First, will the management try to be efficient? Second, can the management operate efficiently if it tries?

The management of a private enterprise wants to produce efficiently, in the sense of getting the most output from any given amounts of the inputs, because it wants to make more profit. Maximization of profit is a most important objective of a private enterprise. In contrast, the main assignment of the manager of a state-owned enterprise in China is to follow orders, not to maximize profit. The central planning authority sets certain production targets for different industrial products and asks the manager of a factory to fulfill the production targets assigned to that factory. As we pointed out in Section 4.5, in different periods in China factory managers have been given different targets, which always included output in physical terms, but might also include value of output, total wage, material supplies, costs, and other performance indices. Ignoring the frequent inconsistency of these targets, we wish to emphasize that a set of consistent targets is essentially a set of orders to follow. Following orders is different from trying to make a factory economically efficient. Although profit may be one of the targets, managers cannot operate efficiently because they are asked to fulfill other targets as well. Maximizing profit requires taking one's own initiative, or "doing one's own thing." If managers are ordered to produce specified quantities of different outputs, are given the supplies of different inputs at specified prices, are assigned the laborers and the capital equipment to be used in production, and so on, they have no opportunity to become efficient. They cannot then be criticized for being inefficient, because they are simply following orders.

Is it possible to set the targets in such a way as to make the operation of a state-owned factory efficient? The answer is no, because the staff of the central planning authority and its administrative units do not know the economic conditions of an individual enterprise. It has to depend on the factory manager to describe the economic conditions and draft the plan for the factory. If the manager is judged by how well he can fulfill the production targets, he will tend to underestimate the production capabilities of his factory and overestimate the quantities of inputs required to fulfill his production targets. In fact, there is an incentive for him to produce inefficiently, requesting more inputs than are really needed and producing less output than is actually possible, to avoid having the production targets raised in future periods. Likewise, managers have little incentive to try new products or to make innovations in the production process. If such experiment failed, the manager would be penalized. If it succeeded, the manager might receive only a small reward, as judged by the economic value of the new product or new production process, and might be asked to achieve higher targets in the future.

Even if, for patriotic or other reasons, a manager wants to operate efficiently, there is no way for him to do so. We have just pointed out that treating a manager as a subordinate by assigning him targets to fulfill will discourage him from being efficient. Now let us assume, somewhat unrealistically, that he wants to be efficient anyway. He still has to go through the bureaucracy to get funds to improve his plant, to obtain supplies of materials, to increase or decrease his labor force, and to sell his products.

His hands are tied by this red tape. Furthermore, the prices of outputs and inputs are fixed by the government and do not necessarily reflect the economic value of these products as measured by the production-transformation curve (see Figure 1.6). A manager can thus be misled into using an input that is cheap just because the government happens to assign a low price to it. He does not have the correct information to perform the economic calculations required for efficiency.

The essence of this discussion is that under a system of central planning, it is not easy to find adequate substitutes to perform the economic functions of the market, which are fourfold. First, the market evaluates the output of an enterprise, assessing how much is needed and what quality is acceptable. Under central planning, a government administrator performs this task. The manager of a state-owned enterprise delivers the product to an administrator, who decides whether the manager has fulfilled the output target in terms of both quantity and quality. Some product may have very little economic value as input for production or as final output for consumption. Economists in China have recognized the difference between industrial production as measured by the gross output index and the economically useful output. Without the market, it is difficult to assess the economic value of the output of an enterprise.

Second, the markets for labor and capital goods serve to evaluate the economic costs of these inputs. By assigning these inputs to different factories and not allowing their prices to be determined in the market, the government economic planners deprive the factory managers of the correct information for economizing in the use of these inputs. The same is true for the central allocation and price fixing of the materials used in industrial production.

Third, side by side with providing information on the values and costs of outputs and inputs, the market allocates these products to their users. A government administrator is a poor substitute for the market in performing the allocation. He and his staff do not have the required knowledge. A market has many potential buyers who examine the product for its quality and who decide how much of the product is needed. Even if a government administrator has this knowledge of the desired quality and quantity, it is more difficult for him to administer the allocation. If a factory manager cannot sell his product in the market, then either his product is of poor quality or he has produced too much. The market would determine this objectively; but when the output is allocated administratively, the manager can argue with the administrator that his output is of good quality, and if told otherwise he can blame an unclear product specification, a poor piece of equipment, or an inadequate material supply. When it comes to allocation of inputs, managers under central planning will request more than needed and will use political pressure or personal connections to get more from administrators. In a market economy, managers must simply compete in the market for the inputs by offering to pay for them.

Fourth, the market provides rewards to the successful manager who, through innovations and efforts to economize, makes a profit for his or her enterprise. The manager of a large state-owned enterprise in China does not receive a significant fraction of any profits of the enterprise. He or she has no incentive to, and is not supposed to, maximize the profit of the enterprise.

The First Lathe Factory of Beijing reported sizeable profits, as we saw in Section 4.5. Those figures do not necessarily show economic efficiency, however, for five reasons. First, an appropriate return on the capital invested was not included in the calculation of cost. Second, all prices of outputs and inputs were fixed by the government. The *Survey* (1961, p. 69) points out that the increase in profits was due to the reduction in the prices of material supplies without any accompanying reduction in the prices of outputs and therefore should not be interpreted as an improvement in management efficiency. It even recommends a reduction in the prices of the outputs of this factory. Third, production in the factory was often disrupted by the inadequate supply of materials. Fourth, waste of materials occurred because of faulty specifications. Fifth, management was hampered by the ambiguous leadership role given to the secretaries of the party committees at various levels.

The economic problems of central planning in China are well recognized by Chinese economists. In a collection of essays edited by Ma Hong and Sun Shangqing entitled *Studies of the Problems of China's Economic Structure* (1982), many of these problems are discussed. The first chapter, by Zhou Xulian, provides a good survey. The following excerpt from Zhou's paper (p. 53) summarizes the problems of central economic planning in China:

> The system of economic administration practiced in our country today was adopted from the Soviet Union in the early 1950s. The particular characteristic of this administrative system is to stress the extremely centralized leadership of the economy by the state. The state directs and manages the affairs of state-owned enterprises, large or small. The state transmits to the enterprises its authoritative planning targets. It centrally organizes the distribution of material inputs required by the enterprises. It centrally manages the purchases and sales of their products. It centrally determines the prices of commodities. It takes a large fraction of the profits of the enterprises and subsidizes their losses. It approves the funds requested by the enterprises for capital construction and expansion. Under this administrative system an enterprise is not a self-propelling entity but rather a bead of the abacus of the state administration, lacking a necessary sense of independence and a strong economic motivation. In the meantime the regulatory functions of the market have been abolished. Enterprises have neither initiative nor authority to produce according to the need of the market, which results unavoidably in the disconnection between production and the need of society and in an economy operating out of proportion. Under such a system the society lacks an automatic regulatory mechanism. It cannot prevent the economy from getting out of proportion and, when it happens, has no way to discover and correct the problem.

Earlier in this paper, Zhou (1982, pp. 38–39) describes some of the undesirable consequences of the Chinese system of central planning:

> Our productive capacity is underutilized. We have excess of inventories. There are many people waiting for job assignments. All these are manifestations of the malfunctioning of our productive system. Let us compare our rates of capacity utilization and of unemployment with those of a capitalist economy. Many of our enterprises use about 3 to 4 sevenths of their capacities. The rate of utilization of metal lathes in the entire country was 54.6 percent in 1977 and 55.6 percent in 1978. During the Great Depression in the United States the rate of capacity utilization was 42 percent in 1932 (the worst year), 52 percent in 1933, 53 percent in 1931, and 58 percent in 1934, but

was always above 65 percent in other years. Certain material in our country was imported in large quantity while its inventory was accumulating. For example, the inventory of steel was 12.0 million tons at the end of 1976, 12.6 at the end of 1977, 15.5 at the end of 1978, and 18.65 million tons at the end of June 1979, an amount sufficient for use in eight months. The steel inventory is less than the amount used in 90 days in Rumania and is about the amount used in one month in Japan.

Early in 1979 the number of people requesting job assignments was 20 million. During the Great Depression in the United States the highest unemployment rate was 24.9 percent in 1933, followed by 23.6 percent in 1932, 21.7 percent in 1937, 20.1 percent in 1935, 16.9 percent in 1936, 15.9 percent in 1931, and 8.7 percent in 1930. In the 1950s the highest unemployment rate in the United States reached 6.8 percent in 1958, the lowest being 2.5 percent in 1954. At the beginning of 1979 the total number of workers and staff in the labor force was 94.99 million. The 20 million waiting for jobs constituted a large fraction of this total. In many enterprises in our country, the fractions of labor hours actually utilized are low. The average for Beijing in 1978 was 84.3 percent, and the average for the enterprises under the Third, Fourth, and Fifth Machine-Building Ministries was only 74.5 percent. Our economy was subject to large fluctuations. Total gross agricultural and industrial output value increased 54.8 percent in 1958 and 36.1 percent in 1959; it decreased 38.2 percent in 1961 and 16.6 percent in 1962. Gross agricultural output value decreased 13.6 percent in 1959 and 12.6 in 1960. . . .

How to make the Chinese economy efficient remains an unsolved problem today. In the next section we report on the reforms of Chinese industry since 1979 and their economic effects.

4.8   ECONOMIC REFORMS IN INDUSTRY AND THEIR EFFECTS

Chinese economic planners have recognized some of the economic problems described in the preceding section. They realized that industrial production was overly centralized. A front-page article in the *New York Times* (August 31, 1980) entitled "Peking Congress Meets to Adopt Economic Change, New Leaders" reports:

With words and phrases such as "profit," "increased competition" and "market forces" echoing through the Great Hall of the People, Chinese leaders met today in what they said would be a historic session of the National People's Congress to transfer governmental power to a new generation of leaders and further loosen central control of the economy. . . .

It was the third annual session of the Fifth Congress—each congress lasts five years —and the first to which both foreign journalists and diplomats have been invited for 20 years. . . .

As Chairman Hua sipped tea, Deputy Prime Minister Deng, next to him, puffed cigarettes, and 3,478 other deputies shuffled papers on the podium and in the 10,000-seat auditorium, Deputy Prime Minister Yao Yilin, who is in charge of the State Planning Ministry, said the economy "as a whole is becoming livelier" after decades of stagnation. He said sluggish growth in agricultural production and light industry was finally being overcome, adding that the experiments of free enterprise, factory autonomy, local decision-making and competition would be greatly expanded in the next two years.

abolishing the bureaus and delegating to its economic commission the authority over personnel, finance, material supplies, production, and sales. All directives from the ministries to the individual enterprises need to go through only the economic commission. The commission, in turn, gave the enterprises some discretion in the disposition of retained profits, the use and addition of capital equipment, the planning of production, the sales of products above quota, the giving of bonuses, and the hiring and disciplining of workers. These administrative changes appeared to yield positive economic results, as the total profits of all industrial enterprises in this county more than doubled in 1979.

Fifth, the establishment of collectively owned enterprises was encouraged, reversing the previous trend to convert collectively owned enterprises to state-owned enterprises. While both types of enterprises can be controlled by the government through the assignment of production quotas and the control of material supplies, the profits of state-owned enterprises, except for the part retained, constitute revenues of the state budget. More important, a group of citizens can take the initiative to establish a collectively owned industrial enterprise subject to the regulation of the government. Collectively owned enterprises accounted for 40 percent of the increase in total gross industrial output value in 1980. They are responsible for 90 percent of the output value of the handicraft industry, which is more than 50 percent of the output value of all light industry.

To summarize, institutional reforms in Chinese industry since 1979 have consisted of giving over 6000 state-owned enterprises some autonomy in their operations, granting some enterprises a lease under the "economic responsibility system" to operate more or less on their own, extending the role of the markets, and encouraging the expansion of usually small collectively owned enterprises. In addition, the administration of the state-owned enterprises in certain counties and cities has been streamlined to avoid the division of authority among many bureaus. Can we find evidence of increase in productivity resulting from these reforms?

Consider the trend of the index of gross industrial output value as shown in column 1 of Table 4.1. The growth from 100 in 1952 to 1,734.4 in 1979 amounted to an exponential growth rate of .1057. The growth from 1,734.4 in 1979 to 1,962.7 in 1981 amounted to an exponential growth rate of .0618, much lower than the former rate. Some of the reduction in the growth rate of industrial output since 1979 may be due to the change in policy to expand the agricultural sector at the expense of heavy industry. Furthermore, the expansion of light industry at the expense of heavy industry may slow down the increase in total gross industrial output value, because gross output of heavy industry probably involves more double counting and includes more products with little economic value as judged by the user. If we consider national income generated by industry as shown in column 3 of Table 3.5, we find the increase from 11.5 billion yuan in 1952 to 153.6 billion in 1979 to imply an exponential rate of .0960, whereas the increase from 153.6 billion in 1979 to 171.9 billion in 1981 implies an exponential rate of .0563, much smaller than the former rate. Note that these figures are in current yuan. The general ex-factory price index of industrial products increased slightly from 82.9 in 1979 to 83.6 in 1981, while it had decreased from 113.2 in 1952 to 82.9 in 1979, making the comparison in constant prices even more unfavorable for the period after 1979.

To measure productivity, one should observe not merely output but the ratio of output to inputs. One such measure is labor productivity, or output per unit of labor. According to column 3 of Table 4.1, output per person in state-owned industrial enterprises increased hardly at all from 1979 to 1981, while it had increased significantly from 1952 to 1979. However, this measure ignores the possible effect of capital. A better way to detect possible changes in productivity is to examine the residuals in a production function explaining output by the relevant inputs. If the residuals for the years 1979 to 1981 are large and positive, the outputs in these years are higher than those that can be predicted by a stable relation between output and inputs, suggesting that some other factors have contributed to the large outputs. Using the data given in equation 4.29 and the regression equation

$$\hat{y} = 2.52183 + .52401\, x_1 + .53468\, x_2 \tag{4.44}$$

estimated in Section 4.2, where y, x_1, and x_2 denote the natural logarithms of industrial output, labor, and capital of state-owned enterprises, respectively, we find the predicted values $\hat{y}$ for 1979, 1980, and 1981 to be 7.416, 7.512, and 7.579, respectively. The observed values y for these three years are 7.453, 7.516, and 7.546, yielding the residuals .037, .004, and $-.033$. These residuals are extremely small as compared with the standard error of regression $s = .04674$ given by equation 4.38, and one residual is even negative. Therefore, there is no evidence that the outputs in the years 1979 to 1981 were higher than can be accounted for by the labor and capital inputs, using a production function estimated for the period 1952 to 1981.

However, this analysis fails to include materials as an input in the production function. It might be argued that more output was produced in 1979 to 1981 than before in relation to the amounts of labor, capital, *and* current inputs. Byrd (1983, p. 331) considers the quantity of output in relation to current inputs. He writes, "There was a perceptible decrease in the estimated ratio of current input consumption to gross output value of Chinese state industry between 1975 and 1978, and in each of the three years 1979, 1980, and 1981. The ratio fell from .650 in 1978 to .632 in 1981, a reduction of almost 3 percent." He then suggests that "the reduction in the ratio of 'real' input consumption to gross output value was between 4 and 7 percent" by assuming that the prices of agricultural products used as inputs in the state-owned industrial sector increased by 10 to 20 percent. It would be preferable to include all relevant inputs in the production function to evaluate possible changes in productivity. Byrd's estimate would then require a closer examination, in view of the fact that the estimated ratio of current input consumption to gross output value decreased perceptibly between 1975 and 1978, before the introduction of institutional reforms in Chinese industry.

The crude analyses of productivity in Chinese industry presented above serve to demonstrate the method involved rather than providing precise results. It appears difficult to find evidence from aggregate data to show an increase in productivity as a result of the reforms in Chinese industry. Disaggregate data can show the economic effects of certain reforms. For example, in Shandong Province, which led the introduction of the "economic responsibility system," the coal industry was budgeted to have a loss of 13.57 million yuan in 1981. After the system was introduced in March 1981, a loss was turned to a profit of .57 million in April and a profit of 9.02 million in May and June, according to the *Public Daily* of July 30, 1981, as quoted by Ma (1982, p.

83). Perhaps more conclusive results can be found by analyzing disaggregate data. It may also be true that certain reforms have yielded positive economic results in the sectors or regions adopting them, while the reforms as a whole might not have yielded sizeable effects on aggregate industrial output in China.

We will conclude this section by considering the economic effects of industrial reforms from the theoretical point of view. Our discussion of the operation of Chinese industry in Sections 4.5 and 4.7 has pointed to certain elements in the previous system of central planning that had an adverse effect on economic efficiency. Since the reforms are aimed at granting enterprises more discretionary power and allowing some of them to operate as independent economic entities while extending the role of the markets, they are heading in the right direction for the purpose of correcting the harmful effects of overcentralized economic planning. The ultimate success of the reforms will depend on whether the following questions are satisfactorily answered.

First, while it is encouraging to see the markets gradually expand, covering some 15 percent of industrial output in 1981, the question is, Will they become extensive enough to provide outlets for the products of, and furnish the inputs used by, the majority of industrial enterprises? If the prices of substantial fractions of the outputs and inputs are determined by the market, enterprises can produce products of economic value by employing inputs in an economically efficient manner. Depending on administrators to evaluate the outputs and supply the required inputs of industry has been shown by the Chinese experience to be economically inefficient.

Second, perhaps as a corollary to the first, will labor, land, and capital equipment be paid their proper economic values when used as inputs in industrial production? If markets for these factors of production are established, wages and rents determined by the market will measure their economic costs. If not, it would be difficult to find other means of determining their economic costs, which the enterprises need in order to perform efficient calculations.

Third, will the managers and workers of industrial enterprises be given sufficient incentives to produce the best products most efficiently? The economic responsibility system, if it comes to be practiced by the majority of enterprises, will provide a satisfactory answer to this question. This system has shown remarkable results when applied to agriculture, where farm households can operate as independent economic units, receiving all the profits of farming after paying a fixed amount to the government. This system has been extended to small industrial enterprises. The question is whether large industrial enterprises will be allowed to operate in this fashion and, if so, how much of the profits will be available to be freely used by the managers and workers of the enterprises.

In addition to the size of the enterprise, a second difference between industry and agriculture is that many essential inputs of industrial production have to be supplied from outside. It would not be economically efficient to allow an industrial enterprise to keep all its profits after a lump-sum payment to the government if its inputs are also cheaply supplied by the government and its outputs are sold at high prices determined by the government. Production in agriculture is simpler, the major inputs being the labor of the farmers, the land, some equipment, and current inputs such as fertilizer. Once an independent farm household is asked to pay a fixed amount dependent on the productivity of the land it uses, the profit of the farm will largely reflect its efficiency rather than the possibly low costs of the material inputs. In the case of a large industrial enterprise, its profit can measure efficiency only if its outputs and inputs are properly priced. Without extensive markets for these products, therefore, it may be undesirable to let certain large industrial enterprises operate under the economic responsibility system.

This last point is supported by some experience in Chinese industry. In 1981 many small factories were established in the rural areas to produce sugar, cigarettes, wine, soap, and leather products using materials supplied locally (see Ma and Sun, 1982, p. 199). Some of these enterprises were considered economically inefficient and were said to take away the supply of materials from the presumably more efficient factories in the cities. If free markets for both the material inputs and the final products were established, alleged inefficient production by the small rural factories could hardly occur. For example, if a large urban factory can really produce cigarettes more efficiently than a small rural factory, it can afford to pay a higher price (in addition to transportation costs) for the tobacco, and the growers of tobacco will find it more profitable to sell to the large factory than to a small rural factory or to produce cigarettes in small factories themselves. If an urban cigarette factory cannot afford to buy tobacco in a rural market, perhaps it is less efficient than the small rural factories. Without markets for outputs and inputs, it is difficult to measure efficiency, and it might be inefficient to allow large industrial enterprises to operate under the economic responsibility system.

A third major difference between agriculture and state-owned industry is that the livelihood of the members of a production unit in agriculture depends on the output of the unit, whereas the incomes of the managers and workers of a state-owned industrial enterprise are hardly affected by its output or profit. The purpose of the responsibility system is to make the incomes of the managers and workers dependent on the productivity of the enterprise (see Problem 15).

An optimistic observer can hope that free markets in China will greatly expand in the 1980s and the economic responsibility system will be extended to a large number of industrial enterprises. The Chinese government will continue to practice economic planning to a significant extent, but it has recognized the shortcomings of centralized economic planning and has decided to supplement planning with regulation by markets. It has also decided to encourage the establishment of collectively owned enterprises. If the market sector is allowed to grow, if the prices of most outputs and inputs are determined by market forces, and if more collectively owned and state-owned enterprises can operate as lessees from the government under the economic responsibility system, efficiency in Chinese industry and in the Chinese economy as a whole can be expected to improve in the 1980s.

PROBLEMS

1. Using the data of column 4, Table 3.12, find the mean and standard deviation of gross agricultural output values per capita of the 29 provinces and municipalities of China. Mark them in Figure 3.1.
2. Compute the seven residuals $(y_i - \hat{y}_i)$ for the regression shown in Figure 4.1 and check the result (equation 4.21).

3. Divide both sides of equation 4.2 by X_2 to obtain an equation explaining the ratio Y/X_2 by X_1/X_2. Let $y = \log(Y/X_2)$ and $x = \log(X_1/X_2)$. Using the data in columns 2, 4, and 5 of Table 4.1, compute (x_i, y_i) for $i = 1, \ldots, 6$. Plot these six observations in a diagram. Estimate the regression equation $\hat{y} = a + bx$. What is your estimate of β in equation 4.2? How does it compare with the estimate of .602 for $(1 - \beta)$ presented in Section 4.1?

4. Continuing the calculations for problem 3, find the standard error of the regression, the standard error of the coefficient b, and the correlation coefficient between y and x.

5. Find the correlation coefficient between y_i and $\hat{y}_i$ using the regression equation estimated in Section 4.2.

6. If annual data from 1952 to 1981 on all the variables of Table 4.1 are available, how can you decide whether there has been technological change in industrial production in China?

7. Generalize equations 4.28 to the case of three regression coefficients b_1, b_2, and b_3.

8. In what ways would a manager of a Chinese state-owned industrial enterprise in the early 1960s behave differently from a manager of an American enterprise? Explain.

9. In what ways was industrial production in China inefficient prior to 1979? Provide some evidence of inefficiency.

10. Explain how a market system can promote economic efficiency. What are the essential functions performed by the market? Can these functions be performed without the use of markets? Explain.

11. What are the main elements of institutional reforms in Chinese industry since 1979? Explain the rationale of these reforms.

12. How can possible improvement in economic efficiency in Chinese industry since 1979 be measured statistically?

13. Design a statistical study to measure the possible change in economic efficiency in Chinese industry since 1979, assuming that you are allowed by the Chinese government to obtain any necessary data.

14. What are the reasons for the residuals in the regression plotted in Figure 4.1 to be different from the residuals of equation 4.44? Would they be different if equation 4.44 were changed to

$$\hat{y} = 3.762 + .398\, x_1 + .602\, x_2$$

15. In Section 3.7 it was suggested that the law of supply applies to Chinese agriculture even under the commune system. Is the law of supply applicable to state-owned industry in China before the institutional reforms? Why or why not? Is the law applicable to collectively owned industry in China after the institutional reforms? Why or why not?

REFERENCES

Byrd, W. 1983. Enterprise-level reforms in Chinese state-owned industry. *American Economic Review* 73:329–332.

Cheng, C.-Y. 1982. *China's economic development: Growth and structural change.* Boulder, Colo.: Westview Press.

Chinese State Statistics Bureau. 1982. *Statistical yearbook of China, 1981.* Hong Kong: Hong Kong Economic Review Publishing House.

Chow, G. C. 1983. *Econometrics.* New York: McGraw-Hill.

Economic Research Center, State Council of the People's Republic of China. 1982. *Almanac of China's economy, 1981.* Hong Kong: Modern Cultural Company Limited. Hong Kong.

Ma Hong. 1982. *Shilun woguo shehuizhuyi jingji fazhan de xin zhanlue* [On the new strategies for the socialist economic development of our country]. Beijing: Chinese Social Science Publishing House.

————— and Sun Shangqing, eds. 1982. *Zhongquo jingji jiegou wenti yanjou* [Studies of the problems of China's economic structure]. 2 vols. Beijing: People's Publishing Society.

Riskin, C. 1975. Workers' incentives in Chinese industry. In *China: A reassessment of the economy.* United States Congress Joint Economic Committee, ed. Washington, D.C.: U.S. Government Printing Office.

Survey of the First Lathe Factory of Beijing. 1980. (In Chinese.) Prepared by the Survey Team of Beijing's First Lathe Factory. Beijing: Chinese Social Science Publishing Company.

United States Congress Joint Economic Committee, ed. 1975. *China: A reassessment of the economy.* Washington, D.C.: U.S. Government Printing Office.

Wang Haibo and Wu Jiajun. 1982. China's industry in 1980. In Economic Research Center, State Council of the People's Republic of China, *Almanac of China's economy, 1981.* Hong Kong: Modern Cultural Company Limited. Pp. 444–455.

Xue Muqiao. 1981. *China's socialist economy.* China Knowledge Series. Beijing: Foreign Language Press.

Zhou Shulian (1982): Sanshinian lai woguo jingji jiegou de huigu [A review of our country's economic structure in the past thirty years], Chapter 1 of Ma and Sun, eds., *Zhongquo jingji jegou wenti yanjou* [Studies of the problems of China's economic structure], Vol. 1. Beijing: People's Publishing Society. Pp. 23–55.

chapter 5

Consumption

5.1 TRENDS IN PER CAPITA CONSUMPTION

Economists in China agree that the main objective of all socialist economic activities is to satisfy the people's consumption needs. (See Ma and Sun, 1982, p. 10, and Yang, 1982, p. 543.) They recognize that among the major causes of the distortions in the economic structure existing in China today are the overemphasis on developing heavy industry at the expense of agriculture and light industry and the excessively high rate of accumulation at the expense of consumption (see Ma and Sun, 1982, p. 7). While heavy industry greatly expanded from 1952 to 1978, per capita consumption in China advanced only slowly. Since 1978, consumption has increased more rapidly. We will elaborate on these two statements in this section.

To examine the trends in per capita consumption in China, it will be informative to treat urban and rural consumption separately. As we pointed out in Section 4.6, real wages in all state-owned enterprises in China were about the same in 1981 as in 1957. The average wage was 637 yuan in 1957 and 812 yuan in 1981. Deflated by the cost of living index of staff and workers, these figures become 503 and 500 1950 yuan, respectively (see Table 4.8). In 1977 the real wage of all state-owned units was only 602/1.437, or 419, 1950 yuan, not much higher than the 446/1.155, or 386, 1950 yuan in 1952. As column 1 of Table 4.8 shows, the wage rate was held low for more than two decades up to 1977 and was allowed to increase from 1978 to 1980 when economic policy was changed to expand the production of consumer goods. These data on wages might be interpreted to mean that per capita consumption of urban workers and their family members was held practically constant for more than two decades terminating in 1977.

The data of Table 4.8 have been used by Yang (1982, p. 553) to point out that the average real wage in China declined between 1957 and 1978: "In 1978, the average

157

money wage in all state-owned units was 644 yuan, which was higher than the 1957 average wage of 637 yuan by 1.1 percent. . . . The cost of living index (inclusive of items traded in markets) of staff and workers increased by 11.3 percent during the same period. Accordingly the 644 yuan in 1978 was equivalent to 578.6 yuan in 1957." Yang's conclusion is the same as the one we reached in the preceding paragraph. The only minor discrepancy is in the increase in the cost of living index of 11.3 percent quoted by Yang, as compared with the increase from 126.6 in 1957 to 144.7 in 1978, or 14.3 percent, according to the data of Table 4.8.

It is necessary to reconcile the data quoted in the two preceding paragraphs with the index of annual consumption per capita for nonagricultural residents given in column 9 of Table 3.7. The latter index, according to its source, the *Almanac of China's Economy, 1981* (Economic Research Center, 1982, p. 985), is "at comparative prices, 1952 = 100," and is "calculated by dividing private consumption expenditure (excluding services) from available national income by mean population of the year." This index increased from 126.3 in 1957 to 136.5 in 1965, to 181.1 in 1975, and to 214.5 in 1979. From 1957 to 1975, the average money wage of all state-owned units shown in column 1 of Table 4.8 decreased from 637 yuan to 613 yuan, while the cost of living index of staff and workers shown in column 5 of Table 4.8 increased from 126.6 to 139.5. How could the index of per capita consumption of nonagricultural residents increase from 126.3 to 181.1, or by 43.4 percent, between 1957 and 1975?

The main explanation for increase in the index of per capita consumption expenditure while the average real wage declined is the increase in the ratio of the number of wage earners to the total urban population. According to Rawski (1979, pp. 29–30):

> The population-weighted average of employment rates for four major urban areas during the 1950's is calculated at 33.3 percent, which is nearly identical with the figure of 32.6 percent compiled from a national sample survey conducted in 1956. It can therefore be assumed with reasonable confidence that approximately 33 percent of urban residents were employed in 1957. . . .

> Repeated campaigns to resettle idle town dwellers in the countryside and the emergence of new employment opportunities for urban housewives in neighborhood industries lead to the expectation that both employment rates and participation rates should be higher in urban areas for the 1970's than for the 1950's. This expectation is confirmed by the data . . . , which show that employment rates in Nanking and Shanghai jumped from about 33 percent to more than 50 percent between the late 1950's and the mid-1970's. Survey results . . . show that urban employment rates of 50 percent or higher are common except in mining centers, where women find only limited employment opportunities, and in cities performing unspecified "special functions." On the basis of these data, an employment rate of 50 percent can be assumed for urban residents in 1975. . . .

Thus, the increase from 33 percent to 50 percent of urban population employed would by itself raise the wage income per person by a factor of 50/33, or 51.5 percent. From 1957 to 1975, real wage decreased from 637/1.266, or 503, 1950 yuan to 613/1.395, or 439, 1950 yuan, according to Table 4.8. These two factors combined yield a factor of $(50/33) \times (439/503)$, or 1.32, for the ratio of real wage per member of the urban population between 1975 and 1957. Taking into account possible errors in the quoted figures, we can conclude that the increase in per capita consumption of the nonagricultural residents by approximately 43 percent between 1957 and 1975 is due mainly to the increase in the ratio of employed to total urban population by over 50 percent, combined with a small reduction in the real wage rate.

Concerning the consumption rate of Chinese peasants, Yang (1982, pp. 549–552) presents four sets of evidence to suggest a widening of the gap between the consumption rates of workers and peasants from the 1950s to the 1970s. Yang (1982, p. 551) quotes a Chinese census as showing that in 1955 the average income per person was 148 yuan for all workers' families and 98 yuan for all farm families. If the workers accounted for 33 percent of the urban population in 1955, the 148 yuan figure would be equivalent to 448 yuan per worker, somewhat lower than the 534 yuan given in column 1 of Table 4.8 for the average wage of all *state-owned* units. The ratio of per capita incomes of workers' and peasants' families was 148/98, or 1.51, in 1955. According to a census of 15 provinces and municipalities quoted by Yang, in 1965 the per capita income was 219 yuan for workers' families and 110 yuan for families in the rural communes, their ratio being 1.99; in 1977 the per capita incomes of these two groups were 260 yuan and 114 yuan, respectively, their ratio being increased to 2.28. Hence Yang claims that from 1955 to 1977, the ratio of workers' per capita income to the farmers' increased by a factor of 2.28/1.51, or 1.50. Since, according to the figures quoted in the preceding paragraph, the per capita real income of workers' families increased by about 43 percent from 1957 to 1975 and thus could not have increased much more than 51 percent from 1955 to 1957, Yang's claim would imply that the per capita real income of farm families did not materially increase from 1955 to 1977.

Is Yang's claim valid? For the years 1955, 1965, and 1977, he cites per capita income figures of 148, 219, and 260 yuan respectively for workers' families and 98, 110, and 114 yuan respectively for farm families. The 1955 figures are for all China, whereas the 1965 and 1977 figures are from 15 out of a total of 29 provinces and municipalities. The question is not whether the figures from the 15 provinces are close to the figures for all China. It is whether the ratio 2.28 for the year 1977 is close to the ratio of per capita incomes of the two groups for all China. Our second question, alluded to above, is whether per capita income of all workers' families was 148 yuan in 1955. If we assumed only 30 percent of the urban population were employed, instead of 33 percent, the 148 yuan would imply an average income of 493 yuan per worker, not inconsistent with the average wage of 534 yuan for all workers in state-owned units. The third question is whether the ratio of money incomes of the workers and the farmers is the same as the ratio of their real incomes, since the cost of living indices for the two groups may be different. These questions notwithstanding, the evidence cited by Yang leads one to take seriously his claim that from 1955 to 1977 the ratio of workers' to farmers' per capita income increased by about 50 percent. If the workers' per capita income increased by more than that, the farmers' per capita income would have increased from 1955 to 1977.

The index of per capita private consumption of all peasants, given in column 8 of Table 3.7, shows an increase of 22.2 percent, from 117.1 in 1957 to 143.1 in 1975. These figures need to be reconciled with the figures cited by Yang. Since the index of per capita private consumption of all nonagricultural residents, given in column 9 of Table 3.7, shows an increase of 43.4 percent, from 126.3 in 1957 to 181.1 in 1975, the ratio of workers' to farmers' per capita income increased by a factor of 143.4/122.2, or 1.173, from 1957 to 1975. Between 1955 and 1957 the average wage of all state-owned units, as given in column 1 of Table 4.8, increased from 534 to 637, or by a factor of 1.193. These two factors combined would account for an increase in the ratio of workers' to farmers' per capita income of 40 percent between 1955 and 1975, not very different from Yang's estimate of 50 percent between 1955 and 1977.

Can the slow increase in per capita consumption of all farm families between 1957 and 1975 also be explained by an increase in the ratio of the number of farm laborers to total farm population? The answer is no. Column 6 of Table 5.1 shows that the percentage of population in rural communes classified as employed laborers did not increase from 1957 to 1978. Column 7 of Table 5.1 shows that the percentage of employed population in cities and towns increased from 32.6 in 1957 to 38.3 in 1965 and then to 61.4 in 1978. The 1957 figure is the same as reported by Rawski (1979, p. 29). The 1978 percentage of 61.4 is much higher than the 50 percent figure reported by Rawski for 1975, but there probably was an increase in this percentage from 1975 to 1978. The population figure used to compute this percentage is obtained by subtracting the population of rural communes from total population. The "urban population" figures given on page 89 of the *1981* (Chinese State Statistics Bureau, 1982) *Statistical Yearbook of China,* are lower, being 119.94 as compared with 154.89 used in Table 5.1 for the year 1978, and would yield an even higher percentage of employed persons in cities and towns.

From this discussion we can conclude that per capita consumption of the non-agricultural population in China increased from 126.3 to 181.1 1952 yuan, or by 43.4 percent, as a result of a 52 percent increase in the employment rate of the population from .33 to .50, together with a decrease in the average real wage per worker. Per capita consumption of the agricultural population increased from 117.1 to 143.1 1952 yuan, or by 22.2 percent, with no change in the employment rate of the population. The above

Table 5.1   **TOTAL AND EMPLOYED POPULATION IN RURAL COMMUNES AND OTHERWISE**
(Millions at Year-End)

Year	1 Total population	2 Total labor force employed	3 Population in rural communes	4 Labor force employed in rural communes	5 Percentage of total population employed	6 Percentage of population employed in rural communes	7 Percentage of population employed in cities and towns
1957	646.53	237.71	548.27	205.56	36.8	37.5	32.6
1965	725.38	286.70	591.22	235.34	39.5	39.8	38.3
1978	958.09	398.56	803.20	303.42	41.6	37.8	61.4
1981	996.22	432.80	818.81	322.27	43.4	39.4	62.3

Source: Column 1 is from *Statistical Yearbook of China, 1981,* p. 89. Columns 2 and 4 are from ibid., p. 105. Column 3 is from ibid., p. 133, except for the 1957 figure, which is estimated by dividing the 1958 figure 560.17 by 1.0217, .0217 being the population growth rate in 1957 given in ibid., p. 89. (This estimate for 1957 differs from the estimate 518.59 given in column 3 of Table 3.7. The latter estimate makes columns 2, 4, and 6 of Table 3.7 consistent, but would yield 25.1 for the percentage of population employed in cities and towns in 1957.) Column 5 is the ratio of column 2 to column 1. Column 6 is the ratio of column 4 to column 3. Column 7 is the ratio of labor force employed in cities and towns (column 2 minus column 4, also given separately in ibid., p. 105) to population in cities and towns (column 1 minus column 3). Strictly speaking, the communes had not yet been organized in 1957, so the 1957 figures refer to agricultural cooperatives.

consumption expenditure figures are weighted averages of physical quantities, with some quantities increasing more rapidly than others. The main items contributing to the increase in consumption expenditures are consumer durable goods, including sewing machines, bicycles, and watches (see columns 2, 3, and 4 of Table 4.5), and certain food items such as sugar, tea, and meat (see *Statistical Yearbook of China, 1981*, pp. 147 and 165).

There are two important qualifications to the increase in per capita consumption. First, average housing space for the population in cities and towns decreased from 4.5 square meters in 1952 to 3.6 square meters in 1977 (see Yang, 1982, p. 548). Housing has been rationed to urban residents at extremely low cost and has almost no weight in the statistics on consumption expenditures. Second, to the extent that an increase in per capita consumption is due to an increase in labor participation, increase in consumer welfare is less because there is less leisure time and less time to produce nonmarket consumer goods and services at home (such as home-cooked meals, laundry, and child care). Given these two qualifications, the increase in per capita consumption in China in the two decades after 1957 was quite modest, as compared with the large increase in the output of heavy industry reported in Chapter 4.

Realizing the need to raise the people's level of consumption, the Chinese government changed its policy in 1978 to increase the production of consumer goods by expanding the output of agriculture and light industry at the expense of heavy industry. The improvement in the people's living standard resulting from this change in policy is indicated in the data recorded in the accompanying table (*Statistical Yearbook of China, 1981*, pp. 429–430).

	1978	1981	1981/1978 %
Income per capita of peasants (yuan)	134	223	166.4
Average annual wage of staff and workers	614	772	125.7
Spendable monthly income per family member of staff and workers (yuan)	26.3	38.6	146.8
(after adjustment for price increase)			130.8
Grain consumption per capita (jin = $\frac{1}{2}$ kg.)	391	438	112.0
Vegetable oil consumption per capita (jin)	3.2	5.9	184.4
Pork consumption per capita (jin)	15.3	22.2	145.1
Cotton and chemical-fiber cloth p.c. (chi = $\frac{1}{3}$ m.)	24.1	30.9	128.2
Consumer goods for daily use (yuan)	28.8	45.0	156.2
Bicycles per 100 persons	7.7	11.2	145.5
Buses per 10,000 persons in cities	3.3	3.7	112.1
TV sets possessed per 100 persons:	0.3	1.6	533.3
Of which in cities and towns	1.3	5.6	430.8
Radio sets possessed per 100 persons	7.8	14.9	191.0
Books and magazines per person per year	4.77	7.12	149.3

	1979	1981	1981/1979 %
Living floor space p.c., cities and towns	4.4 m^2	5.3 m^2	120.5
Living floor space p.c., rural areas	8.4 m^2	10.2 m^2	121.4

5.2 HOUSEHOLD EXPENDITURE PATTERNS

In the preceding section we discussed the changes in total consumption per capita through time. This is an example of *time-series analysis*. In this section we study the composition of family consumption expenditures at the same time among different groups of consumers. This exemplifies a *cross-section analysis*. It is of interest to examine how households increase their expenditures on different kinds of consumption goods as their total consumption expenditure increases. Such studies of consumer expenditure patterns originated more than 100 years ago. As Houthakker (1957, p. 532) writes:

> Few dates in the history of econometrics are more significant than 1857. In that year Ernst Engel (1821–1896) published a study on the conditions of production and consumption in the Kingdom of Saxony, in which he formulated an empirical law concerning the relation between income and expenditure on food. Engel's law, as it has since become known, states that the proportion of income spent on food declines as income rises. Its original statement was mainly based on an examination of about two hundred budgets of Belgian laborers collected by Ducpétiaux. Since that date the law has been found to hold in many other budget surveys; similar laws have also been formulated for other items of expenditure.

> With the formulation of Engel's law an important branch of econometrics took its start, though it was not until our days that consumption research was placed on a sound theoretical and statistical basis. . . . His successful attempt to derive meaningful regularities from seemingly arbitrary observations will always be an inspiring example to the profession, the more so because in his day economic theory and statistical techniques were of little assistance in such an attempt. . . .

Econometrics is the art and science of using statistical methods for the measurement of economic relations. Our study of production relations in Chinese industry presented in Sections 4.1 and 4.2 is an econometric study. Our present task is to study the relations between total consumption expenditures of Chinese households and expenditures on food and other major consumption categories.

Data on per capita consumption expenditure of Chinese peasants and its four major components—food, clothing, housing and fuel, and all other items—for 28 provinces and municipalities (with the exception of Tibet) are found in Table 5.2. The data are based on a sample survey of 18,529 farm households conducted in 1981 and is reported in the *Statistical Yearbook of China, 1981* (pp. 441 and 445–446). Observations for the 28 provinces permit us to examine how per capita expenditures on the four categories of consumption change as total consumption expenditure changes. We have

Table 5.2 **CONSUMPTION EXPENDITURE PER CAPITA AND ITS COMPONENTS BY PROVINCE, 1981**
(Yuan)

	Province	1 Total expenditure	2 Food	3 Clothes	4 Housing and fuel	5 All other items
	Total	190.81	113.83	23.57	29.26	24.15
1	Beijing	312.99	163.11	36.00	58.43	55.45
2	Tianjin	249.17	126.42	37.49	51.50	33.76
3	Hebei	164.66	85.93	23.48	28.07	27.18
4	Shanxi	147.78	85.86	23.88	17.70	20.34
5	Inner Mongolia	177.12	110.74	24.77	16.08	25.53
6	Liaoning	258.50	139.06	35.88	41.60	41.96
7	Jilin	246.07	152.39	34.04	28.94	30.70
8	Heilongjiang	175.23	101.98	29.97	19.08	24.20
9	Shanghai	389.85	198.10	43.25	95.86	52.64
10	Jiangsu	225.54	128.22	25.80	42.64	28.88
11	Zhejiang	266.46	147.01	31.75	54.96	32.74
12	Anhui	193.26	117.90	21.49	30.79	23.08
13	Fujian	199.25	123.50	19.98	31.34	24.43
14	Jiangxi	194.17	117.99	20.52	36.35	19.31
15	Shandong	178.95	89.56	27.03	31.69	30.67
16	Henan	165.57	89.08	24.51	28.64	23.34
17	Hubei	183.78	114.75	22.58	25.90	20.55
18	Hunan	207.59	135.98	23.06	27.87	20.68
19	Guangdong	266.05	157.72	21.32	50.26	36.75
20	Guangxi	171.45	115.93	14.93	20.22	20.37
21	Sichuan	184.07	121.21	20.65	22.51	19.70
22	Guizhou	162.51	105.16	18.93	23.48	14.94
23	Yunnan	137.75	91.83	15.90	16.75	13.27
24	Shaanxi	148.46	92.10	18.82	18.88	18.66
25	Gansu	135.23	92.99	16.37	12.28	13.59
26	Qinghai	153.48	103.43	18.90	14.91	16.24
27	Ningxia	141.68	89.06	20.11	13.22	19.29
28	Xinjiang	168.58	98.98	35.08	15.21	19.31

Source: Statistical Yearbook of China, 1981, pp. 445–446.

plotted the four types of expenditures against total expenditure in Figures 5.1, 5.2, 5.3, and 5.4, respectively, where the axes are measured in logarithmic scale. Each data point is marked by a number corresponding to the province or municipality shown in Table 5.2—1 for Beijing, 2 for Tianjin, and so on. These figures indicate that the relations between the logarithms of the four categories of expenditures and the logarithm of total expenditure are approximately linear. Therefore, for each category j ($j = 1,2,3,4$) we can postulate a regression relation

$$\log y_{ij} = \alpha_j + \beta_j \log x_i + \epsilon_{ij} \qquad (i = 1,...,28) \qquad (5.1)$$

where y_{ij} denotes per capita consumption expenditure in the ith province for the jth consumption category, x_i denotes per capita total consumption expenditure in the ith province and β_j is the elasticity of demand for the jth consumption category with respect to total expenditure. ϵ_{ij} is the residual pertaining to the ith province in the regression for the jth consumption category; it is assumed to be a random drawing

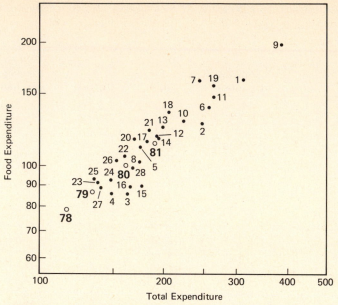

Figure 5.1 Relation between per capita food expenditure and total expenditure of peasants by province—sample survey, 1981.

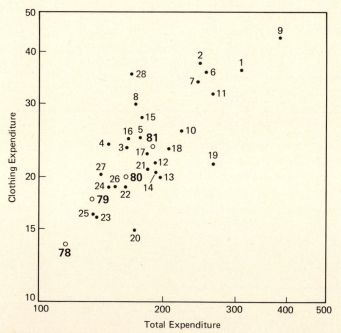

Figure 5.2 Relation between per capita clothing expenditure and total expenditure of peasants by province—sample survey, 1981.

Table 5.4 *(Continued)*

| Country | Food | | Clothing | Housing | Miscella-neous |
	Unad-justed *b*	Adjusted *b*	Unad-justed *b*	Unad-justed *b*	Unad-justed *b*
India, Punjab	.943 (.027)	.811	1.161 (.252)	.764 (.037)	1.391 (.024)
Ireland	.775 (.052)	.621	1.224 (.194)	.583 (.038)	1.358 (.039)
Italy	.615 (.026)	a	1.219 (.034)		
Japan 1953	.648 (.017)	.563	1.398 (.149)	.906 (.031)	1.387 (.011)
Libya	.895 (.073)	.805	1.830 (.165)	.900 (.165)	1.403 (.329)
Northern Rhodesia	.514 (.109)	.393	1.081 (.093)	.229 (.131)	1.308 (.040)
Panama, Panama City	.790 (.055)	.717	1.226 (.064)	.932 (.072)	1.232 (.030)
Philippines, Manila	.810 (.028)	.757	1.141 (.037)	.874 (.047)	1.312 (.026)
Portugal, Porto	.779 (.047)	.623	1.296 (.445)	.564 (.301)	1.246 (.122)
Puerto Rico, San Juan	.699 (.040)	.692	.957 (.026)	1.049 .083	1.177 (.076)
Puerto Rico, Whole Territory	.812 (.031)	a	1.147 (.055)	.963 (.108)	1.315 (.019)
Sweden	.843 (.092)	.652	1.139 (.077)	.749 (.061)	1.261 (.087)
United States 1950	.816 (.025)	.642	1.336 (.048)	.731 (.273)	1.222 (.037)

*a*Adjustment not possible.
Source: Table III of Houthakker, 1957, pp. 546–547.

Houthakker's estimates of the elasticities for the four expenditure categories with respect to total expenditure are given in Table 5.4. The author concludes his multicountry study (p. 551) as follows:

Some final comments are in order. What has been shown is mainly that the elasticities of the four main items of expenditure with respect to total expenditure are similar but not equal, and that the elasticities with respect to family size are rather similar (but also unequal) for food and miscellaneous items, and irregular for clothing and housing. To return to the problem of development planning mentioned in the beginning of the paper: if no data on the expenditure patterns of a country are available at all, one would not be very far astray by putting the partial elasticity with respect to total expenditure at .6 for food, 1.2 for clothing, .8 for housing, and 1.6 for all other items combined, and the partial elasticity with respect to family size at .3 for food, zero for housing and clothing, and −.4 for miscellaneous expenditures. But it would be prudent not to use those guesses for wide extrapolations, and more prudent still to organize a survey and cross-classify the results.

The total expenditure elasticity of demand for food estimated from the survey of Chinese peasants is somewhat higher than the .6 figure proposed by Houthakker. This difference may be explained by the suggestion of Houthakker (p. 547) that "the elasticity for food with respect to total expenditure might be higher for the countries and time periods with lower total expenditure, though the evidence is equivocal." The estimate of elasticity for clothing is somewhat lower, and for housing somewhat higher, in the case of the Chinese peasants surveyed in 1981 than the corresponding average figures used by Houthakker. Two related explanations for the differences can be offered. First, the surveys used by Houthakker are mainly for urban families, and it is reasonable to suppose that urban people tend to spend more on clothing than peasants do as their incomes increase. To the extent that people spend less on clothing, they will spend more on other things, including housing. Second, the demand for housing by Chinese farmers is perhaps subject to fewer restrictions than the demand for clothing. Chinese peasants are relatively free to build their own houses, while the supply of clothing may be more limited. Observe that the elasticities for clothing and housing estimated from urban families in Peiping (in 1927) and in Shanghai (in 1929–1930) as given in Table 5.4 are much closer to the international averages. The higher elasticity for clothing in Shanghai than in Peiping is noteworthy because the residents of the cultural city of Peiping in the late 1920s were known to dress more modestly than the residents of the cosmopolitan Shanghai. There is no reason to believe, and no evidence to suggest, that the consumption behavior of the Chinese people is very different from that of the other people in the world. In fact, the regularities documented in Table 5.4 and in equations 5.2 to 5.5, with the differences reasonably explained, are encouraging to students in their search for universal laws in economics.

*5.3   UTILITY THEORY OF DEMAND

In the preceding section we studied the relation between the demand for one commodity and income (or total expenditure). Such a relation is called an Engel curve, in honor of Ernst Engel (1821–1896). According to the theory of consumer demand expounded in Section 1.3, the demand for a commodity is a function of the prices of all commodities and income, as given in equation 1.5. A demand curve is the relation between the demand for a commodity and its own price, holding all other prices and real income constant. In Section 1.3 we assumed that the preferences of a consumer are summarized by a set of indifference curves, and derived a demand curve from a set of indifference curves graphically (see Figure 1.2). In this section we propose to summarize the preferences of a consumer by a utility function with the quantities of the different consumption goods as arguments. We will derive a set of demand functions from the utility function mathematically.

Referring to Section 1.3 and the discussion of an individual's demand for only two commodities, rice and cloth, with their quantities denoted by x_1 and x_2, observe that the indifference curves depicted in Figure 1.2 can be represented by the *utility function*

$$u(x_1, x_2) = x_1 x_2 \tag{5.6}$$

which gives the utility of the bundle (x_1, x_2) of consumer goods to the individual consumer. For example, the bundle (50,10) as depicted by point b in Figure 1.2 has a utility of $50 \times 10 = 500$. Similarly, the bundles (40,12.5) and (100,5) also have a utility of 500. These points are on the same indifference curve that passes through point *b* in Figure 1.2. The consumer is assumed to prefer a bundle with a higher utility to a bundle with a lower utility. Given income I and prices p_1 and p_2 of the two commodities, the consumer is subject to the budget constraint

$$I - p_1x_1 - p_2x_2 = 0 \qquad (5.7)$$

The consumer will choose that bundle (x_1, x_2) that satisfies the budget constraint (equation 5.7) and that maximizes the utility function $u(x_1, x_2)$.

To solve the mathematical problem of determining which bundle the individual will choose, given his utility function (equation 5.6) and his budget constraint (equation 5.7), we can use equation 5.7 to express x_2 as a function of x_1, namely

$$x_2 = \frac{I}{p_2} - \frac{p_1}{p_2}x_1 \qquad (5.8)$$

and substitute for x_2 in the utility function

$$u = x_1x_2 = \frac{I}{p_2}x_1 - \frac{p_1}{p_2}x_1^2 \qquad (5.9)$$

Equation 5.9 is a function of x_1 alone. We can then maximize 5.9 by setting its derivative with respect to x_1 equal to zero.

$$\frac{du}{dx_1} = \frac{I}{p_2} - 2\frac{p_1}{p_2}x_1 = 0$$

and solving for x_1 to yield the demand function

$$x_1 = \frac{I}{2p_1} \qquad (5.10)$$

which is the demand function (equation 1.33) used in Section 1.6. We can derive the demand function for x_2 in a similar fashion.

Let us restate the above method for deriving demand functions from a general utility function $u(x_1, x_2)$ of two commodities. First, the budget constraint equation 5.7 is used to express x_2 as a function of x_1, yielding equation 5.8. Second, equation 5.8 is substituted for x_2 in the utility function to get

$$u(x_1, x_2) = u(x_1, \frac{I}{p_2} - \frac{p_1}{p_2}x_1) \qquad (5.11)$$

Third, equation 5.11 is maximized with respect to x_1 by differentiation:

$$\frac{\partial u}{\partial x_1} + \frac{\partial u}{\partial x_2}\frac{dx_2}{dx_1} = \frac{\partial u}{\partial x_1} + \frac{\partial u}{\partial x_2}\left(-\frac{p_1}{p_2}\right) = 0 \qquad (5.12)$$

Similar steps can be used to express x_1 as a function of x_2, substitute for x_1 in the utility function, and maximize with respect to x_2, yielding

$$\frac{\partial u}{\partial x_2} + \frac{\partial u}{\partial x_1}\frac{dx_1}{dx_2} = \frac{\partial u}{\partial x_2} + \frac{\partial u}{\partial x_1}\left(-\frac{p_2}{p_1}\right) = 0 \qquad (5.13)$$

Two equations for the unknowns x_1 and x_2 are provided by 5.12 and 5.13. The solution of these equations gives the demand functions for x_1 and x_2.

The partial derivatives $\partial u / \partial x_1$ and $\partial u / \partial x_2$ are called the *marginal utilities* of consuming good 1 and good 2; they measure the increases in utility per unit increase in the quantities x_1 and x_2. Both 5.12 and 5.13 assert that for the consumer to maximize utility, he must choose the quantities x_1 and x_2 in such a manner that the ratio of the marginal utilities is equal to the ratio of the prices:

$$\frac{\dfrac{\partial u}{\partial x_1}}{\dfrac{\partial u}{\partial x_2}} = \frac{p_1}{p_2} \tag{5.14}$$

Geometrically, the left-hand side of equation 5.14 is the negative of the slope of the indifference curve, with x_1 measured along the horizontal axis and x_2 along the vertical axis; it is the *marginal rate of substitution* of x_2 for x_1, showing the quantity of commodity 2 that is required to compensate for a loss of one unit of commodity 1 in order to keep the consumer equally satisfied. The right-hand side of equation 5.14 is the negative of the slope of the budget line. Equation 5.14 thus asserts that for the consumer to maximize utility, the slope of the indifference curve must equal the slope of the budget line.

Another way to interpret the condition equation 5.14 for maximizing utility is to write

$$\frac{\dfrac{\partial u}{\partial x_1}}{p_1} = \frac{\dfrac{\partial u}{\partial x_2}}{p_2} = \lambda \tag{5.15}$$

The ratio on the left of equation 5.14 is the marginal utility per dollar spent on commodity 1, since $\partial u / \partial x_1$ is the marginal utility per unit of commodity 1 and $1/p_1$ is the quantity of commodity 1 obtained per dollar. Equation 5.15 asserts that the marginal utility per dollar spent on commodity 1 must equal the marginal utility per dollar spent on commodity 2. If the former marginal utility were larger, the consumer could do better by spending another dollar on commodity 1 instead of commodity 2. In equation 5.15 we denote the commodity ratio by λ, which is called the *marginal utility of income* because it shows the extra utility obtainable per additional dollar of income. Equations 5.12 and 5.13 can then be written respectively as

$$\frac{\partial u}{\partial x_1} - \lambda p_1 = 0 \tag{5.16}$$

$$\frac{\partial u}{\partial x_2} - \lambda p_2 = 0 \tag{5.17}$$

If we note in equations 5.16 and 5.17 that $-p_1$ and $-p_2$ are respectively the derivatives of the budget constraint (equation 5.7) with respect to x_1 and x_2, we can obtain the same set of conditions as in equations 5.16 and 5.17 for maximizing utility by setting the partial derivatives of the expression

$$L = u(x_1, x_2) + \lambda(I - p_1 x_1 - p_2 x_2) \qquad (5.18)$$

with respect to x_1, x_2 and λ equal to zero. The resulting equations are 5.16, 5.17, and the budget constraint (5.7). These equations can be solved for x_1, x_2, and λ, yielding the demand functions for x_1 and x_2. λ is called a *Lagrange multiplier.* We have just described a method for maximizing a function $u(x_1, x_2)$ subject to the budget constraint (equation 5.7) by introducing the Lagrange multiplier λ, forming the Lagrangian expression of equation 5.18, and differentiating the Lagrangian expression with respect to x_1, x_2, and λ.

To illustrate the method of Lagrange multipliers, let the utility function be $x_1 x_2$. The Lagrangian expression 5.18 becomes

$$L = x_1 x_2 + \lambda(I - p_1 x_1 - p_2 x_2) \qquad (5.19)$$

Setting the partial derivatives of L with respect to x_1, x_2, and λ yields

$$x_2 - \lambda p_1 = 0$$
$$x_1 - \lambda p_2 = 0$$
$$I - p_1 x_1 - p_2 x_2 = 0 \qquad (5.20)$$

The first two equations of 5.20 imply $\lambda = x_2/p_1 = x_1/p_2$, or $p_2 x_2 = p_1 x_1$. Substitution into the last equation of 5.20 gives

$$I - 2p_1 x_1 = I - 2p_2 x_2 = 0$$

and the demand functions

$$x_1 = \frac{I}{2p_1}$$

$$x_2 = \frac{I}{2p_2} \qquad (5.21)$$

from which we obtain the marginal utility of income

$$\lambda = \frac{x_1}{p_2} = \frac{I}{2p_1 p_2} \qquad (5.22)$$

Using the method of Lagrange multipliers, we can solve the problem of maximizing a utility function $u(x_1, \ldots, x_n)$ of n commodities subject to the budget constraint

$$I - \sum_{i=1}^{n} p_i x_i = 0 \qquad (5.23)$$

by introducing the Lagrangian expression

$$L = u(x_1, \ldots, x_n) + \lambda\left(I - \sum_{i=1}^{n} p_i x_i\right) \qquad (5.24)$$

Denoting the partial derivative $\partial u/\partial x_i$ by u_i $(i = 1, \ldots, n)$, we set the partial derivatives of L with respect to $x_1, \ldots, x_n$ and λ equal to zero, obtaining

$$u_1 - \lambda p_1 = 0$$
$$u_2 - \lambda p_2 = 0$$
$$\cdots$$
$$u_n - \lambda p_n = 0$$
$$I - \sum_{i=1}^{n} p_i x_i = 0 \qquad\qquad\qquad (5.25)$$

Equation 5.25 is a set of $n+1$ equations for the unknowns $x_1,\ldots,x_n$ and λ. The solution of these equations gives the demand functions for $x_1,\ldots,x_n$.

Without specifying the mathematical form of the utility function, one cannot obtain explicit expressions for the demand functions, but one can study their properties. In particular, one would like to investigate how the demand x_i changes as prices and income change. To do so, we take the differential of each equation of 5.25. Denoting the second partial of u with respect to x_i and x_j by u_{ij}, we can write the total differentials of the $n+1$ equations 5.25 as

$$u_{11}dx_1 + u_{12}dx_2 + \ldots + u_{1n}dx_n - p_1 d\lambda = \lambda dp_1$$
$$u_{21}dx_1 + u_{22}dx_2 + \ldots + u_{2n}dx_n - p_2 d\lambda = \lambda dp_2$$
$$\cdots$$
$$u_{n1}dx_1 + u_{n2}dx_2 + \ldots + u_{nn}dx_n - p_n d\lambda = \lambda dp_n$$
$$-p_1 dx_1 - p_2 dx_2 - \ldots - p_n dx_n + 0 d\lambda = -dI + \sum_{i=1}^{n} x_i dp_i \quad (5.26)$$

Equation 5.26 is a system of $n+1$ equations for the unknowns $dx_1,\ldots,dx_n$ and $d\lambda$, with $dp_1,\ldots,dp_n$ and dI treated as given. College algebra can be used to solve these equations.

Denote by Δ the determinant

$$\begin{vmatrix} u_{11} & \cdots & u_{1n} & -p_1 \\ & \cdots & & \vdots \\ u_{n1} & \cdots & u_{nn} & -p_n \\ -p_1 & \cdots & -p_n & 0 \end{vmatrix} \qquad\qquad (5.27)$$

The solution for the jth variable dx_j in the system of linear equations 5.26 equals the ratio of two determinants. The denominator of the ratio is Δ. The numerator is obtained by replacing the jth column of Δ by the column consisting of the right-hand side of equation 5.26. This determinant can be expanded using this column and the cofactors of its elements. Denote by Δ_{ij} the cofactor of the element in the ith row and the jth column of Δ. The solution of 5.26 for dx_j is therefore

$$dx_j = \Delta^{-1}\left[\sum_{i=1}^{n} \lambda\Delta_{ij}dp_i + (-dI + \sum_{i=1}^{n} x_i dp_i)\Delta_{n+1,j} \right] \qquad (5.28)$$

The partial derivative of x_j with respect to p_i is obtained from equation 5.28 by setting all terms on the right-hand side equal to zero except dp_i, yielding

$$\frac{\partial x_j}{\partial p_i} = \Delta^{-1}\left[\lambda\Delta_{ij} + x_i\Delta_{n+1,j}\right] \qquad (i = 1,. . .,n) \qquad (5.29)$$

Similarly, the partial derivative of x_j with respect to income I is obtained from equation 5.28 by letting only the change dI be nonzero.

$$\frac{\partial x_j}{\partial I} = \Delta^{-1}(-\Delta_{n+1,j}) \qquad (5.30)$$

Thus, although we cannot obtain the demand function

$$x_j = f_j(p_1, p_2, . . .,p_n, I) \qquad (5.31)$$

explicitly without assuming a specific utility function, we can study its derivatives with respect to the prices $p_1, . . .,p_n$ and to income I using equations 5.29 and 5.30.

The *income effect* on the demand for x_j is given by equation 5.30, which gives the derivative of the Engel curve. This derivative may be positive or negative. If the income effect is positive, the commodity is called a *superior good;* if negative, the commodity is called an *inferior good.* Essentially, an inferior good is consumed by an individual when her income is low, and its consumption is reduced when her income increases. The last equation of 5.26 tells us that when all prices are held fixed, or when $dp_i = 0$ for all i, then

$$p_1 \frac{\partial x_1}{\partial I} + p_2 \frac{\partial x_2}{\partial I} + . . . + p_n\frac{\partial x_n}{\partial I} = 1 \qquad (5.32)$$

which can be obtained by differentiating the budget constraint (5.23) with respect to income I. Although some commodities may be inferior goods, with $\partial x_j/\partial I$ negative, the weighted average of the income effects given by equation 5.32 has to be positive. The normal case is to have a positive income effect, because as income increases total expenditure increases by the same amount, according to the above theory.

Substituting equation 5.30 into equation 5.29, we obtain

$$\frac{\partial x_j}{\partial p_i} = \lambda \frac{\Delta_{ij}}{\Delta} - x_i \frac{\partial x_i}{\partial I}$$
$$= \left(\frac{\partial x_j}{\partial p_i}\right)_{I \text{ const.}} + \left(\frac{\partial I}{\partial p_i}\right) \frac{\partial x_j}{\partial I} \qquad (5.33)$$

which is the celebrated Slutsky equation (see Slutsky, 1915). Equation 5.33 breaks down the effect of a change in p_i on the demand x_j into two components. The first

$$\left(\frac{\partial x_j}{\partial p_i}\right)_{I \text{ const.}} = \lambda\frac{\Delta_{ij}}{\Delta} \equiv K_{ji} \qquad (5.34)$$

is the *substitution effect.* The second

$$\left(\frac{\partial I}{\partial p_i}\right) \frac{\partial x_j}{\partial I} = -x_i \frac{\partial x_j}{\partial I} \qquad (5.35)$$

is the *income effect* of a change in p_i. Review the discussion of these two effects in Section 1.3. The income effect arises because when p_i increases by dp_i, the consumer is no longer able to buy the same bundle of goods as before, or his real income is in effect reduced. This change in real income *resulting from an increase in p_i* has an effect on the demand for x_j, called the *income effect.* The income effect is a product of $\partial I / \partial p_i$ and $\partial x_j / \partial I$, where $\partial I / \partial p_i = -x_i$ shows how much real income is changed by dp_i. If the consumer is buying x_i units of commodity i, and the price of this commodity is increased by dp_i, the consumer in effect loses $x_i dp_i$ in real income, which is the extra amount the x_i units would cost after the price change. The rate of change in real income with respect to p_i is therefore $-x_i$. The rate of change in the demand for x_j due to the income effect is the product of $-x_i$ and the rate of change of x_j with respect to real income.

The substitution effect K_{ji} of a change in p_i on the demand x_j is given by equation 5.34. It is the rate of change of x_j with respect to p_i *holding real income constant;* for small dp_i, this is the same as the rate of change of x_j with respect to p_i holding utility constant. Since for the determinant 5.27 the cofactors Δ_{ij} and Δ_{ji} are equal, we have

$$K_{ji} = \lambda \frac{\Delta_{ij}}{\Delta} = \lambda \frac{\Delta_{ji}}{\Delta} = K_{ij} \tag{5.36}$$

Hence, the substitution effect of a change in p_j on the demand x_i is the same as the substitution effect of a change in p_i on the demand x_j. If the substitution term is positive, the goods i and j are called *substitutes.* For example, cotton cloth and nylon cloth are substitutes. When the price of cotton cloth increases, people tend to buy more nylon cloth. When the price of nylon cloth increases, people tend to buy more cotton cloth. The two substitution effects K_{ji} and K_{ij} are equal, according to the utility theory of demand. If the substitution term is negative, the goods i and j are called *complements.* Complementary goods tend to be consumed together, such as automobiles and gasoline. When the price of one good increases, with real income held constant, the demand for the other good decreases. For $i=j$ the substitution effect (equation 5.34) becomes

$$K_{jj} = \left(\frac{\partial x_j}{\partial p_j} \right)_{I \text{ const.}} = \lambda \frac{\Delta_{jj}}{\Delta} < 0 \tag{5.37}$$

which is always negative, because a second-order condition for the solution of equation 5.25 to give a maximum of $u(x_1, \ldots, x_n)$ subject to the budget constraint of equation 5.23 is for Δ and Δ_{jj} to have opposite signs, and because the marginal utility of income is positive. Thus, the *substitution effect of a change in p_j on the demand x_j is always negative.* In other words, the slope of the demand curve for x_j, holding real income constant, is always negative.

Before concluding our discussion of the theory of consumer demand, we should point out that if a utility function $u(x_1, \ldots, x_n)$ can explain the behavior of a consumer, so can any monotone increasing function of u, such as $\log u$, u^2, u^4. It is possible to change the utility function $u = x_1 x_2$ in our earlier example to

$$u^* = \log u = \log x_1 + \log x_2 \tag{5.38}$$

and to convince oneself that the resulting demand functions are the same as given by equation 5.21 (see Problem 3). The reason is that both utility functions u and u^* imply the same set of indifference curves that can be used to derive the demand equations. Hence, the utility function used in the theory of demand in this section is an *ordinal utility function,* meaning that it gives the order of preference for the bundles of goods $(x_1, \ldots, x_n)$. If the utility of one bundle is larger than the utility of a second bundle, we know that the first is preferred, but we cannot say by how much. We may assign utilities 2 and 1 to the first and second bundle respectively, but we can equally well assign the utilities 4 and 1, or $\sqrt{2}$ and 1.

*5.4   CONSUMER BEHAVIOR UNDER RATIONING

The Chinese population is living under a system of rationing for the key consumer goods. To study consumer behavior under rationing, the use of mathematics is unavoidable. One reason for presenting the mathematical treatment of the theory of consumer demand in the preceding section, besides its own importance, is to pave the way for studying demand behavior under rationing. The reader should refer to Tobin (1952) for a survey of the theory of rationing and to the references therein.

   Three major kinds of rationing have been put into practice and have been studied theoretically. First, *straight rationing* allows each consumer unit to buy not more than a given quantity of a certain commodity, usually a homogeneous commodity such as rice. Straight rationing is practiced in China, where food grain, vegetable oil, meat, sugar, and cotton cloth are among the rationed commodities. Second, *point rationing* assigns points to each rationed commodity, which can be purchased by points together with money. Thus, a rationed commodity has two prices, a point price and a money price. As an example, textiles were under point rationing in Great Britain during the Second World War. Third, *value rationing* is a special case of point rationing. Each consumer unit is allowed to buy no more than a certain money value of the rationed commodities. In this case, point prices equal money prices. The rationing of meat in England during and immediately after the Second World War is an example of value rationing.

   Consumer behavior under the three kinds of rationing can be studied by modifying the theory of Section 5.3. The consumer is assumed to maximize a utility function $u(x_1, \ldots, x_n)$ subject to the budget constraint $\sum_{i=1}^{n} p_i x_i = I$ *and* additional restrictions resulting from rationing. For *straight rationing,* the additional restrictions are

$$x_i \le q_i \qquad (i \in S) \tag{5.39}$$

where the ith commodity belongs to the set S of rationed commodities and q_i is the maximum quantity of the ith commodity that the consumer unit can buy. For *point rationing,* the additional restriction is

$$\sum_{i \in S} p_i^* x_i \le R \tag{5.40}$$

where p_i^* is the point price of the ith rationed commodity in the set S of rationed commodities and the total point value of all rationed commodities cannot exceed R. The additional restriction for *value rationing* is

$$\sum_{i \epsilon S} p_i x_i \leq R \tag{5.41}$$

which is a special case of equation 5.40, with the point prices equal to the money prices p_i. The theory of consumer behavior under point rationing has been worked out by Chow (1957, Chapter III) in connection with a theory of consumer demand for durable goods and will not be discussed here. Since straight rationing is practiced in China, we will present a theory of consumer behavior under straight rationing based on the work of Tobin and Houthakker (1951).

To begin the presentation, let only the nth commodity be under straight rationing. The consumer is assumed to maximize a utility function $u(x_1, \ldots, x_n)$ subject to the budget constraint $\sum_{i=1}^{n} p_i x_i = I$ and the restriction $x_n \leq q_n$. Tobin and Houthakker (1951) introduce two additional assumptions. First, rationing is effective, namely $x_n = q_n$. This assumption is realistic because the quantities of rationed commodities made available to the consumer are usually smaller than the amounts she would buy in a free market. Second, the analysis will be restricted to small changes from the original equilibrium point—that is, the solution of the consumer's problem of maximizing utility, subject to the original budget constraint.

The first question to be asked is how a change in the quantity q_n of the ration affects the demand for other commodities. To study the effects of a change in q_n, imagine a hypothetical change dx_n in the demand for x_n in the free market that equals the change dq_n in the ration—that is,

$$dx_n = dq_n \tag{5.42}$$

—and that would result from a combination of a price change dp_n and an income change dI—that is,

$$dx_n = \frac{\partial x_n}{\partial p_n} dp_n + \frac{\partial x_n}{\partial I} dI \tag{5.43}$$

The income change dI, which in a free market would just compensate for the income effect of a price change dp_n, is

$$dI = x_n dp_n$$

Therefore, the price change dp_n, which in a free market would be equivalent to the change dq_n in the ration, must satisfy

$$dq_n = \frac{\partial x_n}{\partial p_n} dp_n + x_n \frac{\partial x_n}{\partial I} dp_n$$

$$= \left(\frac{\partial x_n}{\partial p_n} + x_n \frac{\partial x_n}{\partial I} \right) dp_n = K_{nn} dp_n \tag{5.44}$$

where the last equality sign is due to equations 5.33 and 5.34. Thus, the free-market price change equivalent to the change dq_n in ration is given by $dp_n = dq_n/K_{nn}$. "Free market" here means only the absence of rationing constraints and permits government control of some prices in the budget constraint.

To study the effect of a small change in ration on the demand for commodity i, we can consider the effect of its equivalent price change. Following the development of equations 5.43 and 5.44, the change in x_i can be written as

$$dx_i = \frac{\partial x_i}{\partial p_n}dp_n + \frac{\partial x_i}{\partial I}dI = \frac{\partial x_i}{\partial p_n}dp_n + x_n\frac{\partial x_i}{\partial I}dp_n$$

$$= \left(\frac{\partial x_i}{\partial p_n} + x_n\frac{\partial x_i}{\partial I}\right)dp_n = K_{in}dp_n = \frac{K_{in}}{K_{nn}}dq_n \tag{5.45}$$

where the last equality sign has used the free-market equivalent price change $dp_n = dq_n/K_{nn}$. Equation 5.45 implies that the compensated rate of change of the demand x_i with respect to the ration q_n is

$$\frac{\partial x_i}{\partial q_n} = \frac{K_{in}}{K_{nn}} \tag{5.46}$$

Given that K_{nn} is negative, the effect $\partial x_i/\partial q_n$ of a change in ration on x_i is negative if K_{in} is positive—that is, if the ith and nth goods are substitutes. This conclusion agrees with common sense. If the ration of the nth commodity is increased, the demand for its substitutes will fall and the demand for its complements (with $K_{in} < 0$) will rise. In China an increase in the ration of cotton cloth will reduce the demand for nylon fabric and will increase the demand for thread and possibly tailors' services.

Second, Tobin and Houthakker compare the effect $\partial x_i/\partial I$ of a change in income on the demand for the ith commodity under a free market with the corresponding effect $\partial\!\!\!/x_i/\partial I$ under rationing (the slash through the partial-derivative sign indicates rationing). In deriving theorems concerning demand in Section 5.3, we used the determinant Δ given by equation 5.27, which resulted from differentiation of the first-order equilibrium conditions (equation 5.25). When the nth commodity is rationed, $x_n = q_n$ is fixed and we cannot differentiate the utility function with respect to x_n. The determinant corresponding to 5.27 becomes Δ_{nn}, which is the cofactor obtained by deleting the nth row and the nth column from Δ. We use the symbol $\Delta_{nn;ij}$ to denote the cofactor obtained by deleting the ith row and the jth column from Δ_{nn}. Using equation 5.30, we can write

$$\frac{\partial x_i}{\partial I} - \frac{\partial\!\!\!/x_i}{\partial I} = \frac{-\Delta_{n+1,i}}{\Delta} - \frac{-\Delta_{nn;n+1,i}}{\Delta_{nn}} \tag{5.47}$$

By Jacobi's Theorem,

$$\Delta\,\Delta_{nn;n+1,i} = \Delta_{nn}\,\Delta_{n+1,i} - \Delta_{ni}\,\Delta_{n+1,n} \tag{5.48}$$

which can be used to substitute for $\Delta_{nn;n+1,i}$ in equation 5.47 to obtain

$$\frac{\partial x_i}{\partial I} - \frac{\partial\!\!\!/x_i}{\partial I} = \frac{-\Delta_{n+1,i}}{\Delta} + \frac{\Delta_{nn}\,\Delta_{n+1,i} - \Delta_{ni}\,\Delta_{n+1,n}}{\Delta_{nn}\,\Delta}$$

$$= \frac{\Delta_{ni}}{\Delta_{nn}}\left(\frac{-\Delta_{n+1,n}}{\Delta}\right) = \frac{\partial x_i}{\partial q_n}\frac{\partial x_n}{\partial I} \tag{5.49}$$

where the last equality sign has made use of equations 5.46, 5.34, and 5.30. From equation 5.49, we conclude that, if the ith and the nth goods are substitutes ($\partial x_i/\partial q_n < 0$) and if the nth good is a superior good ($\partial x_n/\partial I > 0$), the product

$$\frac{\partial x_i}{\partial q_n} \frac{\partial x_n}{\partial I}$$

is negative and therefore

$$\frac{\partial x_i}{\partial I} < \frac{\cancel{\partial} x_i}{\partial I}$$

or rationing will increase the income derivatives of the unrationed commodities. Since the consumer cannot spend his income on x_n, he may be expected to spend it on other goods that are substitutes for x_n, assuming that x_n is a superior good.

A similar method can be used to compare the effects of a change in the price p_j on the demand for x_i in a free market and under straight rationing, the result being

$$\frac{\partial x_i}{\partial p_j} - \frac{\cancel{\partial} x_i}{\partial p_j} = \frac{\partial x_i}{\partial q_n} \frac{\partial x_n}{\partial p_j} \qquad (5.50)$$

(see Problem 4). From equation 5.50, we conclude that if goods i and n are substitutes ($\partial x_i / \partial q_n < 0$) and if goods j and n are also substitutes ($\partial x_n / \partial p_j > 0$), the product on the right-hand side of equation 5.50 is negative and therefore

$$\frac{\partial x_i}{\partial p_j} < \frac{\cancel{\partial} x_i}{\partial p_j}$$

or rationing will increase the effect of p_j on x_i. When p_j increases and if the consumer is prevented by rationing from buying more of the substitute good x_n, she will tend to buy more of other substitutes x_i. When the price of nylon cloth increases and if the consumer cannot buy more of the rationed cotton cloth, she will tend to buy more of another synthetic clothing material.

Theorems 5.49 and 5.50 have been generalized by Tobin and Houthakker to the case of several commodities under straight rationing. Let the first m $(m < n)$ commodities be not subject to rationing and the commodities $m+1, m+2, \ldots, n$ be subject to straight rationing, with $x_k = q_k$ $(k = m+1, \ldots, n)$. Theorems 5.49 and 5.50 will become, respectively,

$$\frac{\partial x_i}{\partial I} - \frac{\cancel{\partial} x_i}{\partial I} = \sum_{k=m+1}^{n} \frac{\partial x_i}{\partial q_k} \frac{\partial x_k}{\partial I} \qquad (5.51)$$

and

$$\frac{\partial x_i}{\partial p_j} - \frac{\cancel{\partial} x_i}{\partial p_j} = \sum_{k=m+1}^{n} \frac{\partial x_i}{\partial q_k} \frac{\partial x_k}{\partial p_j} \qquad (5.52)$$

Interested readers should translate these theorems into words.

This discussion has been concerned with comparing the income and price effects on demand under rationing with those in the free market. To compare the substitution term K_{ii} prevailing when the nth commodity is under straight rationing with the corresponding term under a free market, one can ascertain the sign of the difference between these substitution terms

$$\left(\frac{\partial x_i}{\partial p_i} + x_i \frac{\partial x_i}{\partial I}\right) - \left(\frac{\partial x_i}{\partial p_i} + x_i \frac{\partial x_i}{\partial I}\right) = \lambda \frac{\Delta_{nn,ii}}{\Delta_{nn}} - \lambda \frac{\Delta_{ii}}{\Delta}$$

$$= \lambda \frac{\Delta \, \Delta_{nn,ii} - \Delta_{ii} \, \Delta_{nn}}{\Delta \, \Delta_{nn}} = -\lambda \frac{\Delta^2_{ni}}{\Delta \, \Delta_{nn}} > 0 \qquad (5.53)$$

where the first equality sign results from applying equation 5.34 to the rationing and free-market regimes and the last equality sign results from applying Jacobi's Theorem (equation 5.48, with i replacing $n+1$). One might think that the marginal utility of income λ under rationing is different, but it is not because we are considering only small changes from the original free-market equilibrium. Because Δ and Δ_{nn} have opposite signs by the second-order condition of the constrained maximum, and because the marginal utility of income λ is positive, equation 5.53 is positive. Since both substitution terms in 5.53 are negative, a positive difference means that the absolute value of the first substitution term under rationing must be smaller than the absolute value of the second substitution term under a free market. The proof of 5.53 can be used to compare the substitution terms when both commodities $n-1$ and n are rationed and when only commodity n is rationed; Δ_{nn} will replace Δ, and $\Delta_{nn;n-1,n-1}$ will replace Δ_{nn}, and so on. Thus, the result applies to the introduction of one more rationed commodity. This result illustrates the Le Chatelier Principle, which asserts that, as a new commodity is introduced into a rationing regime or as an additional constraint is imposed, the substitution term will become smaller in absolute value, or the consumer's demand for x_i will respond less to a change in its own price. The Le Chatelier Principle in physics was introduced to economics by Samuelson (1948). We have seen that rationing makes the consumer less responsive in terms of her demand curves. We have also studied the effects of a change in the quantity of the rationed commodity on the demand for other commodities, and we have compared the effects of changes in income and prices on demand under rationing with the corresponding effects in a free market or in the absence of rationing.

*5.5 IS RATIONING A GOOD SYSTEM?

China probably has the longest record of enforcing a fairly comprehensive rationing regime. Rationing was introduced during the Second World War by some Western countries, including Great Britain and the United States, but was abolished soon after the war. Rationing was introduced in China in 1955 and has remained in effect for the ensuing three decades. One may ask whether rationing is a good system to achieve the intended objectives and whether there are better ways to achieve the same objectives.

One major objective of introducing a rationing system is to restrict the demand for certain commodities when their supplies are limited. But we know that prices as determined in a free market will automatically restrict the demand for commodities with limited supplies. When the supply of a commodity is short relative to demand, its price will rise to equate demand and supply, leaving no shortage. In China, if rationing is abolished, the prices of the currently rationed commodities will go up to equate demand and supply. Furthermore, when the prices go up, the quantities supplied will tend to increase insofar as the producers are allowed some autonomy in their production decisions and are able to retain some profits from the increase in output. What, then, is wrong with the free-market solution? One answer is that the resulting price increases may lead to inflation, which is deemed undesirable. A second answer is that as the prices of certain necessities increase, the people with high incomes will buy more of them and the people with low incomes will get less. This means that the rich will benefit more than the poor. In China, however, the second answer is probably not valid, at least as far as the possible derationing of food grain is concerned. As we pointed out in Section 5.1, the urban population is much richer than the rural population. Derationing food grain and letting the urban population pay a higher price for it would only help redistribute income from the richer urban population to the poorer farm population if the latter were allowed to receive a higher price for the food grain. Furthermore, allowing the price of food grain to go up would increase its supply, which would benefit both the farmers and the urban population.

If we leave out the effect of derationing food grain on income redistribution between the urban population and the farmers (which appears to be desirable) and consider only the possible effect on inflation, we can achieve the same objective of preventing inflation without the use of rationing by imposing a spending tax on the currently rationed commodities. Let us compare the rationing scheme with an alternative tax scheme, assuming that the supply of the rationed commodities is fixed at the same amount in both cases. In the alternative scheme the consumer is asked to pay a tax on the purchase of the currently rationed commodities so that he will end up buying exactly the same amount as the current ration. Tobin (1952) has compared these two schemes and found that the alternative scheme is better because it has a less damaging effect on the consumer's incentive to work than the rationing scheme does. We will present Tobin's analysis below, not only because its result is interesting but also because it provides another illustration of the usefulness of the utility analysis of demand behavior.

Let the consumer unit maximize a utility function $u(x_1, x_2, x_3)$ of the quantities x_1 of a rationed commodity (or a group of rationed commodities), x_2 of the remaining group of commodities, and x_3 of leisure time. Assume that the consumer has an income Y from sources other than his own labor and has a given number M of man-hours at his disposal. These man-hours can be devoted either to leisure time x_3 or to working time $(M-x_3)$ with a wage rate p_3. His income is $p_3(M-x_3) + Y$, which can be used to buy x_1 and x_2 at prices p_1 and p_2. Therefore, his budget constraint is

$$p_1 x_1 + p_2 x_2 = p_3(M-x_3) + Y$$

or

$$p_1 x_1 + p_2 x_2 + p_3 x_3 = p_3 M + Y \qquad (5.54)$$

(Here the prices p_1, p_2, and p_3 might be subject to government control.) We specify that the consumer's demand for x_1 must be limited to a given amount q_1 either by a rationing scheme (r) or by a proportional spendings tax (s), so that the consumer would in effect pay a price p_{1s} inclusive of the tax per unit of commodity 1. Let x_{10}, x_{20}, and x_{30} be the quantities of the three consumption goods that maximize utility subject to the constraint determined in equation 5.54. The additional constraint under the rationing scheme (r) is

$$x_1 = q_1 \tag{5.55}$$

The revised budget constraint under the spending-tax scheme is

$$p_{1s}x_1 + p_2x_2 + p_3x_3 = p_3M + Y \tag{5.56}$$

Let (q_1, x_{2r}, x_{3r}) maximize utility subject to equations 5.54 and 5.55 under the rationing scheme. Let p_{1s} be so chosen that maximizing utility subject to equation 5.56 yields (q_1, x_{2s}, x_{3s}). The problem is to compare x_{3r} and x_{3s}, the amounts of leisure purchased under the two schemes.

Tobin assumes that the utility function can be approximated by a quadratic function:

$$u(x_1, x_2, x_3) = \frac{1}{2}\sum_{i=1}^{3}\sum_{j=1}^{3} a_{ij}x_ix_j - \sum_{i=1}^{3} a_ix_i \qquad (a_{ij} = a_{ji}) \tag{5.57}$$

Under the first regime, with neither rationing nor a spending tax, the consumer would maximize 5.57 subject to 5.54. Introducing the Lagrangian expression

$$L = \frac{1}{2}\sum_{i=1}^{3}\sum_{j=1}^{3} a_{ij}x_ix_j + \sum_{i=1}^{3} a_ix_i + \lambda(p_3M + Y - \sum_{i=1}^{3} p_ix_i) \tag{5.58}$$

we differentiate with respect to x_1, x_2, x_3, and λ to obtain the first-order conditions for minimization:

$$a_{11}x_{10} + a_{12}x_{20} + a_{13}x_{30} - p_1\lambda = a_1$$
$$a_{21}x_{10} + a_{22}x_{20} + a_{23}x_{30} - p_2\lambda = a_2$$
$$a_{31}x_{10} + a_{32}x_{20} + a_{33}x_{30} - p_3\lambda = a_3$$
$$-p_1x_{10} - p_2x_{20} - p_3x_{30} = -p_3M - Y \tag{5.59}$$

The solution of equations 5.59 for x_{10}, x_{20}, x_{30}, and λ will give the demand functions, where the subscript 0 denotes the first regime.

Under the rationing regime, the consumer would maximize 5.57 subject to 5.54 and $x_1 = q_1$. Replacing x_1 and λ in the Lagrangian expression shown in 5.58 by q_1 and λ_r, respectively, and differentiating the resulting expression with respect to x_2, x_3, and λ_r, we obtain the first-order conditions

$$a_{21}q_1 + a_{22}x_{2r} + a_{23}x_{3r} - p_2\lambda_r = a_2$$
$$a_{31}q_1 + a_{32}x_{2r} + a_{33}x_{3r} - p_3\lambda_r = a_3$$
$$-p_1q_1 - p_2x_{2r} - p_3x_{3r} = -p_3M - Y \tag{5.60}$$

which can be solved for x_{2r}, x_{3r}, and λ_r, where the subscript r signifies the rationing regime.

Under the spending-tax regime, the consumer would maximize 5.57 subject to 5.56 and $x_1 = q_1$. Replacing p_1 and λ in the Lagrangian 5.58 by p_{1s} and λ_s, respectively, and differentiating the resulting expression with respect to x_1, x_2, x_3, and λ_s, we obtain a set of first-order conditions. Since we specify that the solution to these first-order conditions should yield $x_1 = q_1$, we can write

$$a_{11}q_1 + a_{12}x_{2s} + a_{13}x_{3s} - p_{1s}\lambda_s = a_1$$
$$a_{21}q_1 + a_{22}x_{2s} + a_{23}x_{3s} - p_2\lambda_s = a_2$$
$$a_{31}q_1 + a_{32}x_{2s} + a_{33}x_{3s} - p_3\lambda_s = a_3$$
$$-p_{1s}q_1 - p_2 x_{2s} - p_3 x_{3s} \qquad = -p_3 M - Y \qquad (5.61)$$

where the subscript s signifies the spending-tax regime. We would like to compare the solution x_{3s} from equation 5.61 with the solution x_{3r} from equation 5.60 under the rationing regime in order to determine under which regime the consumer would choose more leisure time x_3.

Let Δ be the determinant of the equations 5.59,

$$\Delta = \begin{vmatrix} a_{11} & a_{12} & a_{13} & -p_1 \\ a_{21} & a_{22} & a_{23} & -p_2 \\ a_{31} & a_{32} & a_{33} & -p_3 \\ -p_1 & -p_2 & -p_3 & 0 \end{vmatrix} \qquad (5.62)$$

and Δ_{ij} be the cofactor of the element in the ith row and the jth column. The relationships between the change in leisure time x_3 and the change in the purchase of scarce consumption goods x_1 under the two regimes can be shown to be

$$\frac{x_{3r} - x_{30}}{q_1 - x_{10}} = \frac{\Delta_{13}}{\Delta_{11}} \qquad (5.63)$$

$$\frac{x_{3s} - x_{30}}{q_1 - x_{10}} = \frac{\lambda_s \Delta_{13} + q_1 \Delta_{43}}{\lambda_s \Delta_{11} + q_1 \Delta_{41}} \qquad (5.64)$$

To prove 5.63, we subtract from each equation in 5.60 the corresponding equation in 5.59 to yield

$$a_{22}(x_{2r} - x_{20}) + a_{23}(x_{3r} - x_{30}) - p_2(\lambda_r - \lambda) = -a_{21}(q_1 - x_{10})$$
$$a_{32}(x_{2r} - x_{20}) + a_{33}(x_{3r} - x_{30}) - p_3(\lambda_r - \lambda) = -a_{31}(q_1 - x_{10})$$
$$-p_2(x_{2r} - x_{20}) - p_3(x_{3r} - x_{30}) \qquad = +p_1(q_1 - x_{10}) \quad (5.65)$$

The solution of these three equations for $(x_{3r} - x_{30})$ is the ratio of two determinants. The denominator of the ratio is Δ_{11}. The numerator is

$$\begin{vmatrix} a_{22} & -a_{21}(q_1 - x_{10}) & -p_2 \\ a_{32} & -a_{31}(q_1 - x_{10}) & -p_3 \\ -p_2 & p_1(q_1 - x_{10}) & 0 \end{vmatrix} = -(q_1 - x_{10}) \begin{vmatrix} a_{22} & a_{21} & -p_2 \\ a_{32} & a_{31} & -p_3 \\ -p_2 & -p_1 & 0 \end{vmatrix}$$

which equals $-(q_1 - x_{10})(-\Delta_{13})$, since the determinant on the right-hand side is obtained by interchanging the first and second columns of Δ_{13}. This solution for $(x_{3r} - x_{30})$ yields equation 5.63.

To prove 5.64, we subtract from each equation in 5.61 the corresponding equation in 5.59 to yield

$$a_{11}(q_1 - x_{10}) + a_{12}(x_{2s} - x_{20}) + a_{13}(x_{3s} - x_{30}) - p_1(\lambda_s - \lambda) = \lambda_s(p_{1s} - p_1)$$
$$a_{21}(q_1 - x_{10}) + a_{22}(x_{2s} - x_{20}) + a_{23}(x_{3s} - x_{30}) - p_2(\lambda_s - \lambda) = 0$$
$$a_{31}(q_1 - x_{10}) + a_{32}(x_{2s} - x_{20}) + a_{33}(x_{3s} - x_{30}) - p_3(\lambda_s - \lambda) = 0$$
$$-p_1(q_1 - x_{10}) - p_2(x_{2s} - x_{20}) - p_3(x_{3s} - x_{30}) \qquad = q_1(p_{1s} - p_1)$$
$$(5.66)$$

The solution of these equations yields

$$(x_{3s} - x_{30}) = \frac{\lambda_s(p_{1s} - p_1)\Delta_{13} + q_1(p_{1s} - p_1)\Delta_{43}}{\Delta}$$

and

$$(q_1 - x_{10}) = \frac{\lambda_s(p_{1s} - p_1)\Delta_{13} + q_1(p_{1s} - p_1)\Delta_{41}}{\Delta}$$

The ratio of these two expressions is shown in equation 5.64.

Finally, to compare the demand for leisure under the rationing and spendings-tax regimes, we take the ratio of 5.63 to 5.64

$$\frac{x_{3r} - x_{30}}{x_{3s} - x_{30}} = \frac{(-\lambda_s\Delta_{11}\Delta_{13} - q_1\Delta_{41}\Delta_{13})/\Delta^2}{(-\lambda_s\Delta_{11}\Delta_{13} - q_1\Delta_{43}\Delta_{11})/\Delta^2}$$

$$= \frac{-\lambda_s K_{11}K_{13}\lambda^{-2} + q_1\ (\partial x_1/\partial I)K_{13}\lambda^{-1}}{-\lambda_s K_{11}K_{13}\lambda^{-2} + q_1\ (\partial x_3/\partial I)K_{11}\lambda^{-1}} \quad (5.67)$$

where the last equality sign has used the substitution and income effects defined by equations 5.34 and 5.30. We know that the marginal utilities of income λ and λ_s are positive and that the substitution term K_{11} is negative. We assume that x_1 and x_3 are substitutes (that is, K_{13} is positive) and that x_1 and x_3 are superior goods (that is, $\partial x_1/\partial I$ and $\partial x_3/\partial I$ are positive). Therefore, the first term $-\lambda_s K_{11}K_{13}\lambda^{-2}$ is positive. The second term $q_1\ (\partial x_1/\partial I)K_{13}\lambda^{-1}$ in the numerator of 5.67 is positive, whereas the second term $q_1\ (\partial x_3/\partial I)K_{11}\lambda^{-1}$ in the denominator of 5.67 is negative. Hence, the numerator of 5.67 is larger than the denominator, implying

$$x_{3r} - x_{30} > x_{3s} - x_{30} \quad (5.68)$$

where we know, from solving equation 5.65, that

$$x_{3r} - x_{30} = \frac{(x_{10} - q_1)(-\Delta_{13})}{\Delta_{11}} = \frac{(x_{10} - q_1)(-K_{13})}{K_{11}} > 0 \quad (5.69)$$

From 5.69 we conclude that under the rationing regime, the consumer would choose to consume more leisure time x_{3r} (or choose to work less) than under the first regime without rationing. From 5.68 we conclude that under the rationing system, the consumer would choose to consume more leisure time x_{3r} than under the alternative spending-tax system, which would restrict the consumption of x_1 to the same level q_1. In other words, the consumer would be induced to work more under the alternative tax scheme. The assumptions used in the proof are that the rationed goods and leisure are substitutes and that both are superior goods.

When the above analysis is applied to the Chinese economy, one qualification should be noted. The analysis assumes that the consumer can choose the number of working hours. This is true for a farm laborer and for a worker who can earn more by working more. The analysis would not be applicable to workers who have no choice in the number of working hours and who receive the same payment regardless of the amount of work done. The main purpose of presenting the above comparison is to demonstrate that economic institutions such as rationing and tax systems can be evaluated by means of economic analysis. We have found that for the purpose of inducing workers to work more, the alternative spending-tax system, which limits the consumer to consume the same amount of the rationed good, is better than the rationing system and that both the tax system and the rationing system will discourage the worker from working as much as before.

To the majority of economists who believe that the consumer can decide which of two alternatives is better by actually choosing one of them, there is an easy way to improve the rationing system. This is to allow the ration coupons to be freely traded. If consumer A is willing to trade one ration coupon good for one kilogram of rice for 5 cents and B is willing to pay 5 cents for the coupon, both parties will benefit from the trade and social welfare will be improved. A's utility is higher because he chooses to have the extra 5 cents instead of the coupon. B's utility is also higher because she chooses to have the coupon instead of the 5 cents. Both are better off and no one else is worse off. Hence, social welfare is increased by the trade.

One day the Chinese government may decide to abolish rationing of some or all commodities, perhaps by instituting spendings taxes as discussed in this section or by letting the prices rise to equate demand and supply. For any rationed commodity, by how much would the price rise after derationing? Or if price remains fixed, how much will the free demand be? The latter question has been answered for the United Kingdom after the Second World War by Houthakker and Tobin (1952), who have estimated the free demand for rationed foodstuffs assuming the prices to be the same as those prevailing in the middle of 1951. The method consists of estimating the elasticities of demand with respect to income, own-price, and price of a related product, and applying the elasticities to the actual changes in these variables between 1938 and 1951, thus arriving at an estimate of the change in demand between 1938 and 1951 (see Problem 11). Leon Podkaminer (1982) has estimated consumer demand functions for Poland under rationing, using annual data from 1965 to 1978. The methods of these studies are useful for estimating the increases in demand or the increases in prices of derationed commodities in China. For an attempt to estimate a statistical demand function for pork in Shanghai, see Fan, Li, and Zuo (1980).

*5.6   ANALYSIS OF URBAN–RURAL INCOME REDISTRIBUTION IN CHINA

A strategy for industrialization in China is to tax the farmers to provide food for the urban workers who produce industrial products. David Bradford (1983) has provided a simple model to describe the mechanism of taxing the farmers and subsidizing the urban workers through the provision of food rations, and has evaluated the welfare effects of this policy of income redistribution.

Bradford (1983) makes the following simplifying assumptions to bring out the essence of the problem. There are only two consumer goods, good 1 being grain (or food) produced in the rural sector r and good 2 being cloth (or industrial consumer good) produced in the urban sector u. Let x_j^i be the consumption of good j ($j = 1,2$) by the resident of sector i ($i = r,u$) and let y_i be the production of good i.

Good 1 is produced according to the production function

$$y_1 = f_1(l^r) \tag{5.70}$$

where l^r is the quantity of rural labor used, the quantity of land being fixed. Good 2 is produced with urban labor l^u and capital, the quantity of capital being assumed to be fixed. The production function of good 2 is

$$y_2 = f_2(l^u) \tag{5.71}$$

The policy of the Chinese government is described by four *policy variables*, also called *policy instruments.* First, a tax of $\bar{y}_1$ units of grain is imposed on the rural sector. In fact, compulsory purchase of grain is paid a below-market price, but it is equivalent to a smaller amount $\bar{y}_1$ delivered to the government at zero price. Second, a subsidy of $\bar{x}_1$ units of grain is provided for urban consumption. Again, the urban ration has a small price, but it is equivalent to a smaller ration $\bar{x}_1$ free of charge. The third and fourth policy variables are the price p_2 of cloth and the wage rate w of urban workers. The values of the policy variables are set by the government. The question is whether the Chinese government sets these policy variables optimally to maximize the welfare of the farmers and the workers, while keeping a given amount g of good 1 for government consumption (which could be traded to provide for national defense and other needs).

Given the values of the policy instruments, the farmers and the workers will respond accordingly. The welfare effects of government policy depend on the responses of the farmers and the workers. To study the responses, Bradford conducts his analysis in terms of one farmer and one worker only, as is often done in economic analysis. This simplification is justified if all farmers have the same utility function and all workers have the same utility function, if all farmers have the same production function and if the tax $\bar{y}_1$ is the same for all farmers and the subsidy $\bar{x}_1$ is the same for all workers. $\bar{y}_1$ will denote the tax per farmer, and so on.

The farmer's behavior is determined by maximizing his utility function $u^r(x_1^r, x_2^r, M - l^r)$, where M is the number of man-hours and $M - l^r$ is leisure time, subject to the budget constraint

$$p_1 x_1^r + p_2 x_2^r = y_1 - \bar{y}_1 = f_1(l^r) - \bar{y}_1 \tag{5.72}$$

where $p_1 = 1$ by definition. Differentiating an appropriate Lagrangian expression with respect to x_1^r, x_2^r, l^r, and λ yields the three demand functions

$$x_1^r = x_1^r(p_2, \bar{y}_1)$$
$$x_2^r = x_2^r(p_2, \bar{y}_1)$$
$$l^r = l^r(p_2, \bar{y}_1) \tag{5.73}$$

the last being the supply function for labor l^r, which is equivalent to the demand function for leisure $M - l^r$. The arguments in these demand functions should be p_1, p_2, and income, but $p_1 = 1$ and income is a function of $\bar{y}_1$ according to equation 5.72, with $y_1 = f_1(l^r)$ being itself a function of p_2 and $\bar{y}_1$. Hence, the arguments are p_2 and $\bar{y}_1$. The net supply of food y_1^n to the urban sector is the difference between production y_1 and rural consumption x_1^r, both being functions of p_2 and $\bar{y}_1$. Hence, net food supply is

$$y_1^n = y_1 - x_1^r = y_1^n(p_2, \bar{y}_1) \tag{5.74}$$

Equation 5.73 shows that government policy on the price of cloth p_2 and the agricultural tax $\bar{y}_1$ will affect the farmer's demand for food, clothing, and leisure time. Since x_1^r, x_2^r, and l^r enter the farmer's utility function, the utility function is indirectly a function of p_2 and $\bar{y}_1$,

$$u^r(x_1^r, x_2^r, M - l^r) = u^r[x_1^r(p_2, \bar{y}_1), x_2^r(p_2, \bar{y}_1), M - l^r(p_2, \bar{y}_1)]$$
$$\equiv v^r(p_2, \bar{y}_1) \qquad (5.75)$$

which is called an *indirect utility function.* A direct utility function $u(x_1, x_2, x_2)$ is a function of the quantities consumed. When the direct utility function is maximized, the demand x_i for each commodity is obtained as a function of all prices and income. When these demand functions are substituted for the x_i in the direct utility function, utility becomes a function of all prices and income. This function is the indirect utility function. In the present application the indirect utility function (equation 5.75) shows how the farmer's welfare depends on the price of cloth p_2 and agricultural tax $\bar{y}_1$, which are determined by government policy.

Similarly, the urban worker maximizes a direct utility function $u^u(x_1^u, x_2^u, M - l^u)$ subject to her budget constraint

$$p_1 x_1^u + p_2 x_2^u = wl^u + \bar{x}_1 \qquad (5.76)$$

where $p_1 = 1$ and the worker's income consists of wage income wl^u and food subsidy $\bar{x}_1$. Maximization yields demand functions and urban labor supply,

$$x_i^u = x_i^u(p_2, w, \bar{x}_1) \qquad (i = 1,2)$$
$$l^u = l^u(p_2, w, \bar{x}_1) \qquad (5.77)$$

as well as an indirect utility function

$$v^u(p_2, w, \bar{x}_1) \qquad (5.78)$$

showing how government policies on p_2, wage w, and food subsidy $\bar{x}_1$ affect the worker's welfare.

To complete the description of the economy, we need to specify the constraints on urban production and on the government. Bradford models urban production as taking place in a single consolidated government enterprise and makes the simplifying approximations that the markets for goods and labor are cleared with demand equal to supply, realizing that these approximations are crude for the Chinese economy. Assume that the government takes any surplus π earned by the enterprise and ignores the problem of retained surplus devoted to investment, which is not our present concern. The constraints of the urban enterprise are

$$y_2 = f_2(l^u)$$
$$p_2 y_2 = wl^u + \pi \qquad (5.79)$$

the first being a simple production function and the second equating revenue with cost plus profit (or surplus).

The government budget is constrained by

$$\bar{y}_1 + \pi = \bar{x}_1 + g \qquad (5.80)$$

which equates total government revenue (from agricultural tax and enterprise profit) with total government expenditure (on urban food subsidy and on government consumption g) if a balanced budget is assumed. (Strictly speaking, if $\bar{y}_1$ and $\bar{x}_1$ denote tax and subsidy per person, $\bar{y}_1$ in equation 5.80 should be multiplied by the number of farmers and $\bar{x}_1$ by the number of workers.) In addition, market clearing for good 1 implies that demand equals net supply.

$$g + x_1^u = y_1^n \tag{5.81}$$

The above analysis provides enough equations in 5.73, 5.74, 5.77, 5.79, and 5.81 to determine the unknowns x_1^r, x_2^r, l^r, y_1^n, x_1^u, x_2^u, l^u, y_2, π, and g. If these equations are solved for the unknowns, the farmer's and the worker's utility will be maximized and government consumption g will be determined as a residual. Since government consumption is important for itself, Bradford asks how, given a specified level of g, the government should choose its policy instruments p_2, w, $\bar{y}_1$, and $\bar{x}_1$ to maximize a weighted average of the farmer's utility and the worker's utility

$$v^r(p_2, \bar{y}_1) + \mu v^u(p_2, w, \bar{x}_1) \tag{5.82}$$

When there are two groups of individuals in a society, a weighted average of their utility functions in the form shown in equation 5.82 is often used to represent social welfare in the study of economic welfare. Although the weight μ in equation 5.82 specifies the importance of the urban worker's utility relative to the farmer's utility in social welfare, the results of the analysis will be made independently of μ. We are concerned only with Pareto optimality, or with a solution in which the farmer's utility cannot be increased without decreasing the worker's utility.

The problem posed for the Chinese government is how to use the indirect means of price p_2, wage w, tax $\bar{y}_1$, and subsidy $\bar{x}_1$ to achieve a Pareto-optimal solution of maximizing equation 5.82 for a given level of government consumption g. A second problem is to choose directly the rural and urban consumptions and labor supplies x_1^i, x_2^i, l^i ($i = r,u$) to maximize the direct social welfare function

$$u^r(x_1^r, x_2^r, M - l^r) + \mu u^u(x_1^u, x_2^u, M - l^r) \tag{5.83}$$

subject to the physical production constraints that total consumptions of grain and cloth cannot exceed their outputs

$$x_1^r + x_1^u + g - f_1(l^r) = 0$$
$$x_2^r + x_2^u - f_2(l^u) = 0 \tag{5.84}$$

For the second problem, one can imagine that the government actually runs the production of grain and cloth and uses the outputs to satisfy the needs of the farmers and the workers in such a way as to maximize a weighted average (equation 5.83) of their utilities. The solution to the second problem gives a Pareto-optimal solution for the Chinese economy so modeled. The question is whether the same Pareto-optimal solution can be obtained indirectly by manipulating p_2, w, $\bar{y}_1$, and $\bar{x}_1$ instead of x_1^i, x_2^i, and l^i ($i = r,u$).

To answer this question, we first solve the second problem to yield its first-order conditions. If these first-order conditions can be achieved by using p_2, w, $\bar{y}_1$, and

$\bar{x}_1$, then a government policy that manipulates these instruments can yield a Pareto-optimal solution. To solve the second problem, we form a Lagrangian expression

$$L = u^r(x_1^r, x_2^r, M-l^r) + \mu u^u(x_1^u, x_2^u, M-l^u)$$
$$+ \lambda_1[f_1(l^r) - x_1^r - x_1^u - g] + \lambda_2[f_2(l^u) - x_2^r - x_2^u] \quad (5.85)$$

and set its derivatives with respect to x_1^i, x_2^i, l^i $(i = r, u)$, λ_1 and λ_2 equal to zero. Using a subscript k of u^r and u^u to denote its partial derivative with respect to the kth argument and a prime to denote derivative, we can write the result as

$$u_1^r - \lambda_1 = 0$$
$$u_2^r - \lambda_2 = 0$$
$$-u_3^r + \lambda_1 f_1'(l^r) = 0$$
$$\mu u_1^u - \lambda_1 = 0$$
$$\mu u_2^u - \lambda_2 = 0$$
$$-\mu u_3^u + \lambda_2 f_2'(l^u) = 0 \quad (5.86)$$

These first-order conditions imply

$$f_1'(l^r) = (u_3^r/\lambda_1) = u_3^r/u_1^r$$
$$(\lambda_2/\mu) = u_2^u = u_3^u/f_2'(l^u)$$
$$(\lambda_1/\lambda_2) = u_1^r/u_2^r = u_1^u/u_2^u \quad (5.87)$$

Now, instead of the government running the show by determining directly the variables x_1^i, x_2^i, and l^i $(i = r,u)$ to maximize equation 5.83, let the government set only p_2, w, $\bar{y}_1$, and $\bar{x}_1$, leaving it to the farmer and the urban worker to maximize their own utilities subject to their budget constraints. The solution of the farmer's maximization problem with constraint (equation 5.72), using the Lagrangian

$$L^r = u^r(x_1^r, x_2^r, M-l^r) + \lambda_1^*[f_1(l^r) - \bar{y}_1 - x_1^r - p_2 x_2^r] \quad (5.88)$$

yields the first-order conditions

$$u_1^r - \lambda_1^* = 0$$
$$u_2^r - \lambda_1^* p_2 = 0$$
$$-u_3^r + \lambda_1^* f_1'(l^r) = 0 \quad (5.89)$$

The solution of the worker's maximization problem with constraint (equation 5.76), using the Lagrangian

$$L^u = u^u(x_1^u, x_2^u, M-l^u) + \lambda_2^*(wl^u + \bar{x}_1 - x_1^u - p_2 x_2^u) \quad (5.90)$$

yields the first-order conditions

$$u_1^u - \lambda_2^* = 0$$
$$u_2^u - \lambda_2^* p_2 = 0$$
$$-u_3^u + \lambda_2^* w = 0 \quad (5.91)$$

The first and third conditions of equation 5.89 imply

$$f_1'(l^r) = (u_3^r/\lambda_1^*) = u_3^r/u_1^r$$

The second and third conditions of equation 5.91 imply

$$u_2^u = \lambda_2^* p_2 = \lambda_2^* w(p_2/w) = u_3^u(p_2/w)$$

The first two conditions of equation 5.89 and the first two conditions of equation 5.91 imply

$$u_1^r/u_2^r = p_2^{-1} = u_1^u/u_2^u$$

The last three conditions are identical with the three conditions of equation 5.87 if the government chooses $w = p_2 f_2'(l^u)$. Thus, by setting the urban wage w equal to the value $p_2 f_2'(l^u)$ of the marginal product of labor, the government can achieve a Pareto-optimal solution for the economy while leaving the farmers and the workers to maximize their own utilities.

It appears worthwhile to examine the Chinese data to find out whether wage equals the value of marginal product and, if not, what policy action can be taken to achieve a Pareto-optimal solution. In Section 4.1, I estimated a Cobb-Douglas production function using data on gross industrial output of state-owned enterprises. The function is

$$\log (Y/X_1) = 3.762 + .602 (X_2/X_1)$$

or

$$Y = 43.0344 \, X_1^{.398} \, X_2^{.602} \tag{5.92}$$

where Y stands for gross value of industrial output in 1970 yuan, X_1 is employment in millions of workers, and X_2 is original value of fixed assets in billion yuan, all of state-owned enterprises. To convert the gross output value in 1970 yuan into net value added in 1980 yuan, I used a factor of .34014, which is the ratio of the 1980 national income 169.8 billion contributed by industry to the 1980 gross industrial output value 499.2 billion in 1970 constant prices (*Statistical Yearbook of China, 1981,* pp. 17 and 20). Multiplying the coefficient 43.0344 in equation 5.92 by .34014 yields a production function

$$Y = 14.638 \, X_1^{.398} \, X_2^{.602} \tag{5.93}$$

for net value added in 1980 yuan in state-owned industrial enterprises. According to equation 5.93, the value of the marginal product of one worker in 1980 was

$$\frac{\partial Y}{\partial X_1} = 5.8259 \, (X_2/X_1)^{.602} = 5.8259 \, (11,492)^{.602} = 1621 \text{ yuan}$$

In 1980, the average annual wage of staff and workers in state-owned industrial enterprises was 854 yuan, only slightly over half of the value of the marginal product. Our analysis suggests that to achieve a Pareto optimum, the Chinese government should increase wage w relative to the price p_2 of industrial products.

To get a rough idea of the aggregate magnitudes involved in terms of the government budget constraint given in equation 5.80, let us interpret g as the value of government consumption minus government revenues from sources (mainly industrial and commercial turnover taxes) other than profits from state-owned enterprises. *Statistical Yearbook of China, 1981,* page 405, gives the following data on revenues and expenditures of the Chinese government in 1980 in billions of RMB.

Total revenue	108.5	Total expenditure	121.3
Enterprises profits, etc.	43.5	Capital construction	41.9
Taxes	57.2	Technical innovation	8.0
Debts and borrowing	4.3	Circulating funds added	3.7
Other revenues	3.5	Education, science	15.6
Deficit	12.8	National defense	19.4
		Administration	6.7
		Other expenditures	26.0

Lardy (1983, p. 37) quotes estimates of the government financial losses in the sales of food grain and edible vegetable oils at 6.8 billion RMB in 1979, 10.3 billion in 1980, and 12.9 billion in 1981, the increases being due to the increases in government procurement prices of farm products or a reduction in the agricultural tax $\bar{y}_1$ in the above model. We will consider g as including all government expenditure items other than food subsidy to the urban population, totaling $121.3 - 10.3 = 111.0$, minus all taxes and revenues other than enterprises' profits, totaling $108.5 - 43.5 = 65.0$. Thus g equals $111.0 - 65.0$, or 46.0 billion. Using the 10.3 billion figure for $\bar{x}_1 - \bar{y}_1$ and the government budget constraint (equation 5.80) revised to include deficits, we have

$$\pi + \text{Deficit} = (\bar{x}_1 - \bar{y}_1) + g$$
$$43.5 + 12.8 = 10.3 + 46.0$$

By increasing the wage rate, the Chinese government could reduce enterprise profits π and the urban food subsidy $\bar{x}_1 - \bar{y}_1$ simultaneously to achieve a Pareto optimum. The workers would have a higher wage but a smaller food subsidy. From the viewpoint of welfare economics, it is better for the government to spend a given amount of subsidy in the form of a wage increase than in the form of provision for a particular commodity such as food grains. Given the wage increase, an urban worker can decide whether to spend it on food grains or other items. Having the wage increase, the worker cannot be worse off than having the food subsidy because he can always spend the additional wage on food grains if he chooses. In 1980, according to Lardy (1983, p. 35), there were about 160 million persons in the nonagricultural population receiving food subsidies, of which about 135 million were urbanites and 25 million were residing in rural areas. In 1980, there were 104 million staff and workers (*Statistical Yearbook, 1981,* p. 105). To replace the food subsidy of 10.3 billion by a wage increase, the average increase would amount to 10,300/104 or 99 yuan per worker per year. This would be added to the actual annual wage of 762 yuan for all staff and workers. This increase would still not make wage equal to the value of marginal product but would be a step in the right direction.

The equality between wage w and the value of marginal product $p_2 f_2'(l^u)$ can be achieved by simultaneously adjusting w and p_2. How should p_2 be determined? To equate the nonfarm demand for grain with its net supply given by equation 5.74, we must have

$$x_1^u(p_2, w, \bar{x}_1) = y_1^n(p_2, \bar{y}_1)$$

If w is set equal to $p_2 f_2'(l^u)$, this equation becomes

$$x_1^u[p_2, p_2 f_2'(l^u), \bar{x}_1] = y_1^n(p_2, \bar{y}_1) \tag{5.94}$$

Given $\bar{x}_1$ and $\bar{y}_1$, this equation determines p_2. [It is true that l^u is itself a function of p_2, w, and $\bar{x}_1$ according to equation 5.77, but w can be eliminated from equation 5.94 again by $p_2 f_2'(l^u)$.] The value of p_2 that satisfies equation 5.94 is that value that equates the demand and supply of grain in a free market. This model determines the relative price of industrial goods p_2 to food grains (the price of the latter being set at 1 for convenience). To the extent that the prices of industrial goods in China are not set by markets, it is difficult for the Chinese government to achieve economic efficiency by introducing the responsibility system to Chinese industry. Under the new system, an inefficient industrial enterprise can be profitable if the prices of its products are set arbitrarily high or the prices of its inputs are set arbitrarily low. This point was stressed in Section 4.8, when we discussed reforms in Chinese industry.

An important point has been demonstrated in this section. The government can achieve its objective of maximizing a social welfare function, or mathematically maximizing the Lagrangian expression L of equation 5.85, without actually controlling the amounts of consumptions and labor supplies, or x_1^i, x_2^i, l^i ($i = r, u$) in our model. It can do so by simply manipulating certain policy instruments including w, p_2, $\bar{x}_1$, and $\bar{y}_1$ in our model, while leaving the farmers and workers to solve their own optimization problems. Furthermore, to achieve efficiency, the government should choose wage increase rather than subsidy on one particular good in order to help a group of consumers, should employ labor by setting wage equal to the value of marginal product (which an industrial enterprise under the responsibility system would do automatically to maximize profits), and should allow prices to be determined by the forces of demand and supply without which autonomy of industrial enterprises would not lead to economic efficiency.

5.7 DISTRIBUTION OF INCOME

One important subject concerning social welfare is the distribution of income. A frequency distribution of income shows the relative frequency, or percentage, of families or individuals in each income group. The *Statistical Yearbook of China, 1981* (p. 438), provides the data in the accompanying table on the distribution of income of urban industrial staff and workers, based on a sample survey of 1981.

	Total	Per Capita Monthly Income Group					
		Less than RMB-20	RMB 20–25	RMB 25–35	RMB 35–50	RMB 50–60	RMB 60+
Number of households	8,715	179	476	2,772	3,685	1,037	566
Percentage of total	100.00	2.05	5.46	31.81	42.29	11.90	6.49

The distribution shows that about 7.5 percent of industrial urban households had per capita income below 25 RMB per month, while about 6.5 percent had income of 60 RMB or more.

When the above distribution is plotted in Figure 5.5 (with the assumptions that the lowest income group had per capita income above 15 RMB and that the highest

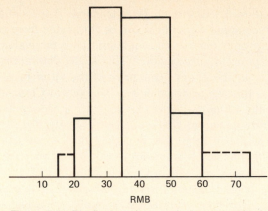

Figure 5.5 Distribution of per capita income of families of urban staff and workers in China.

per capita income per family was below 75 RMB), it is found to be not quite symmetrical and to have a longer tail on the right. The tail would be longer if the maximum
income were assumed to be over 75 RMB. Such a shape is found for the distributions
of income in many other countries. If, instead of measuring a family's per capita
income, we measure the (natural) logarithm of its per capita income, the distribution
of log income will no longer have such a long right tail. The distribution of log income
derived from the above data is shown in Figure 5.6. The longer tail is now on the left.
When the logarithm of income is distributed according to the normal distribution,
which is illustrated by Figure 4.2, the income variable itself is said to have a *lognormal
distribution.* The lognormal distribution turns out to be a reasonable approximation to
the distribution of income in many countries. The distribution of income of Chinese
industrial urban staff and workers is more nearly symmetrical than the lognormal
distribution.

The subject of income distribution has been studied extensively in economics.

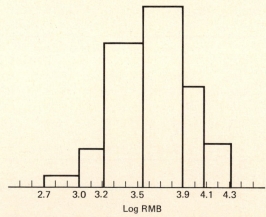
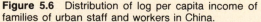

Figure 5.6 Distribution of log per capita income of
families of urban staff and workers in China.

There are different theories to explain it. There are different statistical distributions to approximate it. There are different ways to measure how unequal the incomes specified by a given distribution are. These topics are beyond the scope of this book. We have merely shown in this section the distribution of per capita income of urban families in China, and in Figure 3.1 we have shown the distribution of per capita gross agricultural output of different provinces in China. Some facts concerning the distribution of income in China are contained in Rawski (1982). It is hoped that students of the Chinese economy will pursue these topics in the future.

PROBLEMS

1. Using the time-series data in Table 5.3 for the years 1978 to 1981, estimate the regression equation of per capita consumption for each of the four categories on per capita total consumption expenditure. Compare the elasticities of these equations with the corresponding elasticities in equations 5.2 to 5.5.

2. Let Y_i, X_i, and N_i be respectively the expenditure on a certain commodity, total consumption expenditure, and the size of the ith family in a sample. Assume the relation

$$\log Y_i = \alpha + \beta \log X_i + \gamma \log N_i + \epsilon_i$$

Let y_i be per capita expenditure on the same commodity and x_i be per capita total consumption expenditure. How is the assumption

$$\log y_i = \alpha + \beta \log x_i + \epsilon_i$$

related to the first assumption? Which assumption do you prefer, and why?

3. Let the utility function be $u^* = \log x_1 + \log x_2$. Using the method of Lagrange multipliers, maximize u^* subject to the budget constraint

$$I - p_1 x_1 - p_2 x_2 = 0$$

and derive the demand functions for x_1 and x_2.

4. Derive equation 5.50 for comparing the effects of a change in the price p_j on the demand for x_i in a free market and under straight rationing with $x_n = q_n$.

5. Assume the utility function to be

$$u(x_1, x_2) = \beta_1 \log(x_1 - \gamma_1) + \beta_2 \log(x_2 - \gamma_2) \qquad \begin{array}{l} x_1 > \gamma_1 \; ; x_2 > \gamma_2 \\ \beta_1 + \beta_2 = 1 \end{array}$$

which is used by Klein and Rubin (1947–1948). Derive the demand functions for x_1 and x_2. Also derive the expenditures $p_1 x_1$ and $p_2 x_2$ as functions of income I.

6. Assume a quadratic utility function as given by equation 5.57, with only two commodities. Derive the demand functions for x_1 and x_2 subject only to the income constraint. Also derive the expenditures $p_1 x_1$ and $p_2 x_2$ as functions of income I.

7. Assume a quadratic utility function as given by equation 5.57, with only two commodities. Let x_1 be the quantity of rice (in kilograms) and x_2 be the quantity of cloth (in meters). Assign some reasonable numerical values for the constants $a_{ij} = a_{ji}$ and a_i ($i, j = 1, 2$) in the utility function. Check the reasonableness of these values by examining the demand functions for x_1 and x_2. If the values are unreasonable, revise them until they become reasonable as viewed from the implied demand functions.

8. In comparing the effects of rationing and of an alternative spendings tax on the demand for leisure, Tobin (1952) assumes a quadratic utility function (equation 5.57). How should his

analysis be modified if a general utility function $u(x_1,x_2,x_3)$ is assumed instead? Answer this question by revising equations 5.59 to 5.65 using the more general utility function. Why and to what extent does Tobin's conclusion (equation 5.68) depend on the assumption of a quadratic utility function?

9. Using an Edgeworth diagram (as shown in Figure 1.1) and assuming that both commodities rice and cloth are rationed, explain how the trading of ration coupons for rice and cloth can improve the welfare of both consumers. Explain why the solution before and after the trade is or is not Pareto optimal.

10. Assume some reasonable numerical values for the constants $a_{ij} = a_{ji}$ and a_i ($i = 1,2,3$) in the utility function (equation 5.57), and solve equations 5.60 and 5.61 to obtain the demand functions for x_{3r} and x_{3s}, respectively. (The demand for x_{3r} is a function of p_1, p_2, p_3, M, Y, and q_1.) Assume some numerical values for p_1, p_2, p_3, M, Y, and q_1 and find x_{3r} and x_{3s}, under the assumption that rationing is effective.

11. Assume a demand function with constant elasticities β_1, β_2, and β_3—that is,

$$\log x_i = \alpha + \beta_1 \log I + \beta_2 \log p_i + \beta_3 \log p_j$$

—where x_i is demand for the ith commodity, p_i is its price, I is income, and p_j is the price of the jth commodity. Let $\beta_1 = .70$, $\beta_2 = -.60$, and $\beta_3 = .40$. From a base year 1938, let income be increased by 10 percent, p_i be increased by 5 percent, and p_j be increased by 5 percent. Estimate the demand for x_i relative to the 1938 demand. What are the important assumptions underlying this method of estimation? What modifications, if any, would you introduce if the method were applied to estimate the demand for derationed foodstuffs in China (see Houthakker and Tobin, 1982)?

12. If utility is ordinal, as pointed out at the end of Section 5.3, explain how one can assume a quadratic utility function (equation 5.57) that gives a numerical value (and not just an order) for the utility of a bundle of commodities.

13. Try to make a convincing argument against allowing consumers to trade ration coupons. Discuss the advantages and disadvantages of such trading.

14. Referring to Houthakker (1957), explain how the expenditure elasticities of demand for food in Table 5.4 are adjusted.

15. The source note of Table 5.1 mentions that the estimate of 548.27 million population in rural agricultural cooperatives in China in 1957 differs from the estimate of 518.59 million given in column 3 of Table 3.7. Each of these estimates is consistent with other official figures used in its own table and in its own context. Which estimate would you choose and why? Can you find one estimate that is reasonable in both contexts?

REFERENCES

Bradford, D. 1983. A simple model of urban-rural income redistribution in China. Mimeographed. Princeton, N.J.: Princeton University Press.

Chinese State Statistics Bureau. 1982. *Statistical yearbook of China, 1981.* Hong Kong: Hong Kong Economic Review Publishing House.

Chow, G. C. 1957. *Demand for automobiles in the United States: A study in consumer durables.* Amsterdam: North-Holland Publishing Company.

Economic Research Center, State Council of the People's Republic of China. 1982. *Almanac of China's economy, 1981.* Hong Kong: Modern Cultural Company Limited.

Fan Jin, Li Wuwei, and Zuo Xuejin. 1980. Zhurou de shichang xugou yuce ["Forecasting the market demand for port"]. *Shehui kexue* [*Social Science*], 64–67.

Henderson, J., and R. E. Quandt. 1980. *Microeconomic theory: A mathematical approach.* New York: McGraw-Hill.

Hicks, J. R. 1946. *Value and capital.* 2d ed. London: Oxford University Press.

Houthakker, H. S. 1957. An international comparison of household expenditure patterns, commemorating the centenary of Engel's Law. *Econometrica* 25:532–551.

Houthakker, H. S., and J. Tobin. 1952. Estimates of the free demand for rationed foodstuffs. *The Economic Journal* 62:103–118.

Klein, L. R., and H. Rubin. 1947–1948. A constant-utility index of the cost of living. *Review of Economic Studies* 15:84–87.

Lardy, N. R. 1983. Agricultural prices in China. Working paper no. 606. Washington, D.C.: The World Bank.

Ma Hong and Sun Shangqing, eds. 1982. *Zhongquo jingji jegou wenti yanjou* [*Studies of the problems of China's economic structure*). 2 vols. Beijing: People's Publishing Society.

Podkaminer, L. 1982. Estimates of the disequilibria in Poland's consumer markets, 1965–1978. *Review of Economics and Statistics* 64:423–431.

Rawski, T. G. 1979. *Economic growth and employment in China.* New York: Oxford University Press.

———. 1982. The simple arithmetic of Chinese income distribution. *Keizai Kenkyu* 33:12–26.

Samuelson, Paul A. 1948. *Foundations of economic analysis.* Cambridge, Mass.: Harvard University Press.

Slutsky, E. E. 1915. On the theory of the budget of the consumer. *Giornale degli Economisti* 51:1–26. Also reprinted in American Economic Association, *Readings in Price Theory.* Homewood, Ill.: Irwin, 1952. Pp. 27–56.

Tobin, J. 1952. A survey of the theory of rationing. *Econometrica* 20:521–553.

Tobin, J., and H. S. Houthakker. 1951. The effects of rationing on demand elasticities. *Review of Economic Studies* 18:140–153.

Yang Janming. 1982. Renmin shenghuo xiaofei jiegou [Structure of people's consumption], Chapter 18 of *Zhongquo jingji jegou wenti yanjou* [Studies of the problems of China's economic structure], Vol. 2, Ma Hong and Sun Xianqing, eds. Beijing: People's Publishing Society. Pp. 543–561.

chapter 6

National Income and Capital Formation

6.1 ESTIMATION OF CHINA'S NATIONAL INCOME

Perhaps no other topic has received as much attention from foreign scholars of the Chinese economy in the last three decades as the estimation of China's national income. Only since 1980 has the State Statistics Bureau of the Chinese government published its own estimates of Chinese national income, in the *Almanac of China's Economy, 1981* (Economic Research Center, 1982), and the *Statistical Yearbook of China, 1981* (Chinese State Statistics Bureau, 1982); we summarized these estimates in Table 3.3. Scholars are still digesting and evaluating these official figures. Previously, many attempts had been made to estimate China's national income and its major components. Some of these attempts are discussed in Alexander Eckstein, ed. (1980). A survey chapter by Dwight Perkins in the Eckstein volume (1980, p. 248) compares the estimates of China's gross domestic product (GDP) made by Liu and Yeh (1973), Eckstein (1973), Perkins (1975), Swamy (1973), Hidasi (1971), and Field (1980). For the period 1952–1970, these authors estimate the average annual growth rate of GDP (net domestic product in the case of Swamy and national income in the case of Hidasi) to be 4.1, 4.5, 5.8, 2.6, 6.0, and 5.6 percent, respectively.

Perkins (1980) points out that estimates of China's national product are obtained by various authors essentially by combining the outputs of the agricultural, industrial, and the services sectors, and that the sources of the differences among the various estimates of GDP are (1) differences in the underlying indexes of industrial or agricultural product or both, (2) differences in the assumptions made about the services sector, and (3) differences in the (price) weights used to combine the three sectors. We will have more to say on this point later in this section.

Now that the official figures from the State Statistical Bureau are available, it will be of interest to compare them with the estimates provided by foreign scholars. Chinese official national income figures include only material output and exclude many service items (see p. 91). Futhermore, the details provided are much less than those found for the national income of the United States as provided by the U.S. Department of Commerce in its monthly *Survey of Current Business* (see especially the July issues and the survey's *Supplements on the National Income and Product Accounts*).

Column 1 of Table 6.1 provides the State Statistical Bureau's estimates of Chinese national income in billions of current yuan. For the years covered in Table 3.3 the national income figures in Table 6.1 are identical. For all other years I have accumulated the increments in national income provided by Zhang (1981, p. 727), beginning with the 1957 figure of 90.8 and going forward and backward. (The increment of 12.0 billion for 1953 provided by Zhang appears to be too large and is not used in our calculations backward from 1957 to 1953, leaving intact the figure 58.9 billion for 1952. The results of these calculations agree with the figures given in column 1 of Table 3.3. It is curious why the subtotals of national income for different Five-Year Plan periods given on p., 737 of Zhang do not agree with the corresponding subtotals of column 1, Table 6.1, whether we use 90.8 or 93.5—see column 1 of Table 3.4—for the national income figure in 1957 to start the accumulations.) To estimate the average rate of growth of national income in constant 1952 yuan from 1952 to 1970, we make the assumption that prices are constant from 1965 to 1970, an assumption supported by the price indices given on pages 411–412 of the *Statistical Yearbook of China, 1981.* National income in 1952 yuan for 1965 was given in Table 3.3 as 116.3 billion. National income in 1952 yuan for 1970 is estimated to be 116.3 times (192.6/138.7) the ratio of national incomes in 1970 and 1965 given in Table 6.1, yielding 161.5. The increase from 58.9 in 1952 to 161.5 in 1970 implies an exponential rate of growth of

Table 6.1 NATIONAL INCOME AND CAPITAL ACCUMULATION
(Billion Yuan)

Year	National income	Accumulation	Year	National income	Accumulation
1952	58.9	13.0	1967	148.7	30.4
1953	67.5	16.8	1968	141.5	29.8
1954	71.4	19.5	1969	161.7	35.7
1955	75.4	18.5	1970	192.6	61.8
1956	84.8	21.7	1971	208.2	68.4
1957	90.8	23.3	1972	214.0	64.8
1958	111.8	37.9	1973	232.6	74.1
1959	122.2	55.8	1974	235.1	74.1
1960	122.0	50.1	1975	250.5	83.0
1961	99.6	19.5	1976	243.5	75.6
1962	92.4	9.9	1977	265.9	83.2
1963	100.0	18.3	1978	301.0	108.7
1964	116.6	26.3	1979	335.0	116.1
1965	138.7	36.5	1980	366.7	116.5
1966	158.6	47.0	1981	388.7	109.0

Sources: Column 1 is from Table 3.3 and Zhang, 1981, p. 727. Column 2 is from Table 3.4 and Zhang, 1981, p. 727. Note that according to official data provided in Table 3.4, the sum of capital accumulation and consumption equals "national income available," which is slightly different from "national income," as explained in the note to Table 3.4.

.0560, or an annual rate of growth of 5.76 percent. This rate of growth can be compared with the estimates by the scholars mentioned in the first paragraph of this section.

As Perkins (1980) points out, the use of different price weights can make a difference in the estimates of the rate of growth. To explore this point, let us construct estimates of Chinese national income in 1980 yuan for 1952 and compare its rate of growth with that of national income in 1952 yuan. National income in 1952 yuan was given in column 3 of Table 3.3. It increased from 58.9 billion in 1952 to 300.4 billion in 1980, implying an exponential rate of growth of .0582 or an annual rate of growth of 5.99 percent.

Let us first break down the 300.4 billion of 1952 yuan in 1980 into contributions from the industrial sector and the other sectors, including agriculture, construction, transport, and commerce. We need to use only two sectors to demonstrate the fairly obvious point that the weights assigned to the two sectors in constructing a national income series can make a difference if the rates of growth of these two sectors are different. National income in billions of current yuan in 1980 is 366.7, which consists of 169.8 from industry and 196.9 from all other sectors (see Table 3.5). What would the incomes from these two sectors be in 1952 prices? We have to deflate 169.8 and 196.9 by their price indices, with 1952 = 100. The sum of the two deflated figures should be 300.4 billion. One wishes that the State Statistical Bureau had provided the breakdown of its estimate of national income in 1952 prices into its contributing sectors. Such data not being available, we must choose two price indices to deflate the incomes 169.8 and 196.9 from industry and the other sectors.

For industry let us choose .769162 as the price index for 1980, with 1952 = 100. This figure is the ratio of the gross industrial output value 517.8 for 1981 in 1980 prices to the gross industrial output value 673.2 for 1981 in 1952 prices, both figures being given in Table 3.6. Dividing 169.8 by .769162 yields 220.8 (billion 1952 yuan) for income for industry. According to pages 411–412 of the *Statistical Yearbook of China, 1981*, the general ex-factory price index of industrial products in 1980 equals 83.4/113.2, or .736749. If we were to use this latter figure instead, income from the industrial sector would be larger—169.8/.736749, or 230.5—and more difficult to reconcile with the total income of 300.4. If we accept 220.8 of the total of 300.4 as being contributed by industry, the remainder, 79.6, must be from all the other sectors. The income in current yuan from all other sectors in 1980 is 196.9, implying a price index for these sectors of 196.9/79.6, or 2.47362. This index is not unreasonable compared with the general purchasing price index of farm and sideline products given on pages 411–412 of the *Statistical Yearbook of China, 1981*, which is 284.4/121.6, or 2.33882. We will use the price indices .769162 and 2.47362 for industry and the remaining sectors in 1980 for illustrative purposes, hoping that official deflators will become available in the future. Using 1952 prices, then, national income increases from 58.9 in 1952, with 11.5 from industry and 47.4 from the remaining sectors (see Table 3.5), to 300.4, with 220.8 from industry and 79.6 from the remaining sectors. The exponential rate of growth for the remaining sectors is .01851, a bit lower than the ratio .02395 for grain output, which increased from 163.92 million metric tons in 1952 to 320.56 million in 1980 (*Statistical Yearbook of China, 1981*, p. 145). Such a slow growth rate is combined with a much higher rate for industry to yield an exponential growth rate of .0582 for national income in 1952 prices.

Using 1980 prices, national income equals 366.7 billion in 1980, with 169.8 from industry and 196.9 from the remaining sectors (see Table 3.5). We can evaluate the industrial and other income of 11.5 and 47.4 in 1952 at 1980 prices by the indices .769162 and 2.47362 respectively, yielding 8.8 and 117.2, or a total national income of 126.0 billion 1980 yuan. An increase from 126.0 in 1952 to 366.7 in 1980 implies an exponential growth rate of .03815 or an annual rate of growth of 3.89 percent. This compares with an annual growth rate of 5.99 percent for the same period using 1952 prices instead of 1980 prices. The same point has been made by Perkins (1981, pp. 3–5), who, using industry, agriculture, and others as three sectors contributing to national income, has computed an annual growth rate from 1952 to 1978 of 6.0 percent using 1952 prices and of 4.8 percent using 1978 prices.

The reason for the difference between the growth rates of 5.99 and 3.89 as computed by the two sets of prices used in our illustrative calculation is simple. Both the national income in 1952 prices and the national income in 1980 prices are weighted averages of the same two time series, net income from industry and net income from other sectors. Income from industry increases from 11.5 billion 1952 yuan in 1952 to 220.8 billion 1952 yuan in 1980, or at an exponential rate of .10553 or an annual rate of 11.13 percent. Income from the other sectors increases from 47.4 billion 1952 yuan in 1952 to 79.6 billion in 1980, or at an exponential rate of .01851 or an annual rate of 1.869 percent. Giving a higher weight to the industry series, as is done by using 1952 prices, will produce a higher rate of growth in national income. Note that when 1980 prices are used, income from industry in 1952 equals 8.8 billion yuan and income from the other sectors equals 117.2 billion yuan. Industrial income in 1952 is only 8.8/126.0 or 7.0 percent of total income in 1980 prices, as compared with 11.5/58.9 or 19.5 percent of total income in 1952 prices.

To appreciate the 5.99 percent annual rate of growth in national income in 1952 prices from 1952 to 1980, imagine a hypothetical economy producing only bicycles (from the industrial sector) and grain (from the agricultural sector). In 1952 one bicycle was produced with value added equal to 115 yuan, and 9480 kilograms of grain were produced with unit price of .05 yuan per kilogram or valued at 474 yuan, given a total income of 589 yuan. In 1980 bicycle production increases to 19.2 units, giving a total value added of 2208 yuan at 115 yuan per unit. Grain production increases to 15,920 kilograms, giving a total value of 796 yuan at .05 yuan per kilogram. Total income in 1980 equals 3004 yuan, implying an average annual rate of growth of 5.99 percent from 1952. (According to Table 4.5, the production of bicycles increases from 80,000 in 1952 to 13,024,000 in 1980.) If we change the price of grain from .05 yuan to .1608 yuan per kilogram, grain output would be 1524 yuan in 1952 and 2560 yuan in 1980. National income would be 1639 yuan in 1952 and 4768 in 1980, implying an exponential rate of growth of .03814 or an annual rate of growth of 3.89 percent.

Should 1952 prices or 1980 prices be used to evaluate Chinese national income? Ideally, prices as determined by competitive markets should be used to evaluate different outputs, as we pointed out in Section 1.6. In a competitive market economy, prices reflect the rates of substitution among different products both in consumption and in production, as seen from the tangency of the consumer indifference curve and the production transformation curve in Figure 1.6. Note that if competitive market prices exist, one can still choose to use the prices of either 1952 or 1980 because the relative prices may have changed from 1952 to 1980. In an economy where many prices are not determined by market forces, it is difficult to find appropriate prices to weigh the different products to form an estimate of national income for the purpose of measuring the rate of growth. In the case of China, it is fair to say that the 1952 prices assign values to industrial products that are too high relative to the values of agricultural products because the scarcity of industrial products in 1952 was partly the result of many years of war and because the high prices of industrial products were partly a result of deliberate government policy. In any case, as a country is industrialized, industrial products become easier to produce relative to other products, and their relative prices should be lower. Using the prices in the year 1980 would better reflect the rates of substitution in production in the later, more industrialized period. It is questionable, however, whether the ratio between industrial and other prices in 1952 should be divided by a factor as high as 2.47362/.769162, or 3.2160, as is done in our hypothetical calculation above. The 1980 price indices of .769162 and 2.47362 for the industrial and other sectors, with 1952 = 100, were derived from official data as explained above; they are consistent with the official figure of 300.4 billion 1952 yuan for national income in 1980. It would be desirable to have the official price indices used to deflate the contributions to national income from the different sectors shown in Table 3.5.

6.2   A SIMPLE MODEL OF NATIONAL INCOME GROWTH

If economists were asked to give a single explanation for the growth of national income in any economy, the answer would be capital formation. If a part of income or output in the current year is devoted to augmenting the capital stock, the economy's productive capacity will be increased, thus increasing national income in the future. How fast national income or output will increase depends on two factors. First, how much of current income is devoted to accumulation or capital investment? Second, how much additional output can be produced per unit of capital accumulated? The first is the savings (or investment) ratio. The second is the output–capital ratio. Given the output–capital ratio, the higher the savings ratio, the higher will be the rate of growth of national output. Given the savings ratio, the higher the output–capital ratio, the higher will be the rate of growth of national output.

The above ideas can be formulated in a *mathematical model* of economic growth. A mathematical model in economics is a set of mathematical relations describing the working of an economy. Different models are used to answer different questions. To get a crude picture, a simple model consisting of a small number of equations is used. To answer more complicated and more detailed questions, a more complicated model consisting of many equations is used. Given the same set of questions to be answered, the simpler the model the better. Given the same economic phenomena to be explained, one would prefer to use fewer equations if they can explain the phenomena as well as a model using more equations. Simplicity is a desirable characteristic of any scientific theory, and a mathematical model is a theory in mathematical form.

To explain the average rate of growth of national income, one can use the model of Harrod (1948) and Domar (1957). The Harrod-Domar model incorporates the savings ratio and the output–capital ratio in explaining the rate of growth of national income. Let y_t be national income in year t, k_t be capital stock at the end of year

t, and j_t be net investment during year t. All variables are measured in constant dollars or yuan. First, we have the *identity* or definitional relation

$$j_t = k_t - k_{t-1} = \Delta k_t \tag{6.1}$$

where Δk_t denotes the first difference in k_t, or $k_t - k_{t-1}$. Equation 6.1 states that net investment in year t equals the change in capital stock during the year. Second, assume that output is a fraction θ of capital

$$y_t = \theta k_t \tag{6.2}$$

where θ is the output–capital ratio, or θ^{-1} is the capital–output ratio. Third, investment is assumed to be a fraction σ of income

$$j_t = \sigma y_t \tag{6.3}$$

where σ is the savings ratio, with savings and investment both equal to income minus consumption. Equations 6.1, 6.2, and 6.3 are a system of three equations to determine the three unknowns j_t, k_t, and y_t through time.

Let the initial capital stock k_{t-1} at the beginning of period t (or the end of period $t-1$) be given. Equation 6.1 gives

$$k_t = j_t + k_{t-1} \tag{6.4}$$

while equations 6.2 and 6.3 imply

$$j_t = \sigma y_t = \sigma \theta k_t \tag{6.5}$$

Substituting $\sigma \theta k_t$ for j_t in equation 6.4 yields

$$k_t = \sigma \theta k_t + k_{t-1}$$

or

$$k_t = (1-\sigma\theta)^{-1} k_{t-1} = a k_{t-1} \tag{6.6}$$

where $a = (1-\sigma\theta)^{-1} > 1$, provided $0 < \sigma < 1$ and $0 < \theta < 1$. According to equation 6.6, capital k_t at the end of year t equals a constant $a = (1-\sigma\theta)^{-1}$ times the capital stock k_{t-1} at the end of year $t-1$. The constant a is larger than 1; it increases as the output-capital ratio θ increases, and as the savings ratio σ increases. Since, by equation 6.2, $k_t = \theta^{-1} y_t$ and $k_{t-1} = \theta^{-1} y_{t-1}$, substituting for k_t and k_{t-1} in equation 6.6 and multiplying through by θ yields

$$y_t = (1-\sigma\theta)^{-1} y_{t-1} = a y_{t-1} \tag{6.7}$$

Thus, income y_t in period t equals a constant $a = (1-\sigma\theta)^{-1}$ times income y_{t-1} in period $t-1$, the constant increasing with the output–capital ratio θ and the savings ratio σ. The growth of national income is thus explained by equation 6.7. Since net investment j_t is a fraction of income y_t according to equation 6.3, substitution of equation 6.3 into equation 6.7 will yield

$$j_t = (1-\sigma\theta)^{-1} j_{t-1} = a j_{t-1} \tag{6.8}$$

The model consisting of equations 6.1 to 6.3, or equations 6.6 to 6.8, is a *dynamic model*. A dynamic model explains the evolution of a set of economic variables through time. It is a dynamic model in *discrete time* because the time subscript for the variables takes only discrete values, or is an integer. If the time subscript is continuous, we have a dynamic model in *continuous time.* Equations 6.1 and 6.7 are examples of *different equations* because the first differences Δk_t and Δy_t are involved; equation 6.7 could be written as

$$\Delta y_t = y_t - y_{t-1} = (a-1)y_{t-1} \tag{6.9}$$

A dynamic model in discrete time can be represented by a system of difference equations, as in the case of equations 6.6, 6.7, and 6.8. A dynamic model in continuous time is often represented by a system of differential equations. The original Harrod-Domar model is in continuous time, with equation 6.1 replaced by the differential equation

$$\frac{dk}{dt} = j \tag{6.10}$$

We have converted the model to discrete time to simplify exposition.

By a *solution* to a system of difference equations, or a system of differential equations, is meant the expression of each variable as a function of time that is consistent with the original system of difference or differential equations. Difference equations can be solved numerically by solving a system of algebraic equations involving all variables at time t, treating their values at $t-1$ and all past periods as given. For example, the difference equation 6.7 or 6.9 can be solved numerically for y_t once the value of y_{t-1} is treated as given. Let the initial value y_0 of the variable y at time zero be given. Equation 6.7 implies, by repeated substitutions backward in time,

$$y_t = ay_{t-1} = a(ay_{t-2}) = a^2 y_{t-2} = \ldots = a^t y_0 \tag{6.11}$$

Thus, $y_t = a^t y_0$ is a *solution* of the difference equation 6.7 for it expresses y_t as a function of time t. Given $a > 1$, the variable y_t increases through time at an annual rate of $a-1$, where $a = (1-\sigma\theta)^{-1}$.

To apply the discrete version of the Harrod-Domar model to explain the growth of national income in China, let us first choose a rate of growth to be explained. Our analysis in Section 6.1 suggests that the annual rate of growth probably falls between 3.9 percent and 6.0 percent, depending on whether 1980 prices or 1952 prices are used. Let us try to explain a rate of growth of 4.5 percent, so that $a = 1.045$. Historically, capital accumulation has averaged about .30 of national income, as seen by comparing column 2 and column 1 of Table 6.1. Capital accumulation here refers to net capital investment j_t after the deduction of depreciation, as indicated by the definition of national income quoted in Section 3.4 from p. 509 of the *Statistical Yearbook of China, 1981.* Thus, the savings ratio is $\sigma = .30$. From the assumptions $a = 1.045$ and $\sigma = .30$, we can determine the value of the parameter θ using the definition

$$a = (1-\sigma\theta)^{-1} = 1.045$$
$$\sigma\theta = 1 - a^{-1} = .043062 \tag{6.12}$$

For $\sigma = .30$ the output–capital ratio θ is .1435. Thus, while China has invested .30 of its national income annually on the average, the increase in annual output per dollar increase in capital stock is only 14 cents on the average. Capital is thus not very productive. If we assume the rate of growth of national income to be .06 instead of .045, we have $a = 1.060$ and $\sigma\theta = 1 - a^{-1} = .056604$. Given $\sigma = .30$, we get $\theta = .1887$, a somewhat higher but still small ratio of output to capital stock.

The essence of the above calculations is not difficult to see. We have observed a moderate rate of growth of national income in China, somewhere around 4.5 percent per year, together with a very high ratio of investment to national income of 30 percent. The conclusion must be that the capital invested has not been very productive, yielding only 14 cents of future income per dollar invested. If we assume the observed rate of growth of national income to be higher at 6.0 percent per year, the capital stock will have to be more productive, yielding about 19 cents of future income per dollar invested. The output–capital ratios of .14 and .19 imply capital–output ratios of 7.14 and 5.26, respectively. In other words, to produce one yuan of output, 7.14 yuan and 5.26 yuan of capital, respectively, are required. These estimates of the capital–output ratios are high. For the United States, for example, Simon Kuznets (1961, p. 80) estimates the ratio of net capital stock to net national product in 1929 prices to be 3.6 for the decade of 1869–1878, 3.0 for 1879–1888, 3.6 for 1889–1898, 3.5 for 1899–1908, 3.9 for 1909–1918, 3.8 for 1919–1928, 4.4 for 1929–1938, 3.3 for 1939–1948, and 3.0 for 1946–1955, with the highest ratio 4.4 for the decade 1929–1938, covering the Great Depression and the recession of 1938. A capital–output ratio of 7.14 does not mean that 1 yuan of output can be produced by using 7.14 yuan of capital alone; it means that 1 yuan of output requires the use of 7.14 yuan of capital stock together with the services of labor and other inputs.

The high capital–output ratio for China inferred from the high savings ratio of .30 and a moderate rate of annual growth of national income of between 4.5 and 6.0 means that the capital accumulated in China is not very productive; it requires more capital, together with other inputs, to produce one unit of output than in the United States. One interpretation is that capital invested in the Chinese economy has not been productive; a large quantity of capital recorded in the national income statistics can help raise future output only by a small amount. One way to measure the productivity of capital directly is to divide the increase in national income in constant prices by the associated increase in capital stock in constant prices. This calculation should not be done for a very short period such as one year because the change in national income in a short time may result from many factors other than capital accumulation and because it may take some time for output to change after the capital investment takes place. These measurement problems become less serious when a long period is used to measure the increase in output associated with the observed increase in capital stock. Table 6.1 presents data on national income and capital accumulation, but these data are in current prices, whereas we need data in constant prices. Since we do not have accurate price indices to deflate the income and capital investment data in Table 6.1, we can only perform a calculation of the capital–output ratio using the undeflated data for illustrative purposes. From 1952 to 1981, national income increases from 58.9 billion to 388.7 billion, or by 329.8 billion. In the years from 1952 to 1980, total capital accumulation (unfortunately measured in different prices for different years) amounts to 1436.3 billion. Based on the hypothesis of the Harrod-Domar model given in equation 6.2, the capital–output ratio is 1436.3/329.8, or 4.36. This ratio is lower than the ratios 7.14 and 5.26 estimated earlier from the annual rates of growth in national income of 4.5 and 6.0 percent respectively, because the growth in national income in current prices (column 1 of Table 6.1) from 1952 to 1981 is at an exponential rate of .065 or an annual rate of 6.72 percent, higher than the rate in constant prices.

It is of interest to present the Harrod-Domar model in continuous time by replacing equation 6.1 with equation 6.10. Substituting equations 6.3 and 6.2 into equation 6.10, we obtain the differential equation

$$\frac{dk}{dt} = \sigma\theta k \tag{6.13}$$

where the capital stock k is a function of time t. Solving the differential equation 6.13 yields

$$k = C(\sigma\theta)^{-1} e^{\sigma\theta t} \tag{6.14}$$

The derivative of equation 6.14 equals $\sigma\theta k$, as required by equation 6.13. The constant C can be determined if the initial capital stock k_0 at time zero is known. Given k_0 at $t = 0$ (equation 6.14) implies

$$k_0 = C(\sigma\theta)^{-1} \quad \text{or} \quad C = k_0(\sigma\theta)$$

Substituting for C in equation 6.14 gives

$$k = k_0 e^{\sigma\theta t} \tag{6.15}$$

This solution states that, beginning at time zero with $k = k_0$, the capital stock grows at an exponential rate of $\sigma\theta$. Using equations 6.15 and 6.2, we have

$$y = \theta k = \theta k_0 e^{\sigma\theta t} = y_0 e^{\sigma\theta t} \tag{6.16}$$

where the last equality sign has utilized $y_0 = \theta k_0$. Thus, national income y also grows at an exponential rate of $\sigma\theta$.

To perform an illustrative calculation using equation 6.16, assume that the annual rate of growth of national income in China from 1952 to 1980 is 4.5 percent, which is equivalent to an exponential rate of .0440. Given $\sigma\theta = .044$, a savings ratio σ of .30 implies $\theta = .1467$. Contrast the value $\sigma\theta = .0440$ in this continuous-time model with $\sigma\theta = .0431$ given by equation 6.12 for the discrete-time model. The small difference between these two values is due to the fact that in the present model national income and capital stock change continuously in time, whereas in the previous model these variables are assumed to take only one value each year.

6.3 A MULTIPLIER–ACCELERATOR MODEL OF INCOME DETERMINATION

The Harrod-Domar model is a very simple model for explaining economic growth through capital accumulation, but it does not explain the fluctuations of national income and capital investment. The data in Table 6.1 reveal that national income and capital investment in China have been subject to fluctuations since 1952. Observers would agree that these fluctuations are largely the result of government policies. For example, the decline in national income from 1960 to 1962 can be explained by the failure of the Great Leap Forward. The rapid recovery from 1963 to 1966 can be attributed to the government policies of allowing the farmers more freedom and setting more reasonable targets for industrial production during this period of adjustment. The decline in national income in 1967 and 1968 may be due to the disruptions of the Cultural Revolution. The economic recovery from 1977 to 1981 may be attributed to the government policy of reducing the centralized control of economic activities, discussed in Chapters 2, 3, and 4. Thus to explain economic fluctuations in China from 1952 to 1981, one has to incorporate the effects on the economy of changes in government policy.

After the economic reforms described in Chapters 2, 3, and 4, it is possible that in the future political forces will assert a less disruptive influence on the Chinese economy. Government economic policies may be less subject to abrupt changes. At the same time, the decentralized decisions of farmers and enterprise managers may have a larger influence on economic activities in China. Under these circumstances, future economic fluctuations in China will have to be explained by a combination of government policy and the behavior of the sector where market forces assert an important role. Let us now examine a dynamic model combining government policy and market forces that may explain certain elements of Chinese economic fluctuations and growth in the future. We will begin by presenting some building blocks for such a model in the form of equations explaining the behavior of Chinese consumers and enterprise managers who are given some autonomy in investment decisions. The economic effects of government investment will be incorporated.

First, consider the relation between aggregate consumption and national income, such a relation being called a *consumption function*. Observe that equation 6.3 would imply a relationship between aggregate consumption and income if consumption is defined as income minus investment, or $c = y - j$. Substituting equation 6.3 for j, we have the consumption function

$$c_t = y_t - j_t = y_t - \sigma y_t = \gamma y_t \qquad (6.17)$$

where we have defined $\gamma = (1-\sigma)$. Equation 6.17 states that aggregate consumption equals a fraction γ of national income. Let us consider the justification of this consumption function in the contexts of a market economy and a centrally planned economy. In a market economy where national income equals the sum of incomes of all private citizens, and where a fraction τ of national income is taxed by the government, the hypothesis (equation 6.17) states that private consumers as a group choose to consume a fraction β of their after-tax income $(1-\tau)y$ or, equivalently, a smaller fraction $\gamma = \beta(1-\tau)$ of national income y. In a centrally planned economy where the economic planning authority chooses the total amount of consumption goods available for consumption, the hypothesis (equation 6.17) states that the planning authority decides to devote a fraction γ of national income for consumption.

A constant ratio between consumption and income, hypothesized in equation 6.17, may be a reasonable approximation to the relation between average consumption and average income over long periods, but it is not a good approximation to the relation between annual consumption and annual income. In both market economies and centrally planned economies, national income y_t tends to fluctuate from year to year rather than grow smoothly, whereas consumption c_t tends to fluctuate less than income. Thus, when national income y_t is above its smoothed trend, consumption c_t tends to be a smaller fraction of y_t; when y_t is below its trend, c_t tends to be a larger fraction of y_t. Such tendencies have been observed by Milton Friedman (1957) in his study of the consumption function. In the United States, for example, the ratio between consumption and after-tax income has remained approximately constant at about .90 since the late 1890s. Thus, as consumers become richer through time, they consume the same fraction of income as before. This fact contradicts the view expressed by some pessimists who fear that as an economy gets richer, consumers will buy a smaller fraction of the output and thus create insufficient demand and more unemployment. However, in short periods when national income is increasing faster than its trend or during the upswing of a business cycle, consumption increases less proportionally, leading to a reduction in the ratio of consumption to income. Similarly, during the downswing of a business cycle, consumption decreases proportionally less than income, leading to an increase in the ratio of consumption to income.

A consumption function capable of reconciling the long-run and short-run relations between consumption and income mentioned above is

$$c_t = \gamma_1 y_t + \gamma_2 c_{t-1} \tag{6.18}$$

According to equation 6.18, the short-run ratio of consumption to income is

$$c_t / y_t = \gamma_1 + \gamma_2 (c_{t-1} / y_t)$$

This ratio is not a constant; it is small when y_t is large relative to c_{t-1}, and it is large when y_t is small relative to c_{t-1}. To study the long-run relation between consumption and income, we substitute $\gamma_1 y_{t-1} + \gamma_2 c_{t-2}$ for c_{t-1} in 6.18, a similar expression for c_{t-2}, and so forth, to obtain

$$\begin{aligned} c_t &= \gamma_1 y_t + \gamma_2 (\gamma_1 y_{t-1} + \gamma_2 c_{t-2}) \\ &= \gamma_1 y_t + \gamma_2 \gamma_1 y_{t-1} + \gamma_2^2 \gamma_1 y_{t-2} + \gamma_2^3 \gamma_1 y_{t-3} + \cdots \end{aligned} \tag{6.19}$$

which states that current consumption c_t is a weighted average of current and past incomes; the weights are geometrically declining, the weight for y_{t-k} being $\gamma_2^k \gamma_1 y_{t-k}$. Such a relationship is an example of a *distributed-lag* relationship between consumption and income, showing that consumption is a function of current and past incomes, or that past incomes affect consumption with time lags. If income grows by a factor of ϕ per year, or $y_t = \phi y_{t-1}$, we have $y_{t-1} = \phi^{-1} y_t$ and $y_{t-2} = \phi^{-2} y_t$, etc. Substituting for the lagged y_{t-k} in equation 6.19, we obtain

$$\begin{aligned} c_t &= \gamma_1 y_t + \gamma_1 (\gamma_2 / \phi) y_t + \gamma_1 (\gamma_2 / \phi)^2 y_t + \gamma_1 (\gamma_2 / \phi)^3 y_t + \cdots \\ &= \gamma_1 (1 + r + r^2 + r^3 + \cdots) y_t = \frac{\gamma_1}{1-r} y_t \\ &= \frac{\gamma_1 \phi}{\phi - \gamma_2} y_t \end{aligned} \tag{6.20}$$

where we have let r denote the ratio γ_2 / ϕ and used the formula $(1-r)^{-1}$ for the infinite sum $1 + r + r^2 + \cdots$ of a geometric series, with $|r| < 1$. Hence, if income grows smoothly by a factor of ϕ per year, the consumption function (equation 6.18) implies that consumption is a fraction $\gamma_1 \phi / (\phi - \gamma_2)$ of income no matter what the level of income is. Equation 6.18 is a possible building block for a model explaining the fluctuations and growth of an economy. When applied to a mixed market and planned economy, one has to check whether it is a good approximation to the supply of consumer goods by the economic planning authority.

The consumption function (equation 6.18) and the identity

$$y_t = c_t + j_t \tag{6.21}$$

form a system of two equations that can determine the variables c_t and y_t *if* we take the value of investment j_t as given. Substituting equation 6.18 for c_t in equation 6.21, we have

$$y_t = \gamma_1 y_t + \gamma_2 c_{t-1} + j_t$$

which can be solved for y_t, yielding

$$y_t = (1-\gamma_1)^{-1} j_t + (1-\gamma_1)^{-1} \gamma_2 c_{t-1} \tag{6.22}$$

The coefficient $(1-\gamma_1)^{-1}$ is called the *investment multiplier.* It shows the increase in income per unit increase in investment. The coefficient γ_1 in equation 6.18 is called the *marginal propensity to consume* out of current income; it is the increase in consumption per unit increase of current income. For example, if $\gamma_1 = .6$, consumption will increase by 60 cents when income increases by a dollar, holding c_{t-1} constant. The investment multiplier $(1-\gamma_1)^{-1}$ will be 2.5, showing that income will increase by 2.5 dollars as investment increases by one dollar. The reason for the multiplying effect of investment is that a dollar of investment creates a dollar of income immediately through equation 6.21, which will raise consumption by .6 dollar. The income generated by the .6 dollar will in turn generate (.6) (.6) dollar of consumption through the consumption function, and so forth. The total increase in income resulting from a one-dollar increase in investment is therefore

$$1 + .6 + .6^2 + .6^3 + \ldots = (1-.6)^{-1}$$

The consumption function (equation 6.18) thus generates a multiplier for investment spending.

Our second building block is an equation explaining the investment of autonomous enterprises that exist in a market economy and may exist in a planned economy if permitted by the government, as in the case of China in 1984. To understand why a market economy may generate fluctuations in national income and to provide a stepping stone to a model that incorporates the effects of government investment, let us assume for the time being that all investments in an economy are made by autonomous enterprises (which may be collectively owned or owned by the government granting the autonomous investment decisions). One hypothesis concerning investment behavior is based on equation 6.2, rewritten as

$$k_t = \theta^{-1} y_t = \alpha y_t \tag{6.2a}$$

This hypothesis is interpreted to mean that the capital stock k_t that the autonomous enterprises would like to have is a function of the output y_t that they have to produce, because to produce one unit of output, α units of capital are required. (This hypothesis might also be applicable to explaining the behavior of government economic planners who decide the amount of capital stock and thus indirectly decide the amount of investment of the enterprises under their direction.)

Because of time delays, one may modify the hypothesis (equation 6.2a) by assuming

$$k_t = \alpha_1 y_t + \alpha_2 k_{t-1} \tag{6.23}$$

as we have changed the hypothesis 6.3 or 6.17 to 6.18. Equation 6.23 can be rewritten to express k_t as a weighted average of current and past y_{t-1} ($i = 0, 1, 2, \ldots$), as equation 6.18 is rewritten as 6.19. The explanation of equation 6.23 is that the capital stock desired by the enterprises is a function not of current output y_t alone, which is subject to short-run fluctuations, but of an average of current and past outputs, because such an average measures the requirement for capital stock better than current output y_t. Taking the first difference of equation 6.23 and using the definition (equation 6.1) for net investment j_t, we have

$$
\begin{aligned}
j_t = \Delta k_t &= \alpha_1 \Delta y_t + \alpha_2 \Delta k_{t-1} \\
&= \alpha_1 y_t - \alpha_1 y_{t-1} + \alpha_2 j_{t-1}
\end{aligned}
\tag{6.24}
$$

This investment function states that investment is a function of the first difference in income Δy_t. Such a relation is called *the acceleration relation,* or *the acceleration principle.* When income increases more slowly, or when Δy_t decreases from 1 to .7, say, investment decreases.

Equations 6.18, 6.21, and 6.24 are a system of three difference equations that can explain the evolution of the three variables c_t, j_t, and y_t through time. Note that this system is obtained from the Harrod-Domar model (equations 6.1–6.3) by introducing time lags into the consumption function (equation 6.3) and the capital requirement equation (equation 6.2). The Harrod-Domar model generates time paths for the variables that grow exponentially through time. The model consisting of equations 6.18, 6.21, and 6.24 may generate fluctuations in the variables c_t, j_t, and y_t, as we will explain. This is called a *multiplier-accelerator model,* for it is constructed from a consumption function and an investment function incorporating respectively the multiplier and acceleration relations. Paul Samuelson (1939) first pointed out that such a model may generate oscillations in national income, although the model he used is somewhat different from the above model.

To study the dynamic behavior of c_t, j_t, and y_t generated by the above model, let us simplify the model by substituting 6.21 for y_t and deal with only two variables, consumption c_t and investment j_t. Equations 6.18 and 6.24 become

$$
\begin{aligned}
c_t &= \gamma_1 c_t + \gamma_1 j_t + \gamma_2 c_{t-1} \\
j_t &= \alpha_1 j_t + \alpha_1 c_t - \alpha_1 c_{t-1} - \alpha_1 j_{t-1} + \alpha_2 j_{t-1}
\end{aligned}
$$

or, equivalently,

$$(1-\gamma_1)c_t - \gamma_1 j_t = \gamma_2 c_{t-1} + 0 j_{t-1} \tag{6.25}$$

$$-\alpha_1 c_t + (1-\alpha_1)j_t = -\alpha_1 c_{t-1} + (\alpha_2 - \alpha_1) j_{t-1} \tag{6.26}$$

Equations 6.25 and 6.26 are a system of two simultaneous equations that can be used to explain the two economic variables c_t and j_t, given the lagged values c_{t-1} and j_{t-1}.

A system of simultaneous equations as exemplified by 6.25 and 6.26 is often used by economists to capture the interdependence of economic relations and to determine or explain a set of economic variables. Recall the system of simultaneous equations used in Section 1.6 to determine the prices and output of a hypothetical economy. Variables that are determined by a set of simultaneous equations are called *endogenous variables* or *dependent variables*. The endogenous variables in the system equations 6.25–6.26 are c_t and j_t. The endogenous variables in the system equations 6.18–6.21 are c_t and y_t, when j_t is treated as given, or as an *exogenous variable* not to be determined by the system. There are usually as many simultaneous equations as endogenous variables to be explained. Equations 6.25 and 6.26 are *structural equations*. Each structural equation is derived from some hypothesis about economic behavior, some definition such as $y_t = c_t + j_t$, or from some institutional information such as after-tax income equals $(1-\tau)y$, where τ is the tax rate. In a structural equation more than one endogenous variable may appear, as in the case of equation 6.25 or 6.26, in which both variables c_t and j_t appear.

The simultaneous structural equations can be solved for the endogenous variables. We will solve the linear system of equations 6.25–6.26 using matrix notation, which was introduced in Section 4.2. The system can be written as

$$\begin{bmatrix} 1-\gamma_1 & -\gamma_1 \\ -\alpha_1 & 1-\alpha_1 \end{bmatrix} \begin{bmatrix} c_t \\ j_t \end{bmatrix} = \begin{bmatrix} \gamma_2 & 0 \\ -\alpha_1 & \alpha_2-\alpha_1 \end{bmatrix} \begin{bmatrix} c_{t-1} \\ j_{t-1} \end{bmatrix} \quad (6.27)$$

The inverse of the matrix on the left is

$$\begin{bmatrix} 1-\gamma_1 & -\gamma_1 \\ -\alpha_1 & 1-\alpha_1 \end{bmatrix}^{-1} = [(1-\gamma_1)(1-\alpha_1)-\alpha_1\gamma_1]^{-1} \begin{bmatrix} 1-\alpha_1 & \gamma_1 \\ \alpha_1 & 1-\gamma_1 \end{bmatrix} \quad (6.28)$$

as can easily be checked by the multiplication

$$(1-\alpha_1-\gamma_1)^{-1} \begin{bmatrix} 1-\alpha_1 & \gamma_1 \\ \alpha_1 & 1-\gamma_1 \end{bmatrix} \begin{bmatrix} 1-\gamma_1 & -\gamma_1 \\ -\alpha_1 & 1-\alpha_1 \end{bmatrix} = \begin{bmatrix} 1 & 0 \\ 0 & 1 \end{bmatrix} \quad (6.29)$$

Premultiplying equation 6.27 by equation 6.28 and using equation 6.29, we obtain the solution

$$\begin{bmatrix} c_t \\ j_t \end{bmatrix} = (1-\alpha_1-\gamma_1)^{-1} \begin{bmatrix} (1-\alpha_1)\gamma_2-\alpha_1\gamma_1 & (\alpha_2-\alpha_1)\gamma_1 \\ \alpha_1\gamma_2-\alpha_1(1-\gamma_1) & (\alpha_2-\alpha_1)(1-\gamma_1) \end{bmatrix} \begin{bmatrix} c_{t-1} \\ j_{t-1} \end{bmatrix} \quad (6.30)$$

This expresses each current endogenous variable as a function of the *lagged endogenous variables* and of the *exogenous variables* if the latter variables exist in the system. For example, total investment j_t may be broken down into investment j_{1t} by the enterprises making their own decisions and government investment j_{2t}, yielding the identity

$$y_t = c_t + j_{1t} + j_{2t} \quad (6.31)$$

and j_{1t} may be determined by equation 6.24 with j_{1t} replacing j_t. If j_{2t} is treated as given and not explained by the model, it is an *exogenous variable*. Exogenous variables, if present in the structural equation 6.27, will also appear on the right-hand side of the solution (equation 6.30). The solution (equation 6.30) is called a *reduced form*. Each reduced-form equation expresses one current endogenous variable as a function of current and lagged exogenous variables and of lagged endogenous variables. The set of current and lagged exogenous variables and the lagged endogenous variables are called *predetermined variables*. The values of the predetermined variables are treated as given when the model is used to explain the current endogenous variables. [In the model (equation 6.30), there are no current or lagged exogenous variables.]

To explain the evolution of the variables c_t and j_t through time using the reduced form equation 6.30, let the numerical values of the parameters α_1, α_2, γ_1, and γ_2 of the structural equations be known, and let the initial values c_0 and j_0 at period 0 be given. Using equation 6.30, we can compute c_1 and j_1 in the first period given c_0 and j_0, compute c_2 and j_2 in the second period given c_1 and j_1, and so forth. The time paths c_t and j_t ($t = 1,2,3, \ldots$) can thus be computed numerically.

*6.4   DYNAMIC PROPERTIES OF A SYSTEM OF LINEAR DIFFERENCE EQUATIONS

It is useful to study the dynamic properties of the time paths generated by a reduced form such as equation 6.30 in more general terms than by computations using a specific numerical example. To do so, let us introduce a more general notation for the endogenous variables and treat the case of p endogenous variables. For equation 6.30, $p = 2$. Let y_t denote a column vector consisting of p endogenous variables $y_{1t}, y_{2t}, \ldots, y_{pt}$. A system of first-order difference equations explaining the vector y_t by the vector y_{t-1} can be written as

$$\begin{bmatrix} y_{1t} \\ y_{2t} \\ \vdots \\ y_{pt} \end{bmatrix} = \begin{bmatrix} a_{11} & a_{12} & \cdots & a_{1p} \\ a_{21} & a_{22} & \cdots & a_{2p} \\ & & \cdots & \\ a_{p1} & a_{p2} & \cdots & a_{pp} \end{bmatrix} \begin{bmatrix} y_{1,t-1} \\ y_{2,t-2} \\ \vdots \\ y_{p,t-1} \end{bmatrix} \qquad (6.32)$$

or, more compactly, as

$$y_t = Ay_{t-1} \qquad (6.33)$$

where the matrix A denotes a $p \times p$ matrix with a_{ij} as its element in the ith row and jth column. Equation 6.30 is an example of equation 6.33 with $p = 2$ and with $y_{1t} = c_t$, $y_{2t} = j_t$,

$$a_{11} = (1-\alpha_1-\gamma_1)^{-1}[(1-\alpha_1)\gamma_2-\alpha_1\gamma_1]$$

and so forth. Numerically the time path of the vector y_t can be computed by repeated substitutions for the right-hand side of equation 6.33, namely

$$y_t = Ay_{t-1} = AAy_{t-2} = A^2y_{t-2} = \ldots = A^ty_0 \qquad (6.34)$$

where A^t denotes the product of t As.

It would be of interest to know whether the variables in y_t will increase through time or not, and whether they will fluctuate or not. To study such dynamic properties of the time path y_t, we rewrite the matrix A using its *characteristic roots* and *characteristic vectors* (or *eigen values* and *eigen vectors*). A *right* characteristic vector of a $p \times p$ matrix A is a $p \times 1$ column vector b that satisfies

$$Ab = \lambda b \tag{6.35}$$

where λ is a constant called the *characteristic root* of A associated with the characteristic vector b. Thus, the matrix A times the column vector b equals a constant λ times the column vector b. To find a characteristic root λ, we use equation 6.35 to write

$$Ab - \lambda b = (A - \lambda I)b = 0 \tag{6.36}$$

where I is a $p \times p$ identity matrix. If the system of p equations (6.36) in the p unknowns is to have a nonzero solution for b, the inverse of the matrix $A - \lambda I$ cannot exist. Otherwise we can premultiply equation 6.36 by $(A - \lambda I)^{-1}$ and obtain $b = 0$. The nonexistence of $(A - \lambda I)^{-1}$ is equivalent to the determinant of $A - \lambda I$ being zero. Thus,

$$|A - \lambda I| = 0 \tag{6.37}$$

To write out equation 6.37 for the case $p = 2$, we have

$$\left| \begin{bmatrix} a_{11} & a_{12} \\ a_{21} & a_{22} \end{bmatrix} - \lambda \begin{bmatrix} 1 & 0 \\ 0 & 1 \end{bmatrix} \right| = \begin{vmatrix} a_{11} - \lambda & a_{12} \\ a_{21} & a_{22} - \lambda \end{vmatrix}$$

$$= (a_{11} - \lambda)(a_{22} - \lambda) - a_{12}a_{21}$$
$$= \lambda^2 - (a_{11} + a_{22})\lambda + (a_{11}a_{22} - a_{12}a_{21}) = 0 \tag{6.38}$$

Equation 6.37 is called the *characteristic equation* of the matrix A. For $p = 2$ the characteristic equation is a polynomial of the second degree in the unknown. Let λ_1 and λ_2 be the two roots satisfying the characteristic equation 6.38. When A is $p \times p$, the characteristic equation 6.37 is a polynomial equation of the pth degree in the unknown λ. There are p characteristic roots $\lambda_1, \lambda_2, \ldots, \lambda_p$ associated with the $p \times p$ matrix A. For each characteristic root λ_i, we have a corresponding right characteristic vector b_i satisfying equation 6.35 or 6.36, or

$$Ab_i = \lambda_i b_i \qquad \text{or} \qquad (A - \lambda_i I)b_i = 0 \tag{6.39}$$

Equation 6.39 can be used to find the vector b_i once λ_i is given. Note that if b_i is a characteristic vector corresponding to λ_i, so is a constant times b_i because it also satisfies equation 6.39.

If we place the column vectors $b_1 \ldots b_p$ side by side and denote the resulting $p \times p$ matrix $(b_1 \ldots b_p)$ by B, we can use equation 6.39 to write

$$A(b_1 \; b_2 \; \ldots \; b_p) = (\lambda_1 b_1 \; \lambda_2 b_2 \; \ldots \; \lambda_p b_p) = (b_1 b_2 \ldots b_p) \begin{bmatrix} \lambda_1 & 0 \ldots 0 \\ 0 & \lambda_2 \ldots 0 \\ & \ddots \\ 0 & \ldots \lambda_p \end{bmatrix}$$

or

$$AB = BD_\lambda \tag{6.40}$$

where D_λ is a $p \times p$ matrix with $\lambda_1, \ldots, \lambda_p$ on its diagonal and with zeros elsewhere, such a matrix being called a diagonal matrix. For expositional convenience we assume that the p characteristic roots of A are different, which implies that the inverse of the matrix B exists. Postmultiplying equation 6.40 by B^{-1}, we obtain

$$A = BD_\lambda B^{-1} \tag{6.41}$$

Equation 6.41 is a very useful expression for the matrix A. Using 6.41, we have

$$A^2 = A \cdot A = BD_\lambda B^{-1} BD_\lambda B^{-1} = BD_\lambda^2 B^{-1}$$

and

$$A^t = AA \ldots A = BD_\lambda B^{-1} BD_\lambda B^{-1} \ldots BD_\lambda B^{-1} = BD_\lambda^t B^{-1} \tag{6.42}$$

Substituting 6.42 for A^t in the solution 6.34, we can express the solution to the system (6.33) of difference equations as

$$y_t = A^t y_0 = BD_\lambda^t B^{-1} y_0 \tag{6.43}$$

To appreciate this solution, let us write it out for the case $p = 3$, with b_{ij} denoting the $i-j$ element of B and b^{ij} denoting the $i-j$ element of B^{-1}. In this case 6.43 becomes

$$
\begin{bmatrix} y_{1t} \\ y_{2t} \\ y_{3t} \end{bmatrix} =
\begin{bmatrix} b_{11} & b_{12} & b_{13} \\ b_{21} & b_{22} & b_{23} \\ b_{31} & b_{32} & b_{33} \end{bmatrix}
\begin{bmatrix} \lambda_1^t & 0 & 0 \\ 0 & \lambda_2^t & 0 \\ 0 & 0 & \lambda_3^t \end{bmatrix}
\begin{bmatrix} b^{11} & b^{12} & b^{13} \\ b^{21} & b^{22} & b^{23} \\ b^{31} & b^{32} & b^{33} \end{bmatrix}
\begin{bmatrix} y_{10} \\ y_{20} \\ y_{30} \end{bmatrix}
$$

$$
= \begin{bmatrix} b_{11}\lambda_1^t & b_{12}\lambda_2^t & b_{13}\lambda_3^t \\ b_{21}\lambda_1^t & b_{22}\lambda_2^t & b_{23}\lambda_3^t \\ b_{31}\lambda_1^t & b_{32}\lambda_2^t & b_{33}\lambda_3^t \end{bmatrix}
\begin{bmatrix} b^{11}y_{10} + b^{12}y_{20} + b^{13}y_{30} \\ b^{21}y_{10} + b^{22}y_{20} + b^{23}y_{30} \\ b^{31}y_{10} + b^{32}y_{20} + b^{33}y_{30} \end{bmatrix}
$$

$$
= \begin{bmatrix} b_{11}z_{10}\lambda_1^t + b_{12}z_{20}\lambda_2^t + b_{13}z_{30}\lambda_3^t \\ b_{21}z_{10}\lambda_1^t + b_{22}z_{20}\lambda_2^t + b_{23}z_{30}\lambda_3^t \\ b_{31}z_{10}\lambda_1^t + b_{32}z_{20}\lambda_2^t + b_{33}z_{30}\lambda_3^t \end{bmatrix} \tag{6.44}
$$

where we have defined

$$z_{i0} = b^{i1}y_{10} + b^{i2}y_{20} + b^{i3}y_{30} \qquad (i = 1,2,3) \tag{6.45}$$

The solution 6.44 states that each y_{it} $(i = 1,2,3)$ is a linear combination of λ_1^t, λ_2^t, and λ_3^t. If any root λ_i is larger than 1 in absolute value, the variables y_{1t}, y_{2t}, and y_{3t} will explode, because the absolute value of λ_i^t increases through time. If any λ_i is negative, λ_i^t will oscillate from negative to positive values in successive periods, and the variables y_{1t}, y_{2t}, and y_{3t} themselves will have a component that oscillates. Furthermore, if the roots $\lambda_1, \ldots, \lambda_p$ include a pair of conjugate complex roots, which may be written as

$$
\begin{aligned}
\lambda_1 &= a + bi \qquad i = \sqrt{-1} \\
\lambda_2 &= a - bi
\end{aligned} \tag{6.46}
$$

the variables y_{1t}, y_{2t}, and y_{3t} will show oscillations.

To elaborate on the last remark, let the complex number $\lambda_1 = a + bi$ be represented geometrically by the point (a,b) in Figure 6.1, with the real part a measured

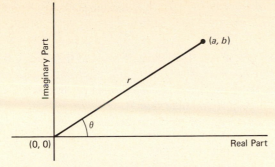

Figure 6.1 Graphic representation of a complex number.

along the horizontal axis and the coefficient b of the imaginary part measured along the vertical axis. Let θ be the angle between the horizontal axis and the line drawn between the origin $(0,0)$ and the point (a,b). Let the length of this line be r. We have, by the Pythagorean theorem and trigonometry,

$$r = \sqrt{a^2 + b^2} \quad ; \quad \tan \theta = b/a \tag{6.47}$$

and

$$a = r \cos \theta \quad ; \quad b = r \sin \theta \tag{6.48}$$

Hence, the pair of conjugate complex numbers in 6.46 can be written as

$$\lambda_1 = a + bi = r(\cos \theta + i \sin \theta) = r\,e^{i\theta}$$
$$\lambda_2 = a - bi = r(\cos \theta - i \sin \theta) = r\,e^{-i\theta} \tag{6.49}$$

where r is defined by 6.47 and is called the *absolute value* or the *modulo* of the pair of complex numbers λ_1 and λ_2, and where

$$e^{i\theta} = \cos\theta + i \sin\theta \quad ; \quad e^{-i\theta} = \cos\theta - i \sin\theta \tag{6.50}$$

as can be checked by expanding $e^{i\theta}$, $\cos\theta$, and $\sin\theta$ in Taylor series.

Consider the linear combination

$$b_{11}z_{10}\lambda_1^t + b_{12}z_{20}\lambda_2^t = c_{11}\lambda_1^t + c_{12}\lambda_2^t \tag{6.51}$$

which is a component of y_{1t}, according to equation 6.44. Let the roots λ_1 and λ_2 be conjugate complex, as given by equation 6.49. The coefficients c_{11} and c_{12} as defined by equation 6.51 can be shown to be conjugate complex (see Chow, 1975, pp. 29 and 36). Let this pair of conjugate numbers be written as

$$c_{11} = s_1 e^{i\psi_1} \quad ; \quad c_{12} = s_1 e^{-i\psi_1} \tag{6.52}$$

Then equation 6.51 becomes

$$\begin{aligned} c_{11}\lambda_1^t + c_{12}\lambda_2^t &= s_1 e^{i\psi}(re^{i\theta})^t + s_1 e^{-i\psi}(re^{-i\theta})^t \\ &= s_1 r^t[e^{i(\psi+\theta t)} + e^{-i(\psi+\theta t)}] \\ &= 2s_1 r^t \cos(\psi+\theta t) \end{aligned} \tag{6.53}$$

where we have used the identity derived from equation 6.50

$$e^{ix} + e^{-ix} = 2\cos x \tag{6.54}$$

From equation 6.53 we see that if two characteristic roots of the matrix A in the system equation 6.33 are conjugate complex, the solution for y_{1t} will have a component that is an explosive (or damped) cosine function $\cos(\psi + \theta t)$ of time if the absolute value r of the pair of roots is larger (or smaller) than 1.

To find the length of the cycle of the function $\cos(\psi + \theta t)$, observe that $\cos 0 = \cos 2\pi = \cos 4\pi = \cos n(2\pi) = 1$, where n is an integer. Thus, the value of $\cos(\psi + \theta t)$ is the same when

$$\psi + \theta t = 0,\ 2\pi,\ 4\pi,\ 6\pi,\ \dots$$

or when

$$t = \frac{-\psi}{\theta},\ \frac{-\psi}{\theta} + \frac{2\pi}{\theta},\ \frac{-\psi}{\theta} + \frac{4\pi}{\theta},\ \frac{-\psi}{\theta} + \frac{6\pi}{\theta},\ \dots$$

In other words, the function $\cos(\psi + \theta t)$ takes the same value every $\frac{2\pi}{\theta}$ time units. The *length of the cycle,* or the *periodicity,* of the function $\cos(\psi + \theta t)$ is $2\pi/\theta$ time units (or $2\pi/\theta$ years if t is measured in years). A function that takes the same value every so many time units is a *periodic function.* $\cos(\psi + \theta t)$ is a periodic function with a periodicity or a cycle length equal to $2\pi/\theta$ time units. In equation 6.53 this periodic function is magnified (or damped) by the factor r^t if r is larger (or smaller) than 1.

To summarize our results on the dynamic properties of a vector y_t generated by a system of first-order linear difference equations (equation 6.33), the solution for each element of y_t is a linear combination of $\lambda_1^t, \lambda_2^t, \dots, \lambda_p^t$, where the λ_i are the characteristic roots of A. If the absolute value of any λ_i is larger than 1, y_t will explode; it will be damped if the absolute values of all λ_i are smaller than 1. If all λ_i are real and positive, y_t will not have prolonged oscillations; it will have oscillating components if some roots are negative or complex, a component generated by a pair of complex roots being given by equation 6.53.

Although we have studied only a first-order system, our results apply to higher-order systems because any higher-order system can be rewritten as a first-order system. An mth-order linear system explaining a vector y_t is

$$y_t = A_1 y_{t-1} + A_2 y_{t-2} + \dots + A_m y_{t-m}$$

It can be rewritten as

$$\begin{bmatrix} y_t \\ y_{t-1} \\ \vdots \\ y_{t-m+1} \end{bmatrix} = \begin{bmatrix} A_1 & A_2 & \dots & A_m \\ I & 0 & \dots & 0 \\ & & & \\ 0 & 0 & \dots I & 0 \end{bmatrix} \begin{bmatrix} y_{t-1} \\ y_{t-2} \\ \vdots \\ y_{t-m} \end{bmatrix}$$

which is a first-order system if the vector of endogenous variables is redefined as the long vector on the left-hand side and the matrix A is defined as the matrix on the right-hand side.

Often the matrices A_i in the above equation contain columns of zeros. If the second column of A_i is a column of zeros, the variable $y_{2,t-i}$ is absent from the model. When many of the variables in the vectors $y_{t-2}, y_{t-3}, \ldots, y_{t-m}$ are absent from the model, a better way to convert a higher-order system into a first-order system is to deal only with those variables in these vectors which appear in the model. For example, if y_t is a column vector of p elements and if $y_{2,t-2}$ and $y_{3,t-2}$ appear in the model, we define two new variables $y_{p+1,t} = y_{2,t-1}$ and $y_{p+2,t} = y_{3,t-1}$. These new variables can be used to write $y_{2,t-2} = y_{p+1,t-1}$ and $y_{3,t-2} = y_{p+2,t-1}$. Thus the two variables with a second-order lag are converted to variables with only a first-order lag. Similarly, if $y_{4,t-3}$ appears, we can define two new variables $y_{p+3,t} = y_{4,t-1}$ and $y_{p+4,t} = y_{t+3,t-1}$ with $y_{4,t-3} = y_{p+3,t-2} = y_{p+4,t-1}$. Thus $y_{4,t-3}$ becomes a new variable with lag $t-1$.

If an intercept b appears in the above model, with elements $b_1, b_2, \ldots, b_p$, we can eliminate it by introducing a new variable $y_{p+5,t}$ that equals 1 for all t. Write a new equation $y_{p+5,t} = y_{p+5,t-1}$, with initial condition $y_{t+5,0} = 1$, and replace each b_i in the model by $b_i y_{t+5,t}$. The model will no longer contain an intercept. Hence a system of high-order linear difference equations with an intercept can be written in the form shown in equation 6.32. Its dynamic properties can be studied by methods presented in this section.

6.5 MODELS OF FLUCTUATIONS AND GROWTH

To use the results of Section 6.4 to study our multiplier-accelerator model (6.30), we observe that if the matrix

$$\begin{bmatrix} a_{11} & a_{12} \\ a_{21} & a_{22} \end{bmatrix} = (1-\alpha_1-\gamma_1)^{-1} \begin{bmatrix} (1-\alpha_1)\gamma_2 - \alpha_1\gamma_1 & (\alpha_2-\alpha_1)\gamma_1 \\ -\alpha_1(1-\gamma_1-\gamma_2) & (\alpha_2-\alpha_1)(1-\gamma_1) \end{bmatrix} \quad (6.55)$$

has a pair of complex characteristic roots, the solutions for $y_{1t} = c_t$ and $y_{2t} = j_t$ will show oscillations. Let us illustrate the solution to the model 6.27 or 6.30 by two numerical examples, one having positive and real roots for the matrix A and the second having a pair of complex roots.

To find some plausible values for the parameters γ_1 and γ_2 in the consumption function 6.18 that might fit the Chinese data, we use equation 6.20 and the fact that in the long run consumption equals .70 times income. By 6.20 we have

$$\frac{\gamma_1\phi}{\phi-\gamma_2} = .70 \quad (6.56)$$

Let the rate of growth of real income be .05 per year, or $\phi = 1.05$. Reasonable values that satisfy equation 6.56 are $\gamma_1 = .50$ and $\gamma_2 = .30$, for

$$\frac{1.05(.50)}{1.05-.30} = .70$$

If the derivation from 6.18 to 6.20 is applied to equation 6.23 for the capital stock k_t, we can find the long-run ratio of capital stock to income to be

$$\frac{\alpha_1 \phi}{\phi - \alpha_2} \tag{6.57}$$

From the discrete version of the Harrod-Domar model, if income grows by 5 percent per year or if $a = 1.05$, we have

$$\sigma\theta = 1 - a^{-1} = .047619$$

which, for a savings ratio $\sigma = .30$, gives an output–capital ratio $\theta = .15873$, or a capital–income ratio of 6.3. Plausible values of α_1 and α_2 that make the ratio shown in 6.57 equal to 6.3, given $\phi = 1.05$, are $\alpha_1 = .30$ and $\alpha_2 = 1.00$. Using the parameter values $\gamma_1 = .50$, $\gamma_2 = .30$, $\alpha_1 = .30$, and $\alpha_2 = 1.00$, we evaluate the matrix A for the model 6.30, as given by 6.55,

$$\begin{bmatrix} a_{11} & a_{12} \\ a_{21} & a_{22} \end{bmatrix} = \begin{bmatrix} .30 & 1.75 \\ -.30 & 1.75 \end{bmatrix} \tag{6.58}$$

The characteristic roots of this matrix satisfy the *characteristic equation*

$$(.30 - \lambda)(1.75 - \lambda) - (-.30)(1.75) = \lambda^2 - 2.05\lambda + 1.05 = 0 \tag{6.59}$$

The roots of equation 6.59 are $\lambda = 1.025 \pm .025$, or $\lambda_1 = 1.05$ and $\lambda_2 = 1.0$.

To construct a numerical example having complex roots that will lead to violent fluctuations, let $\gamma_1 = .50$ and $\gamma_2 = .30$ as before, but let $\alpha_1 = .40$ and $\alpha_2 = .85$. Given $\phi = 1.05$, the capital–income ratio from 6.57 would be

$$\frac{.40(1.05)}{1.05 - .85} = 2.1$$

which is much lower than the ratio 6.3 implied by the Harrod-Domar model with $\sigma = .30$ and $a = 1.05$. Therefore, the values $\alpha_1 = .40$ and $\alpha_2 = .85$ are not economically reasonable; they are used for illustrative purposes only. (More plausible values that generate complex roots are $\alpha_1 = .29$ and $\alpha_2 = 1.0$. See Problem 8.) For the second example, assuming $\gamma_1 = .50$, $\gamma_2 = .30$, $\alpha_1 = .40$, and $\alpha_2 = .85$, we find the matrix A given by 6.55 to be

$$\begin{bmatrix} a_{11} & a_{12} \\ a_{21} & a_{22} \end{bmatrix} = \begin{bmatrix} -.2 & 2.25 \\ -.8 & 2.25 \end{bmatrix} \tag{6.60}$$

The characteristic equation of this matrix is

$$(-.2 - \lambda)(2.25 - \lambda) - (-.8)(2.25) = \lambda^2 - 2.05\lambda + 1.35 = 0 \tag{6.61}$$

The roots of this equation are, using 6.49 and 6.47,

$$\lambda_1 = 1.025 + .54715i = 1.16189\, e^{.4903i}$$
$$\lambda_2 = 1.025 - .54715i = 1.16189\, e^{-.4903i} \tag{6.62}$$

where $\tan(28.093°) = \tan(.4903 \text{ radians}) = .54715/1.025$. These two complex roots would generate a component of the solution which, according to 6.53, is a constant times

$$(1.16189)^t \cos(\psi + .4903t) \tag{6.63}$$

The length of the cycle of $\cos(\psi + .4903)$ is $2\pi/.4903$ or $360°/28.093°$, which is 12.81 years.

This numerical example illustrates the possibility of economic fluctuations resulting from complex roots of the model. However, if 6.63 is the entire solution for an economic variable, and not just a component of the solution, the economic variables will take negative values. The presence of real roots and the existence of intercepts may prevent the variables in a model having complex roots from becoming negative. If we add an intercept α_0 to the investment equation and change 6.24 to

$$j_t = \alpha_1 y_t - \alpha_1 y_{t-1} + \alpha_2 j_{t-1} + \alpha_0 \tag{6.64}$$

the intercept α_0 will also appear in 6.26. Then 6.27 will become

$$\begin{bmatrix} 1-\gamma_1 & -\gamma_1 \\ -\alpha_1 & 1-\alpha_1 \end{bmatrix} \begin{bmatrix} c_t \\ j_t \end{bmatrix} = \begin{bmatrix} \gamma_2 & 0 \\ -\alpha_1 & \alpha_2-\alpha_1 \end{bmatrix} \begin{bmatrix} c_{t-1} \\ j_{t-1} \end{bmatrix} + \begin{bmatrix} 0 \\ \alpha_0 \end{bmatrix} \tag{6.65}$$

Premultiplying 6.65 by 6.28, we obtain its reduced form. This reduced form is the same as 6.30 except for an intercept that equals

$$\begin{bmatrix} 1-\gamma_1 & -\gamma_1 \\ -\alpha_1 & 1-\alpha_1 \end{bmatrix}^{-1} \begin{bmatrix} 0 \\ \alpha_0 \end{bmatrix} = (1-\alpha_1-\gamma_1)^{-1} \begin{bmatrix} \gamma_1\alpha_0 \\ (1-\gamma_1)\alpha_0 \end{bmatrix} \tag{6.66}$$

In the model with $\gamma_1 = .50$, $\gamma_2 = .30$, $\alpha_1 = .40$, and $\alpha_2 = .85$, let $\alpha_0 = 3.0$, so that the two elements of the vector 6.66 are both 15. The reduced form of this model is

$$\begin{bmatrix} c_t \\ j_t \end{bmatrix} = \begin{bmatrix} -.2 & 2.25 \\ -.8 & 2.25 \end{bmatrix} \begin{bmatrix} c_{t-1} \\ j_{t-1} \end{bmatrix} + \begin{bmatrix} 15 \\ 15 \end{bmatrix} \tag{6.67}$$

It may be of interest to trace the time paths of consumption $y_{1t} = c_t$ and investment $y_{2t} = j_t$ generated by 6.67 using the initial values $c_0 = 45.9$ and $j_0 = 13.0$, which are the actual values of consumption and investment for the initial year 1952 given in Table 6.1. The values of c_t and j_t for $t = 1, \ldots, 11$ are

t	c_t	j_t
0	45.9	13.0
1	35.0	7.53
2	24.9285	3.8865
3	18.7589	3.8018
4	19.8023	8.5470
5	30.2702	18.3889
6	50.3208	32.1587
7	77.2928	47.1004
8	105.5172	59.1415
9	126.9650	63.6547
10	132.8300	56.6510
11	115.8988	36.2007

The violent fluctuations of c_t and j_t are easily seen in this numerical example. We have pointed out that the parameter values $\alpha_1 = .40$ and $\alpha_2 = .85$ are unreasonable; they are used only to illustrate the possible economic fluctuations generated by complex roots in the system.

It may be asked whether complex roots can exist if all components y_{it} of national income y_t (not vector) have the same form as the consumption function—that is,

$$y_{it} = \gamma_{i1}y_t + \gamma_{i2}y_{i,t-1}$$

—with $\sum_i y_{it} = y_t$ and if no component y_{it} is dependent on Δy_t according to the acceleration principle. Chow (1968) has shown that all roots of such a system are real and positive and hence the system cannot have prolonged oscillations. In other words, without the acceleration relation, fluctuations cannot occur. Even with the acceleration relation, the roots of the system may all be real and positive, as exemplified by the first example in this section. The acceleration relation is necessary but not sufficient for generating complex and negative roots.

When the numerical values of the parameters of economic models are estimated from actual data, the roots are often found to be real and positive, with absolute values less than 1. How then can prolonged fluctuations in actual economies be explained? One has to introduce *random* or *stochastic* elements in an economic model, for example by adding a *random residual* in each structural equation describing economic behavior. As Frisch (1933, pp. 197 and 202–203) points out:

> The examples we have discussed . . . show that when [a deterministic] economic system gives rise to oscillations, these will most frequently be damped. But in reality the cycles . . . are generally not damped. How can the maintenance of the swings be explained? . . . One way which I believe is particularly fruitful and promising is to study what would become of the solution of a determinate dynamic system if it were exposed to a stream of erratic shocks. . . .

> Thus, by connecting the two ideas: (1) the continuous solution of a determinate dynamic system and (2) the discontinuous shocks intervening and supplying the energy that may maintain the swings—we get a theoretical setup which seems to

furnish a rational interpretation of those movements which we have been accustomed to see in our statistical time data.

The model of economic fluctuations and growth as represented by equation 6.32 is deterministic because no *probabilistic* or *stochastic* elements are involved. To explain actual economic data adequately, probabilistic elements have to be introduced. Stochastic or probabilistic theories of economic fluctuations are too technical to be treated here. Interested readers may refer to Chow (1968, 1975), Chow and Levitan (1969), and Chow and Moore (1972).

If investment by government is treated as an exogenous variable, it is not difficult to modify our model consisting of equations 6.18, 6.21, and 6.24. Equation 6.21 becomes

$$y_t = c_t + j_{1t} + j_{2t} \tag{6.68}$$

where j_{1t} and j_{2t} denote investment by enterprises on their own initiatives and investment by the government, respectively. Equation 6.24 becomes

$$j_{1t} = \alpha_1 y_t - \alpha_1 y_{t-1} + \alpha_2 j_{1,t-1} \tag{6.69}$$

Substituting equation 6.68 for y_t and y_{t-1} in equations 6.18 and 6.69 yields

$$c_t = \gamma_1 c_t + \gamma_1 j_{1t} + \gamma_1 j_{2t} + \gamma_2 c_{t-1}$$
$$j_{1t} = \alpha_1 j_{1t} + \alpha_1 c_t + \alpha_1 j_{2t} - \alpha_1 c_{t-1} - \alpha_1 j_{1,t-1} - \alpha_1 j_{2,t-1} + \alpha_2 j_{1,t-1}$$

or, equivalently,

$$(1-\gamma_1)c_t - \gamma_1 j_{1t} = \gamma_2 c_{t-1} + 0 j_{1,t-1} + \gamma_1 j_{2t} + 0 j_{2,t-1} \tag{6.70}$$
$$-\alpha_1 c_t + (1-\alpha_1)j_{1t} = -\alpha_1 c_{t-1} + (\alpha_2 - \alpha_1)j_{1,t-1} + \alpha_1 j_{2t} - \alpha_1 j_{2,t-1} \tag{6.71}$$

Compare the structural equations 6.70 and 6.71 with 6.25 and 6.26. The new system has a current exogenous variable j_{2t} and a lagged exogenous variable $j_{2,t-1}$.

The reduced form of this model is, using the inverse equation 6.28,

$$\begin{bmatrix} c_t \\ j_{1t} \end{bmatrix} = (1-\alpha_1-\gamma_1)^{-1} \begin{bmatrix} \gamma_2 - \alpha_1(\gamma_1+\gamma_2) & (\alpha_2-\alpha_1)\gamma_1 \\ -\alpha_1(1-\gamma_1-\gamma_2) & (\alpha_2-\alpha_1)(1-\gamma_1) \end{bmatrix} \begin{bmatrix} c_{t-1} \\ j_{1,t-1} \end{bmatrix}$$

$$+ (1-\alpha_1-\gamma_1)^{-1} \begin{bmatrix} 1 \\ \alpha_1 \end{bmatrix} j_{2t} + (1-\alpha_1-\gamma_1)^{-1} \begin{bmatrix} -\alpha_1\gamma_1 \\ -\alpha_1(1-\gamma_1) \end{bmatrix} j_{2,t-1} \tag{6.72}$$

The coefficients of j_{2t} are the *impact multipliers*. They show the changes in the endogenous variables when a *current* exogenous variable is changed by one unit. For example, j_{1t} will change by $(1-\alpha_1-\gamma_1)^{-1}\alpha_1$ units when j_{2t} changes by one unit. The coefficients of $j_{2,t-1}$ are the *delayed multipliers*. They show the changes in the endogenous variables when a *lagged* exogenous variable is changed by one unit. In other words, the impact multipliers show the current-period effects and the delayed multipliers show the delayed effects of the exogenous variables on the endogenous variables as revealed by the model. In our model the only exogenous variable is government investment j_{2t}, which we choose not to explain. We merely trace the effects of government investment j_{2t} on the endogenous variables c_t and j_{1t}.

Is the model equation 6.72 a good first approximation to the Chinese economy in the 1980s, when investment is undertaken partly under the direction of the State Planning Commission and partly by individual enterprises at their own discretion? The answer is no if the variables are all measured in constant prices, as we have assumed. The positive effects of government-directed investment j_{2t} on both consumption c_t and investment of individual enterprises j_{1t} as revealed by the reduced-form model 6.72 may be unreasonable. If the government wants consumption and enterprise investment to grow faster, it only needs to invest more itself, according to the positive impact multiplier of j_{2t} in 6.72. Equation 6.72 is essentially a multiplier-accelerator model with government investment treated as exogenous. As we have explained the multiplier mechanism in equation 6.22, when an exogenous investment increases, consumption and other endogenous components of national income will increase for several rounds through the spending of income that is itself generated by the spending of a previous round. Such a process can lead to an increase in physical output if the resources of the economy are not fully employed, so that some exogenous expenditures can stimulate more production in physical terms. If the resources are fully employed, government-directed investment will be competing with private consumption and enterprise investment for the limited resources. It is not reasonable to claim that the larger j_{2t}, the larger will be c_t and j_{1t}, as implied by 6.72. Equation 6.72 might still be reasonable if the variables are measured in money terms, in which case larger values for these variables only mean inflation but not increases in physical output.

When the variables in 6.72 are measured in constant prices or in real terms, one defect of the model is that it fails to explain how resources are made available for government investment j_{2t}. One has to model the process by which resources are taken away from consumption c_t and enterprise investment j_{1t}. A way to do this is to assume that the government finances its investment j_{2t} by taxation and that consumption and enterprise investment depend on after-tax income. Therefore, when j_{2t} increases, tax will increase and consumption and enterprise investment will decrease. To capture the essence of this process, assume that the government has no other function than investing and that the tax x_t equals government investment j_{2t}. If we replace the income variable y_t in the consumption function 6.18 and the investment function 6.69 by $(y_t - x_t)$, the structural equations of the model are, with $j_{2t} = x_t$,

$$y_t = c_t + j_{1t} + x_t$$
$$c_t = \gamma_1(y_t - x_t) + \gamma_2 c_{t-1}$$
$$j_{1t} = \alpha_1(y_t - x_t) - \alpha_1(y_{t-1} - x_{t-1}) + \alpha_2 j_{1,t-1} \qquad (6.73)$$

Using the first equation of 6.73 to replace $(y_t - x_t)$ by $c_t + j_{1t}$ in the second and third equations, we obtain

$$c_t = \gamma_1 c_t + \gamma_1 j_{1t} + \gamma_2 c_{t-1}$$
$$j_{1t} = \alpha_1 c_t + \alpha_1 j_{1t} - \alpha_1 c_{t-1} - \alpha_1 j_{1,t-1} + \alpha_2 j_{1,t-1}$$

which are identical to the structural equations 6.25 and 6.26, with j_t replaced by j_{1t}. Thus, consumption c_t and enterprise investment j_{1t} generated by the model 6.73

will evolve through time in the same way as the multiplier-accelerator model 6.27 of Section 6.3. National income y_t, however, is now the sum of c_t, j_{1t}, and x_t. Although the tax x_t or government investment j_{2t} has no effect on c_t and j_{1t}, it does add to national income dollar for dollar. In other words, government investment has a multiplier of 1 on national income. Thus, while the model 6.73 yields smaller multiplier effects of j_{2t} on c_t and j_{1t} than the previous model 6.72, it still allows the economy to expand as government investment expands.

Model 6.73 has two limitations. First, even when the resources of the economy are fully employed, it permits government investment to expand the economy. Second, it does not explain how the price level of the economy is determined. Both limitations are related to the fact that it is a model of *aggregate demand,* with the consumption function and the investment function explaining how much c_t and j_{1t} will be demanded by the consumers and enterprise managers. It omits the supply side, which deals with how much the economy is capable of producing. It keeps no record of the capital stock, which helps determine the productive capacity of the economy. It has nothing to say about money and finance, about how inflation may occur, how government investment is financed, and how the financing of government investment may take away resources otherwise available for private consumption and enterprise investment. In fact, one major concern of the Chinese government in the 1980s is the rapid expansion of the investment j_{1t} by individual enterprises using their discretionary funds. The government has allowed these enterprises to retain part of their earnings, which could otherwise have been used for government investment j_{2t}. Whether the rapid expansion of enterprise investment j_{1t} is desirable from the viewpoint of Chinese economic growth deserves careful study. Because of the distorted price structure, some firms investing with their high profits may not be economically efficient, but other firms may be accumulating socially useful capital. We will present a model capable of explaining the price level and the financing of government investment in the next section.

6.6   DETERMINATION OF THE PRICE LEVEL AND FINANCING OF GOVERNMENT INVESTMENT

The topics of Sections 6.1 to 6.5 belong to *macroeconomics,* while the theory of consumer behavior discussed in Chapter 5 belongs to *microeconomics.* Microeconomics deals with the behavior of individual economic units, including consumers, workers, and enterprises. It explains how their decisions affect the production, consumption, distribution, and pricing of individual commodities. Macroeconomics deals with economic aggregates, such as national income, total consumption, total investment, total employment, and the general price level (or a price index for all commodities and services). In Sections 6.2 to 6.5 we have presented several macroeconomic models. The first task of this section is to explain how the price level is determined.

The *quantity theory of money* is a good first approximation to how the price level is determined. It is based on the quantity equation

$$Mv = Py \tag{6.74}$$

where M is the quantity of money, P is the price level, y is national income in physical terms or national product, and v is income velocity of circulation. Py is national income or total expenditure during a period in money terms. M is the quantity of money in existence. If national money income Py is 100 billion yuan during a certain year, and if the stock of money M is 20 billion yuan, the income velocity v is 5. This means that, on the average, each piece of money is used five times during the year to pay for the expenditures totaling Py yuan. The quantity equation is a definition which defines the income velocity $v = Py/M$. Treated as a definition, the quantity equation must hold true in every country every year.

What converts the quantity equation 6.74 from a definition to a theory, called the quantity theory of money, is the hypothesis that for a given economy and for a period as long as several years, the velocity v is approximately constant. The theory states that the stock of money M and money income Py are proportional, at least approximately. The quantity theory of money further assumes that the stock of money M is exogenously determined, so that money income Py is determined by the stock of money M, as a first approximation. If, in a period as short as several years when real output y is not changed by very much while M has changed relatively more, P will be approximately proportional to M, according to the quantity theory. Thus, when output is relatively constant, an increase in M will mainly increase the price level P or create inflation. If output y is determined by some model such as model 6.73 of the preceding section, and if M is treated as exogenous, the quantity theory (equation 6.74) will determine the price level P.

The quantity theory of money provides a fairly good explanation of the price level and inflation in many countries over many different periods. (See Friedman, ed., 1956, for a theoretical and empirical treatment of the quantity theory of money.) Inflation has been mainly caused by the creation of too much money. However, two modifications should be made concerning the quantity theory. First, in periods of hyperinflation when the stock of money is increased very rapidly, such as the period 1947–1949 in China, the price level increases proportionally faster than the stock of money, or the velocity v itself increases. The reason is that people try to get rid of the money they hold, as money is losing real purchasing power. In this case, inflation is still caused by the creation of too much money, except that the price level increases even faster than the stock of money. (See Cagan, 1956, for a study of hyperinflation.) The second modification is to propose a theory that allows money to influence real output y, rather than having output y determined by a separate model and using the quantity theory 6.74 to determine P, given y and M. Many such theories have been proposed in macroeconomics; one theory will be presented here.

As a first step, we modify the quantity theory (6.74) to form an equation explaining the demand for real money balances M/P. According to quantity equation 6.74, with v fixed, the demand for money M/P in real terms is proportional to real income y. An explanation for such a relation is that consumers and business enterprises desire to hold a fraction of their incomes or outputs in the form of money. The modification is that as the rate of interest r increases, the demand for real money balance M/P decreases, because the cost of holding money (which equals the interest forgone by holding money rather than an interest-yielding asset) increases. Thus, the demand for M/P is a function of both y and r. To simplify our discussion, we assume that all money consists of money issued by the government and ignore the creation of money in the form of deposits by commercial banks. When commercial banks exist, they can create money in the form of bank deposits. The deposits in checking accounts are a part of the stock of money, and sometimes deposits in savings accounts of commercial banks are included as money. (According to accepted terminology in the United States, the stock of money M_2 includes savings deposits in commercial banks, but the stock of money M_1 does not.) We simplify our discussion by assuming that money consists only of government-created money, which is called high-powered money because commercial banks can use it to create money in the form of bank deposits. An equivalent assumption is that the deposits in commercial banks have to be backed by 100 percent high-powered money, so that the banks have no power to create money of their own.

To model the financing of government investment j_{2t}, we assume as in model 6.73 that the only function of the government is to invest and that investment j_{2t} in real terms is financed by a net tax x_t (in constant prices), the issuance of new money $(M_t - M_{t-1})/P_t$, and the issuance of new government bonds. A government bond is assumed to pay an interest of one yuan per year perpetually. If the rate of interest is r, the price of one government bond is $1/r$ and the value of B government bonds is B/r (see equation 1.51). Since the holding of money and government bonds is a form of wealth to the public, consumption and the demand for money will be positively influenced by the amount of this wealth. Furthermore, investment by enterprises will be negatively influenced by the rate of interest, as we explained in Section 1.9. The assumptions introduced in this and the preceding paragraph will now be incorporated in the model 6.73 to form a new model that can explain the price level P_t and the financing of government investment j_{2t}.

The model is:

1. $y_t = c_t + j_{1t} + j_{2t}$
2. $x_t = \tau_0/P_t + \tau y_t - B_t/P_t + \tau B_t/P_t$
3. $c_t = \gamma_1(y_t - x_t) + \gamma_2 M_t/P_t + \gamma_3 B_t/P_t + \gamma_4 c_{t-1}$
4. $j_{1t} = \alpha_1(y_t - x_t) - \alpha_1(y_{t-1} - x_{t-1}) + \alpha_2 r_t^{-1} + \alpha_3 j_{1,t-1}$
5. $M_t/P_t = \lambda_0 + \lambda_1 y_t + \lambda_2 B_t/P_t + \lambda_3 r_t^{-1}$
6. $j_{2t} = x_t + (M_t - M_{t-1})/P_t + (B_t - B_{t-1})/r_t P_t$
7. $P_t - P_{t-1} = \delta_0 - \delta_1(\theta k_{t-1} - y_t)$
8. $k_t = j_{1t} + j_{2t} + k_{t-1}$ (6.75)

The first seven equations of this model determine the seven endogenous variables y_t, x_t, c_t, j_{1t}, r_t, B_t, and P_t with j_{2t} and M_t treated as exogenous variables. The last equation determines the capital stock k_t given k_{t-1} once the investments j_{1t} and j_{2t} are known. These equations are explained below.

The first equation is the definition of national income that we used earlier. Note that we are considering a closed economy, with no imports or exports. The second equation explains net tax x_t in constant prices. τ_0 is the amount of tax in money terms, which is independent of national output y_t. The second term τy_t is the amount of tax in real terms, which depends on y_t, τ being the tax rate. If the government has B_t units of bonds outstanding, it has to pay out B_t yuan from the tax revenue, accounting for the third term. The fourth term incorporates the tax τB_t received by the government from the bond interest received by the public; this term vanishes if bond interest is nontaxable. The division by P_t in the first, third, and fourth terms is to convert them into constant prices. The third equation is as before, except that consumption is positively influenced by the money balance M_t/P_t in real terms and by bond interest B_t/P_t. The fourth equation is also the same as before, except that the rate of interest r_t has a negative effect on investment.

In the first four equations explaining the four endogenous variables y_t, x_t, c_t, and j_{1t}, we have introduced three other variables, P_t, B_t, and r_t, which need to be explained. Three more equations are therefore needed. The fifth equation is a demand equation for money, which is a generalization of the quantity theory. Demand for real money balances M_t/P_t is positively influenced by real income y_t and real value of bond interest payment B_t/P_t, and is negatively influenced by the rate of interest r_t. Keynes (1936) introduces such an equation as a crucial equation in macroeconomics. Assuming P_t to be constant (and B_t to be constant also), Keynes uses this equation to explain the rate of interest r_t by the stock of money M_t. By contrast, the quantity theory of money assumes that r_t has a small effect on the demand for money and uses this equation to explain the price level P_t by the stock of money M_t. The truth of the matter is that both variables r_t and P_t exist in this equation and that a change in M_t will affect a combination of these variables. Which will be affected more depends on the solution of the entire system of equations in 6.75. We will say more on this point three paragraphs below.

The sixth equation is a government budget constraint. The importance of such a government budget constraint in macroeconomics has been emphasized by Carl Christ (see his 1979 paper for a survey and the references therein). The point is that government spending for investment (and other purposes) has to be financed by taxation or by an increase in government debt (money being noninterest-bearing and bonds being interest-bearing). Government spending can also be financed by borrowing from foreign countries or by reducing the holding of foreign exchanges, but these are ignored in the present model. In the last term of equation 6, $(B_t - B_{t-1})$ is the number of new bonds issued, and the money value of these new bonds is $(B_t - B_{t-1})/r_t$. As Christ points out, if M_t and j_{2t} are treated as exogenous, the issue of new bonds $(B_t - B_{t-1})$ is endogenously determined by the government budget constraint.

Equation 7 states that the increase in the price level, or inflation, is negatively related to the difference between capacity output θk_{t-1} and actual output. We assume for simplicity that capacity output depends on the capital stock available at the end of the last period. This model fails to incorporate labor as an important factor determining capacity output. An alternative hypothesis is that the rate of change in the money wage rate, and accordingly in the price level, is negatively related to the unemployment rate. A high rate of unemployment means a large difference between the quantity of labor available and the quantity actually used. In equation 7 we use instead the difference between the quantity of capital available and the quantity actually used. The alternative hypothesis is known as the *Phillips curve,* after A. W. Phillips (1958). It is possible to incorporate both labor and capital as factors determining productive capacity. In China, however, for the production of much of the national product, some would consider capital as a more important factor affecting productive capacity, as labor is considered plentiful.

To return to the question of how much a given change in the money stock M_t will affect P_t relative to r_t or y_t, multiplying equation 5 of model 6.75 by P_t yields

$$M_t = \lambda_0 P_t + \lambda_1 p_t y_t + \lambda_2 B_t + \lambda_3 p_t r_t^{-1}$$

or the conclusion that when M_t increases, the right-hand side consisting of $P_t y_t$ and $P_t r_t^{-1}$ must be increased. If λ_3 is very small, the term involving r_t may be dropped, and the effect will be on money income $P_t y_t$. How much will be on P_t as compared with y_t depends on how near actual output is to capacity output θk_{t-1}. According to equation 7, P_t will increase less if national output y_t is much below capacity output. If production is near capacity, P_t will increase more. When we have a system of simultaneous structural equations determining several endogenous variables by several exogenous variables, it is necessary to solve for the reduced form to ascertain the effect of any one exogenous variable on each endogenous variable. When the system of structural equations is nonlinear, as 6.75 is, the reduced form cannot be solved explicitly. One has to resort to numerical analysis or to linearizing the system. Such matters are treated in Chow (1975), but are too technical to be discussed here.

6.7   MACROECONOMIC RELATIONS IN THE CHINESE ECONOMY

In the preceding section we presented a macroeconomic model (6.75) that is capable of explaining fluctuations and growth of an economy. This model consists of three identities or definitions (equations 1, 6, and 8) and five behavioral or institutional equations. Equation 2 is an institutional equation explaining government taxes. Equations 3, 4, 5, and 7 are behavioral, explaining consumption, nongovernment-directed investment, the demand for money, and the adjustment of the general price index, respectively. These equations are applicable to a developed, Western economy. Can these equations, after appropriate modifications, adequately explain the Chinese macroeconomy in the 1980s? Answering this question properly requires constructing an econometric model of the Chinese economy based on these equations.

An econometric model consists of a system of numerical equations describing the working of certain aspects of an economy. The macroeconomic model 6.75 is not econometric because the numerical values of the parameters τ_0, τ, γ_1, γ_2, and so on, are not specified. To construct an econometric model, usually a *random residual* is added to each structural equation that is not an identity. This is done to allow for the fact that the variable on the left-hand side of the equation is not perfectly explained by the function on the right-hand side, leaving a residual that is assumed to be random by the econometrician. Recall from Section 4.2 that the difference between a dependent variable y and the regression function $a+bx$ is also assumed to be a random residual. By the introduction of random residuals the otherwise deterministic equations become *stochastic equations,* and a deterministic model becomes a *stochastic model.* In addition, statistical data and other information are used to estimate the values of the parameters of the stochastic model. Econometric methods will be applied here in a way similar to the way in which the method of least squares was applied in Section 4.2 to estimate the parameters of a regression model, which is a basic example of an econometric model. *Econometric methods* will also help us decide how well the model that we have specified fits the data for a given economy during the period under investigation.

It would be very difficult today to test the empirical validity of all the structural equations in the model 6.75 for the Chinese economy by econometric methods because the data required are not available. The model is specified for the Chinese economy as of the 1980s. Only a very short historical period yet exists for observing this economy, even if all statistical data after 1979 are available. Some of the equations, especially the equation for nongovernment-directed investment, are valid only after the economic reforms of 1979–1980. Therefore, instead of using econometric methods systematically, we have to piece together institutional information and fragmentary data to judge whether model 6.75 is a reasonable first approximation to the working of the Chinese macroeconomy. Our effort may serve as a first step toward the construction, estimation, and testing of an econometric model for the Chinese economy in the 1980s. Let us reexamine the equations of 6.75 from the viewpoint of Chinese economic institutions and data.

Equation 1 requires little comment because it is an identity. Chinese official data, such as those given in Table 6.1, break down national income into consumption and capital accumulation. In view of the expansion of nongovernment-directed investment and the concern that it has recently created among Chinese government officials, data on nongovernment investment j_{1t} and government investment j_{2t} may be separately provided in the future, which will permit economists to study them.

Equation 2 requires a reinterpretation in the Chinese context. The purpose of this equation is to explain total tax revenue of the government net of any transfer payments from the government to the public. The net tax variable will then be used in equations 3 and 4 to form an after-tax income variable, which can explain consumption and nongovernment investment. The idea is that when the government takes away resources from consumers and nongovernment investors in the form of taxation in order to finance its own investments, consumers will consume less and nongovernment investors will invest less. In an economy where all productive resources are owned by the citizen-consumers, all of national income consists of incomes of individual citizens in the forms of wages and salaries, rents, and distributed and undistributed profits of corporations that are owned by them. The government can obtain economic resources from the people by taxation, which reduces the ability of consumers to consume and the ability of private investors to invest. In equation 2 the income variable y_t means national income, which is the total income of all individual citizens, and the net tax variable x_t refers to taxation of the above income by the government net of any transfer payments from the government to the people. This interpretation is essentially valid for the United States, in which the government owns some enterprises producing a very small fraction of national output. If equation 2 is applied to the United States, the tax variable x_t should include profits of government enterprises. (In the national income account of the United States, "current surplus less subsidies of government enterprises" is usually negative, meaning that government enterprises receive more subsidies than the income they earn, leading to an expenditure rather than a revenue for the government.) Here we are assuming that only one equation is used to explain net tax x_t. Otherwise, several equations can be used to explain different components of x_t.

In the Chinese economy most of the productive resources are either state-owned or collectively owned rather than individually owned. Almost all farms are collectively owned, except for some state-owned farms. Most industrial enterprises and all large industrial enterprises are state-owned; some small enterprises are collectively owned, but they are increasing in number and in importance in the 1980s. Therefore, one cannot assume that national output consists essentially of incomes of individual citizens. Spendable income of the citizens is derived from the wages and salaries of workers and staff, distributed income from the communes and income from the farmland separately allotted in the case of farmers (the latter income is becoming increasingly important in the 1980s), and interest from savings deposits. Before the economic reforms initiated in the late 1970s, one can think of Chinese national income as essentially belonging to the government, except for the wages and distributed farm incomes that the government decided to distribute to the people. To the extent that farmers and operators of small enterprises now can earn their own incomes after the economic reforms, the above description has to be modified. Whether one views national income as essentially belonging to the citizens individually except for the tax by the government, or as essentially belonging to the state except for the wage and farm incomes that it decides to distribute, equation 2 can be valid if the net tax variable x_t is interpreted to mean net receipts of the government generated by the economic process producing a national income y_t. For example, if many industrial enterprises are government enterprises, as in the case of China, income from these enterprises should be a part of x_t. The coefficient τ in equation 2 is no longer a purely tax rate, but an average of tax rates and the ratio of government revenue to national income generated by government enterprises. The last ratio will be reduced by the recent decision to allow certain government enterprises to retain a larger fraction of their incomes for their own use and to submit a smaller fraction to the government. If one wishes to have more details, several equations can be formulated to replace equation 2, each equation explaining one component of government revenue. The total of these revenues minus government transfer payments and subsidies will be x_t.

Major components of the revenues and expenditures of the Chinese government in 1980 and 1981 are given in Table 6.2. The variable x_t in equation 2 should include revenues of government enterprises, taxes, and other revenues minus farm subsidies, government administration expenditures, and interest expenses; these are resources generated by national production that are taken by the government from private consumption and nongovernment investment. The model 6.75 does not include government expenditures other than investment expenditures, which are the first three items of expenditures listed in Table 6.2 plus development expenditures for backward areas. Denote government expenditures (in constant prices) on education, health, science, and defense by g_t. Two equations of model 6.75 are affected by the introduction of g_t. First, equation 1 should include g_t on its right-hand side. Second, equation 6 should include g_t on its left-hand side. For equation 2, we assume that the taxes and other revenues minus farm subsidies and government administration expenses are a linear function

$$\tau_0/P_t + \tau y_t$$

of national income y_t, which accounts for the first two terms on the right-hand side of equation 2. The third term on the right-hand side, B_t/P_t, represents interest paid by the government on its debt, which should be subtracted from the above figure to form x_t. The last term of equation 2, $\tau B_t/P_t$, represents tax on the interest income from government bonds. It exists for the United States but should be omitted for China, where no income tax is levied on such interest income received by Chinese citizens. Again, it is possible to break down x_t into two components, one representing taxes and

Table 6.2 **APPROVED CHINESE GOVERNMENT REVENUES AND EXPENDITURES, 1981 AND 1982**

(Billion Yuan)

	1980	1981
Revenues		
Revenues of enterprises	46.06	34.72
Taxes	54.40	60.90
Loans	3.39	8.00
Other revenues	2.44	2.24
Total	106.29	105.86
Expenditures		
Construction	37.35	33.06
Enterprise renovations and innovations	6.98	5.83
Enterprise working capital	3.72	2.20
Farm subsidies and other expenditures	7.74	7.30
Education, health, and science	14.83	17.00
Defense	19.33	16.87
Administration	5.78	7.24
Development of backward areas, geological explorations	.50	2.18
Other expenses—including interest and repayment of foreign loans	4.05	16.90
Total	114.29	108.58

Sources: Figures for 1980 are from *People's Daily,* September 13, 1980. Figures for 1981 are from *Almanac of China's Economy, 1982,* Chinese edition, pp. V-319–320. For the distinctions among the final state account, the draft state budget, and the projected state budget, see *Almanac of China's Economy, 1981,* pp. 128–138. Briefly, the draft state budget is the budget approved by the People's Congress; the final account is an after-the-fact statement of results; the projected state budget is an estimate for the following year. This table provides the draft state budget.

the other representing revenues of government enterprises. The latter variable would require another equation to explain.

Equation 3 is a hypothesis about aggregate consumption, explaining it by after-tax income (or, in the Chinese context, income available to the private sector), money, and bonds held by the public, with a distributed lag relationship captured by the lagged variable c_{t-1}. Such a hypothesis is an assumption about the aggregate *demand* for consumption goods by the people, given their income and monetary assets. It is possible that in a centrally planned economy the total quantity of consumer goods made available is determined mainly by government policy, which is independent of consumer demand. In such a situation the demand equation 3 cannot explain the total quantity of consumer goods produced, which is determined by the supply controlled by the government. However, even in such a situation, a consumption function such as equation 3, if expressed in money terms, can explain consumption expenditures in current prices. Given the level of money income, if consumers decide to spend so many dollars to buy consumer goods and if the government allows only c_t units of consumer goods to be produced, the net effect is for the consumption function to determine the price level P_t, because it determines total consumption expenditure $P_t c_t$, and c_t is fixed by the government. For the Chinese economy in the 1980s, I believe that the consumption function represented by equation 3 is essentially valid, for two reasons. First, the Chinese government now considers consumer demand in determining the production of consumer goods that it supplies. Second, a sizeable fraction of consumer goods, including many agricultural products and products of light industries, is produced at the discretion of the individual farmers and individually or collectively operated enterprises, which will produce to satisfy consumer demand. At least equation 3 is a promising hypothesis to be tested statistically when more data become available.

Equation 4 explains investment j_{1t} by enterprises that have the discretion to expand productive capacity to satisfy demand for profit. Such an equation works well for the American economy (see Chow, 1967 and 1968). If the managers of certain Chinese enterprises are allowed to retain a substantial portion of the profits and are given sufficient discretion to invest, they will behave in the same way as managers of enterprises in the United States and other Western countries. In China, during a period of rapid economic reform in the early 1980s, the price system and the tax system were not working properly in many areas, which led to investment by enterprise managers that may have been socially undesirable. For example, if an enterprise pays a lower-than-market price for an important material used in production, pays a lower-than-market rent for the use of its capital equipment (possibly in the form of a levy by the government), or receives a higher-than-market price for its product because of government protection or price regulation, it may earn a high profit and decide to invest a large fraction of the retained profit. The expansion of such an enterprise may be socially undesirable because its profitability is not the result of its economic efficiency but of the distortion of the price system. In 1983 articles appeared in Chinese newspapers and journals criticizing the large capital investments undertaken by enterprises at their own discretion. The problem of socially undesirable investments deserves careful investigation. If socially undesirable investments occur because prices do not reflect social cost, the solution to this problem is to improve the price system. If the price system functions properly, it is difficult to argue against letting the profitable enterprises expand their productive capacity. A main objective of the economic reform of 1980–1981 to allow enterprises more autonomy in their decisions is to promote economic efficiency in production and investment. Economic efficiency would not result unless prices were allowed to be determined by the forces of demand and supply. If prices are so determined, profitable firms are by and large efficient firms producing to satisfy market demand and should be allowed to expand. In the meantime, investment j_{2t} undertaken by the government will take care of the capital accumulation required by the economy but neglected by the individual enterprises. We will discuss this topic further in the next section.

Concerning equation 4, the interest rate variable r is intended to reflect the cost and availability of credit, which affects investment according to the theory presented in Section 1.9. When the rate of interest is lowered, the same stream of future earnings will have a higher present value, according to equation 1.50. Therefore, an investment project costing an amount larger than the previously calculated present value of its future net earnings may now be undertaken because of the larger present value calculated by a lower interest rate. To put this in another way, if the enterprise can borrow the money from a bank to pay the cost of this investment project, a lower interest rate may make the same future net earnings from the project more than cover the future payments to the bank and thus make the project profitable. As we pointed out in Section 1.9, a main function of banks is to obtain funds from the savings of individual citizens and to lend them to enterprises for investment purposes. In a market economy, the rate of interest is determined partly by the demand for and the supply of loanable funds.

The demand for loanable funds comes mainly from business investment, as explained by equation 4. The supply of loanable funds comes mainly from the savings of consumers, which is the difference between their after-tax income and their consumption, with consumption explained by equation 1. Both demand and supply are functions of the rate of interest. We might therefore choose to modify our model by introducing the rate of interest as an additional variable in equation 3 and introducing private savings $(y-x_t-c_t)$ as an additional variable to reflect the availability of credit in equation 4.

In 1980, as a part of the economic reform to allow enterprises more autonomy, the Chinese banking system began to play a more active role in obtaining savings deposits from the public and extending loans to enterprises for working capital and for investment purpose. Table 6.3 presents the balance sheet of the Chinese banking system at the end of 1979, 1980, and 1981. Note that savings deposits in cities and towns

Table 6.3   BALANCE SHEET OF CHINA'S BANKING SYSTEM
(100 Million Yuan)

	End of 1979	End of 1980	End of 1981
Credit Funds			
Deposits	1,340.04	1,658.64	2,032.97
Deposits by enterprises	468.91	573.09	701.46
Deposits by the treasury	148.68	162.02	194.94
Capital construction funds	131.30	171.75	229.15
Deposits by government departments	184.88	229.45	274.88
Savings deposits in cities and towns	202.56	282.49	354.14
Deposits in rural areas	203.71	239.84	278.40
Deposits by international monetary institutions	—	—	54.05
Currency in circulation	267.71	346.20	396.34
Bank working funds	427.88	477.33	497.05
Bank surplus	49.45	27.19	17.22
Others	77.52	80.63	50.23
Total	2,162.60	2,624.26	3,047.86
Credit Funds Used			
Loans	2,039.63	2,414.30	2,764.67
To industrial production enterprises	363.09	431.58	508.85
To supply and marketing enterprises	242.12	236.03	241.24
Commercial loans	1,232.25	1,437.02	1,639.13
Short, medium-term loans for buying equipment	7.92	55.50	83.73
To urban collective and individual enterprises	57.51	78.29	99.15
To finance down payments on purchases	6.98	7.88	7.39
To state farms	6.86	9.40	16.75
To rural communes and brigades	122.90	158.60	168.41
Gold purchases	12.16	12.16	12.04
Foreign exchange purchases	20.58	−8.47	62.18
Balances with International Monetary Fund	—	36.04	38.74
Money advanced to the Ministry of Finance	90.23	170.23	170.23
Total	2,162.60	2,624.26	3,047.86

Sources: Figures for 1979 and 1980 are from *Almanac of China's Economy, 1981,* p. 997. Figures for 1981 are from *Almanac of China's Economy, 1982,* Chinese edition, p. V-331.

increased from 20.256 billion yuan at the end of 1979 to 35.414 billion at the end of 1981, while deposits in rural areas increased from 20.371 billion to 27.840 billion. Furthermore, outside of the banking system, deposits in rural credit cooperatives increased from 21.588 billion at the end of 1979 to 31.961 billion at the end of 1981 (*Almanac of China's Economy, 1982,* Chinese edition, pp. V-330, V-331). Savings deposits by the nongovernment sector were gaining importance in the early 1980s in providing funds for investment purposes. Observe also that loans to urban collective and individual enterprises increased from 5.751 billion at the end of 1979 to 9.915 billion at the end of 1981. These enterprises are only a small percentage of all enterprises that can use their own discretion to expand their productive capacity.

In 1980 interest rates paid to personal savings deposits of urban and rural residents were 2.88 percent per annum on demand deposits, 4.32 on deposits for six months, 5.40 on deposits for five years. The interest rate on loans to state-owned industrial and commercial enterprises and to urban collective enterprises was 5.04 percent per year. It was 4.32 percent on loans for down payments on purchases of farm and sideline products and on loans to state farms and agricultural communes and brigades to meet production costs and to provide working capital. It was 2.16 percent on loans to communes and brigades for buying production equipment or for constructing hydroelectric power stations, and on loans to credit cooperatives. (*Almanac of China's Economy, 1981,* pp. 662–663.) In April 1982 interest rates paid to personal savings deposits were raised to 0.36 percent per month on deposits for six months and 0.66 percent per month on deposits for five years. Besides using the rates of interest to regulate deposits and loans, the Chinese banking system has discretion to select the kinds of enterprises to which loans will be extended. (For a description of China's banking system, see the 1982 article by the Research Institute of Finance and Banking of the People's Bank of China.) The availability of credits supplied by the banking system could be an additional variable affecting investment in equation 4.

Equation 5 of the model 6.75 is a demand-for-money equation. The demand for money is a subject that has been extensively studied in the United States and other Western countries. One may introduce some distributed lag mechanism to equation 5 by adding a term $\lambda_4 M_{t-1}/P_{t-1}$ on the right-hand side, for instance, or change the functional form to linear in the logarithms (see Chow, 1966), but the basic hypothesis is valid that the demand for real money balances depends positively on real income and negatively on the rate of interest. The same should be true for China. The hypothesis that the demand for real money balances M/P is proportional to real income y constitutes the quantity theory of money. This theory implies that when y changes slowly, an increase in M will essentially lead to an increase in the price level P, or to inflation. Many economic officials of the Chinese government appear to believe in this theory, because after signs of inflation in 1980, the State Council in early 1981 issued a directive ordering the strict control of the supply of money (*Almanac of China's Economy, 1982,* Chinese edition, p. V-326). This directive was followed seriously. Chinese officials probably remembered the inflation in 1947–1949, which was caused by the creation of money.

Observe from Table 6.3 that currency in circulation increased from 26.771 billion yuan at the end of 1979 to 34.620 billion at the end of 1980, or by 29.3 percent; it increased to 39.634 billion at the end of 1981, or by a much slower rate of 16.1 percent.

The general retail price index increased from 138.6 in 1979 to 146.9 in 1980, or by 6.0 percent; it increased to 150.4 in 1981, or by a much slower rate of 2.4 percent (*Statistical Yearbook of China, 1981,* p. 411). The general price index of living costs of staff and workers increased from 147.4 in 1979 to 158.5 in 1980, or by 7.5 percent; it increased to 162.5 in 1981, or by only 2.5 percent. Both price indices are less comprehensive than an index of the general price level, and currency in circulation is only a part of the supply of money, though a large part in China, but there is no question that the above data support the quantity theory of money. The price level increased at a faster rate in 1980, when the stock of money increased faster; it increased at a slower rate in 1981, when the stock of money increased more slowly.

Equation 6 is a form of the government budget constraint. When government expenditure g_t other than investment expenditures j_{2t} is added to its left-hand side, equation 6 states that government expenditures have to be financed by taxes and other revenues x_t, the increase in money supply or the increase in government bonds. The Chinese government understood such a relationship well in 1981, when it tried to slow down the increase in the stock of money. It announced that the expenditures on capital construction j_{2t} should be reduced in 1981 and succeeded in reducing them. Note in Table 6.2 that approved construction expenditures were reduced from 37.35 billion in 1980 to 33.06 billion in 1981, while expenditures for enterprise renovations and innovations were reduced from 6.98 to 5.83 billion. Approved defense expenditures went down from 19.32 to 16.87 billion, while expenditures on education, health, and science went up from 14.83 to 17.00 billion. Table 6.2 shows that the government deficit as approved by the People's Congress was 114.29 minus 106.29, or 8 billion, in 1980, and it was only 108.58 minus 105.86, or 2.72 billion, in 1981, with total approved government expenditure reduced from 114.29 to 108.58 billion. (The U.S. government did not control its deficits as well.) The reduction in government deficit $j_{2t} + g_t - x_t$ in 1981 enabled the stock of money to increase by a smaller amount. Government bonds were also used to finance the deficits. In 1980, while the projected budget deficit was 8 billion, the actual deficit was 12.1 billion, with revenues totaling 106.61 billion and expenditures totaling 118.72 billion (*Almanac of China's Economy, 1981,* p. 644).

Shen and Chen (1982, pp. 644–645) write:

> The large deficits in 1979 and 1980 and the consequent growth of the money supply played a large part in pushing up prices of various commodities, with detrimental effects for the national economy and political stability.

> Late in 1980 the State Council studied the financial and economic situation and decided to take measures to achieve a rough budget balance and a credit balance. . . .

> China's basic budget policy is to maintain an annual balance between revenues and expenditures with a little surplus. . . .

> Deficits have occurred several times. There have been two kinds of budget deficits. One kind was the objective result of wars and natural disaster; the 1950 deficit was of this kind. The other kind was due to subjective errors—in particular, rashness; the deficits that occurred after 1956 were of the second kind.

> In 1956, carried away with the tremendous successes we had achieved in socialist transformation and construction, we quickened the speed of construction. That year

our investments in capital construction increased by more than 50 percent and our expenditures and agricultural loans exceeded their planned levels. As a result we incurred a budget deficit of 1,800 million yuan and a deficit in bank credit. . . .

Equation 7 and equation 5 both contribute to the explanation of the price level. When the stock of money increases, money income tends to increase, according to the quantity theory of money and equation 5. For a given increase in money income, price increases more if real income y increases less. Real income cannot increase substantially if it is already close to capacity output. In such a situation, price will increase more, according to equation 7. Equation 7 can be improved by using a better index for capacity output than θk_{t-1}. For example, a production function can be used, so that both the quantity of capital and the quantity of labor (at least skilled labor) available will jointly determine capacity output. One might question the explanation of the price level implicit in model 6.75 on the ground that the Chinese government still controls the prices of many commodities. To the extent that many prices are not controlled and that government officials would be under pressure to raise the prices they do control when demand exceeded supply, the explanation of the price level by means of an economic model built upon a set of tested economic behavioral relations is a valid procedure.

Equation 8 is an identity, or a definition. It should be applicable to any country. However, when all capital goods are aggregated into one variable k_t and when all investments are grouped in either j_{1t} or j_{2t}, the conceptual problems in the statistical measurement of these variables may be serious. Especially in an economy where many prices are administratively determined, it is difficult to measure the quantities of different capital investments. An expensive investment project may produce a small amount of capital if measured by its productivity. One solution to the problem of too much aggregation is to disaggregate. In China investment and capital stock in agriculture may be treated separately. Much of the investment in agriculture is government-directed and belongs to j_{2t}, but in the future one may find desirable the separation of a component of j_{1t} for agriculture. The statistical measurement of different components of capital stock in China deserves our serious attention.

We have now proposed a system of eight equations to describe the working of the Chinese macroeconomy. These equations are useful definitions or hypotheses about economic behavior that have been tested empirically in other parts of the world and that also seem to be valid for China, from the crude examination of the Chinese institutions and data in this section. Therefore, they are submitted here as a first set of working hypotheses on the Chinese macroeconomy in the 1980s. It is hoped that they will be refined, modified, and improved in the future, and an improved version of these equations will serve as the basis of a macroeconometric model of the Chinese economy.

Just to whet the reader's appetite, I present below a consumption function of the form 6.18 and an investment function of the form 6.24, which make up the simple multiplier-accelerator model of Section 6.3. These functions are estimated by the method of least squares, using the annual data from 1953 to 1981 given in Table 6.1, the data for 1952 serving as the initial values of the lagged endogenous variables. Consumption is defined as national income minus investment (or capital accumulation). In the econometric literature other methods than least squares have been suggested when a right-hand side variable (national income in our case) is endogenous, but we cannot deal with this technical problem here. Furthermore, note that all data are in current prices, whereas data in constant prices might be considered more appropriate. We use capital letters to denote variables in current prices.

The consumption function so estimated is

$$C_t = -.7323 + .2294\ Y_t + .7261\ C_{t-1} \qquad R^2 = .9910$$
$$ (2.8817) \quad (.0724) \qquad (.1219) \qquad\qquad s^2 = 35.299 \qquad (6.76)$$

where standard errors of the estimated coefficients are in parentheses and s^2 denotes the variance of regression residuals. Note that the intercept is very small as compared with its standard error. The two coefficients are very large as compared with their standard errors. The R^2 is also very high, but this is to be expected when an endogenous variable is explained by its own lagged value.

The investment function is

$$J_t = 2.1744 + .7549\ (Y_t - Y_{t-1}) + .8496\ J_{t-1} \qquad R^2 = .9697$$
$$ (2.0870) \quad (.0845) \qquad\qquad\qquad (.0376) \qquad\quad s^2 = 35.170 \quad (6.77)$$

If we replace the variable ΔY_t by two separate variables Y_t and Y_{t-1}, the resulting investment function is

$$J_t = 1.0922 + .7359\ Y_t - .7059\ Y_{t-1} + .7755\ J_{t-1} \qquad R^2 = .9700$$
$$ (2.9789) \quad (.0933) \qquad (.1279) \qquad (.1484) \qquad\quad s^2 = 36.190 \ (6.78)$$

The freely estimated coefficient of Y_{t-1} is approximately the negative of the coefficient of Y_t, as implied by the acceleration principle.

One might be amazed to find how well the consumption function 6.18 and the investment function 6.24 of the multiplier-accelerator model of Section 6.3 fit the Chinese data from 1953 to 1981. These functions have been justified by rational economic behavior on the part of individual consumers and enterprise managers who are in a position to make their own consumption and investment decisions. One might point out that consumption and investment in China from 1953 to 1981 were largely determined by the Chinese government, which was sometimes driven by political forces. The consumption function may still work, because the Chinese consumers were able to determine partially their consumption expenditures out of their incomes and because the Chinese economic planners were planning total consumption based on the national income available. The investment function may still work, because the Chinese enterprise managers submitted their investment plans to accumulate capital to meet the need for producing certain output and because the Chinese economic planners were influenced by the plans so submitted or made their own investment plans in a similar fashion. These behavioral justifications aside, one may simply point out that there are basic empirical relations between consumption and income and between capital stock and income as postulated by the Harrod-Domar model. The consumption function is based on the first relation with a distributed lag. The investment function is the first difference of the second relation with a lag. Therefore, they work in China. A more thorough statistical analysis of this multiplier-accelerator model is found in Chow (1983). Macroeconomic relations are aggregates that hide a lot of things. To study the behavior of individual economic units more thoroughly, one has to resort to microeconometrics.

6.8 COMPOSITION OF CAPITAL INVESTMENT

To complete this chapter on national income and capital accumulation in China, we will describe briefly the composition of investment that has been undertaken by the Chinese government. Partial information is contained in Table 6.4, on the composition of investment by state-owned units, which excludes investment by collective units in towns and in rural communes. Note first that the official data in Table 6.4 show a distinction between the value of newly increased fixed assets and the value of total investment. The former is usually smaller than the latter. The difference is explained in the *Statistical Yearbook of China, 1981* (p. 518): "The purchases of equipment, tools

Table 6.4 COMPOSITION OF INVESTMENT BY STATE–OWNED UNITS
(100 Million Yuan)

Item	1950	1952	1957	1965	1975	1979
1. Newly increased fixed assets	10.09	31.14	129.22	159.93	250.53	418.27
2. Total investment	11.34	43.56	138.29	170.89	391.86	499.88
a) By funding:						
National budget	10.41	37.11	126.45	154.37	318.12	394.97
Self-raised funds of local authorities and enterprises	0.93	6.45	11.84	16.52	73.74	104.91
b) By types:						
Construction and installment works	8.59	28.40	85.06	103.88	218.98	328.30
Purchase of equipment, tools, and implements	2.21	11.07	45.85	55.07	144.63	137.17
Other investment	0.54	4.09	7.38	11.94	28.25	34.31
c) By sectors:						
Industry	—	16.89	72.40	88.96	231.03	256.85
Light industry	—	4.06	11.04	7.01	23.13	30.60
Heavy industry	—	12.83	61.36	81.95	207.90	226.25
Construction	—	0.89	4.62	4.11	6.89	11.47
Transport, post, and telecommunications	—	7.61	20.69	30.51	68.67	64.09
Agriculture, forestry, water conservancy, and meteorology	—	5.83	11.87	24.97	38.40	57.92
Commerce, catering, and service trades	—	1.20	3.72	4.63	12.01	20.57
Science, culture, education, and public health	—	3.34	10.50	9.12	15.12	33.47
Civic public utilities	—	1.64	3.82	4.45	8.25	29.91
Geological exploration	—	0.68	3.02	0.74	2.06	7.40
Others	—	5.48	7.65	3.40	9.43	18.20

Source: Almanac of China's Economy, 1981, p. 979.

Table 6.5   TRANSPORTATION ROUTES IN CHINA
              (in 10,000 km)

| Year | Railway lines | | Highways open to traffic | Navigable inland waterways | Civil aviation routes | | Petroleum and gas pipelines |
	Open to traffic	Total track length			Total	Inter-national routes	
1949	2.20	3.00	8.07	7.36	—	—	—
1952	2.45	3.51	12.67	9.50	1.31	0.51	—
1957	2.99	4.31	25.46	14.41	2.64	0.43	—
1965	3.74	5.89	51.45	15.77	3.94	0.45	—
1975	4.84	7.91	78.36	13.56	8.42	3.71	0.53
1979	5.15	8.68	87.58*	10.78*	16.00	5.13	0.91

Source: Almanac of China's Economy, 1981, p. 977. Asterisked figures refer to the end of October 1979.

and instruments which do not accord with the standard for fixed assets, training expenses, . . . investment on abandoned projects and some other expenses . . . are not counted in newly added fixed assets." This seems to imply that some investment activities do not lead to economically useful assets. Concerning the financing of investment, note the substantial financing from the national budget (compare the 39.5 billion figure for 1979 with the government expenditures on construction for 1980 and 1981 in Table 6.2), but also note the increasing portion financed by self-raised funds of local authorities and enterprises. The data on investment by sectors of the economy are interesting and self-explanatory.

Note the investment in the economic infrastructure, which consists of railroads, highways, waterways, ports, dams, water-conservation projects, urban development projects, and other construction work that provides a basic structure for the functioning of the economy. Table 6.4 also contains figures for government investment in transport, postal service, and telecommunications, for agriculture and forestry, for civic public utilities, and for geological exploration. Many of these investments are related to the building of the economic infrastructure. Further information on the economic infrastructure is contained in Table 6.5, on transportation routes in China. Finally, investments for science, culture, education, and public health are related to the formation of human capital, a subject to be discussed in Chapter 7.

PROBLEMS

1. Let δ be the annual rate of depreciation of capital stock and i_t be gross investment. The relation between i_t and net investment j_t is

$$i_t = j_t + \delta k_{t-1} = k_t - k_{t-1} + \delta k_{t-1} = k_t - (1-\delta)k_{t-1}$$

Incorporate this relation in the Harrod-Domar model of equations 6.1–6.3 and solve the resulting model. Derive an equation for the growth of i_t that is, express i_t as a function of i_{t-1}. Show that the relation between i_t and y_t is

$$i_t = (a-1+\delta)(a\theta)^{-1}y_t = [1 - (1-\delta)(1-\sigma\theta)]\theta^{-1}y_t$$

2. Find the characteristic roots and right characteristic vector of the matrix

$$A = \begin{bmatrix} 5 & -1 \\ 2 & 2 \end{bmatrix}$$

3. Obtain the solution to the following system of difference equations in terms of the relevant characteristic roots:

$$y_{1t} = 5y_{1,t-1} - y_{2,t-1}$$
$$y_{2t} = 2y_{1,t-1} + 2y_{2,t-1}$$

Assume that $y_{1,0} = 0$ and $y_{2,0} = 1$. Plot the solution for y_{1t} and y_{2t} for $t = 1,2,\ldots,5$.

4. Let national income y_t satisfy a second-order difference equation

$$y_t = a_1 y_{t-1} + a_2 y_{t-2}$$

Write this equation as a first-order system. What is the characteristic equation for the system? For what values of a_1 and a_2 will the roots of this characteristic equation be complex? Under what conditions will the above system be explosive and oscillatory?

5. Write the equation

$$y_t = a_1 y_{t-1} + a_2 y_{t-2} + b$$

as a first-order system without an intercept. What is the characteristic equation for the system?

6. How is the Harrod-Domar model related to the multiplier-accelerator model? In what way is each of these models useful or not useful in explaining the Chinese economy?

7. Using the initial values $c_0 = 45.9$ and $j_0 = 13.0$, solve the system 6.58 numerically for $t = 1,2,\ldots,10$.

8. For the model 6.30, let $\gamma_1 = .50$, $\gamma_2 = .30$, $\alpha_1 = .29$, and $\alpha_2 = 1.0$. Find the characteristic roots of the system. What is the length of the cycle of the cosine function generated by the roots? Is the system explosive or damped? Explain. Trace the time paths of c_t and j_t for 10 periods, using the initial values $c_0 = 45.9$ and $j_t = 13.0$.

9. Explain why the rate of growth of real national income in China is different according to whether real income is measured in 1952 prices or in 1980 prices. Which measure do you prefer and for what purposes?

10. Using some reasonable data from whatever source, make an estimate of the rate of growth of Chinese national income in 1980 prices from 1952 to 1980.

11. Using some reasonable data from whatever source, make a rough estimate of the capital stock of the Chinese economy in the constant prices of any year of your choice. Hint: You may find a reasonable price index to deflate the capital accumulation figures in Table 6.1 and add them up through the years, starting from an estimate of capital stock in the initial year 1952. Note the difference between investment and increase in fixed assets shown in Table 6.5. Refer also to the original value of fixed assets of state-owned enterprises on page 964 of the *Almanac of China's Economy, 1981*.

12. Review each equation of model 6.75 and the discussion of it in Section 6.7. Select one equation and comment on it critically for application to China. Can you suggest an improvement, or should the entire equation be discarded? Explain.

13. How can distributed lags be introduced in the demand-for-money equation 5 of model 6.75? Discuss two different ways of introducing lags.

14. The particular linear function to explain price adjustment in equation 7 of model 6.75 may be considered unsatisfactory. Can you suggest a different mathematical form? See the classic article by Phillips (1958).

15. Using 6.76 and 6.77 as two structural equations, find the reduced-form equations for C_t and I_t. Using the reduced-form equations: (a) estimate C_t and I_t given the values of C_{t-1} and I_{t-1} from Table 6.1 for $t = 1953,\ldots,1981$; (b) estimate C_t and I_t given only the values of C_{1952} and I_{1952} from Table 6.1. The estimates in (a) are one-period-ahead forecasts. The estimates in (b) are multi-period forecasts. Compare the one-period forecasts with the actual values of C_t and I_t in Table 6.1 ($t = 1953,\ldots,1981$) and comment on the forecasting errors.

16. Find the characteristic roots of the two-by-two matrix A in the two reduced-form equations of Problem 15. Is the system explosive? Is the system oscillatory? Find the right characteristic vectors corresponding to the two characteristic roots. Introduce a new variable to get rid of the intercept terms in the above reduced-form equations.

17. For a term project (possibly by a group), put in some plausible values for the parameters of model 6.75, with modifications suggested in Section 6.7 or of your own, and solve the model numerically for 10 periods, starting from some estimates of the initial values of the variables in 1980.

REFERENCES

Cagan, P. 1956. The monetary dynamics of hyperinflation. In *Studies in the quantity theory of money,* Milton Friedman, ed. Chicago: University of Chicago Press.

Chinese State Statistics Bureau. 1982. *Statistical yearbook of China, 1981.* Hong Kong: Hong Kong Economic Review Publishing House.

Chow, G. C. 1966. On the long-run and short-run demand for money. *Journal of Political Economy* 74: 111–131.

———. 1967. Multiplier, accelerator, and liquidity preference in the determination of national income in the United States. *The Review of Economics and Statistics* 44:1–15. Also Chapter 30 in *Readings in macroeconomics,* M. G. Mueller, ed. New York: Holt, Rinehart and Winston.

———. 1968. The acceleration principle and the nature of business cycles. *Quarterly Journal of Economics* 82:403–418.

———. 1975. *Analysis and control of dynamic economic systems.* New York: Wiley.

———. 1983. A model of Chinese national income determination. Research Memorandum No. 309. Princeton, N.J.: Princeton University, Econometric Research Program.

Chow, G. C., and R. E. Levitan. 1969. Nature of business cycles implicit in a linear economic model. *Quarterly Journal of Economics* 83:504–517.

Chow, G. C., and G. H. Morre. 1972. An econometric model of business cycles. In *Econometric models of cyclical behavior,* B. G. Hickman, ed. New York: Columbia University Press. pp. 739–809.

Christ, C. F. 1979. On fiscal and monetary policies and the government budget restraint. *American Economic Review* 69:526–538.

Domar, E. D. 1957. *Essays in the theory of economic growth.* New York: Oxford University Press.

Eckstein, A. 1973. Economic growth and change in China: A twenty-year perspective. *The China Quarterly* 54:232.

———, ed. 1980. *Quantitative measures of China's economic output.* Ann Arbor: University of Michigan Press.

Economic Research Center, State Council of the People's Republic of China. 1982. *Almanac of China's economy, 1981.* Hong Kong: Modern Cultural Company Limited.

Field, R. M. 1980. Real capital formation in the People's Republic of China. In *Quantitative measures of China's economic output,* A. Eckstein, ed. Ann Arbor: University of Michigan Press. Pp. 194–245.

Friedman, Milton. 1957. *A study of the consumption function.* Princeton, N.J.: Princeton University Press.

———, ed. 1956. *Studies in the quantity theory of money.* Chicago: University of Chicago Press.

Frisch, R. 1933. Propagation problems and impulse problems in dynamic economics. *Economic essays in honor of Gustav Cassel.* London: Allen and Unwin.

Harrod, R. F. 1948. *Toward a dynamic economics.* London: Macmillan.

Liu, T. C., and K. C. Yeh. 1973. Chinese and other Asian economies: A quantitative evaluation. *American Economic Review* 63:215–223.

Liu Zhicheng. 1982. China's taxation in 1980. In Economic Research Center, State Council of the People's Republic of China, *Almanac of China's economy, 1981.* Hong Kong: Modern Cultural Company Limited. Pp. 655–656.

Keynes, John Maynard 1936. *The general theory of employment, interest and money.* New York: Harcourt Brace Jovanovich.

Kuznets, S. 1961. *Capital in the American economy: Its formation and financing.* Princeton, N.J.: Princeton University Press.

Ma Hong and Sun Xianqing, eds. 1982. *Zhongquo jingji jiegou wenti yanjou* [Studies of the problems of China's economic structure]. 2 vols. Beijing: People's Publishing Society.

People's Bank of China, Research Institute of Finance and Banking. 1982. China's banking system. In Economic Research Center, State Council of the People's Republic of China, *Almanac of China's Economy, 1981.* Hong Kong: Modern Cultural Company Limited. Pp. 657–664.

Perkins, D. H. 1975. Growth and changing structure of China's twentieth-century economy. In *China's modern economy in historical perspective,* D. H. Perkins, ed. Stanford, Calif.: Stanford University Press. Pp. 139–141.

———. 1975. Issues in the estimation of China's national product. in *Quantitative measures of China's economic output,* A. Eckstein, ed. Ann Arbor: University of Michigan Press. Pp. 246–273.

———. 1981. An American view of the prospects for the Chinese economy. In *Guowai jingji xueji lun zhongguo ji fajanzhong guojia jingji* [Essays on the Chinese and other developing economies by foreign economists]. Beijing: Editorial Board of *Jingji Yanjiu.* Pp. 2–23.

Phillips, A. W. 1958. The relation between unemployment and the rate of change of money wage in the United Kingdom, 1861–1957. *Economica,* New Series, 25:283–299.

Samuelson, Paul A. 1939. Interactions between the multiplier analysis and the principle of acceleration. *The Review of Economic Statistics* 21:75–78.

Shen Jingnong and Chen Baosen. 1982. China's financial system. In Economic Research Center, State Council of the People's Republic of China, *Almanac of China's economy, 1981.* Hong Kong: Modern Cultural Company Limited. Pp. 643–654.

Swamy, Subramanian. 1973. Economic growth in China and India, 1952–70: A comparative appraisal. *Economic Development and Cultural Change* 21:62.

Zhang Shuguang. 1981. Jingji jiegou bienhua de jingji xiaoguo fenxi [Analysis of the economic effects of change in economic structure]. In *Zhongquo jingji jiegou wenti yanjou* [Studies in China's economic structural problems], Vol. 2, Ma Hong and Sun Xianqing, eds. Beijing: People's Publishing Society. Pp. 724–759.

chapter *7*

Population and Human Capital

7.1 THE ROLE OF POPULATION AND HUMAN CAPITAL IN ECONOMIC DEVELOPMENT

Among economists known for their pessimistic predictions for the world, one of the best known is the English economist and clergyman Thomas R. Malthus (1766–1834). In *An Essay on the Principle of Population* (1798) Malthus argued that if left unchecked, population would grow faster than the food supply, leading to starvation and economic stagnation. His prediction failed to materialize, however, partly because technological progress increased the supply of food and other consumer goods and partly because population growth slowed down when people's incomes increased. Although Malthus' theory turned out to be wrong, it contains some partial truths for some countries that had difficulty in achieving economic development for fairly long periods. For these countries, population growth was as fast as, if not faster than, the growth in food supply. An increase in per capita national income or output in these countries would require a reduction in the rate of population growth or an increase in the rate of output growth or both.

Chairman Mao Zedong made a statement in 1949 that encouraged the growth of China's population in the late 1950s and the 1960s:

> A large population in China is a very good thing. With a population increase of several fold we still have an adequate solution. The solution lies in production. The fallacy of the Western capitalist economists like Malthus that the increase of food lags behind the increase of population was long ago refuted in theoretical reasoning by the Marxists; it has also been disproved by the facts existing after the revolution of the Soviet Union and in the liberated region of China.

242

In 1958 Mao's statement was used as a basis for criticizing Professor Ma Yin-Chu for advocating family planning and population control. In 1975 Ma was rehabilitated, and the earlier criticism of him was recognized to be a mistake. Most economists in China believe that if not for the mistaken population policy, per capita income in China would be much higher in the 1980s. Since the early 1970s, Chinese leaders have tried to curtail the growth of population, hoping to undo the harm of the population policy in the 1960s. We will say more on this reversal in policy later in this chapter.

Why does a larger population imply a smaller output per capita? In the United States, some would argue that the increase in population from immigration during the first half of the twentieth century actually helped increase national output to the extent that per capita output became higher than otherwise. Although such a conjecture might be mistaken, it makes one think twice before jumping to the conclusion that an increase in population necessarily means a reduction in national output per capita. This conclusion is likely to be valid for countries with very limited resources as compared with the size of their populations. Imagine many people farming on a small piece of land. The marginal product of labor declines as the number of farmers increases. (Review the discussion of marginal product in Section 3.2 and especially equation 3.11.) When the marginal product of labor declines, the increase in output by adding the fifteenth farmer is smaller than the increase in output by adding the fourteenth farmer. As we pointed out in Section 3.4, Lewis (1954) makes the strong assumption that for some less developed countries with a large population relative to land, the marginal product of agricultural labor is practically zero. If more people mean only more mouths to feed and very little extra output, output per person will decrease as the number of people increases.

How is it possible for output per person to increase when population increases? Economic development has been observed in many countries, including China, where national income per capita increased while total population also increased. As we pointed out in Sections 1.1 and 3.11, output per person can increase even when the number of persons engaged in production increases, provided that the quantities of other inputs become larger relative to the quantity of labor. Given the ratio of the quantity of other inputs to labor, output per person can also increase when there is technological change or when the quality of labor improves. Improvement in the quality of labor occurs through education, on-the-job training, and better health care. These are different forms of investment in human capital. While population measures the quantity of labor without adjustment for quality, the amount of human capital measures the quantity of labor after adjustment for quality. Holding the quality of labor fixed, one finds that an increase in the quantity of labor or population leads to a reduction in output per person unless it is matched by increases in other inputs or by the improvement of technology. Holding population fixed, one finds that investment in human capital leads to an increase in output per person in the short run. In the long run it can lead to improvement in technology. The productivity of a given population is likened to the productivity of a given piece of land: It can be increased greatly by investment. Just as fertilizer, irrigation, and crop-rotation increase the productivity of land, so do education, on-the-job training, and better health care increase the productivity of people.

In Section 7.2 we present estimates of population in China from 1952 to 1982 and the associated birth rates and death rates. Section 7.3 is concerned with current population policy in China and its possible effect on population growth. In section 7.4 population projection is discussed and the influence of current policy on the size and age distribution of future population is examined, drawing from the work of Coale (1981). Section 7.5 treats the supply of labor and the demand for labor, which is affected in essential ways by government policy. While the size of the population of working age sets limits to the supply of labor, the actual supply is determined by economic considerations. Section 7.6 deals with investment in human capital and education in China. Such investment improves the quality of the labor force. Section 7.7 deals with health care, while Section 7.8 discusses some economic explanations of the birth rate.

7.2 ESTIMATES OF CHINESE POPULATION AND ITS RATE OF GROWTH

Official data on Chinese population are fragmentary, but more are becoming available in the 1980s. Column 4 of Table 3.3 contains official year-end population figures for selected years from 1952 to 1981, which are published in *Statistical Yearbook of China, 1981* (Chinese State Statistics Bureau, 1982). Table 7.1 contains a set of estimates of Chinese population, together with the associated birth rates and death rates. Column 1 of Table 7.1 gives mid-year population figures estimated by Ansley Coale through interpolations of official figures, as explained in note *c* to the table. Column 2 gives the number of births in China, which John Aird obtained from a graph in an article by Wang Naizong published in April 1980. Column 3 is the birth rate, or the number of births per 1000 persons per year, calculated as the ratio of column 2 to column 1. The birth rates in column 3 can be compared with the birth rates in column 4, which were presented in a 1980 paper by Liu Zheng, director of the Institute of Population Research at the People's University in Beijing. The two sets of estimates are close. Column 5 records the death rates of selected years, as given in Liu's paper. Finally Column 6 lists the total population, based on the official Chinese source.

The rate of population growth, usually expressed as the increase per 1000 persons per year, is the difference between the birth rate and the death rate, provided that there is no net migration to or from the country concerned. According to Table 7.1, the death rate in China decreased from 13.1 per 1000 in 1954 to 6.2 per 1000 in 1979. This is an indication of the great improvement in health care in China during this period. In many countries, as the economy developed, the death rate declined. In Taiwan, for example, the death rate decreased from 9.9 per 1000 in 1952 to 4.7 in 1979, while the infant death rate decreased from 37.2 per 1000 to 9.8 during the same period (see *Statistical Yearbook of of the Republic of China, 1982,* p. 3).

A most important result of economic development is that while the death rate declines, the birth rate will eventually decline by even more, so that the natural rate of population growth ("natural" meaning not counting net migration) will decrease significantly. This has happened in country after country in Western Europe and in the United States. In Taiwan, the birth rate decreased from 46.6 per 1000 in 1952 to 24.4 in 1979, resulting in a natural rate of increase of 46.6 − 9.9, or 36.7, in 1952 as compared with a natural rate of increase of 24.4 − 4.7, or 19.7, in 1979 (see *Statistical Yearbook of the Republic of China, 1982,* p. 3). In recent years economists have devoted much attention to explaining why the birth rate declines during economic development.

Table 7.1   ANNUAL BIRTH AND DEATH RATES IN THE PEOPLE'S REPUBLIC OF CHINA, 1953–1979

Year	1 Rough estimate of population (millions)	2 Number of births (millions)[a]	3 Calculated birth rate (per 1000)	4 Birth rates given by Liu (per 1000)	5 Death rates given by Liu (per 1000)	6 Population at year-end (millions)
1953	583[b]	20.0	34.3			587.96
1954	592	22.0	37.2	38.1[d]	13.1[d]	602.66
1955	601	20.1	33.4			614.65
1956	610	20.6	33.8			628.28
1957	620	21.1	34.0	34	11	656.63
1958	630	18.6	29.5			659.94
1959	640	16.2	25.3			672.07
1960	650	12.6	19.4			662.07
1961	660	11.1	16.8			658.59
1962	670	24.1	36.0	37.3[d]	10.2[d]	672.95
1963	681	29.0	42.6	43.6[d]	10.2[d]	691.72
1964	691[b]	27.2	39.4	39.4[d]	11.6[d]	704.99
1965	712	27.8	39.0	38	9.6	725.38
1966	732	25.1	34.3	35.0[d]	9.1[d]	742.06
1967	752	25.0	33.2			760.32
1968	773	27.2	35.2			781.98
1969	795	27.0	34.0			803.35
1970	818	27.3	33.4	33.6	7.6	825.42
1971	839	24.9	29.7	30.7	7.3	847.79
1972	859	24.9	29.0	29.9	7.65	867.27
1973	879	24.4	27.8	28.1	7.08	887.61
1974	896	23.5	26.2	25.0	7.38	904.09
1975	912	21.0	23.0	23.1	7.36	919.00
1976	926[c]	18.2	19.7	20.0	7.29	932.67
1977	939[c]	16.2	17.3	19.0	6.91	945.24
1978	952[c]			18.3	6.2	958.09
1979	965[c]			17.9	6.2	970.92

[a]Read from graphs by John Aird (see text).
[b]Census figure.
[c]Interpolated between official year-end estimates. For 1954–63, rough estimates are calculated by constant average rate of increase. For 1965–75, interpolation is accomplished with the help of Professor Liu's figures for birth and death rates.
[d]Weighted average of rural and urban rates.
Sources: Coale, 1981, p. 86, except for the last column, which appears in *Labor Economics and Population* 11 (1982):75.

It may be pointed out that in some countries government policy concerning family planning has contributed to the decline in birth rate. However, in most Western countries where the decline occurred, there was no government intervention in family planning. What made the potential parents voluntarily limit the number of children in the family is an interesting economic question that will be discussed later in this chapter.

For China, column 3, supported by column 4, of Table 7.1 shows that the birth rate declined from 37.2 per 1000 in 1954 to 29.5 in 1958 and then to 16.8 in 1961, rose rapidly to 36.0 in 1962 and to the peak rate of 42.6 in 1963, and declined more or less constantly (except for an increase in 1968) to 17.3 (or 19.0, according to Liu) in 1977.

What explains the moderate decline in the Chinese birth rate from 1954 to 1958? These were years of fairly rapid industrialization and very little government intervention in family planning. According to the survey article (1982) on family planning by the Policy Research Section of the Family Planning Office of the State Council published in the *Almanac of China's Economy, 1981* (p. 761), although the Chinese government advocated family planning as early as the 1950s, not much in the way of a concrete program and economic policy was implemented until the 1970s: "Although we advocated family planning work, we did not devise specific measures to implement it" (p. 762). Therefore, it is difficult to attribute the decline in birth rate between 1954 and 1958 to the government policy on family planning. It is even more difficult to look to a government program for family planning to explain the rapid drop in the birth rate between 1958 and 1961 and the subsequent rapid rise. It was in 1958 that Ma Yin-Chu was criticized for advocating family planning. A casual economic observer may view these events as the consequences of the great economic disaster of the Great Leap Forward, which began in 1958, and of the economic recovery after 1961, but more careful study of this issue is required.

After the peak of 42.6 per 1000 in 1963, why did the birth rate continue to decline? The first few years, up to 1968 say, might be considered simply as a return to normality after the abnormally high rate of 1963, which was higher than the rate in the mid-1950s. But the decline continued from the late 1960s on. Although the government advocated family planning from the early 1970s on, strong measures were not taken until the late 1970s. In view of the continued drop in the birth rate beginning in 1963, it may not be easy to attribute the drop entirely to government policy. In any event, when the birth rate decreased from 37.2 in 1954 to 17.3 in 1977, while the death rate decreased from 13.1 to 6.9, the natural rate of population increase was reduced from 24.1 (37.2 − 13.1) in 1954 to 10.4 (17.3 − 6.9) in 1977, according to Coale's estimates in Table 7.1. According to Liu's figures in Table 7.1, which are based on official Chinese figures, the natural rate of population increase was reduced from 25.0 (38.1 − 13.1) in 1954 to 12.1 (19.0 − 6.9) in 1977.

More recent Chinese official data on population, birth rate, death rate, and natural growth rate for selected years are provided in Table 7.2. The figures for 1981 and 1982 may be very accurate, the latter being based on a census conducted with

Table 7.2 POPULATION, BIRTH RATES, AND DEATH RATES IN CHINA IN SELECTED YEARS

Year	Population (millions at year-end)	Birth rate (per 1000)	Death rate (per 1000)	Natural rate of increase
1949	541.67	36.0	20.0	16.0
1952	574.82	37.0	17.0	20.0
1957	646.53	34.0	10.8	23.2
1965	725.38	38.1	9.6	28.5
1978	962.59	18.3	6.3	12.0
1979	975.42	17.9	6.2	11.7
1981	1,000.72	20.9	6.4	14.5
1982	1,015.41	21.1	6.6	14.5

Source: Chinese Statistical Abstract, 1983, p. 13.

technical assistance from the United Nations. Note that the population figures from 1978 on are larger than those of Table 3.3. From 1949 to 1982 both the birth rate and the death rate as shown in Table 7.2 declined by some 14 to 15 points, and their difference (the natural rate of increase) was reduced only slightly, from 16.0 to 14.5.

7.3 POPULATION POLICY

According to a survey article on family planning in China published by the Family Planning Office in the *Almanac of China's Economy, 1981* (pp. 762–763), guidelines and policies of the Communist party and the Chinese government related to family planning have become more explicit since 1978. In 1980 the government called for stricter controls on population growth with the slogan "one couple, one child." Practical measures were devised to reward couples who agreed to have only one child. This article states (pp. 763–764):

> On September 25, 1980, the Central Committee of the CPC [Chinese Communist Party] issued an open letter calling on Communist Party and Youth League members to take the lead in limiting population growth to one child per couple. This letter spelled out the general target and the policies of population control in China. Each province, municipality, autonomous region, prefecture, county and commune appointed one leading comrade—sometimes even the top leader—to take responsibility for family planning work. The work was to be put often on the agenda for discussion and review, so that problems in connection with the implementation of family planning could be solved promptly. . . .
>
> The effective control of the birth rate in 1980 was ensured by the following measures:
>
> (1) *We launched a popular educational campaign via mass media to provide information about family planning and to encourage couples of childbearing age to volunteer to practice birth control.* . . .
>
> (2) *We practiced family planning by implementing economic measures.* In 1980, economic rewards and penalties were introduced. Rewards were given to those units and individuals who had done good work on family planning. Those couples who volunteered to have only one child received regular child care allowances. Economic penalties were levied on the few who, after patient ideological education, still paid no attention to family planning and the very few individuals who undermined this work were punished. . . .
>
> (3) *We used models in family planning.* Cadres at all levels and the broad masses of party and Youth League members conscientiously took the lead in having only one child. Parents who had passed childbearing age persuaded their married children to have only one child. . . .
>
> (4) *We stressed knowledge about eugenics.* . . .
>
> (5) *We paid attention to the study of new trends and to the solution of new problems.* . . .
>
> (6) *We have intensified our cooperation with other countries in family planning work.* . . .
>
> In summary, family planning work achieved good results in 1980, mainly through renewed ideological education supplemented by appropriate and necessary eco-

nomic measures. However, there are still problems to be tackled, such as: the uneven development of the work; relatively more multiple births in remote and mountainous regions; the shortage of technical personnel; bad management and primitive, coercive working methods; the shortage of contraceptives and their poor quality; and inadequate implementation of the "one couple, one child" policy. . . .

The Constitution adopted at the Fifth National People's Congress in 1978 stipulates in Article 53: *The State advocates and encourages family planning.* Article 12 of the marriage law adopted at the Third Session of the Fifth National People's Congress in 1980 stipulates: *Husband and wife are duty bound to practice family planning.* It is the legal oblication of every Chinese citizen to abide by the law and practice family planning, including the practice of late marriage and birth control. (Copyright 1982, Modern Cultural Company Limited. Reprinted with permission of Ballinger Publishing Company.)

How much effect the policy spelled out here has had on population growth in China is difficult to ascertain. There are reports that the Chinese people were affected by the strict measures of population control. For example, *People's Daily,* April 7, 1983, carried an article with the headline, "Anhui Provincial Women's Association Survey Reports: Drowning of Female Infants in Rural Areas Serious, Affecting the Balance of Sex Ratio Among Infants." The article reports that, according to a survey of Suixi and Huaiyuan counties conducted by the Anhui Provincial Women's Association, in some areas the number of reported male births far exceeded the number of female births, by a ratio of as much as 5 to 1 in some cases. The article attributes this situation to the traditional preference for male children, which led to the infanticide by drowning of many female infants. In one production brigade in Huaiyuan County, more than 40 female infants were drowned in 1980 and 1981. In the Meizhuang brigade of Junwang Commune, eight children were born in the first quarter of 1982; while three males survived, three of the five females were drowned, and the other two females were abandoned. In view of the above, the Anhui Provincial Women's Association proposed to strengthen socialist education, making the people realize that the drowning of infants is a crime. At the same time, the association declared that people should be taught that males and females are equal and the traditional prejudices against females should be criticized. The numbers of male and female births in the two counties and selected communes are recorded in Tables 7.3A and 7.3B.

This news report is just one example, albeit a very dramatic one, of the reactions of the Chinese people to the family planning measures of the government. To what

Table 7.3A   COMPARISON OF MALE AND FEMALE BIRTHS IN SUIXI AND HUAIYUAN COUNTIES

Location	Year	Births					Difference in %
		Total	Male	% Male	Female	% Female	
Suixi	1979	11,522	5950	51.6	5572	48.4	3.2
County	1980	11,554	6115	52.9	5439	47.1	5.8
Huaiyuan	1980	13,487	7593	56.3	5894	43.7	12.6
County	1981	10,768	6266	58.2	4502	41.8	16.4

Source: People's Daily, April 7, 1983.

Table 7.3B COMPARISON OF MALE AND FEMALE BIRTHS IN SELECTED COMMUNES IN HUAIYUAN COUNTY, 1981

Location	Births					Difference in %
	Total	Male	% Male	Female	% Female	
Commune S	133	83	62.4	50	24.8	24.8
Commune L1	104	66	63.5	38	36.5	27.0
Commune L2	231	145	62.8	86	37.2	25.6
Commune H	285	164	57.5	121	42.5	15.0
Brigade Z	9	7	77.8	2	22.2	55.6
Brigade N	8	7	87.5	1	12.5	75.0
Brigade Q	10	9	90.0	1	10.0	80.0

Source: People's Daily, April 7, 1983.

extent such measures have affected the birth rate (excluding infanticide) is difficult to measure. Column 2 of Table 7.2 shows that in spite of the stricter measures introduced in 1980, the birth rates in 1981 and 1982 were higher than they had been in 1978 and 1979. One possible explanation of the increase in the birth rate is the agricultural reforms, which permitted farm families to operate independently, thus increasing the value of children in terms of their marginal product accrued to the family. It is possible that economic forces are at work that may have stronger effects on the birth rate than the political and economic measures of the government family planning program.

Another aspect of the government program is to encourage people to marry at later ages. Since 1971 the government had advocated a marriage age of 28 or above for males and 25 or above for females. In 1981 a new marriage law went into effect raising the legal minimum marriage age, but there was reportedly a reduction in local pressure on people to marry even later than the legal minimum age, partly to compensate for the continued strong pressure toward the one-child family. Ansley Coale, in a letter dated January 1983 to Song Jian, Vice-President of the Chinese Demographic Association, comments on the effects on the birth rate of the new policy regarding marriage.

I suspect that the effect of changing mean age of childbearing is not fully appreciated in China, and that there may have been some errors in policy that come from this lack of full understanding. The point is as follows: Suppose over a long period of time that each cohort of women (those born in the same year) bears an average of 3/10 of a child annually as each cohort passes from age 23 to age 28. The women in these cohorts would bear, on average, a total of 1.5 children, more or less in line with the childbearing targets of Chinese policy. Now suppose that in a given year (say 1981) because of a sudden decline in age at marriage, the women reaching age 22 in this year begin childbearing at that age, and then continue for five years (to age 27) at the rate of 3/10 of a child annually. Each cohort of women continues to bear an average total of 1.5 children. But in the calendar year of 1981, childbearing begins at age 22 (the younger women start earlier) and extends to age 27 (the older women are still following the old regime). Thus the total fertility rate for 1981 is not 1.5 but 20 percent higher, at 1.8. This increase in total fertility rate during each calendar year lasts for five years, until the cohorts following the old regime have finished their childbearing. Moreover, the extra births occurring during this time would not be offset by any subsequent reduction, unless there were a subsequent increase in the mean age of childbearing. The extra births would be a permanent addition to the population of China, and would in turn contribute to more births in the future.

Thus, a relaxation in the efforts to maintain a high age at marriage leads to a temporary increase in the birth rate, even if the efforts to restrict the number of children born per family to a level of 1.5 remain fully successful. I have heard, although I am not sure that my information is correct, that Chinese authorities have felt that the efforts to restrict childbearing to one or at most two children, is so successful that there was no need any longer to maintain the pressure towards late marriage. For the reasons outlined above, a relaxation in pressure to keep marriage late in fact produces a temporary increase in the birth rate of possibly substantial magnitude.

According to an article in *People's Daily,* March 14, 1982, the new marriage law had the effect of increasing the number of marriages in 1981 as compared with 1980. This increase, however, probably could not explain the increase in the birth rate in 1981 itself as reported in Table 7.2. One possibility is that the reporting of births and deaths became more nearly complete in 1981, thus increasing both the recorded birth rate and death rate. In any case, from Table 7.2 alone, it is difficult to judge the effectiveness of the strong family planning measures introduced in 1980. Whatever the effects on current birth rates, the changes in the numbers of births in the early 1980s will have a lasting effect on the size and the age composition of the Chinese population for years to come. In the next section we will discuss some elementary aspects of population projections and the effects of current births on future population.

7.4 POPULATION PROJECTION

It is well known that China is the most populous country in the world, accounting for about one-quarter of the world's population. How fast the Chinese population will grow is of concern not only to the Chinese but to the world as a whole. This section presents only the most elementary arithmetic of population projection and discusses some projections resulting from different assumptions about the birth rates in the near future.

Although demography is a technical subject, it is not difficult to get a rough picture of the major components of a population projection. Given the population in each age group (called a cohort) at the initial year, the population in each age group in all subsequent years will be known *if* (1) the number of births in each future year is known, and (2) the survival rate of each age group in each future year is known. This is a big *if.* Essentially, it involves following all persons born in a given year throughout their lives. For example, starting from the beginning of 1983 we have counted the number of (surviving) people born in 1980, or the people between 2 and 3 years of age at the time of our count. A year later, at the beginning of 1984, people in this cohort will be between 3 and 4 years old if they survive. Thus, the number of people in the latter age group at the beginning of 1984 equals the number of people in the former age group at the beginning of 1983 times its survival rate for one year. The number of persons in each age group at a given time equals the number of persons who were one year younger one year ago, times their survival rate for one year. This statement is a definition of the survival rate as the ratio of the former number to the latter number. If the survival rate of each age group in each future year is known, the number of persons in each (older) age group in each subsequent year can be calculated. In the meantime, the youngest age group is being generated each year by birth. If the number of births in each subsequent year is known, we can start keeping track of these new entrants each year as time goes on.

The survival rate of each age group is not extremely difficult to forecast when there are no violent social and economic changes. As the economy develops and health care improves, the survival rate will increase, but the increase is gradual and for a developing country can be estimated from the experience of more developed countries that have already gone through a similar development process. Birth rates appear to be more difficult to forecast. Although each developed country has experienced a period when the birth rate went down, when and how fast a developing country's birth rate will go down is not easy to foretell. Furthermore, even for a developed country like the United States, birth rates could increase in a later stage of development and could be influenced by cyclical changes in economic activities. From a demographic point of view, in predicting the number of births it is important to exploit the information available on the number of women in each childbearing age group and their childbearing history. To study the effects of different population policies on the size and composition of future population, however, we need not forecast the future fertility rates of women of childbearing age, but we will utilize the assumed fertility rates under each policy option to forecast the future. Such an exercise has been performed by Coale (1981).

Coale has made three projections, all starting with a population of 910 million in 1975. The age distribution of the population (combining both sexes) was found in a large epidemiological survey conducted in that year. The sex ratio for each cohort was estimated by assuming a sex ratio at birth of 106 males for every 100 females and using the sex ratios by age recorded in the 1953 and 1964 censuses. To start the projections, the birth rate was estimated to be 24.6 per 1000 in 1975 and to fall to 19 per 1000 in 1980. Life expectancy at birth was assumed to be about 65 years for the two sexes combined in 1975–1980, and to rise to 70 years by 1995–2000. Projection I was motivated by a speech given by Vice Premier Chen Muhua in 1979, in which she asserted that the goal of the first stage of the Planned Birth Program was to reduce the annual rate of population growth from 12.1 per 1000 in 1978 to 5 per 1000 in 1985 and the goal of the second stage was to reduce it to zero by the year 2000. Coale (1981) writes:

> In Projection I, fertility was reduced so as to yield a growth rate of 5 per thousand in 1985 and then to change so that the growth rate fell linearly to zero in 2000. After 2000, the annual number of births is held fixed. In Projection II, the birth rate is assumed to fall to 16 per thousand in 1985, and thereafter projected fertility is adjusted to hold the annual number of births fixed. In Projection III, the same sequence of fertility is assumed as in II until 1985; then the total fertility rate becomes 1.7 in 1990, where it remains until 2020, thereafter moving up to 1.9.

Figure 7.1 shows the three population projections together with the associated total fertility rates per woman which were assumed to generate the projections. Note that the fertility rate of Projection I reflects the policy of one-child families. The result

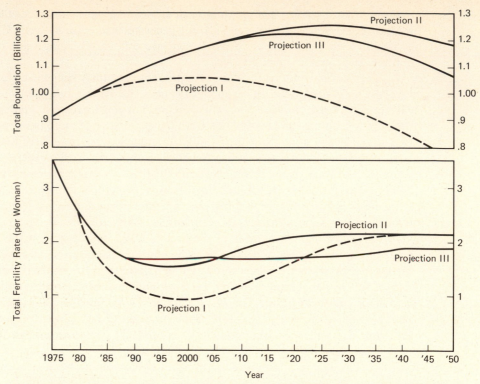

Figure 7.1 Coale's projections of Chinese population, 1975–2050. (*Source:* Coale, 1981, p. 93. By permission.)

is that while population stops growing in the year 2000, it will decline afterwards because after 2000 the fraction of women of child-bearing age will become smaller as a result of the low birth rates some 25 to 35 years earlier.

Coale (1981) emphasizes the drastic change in the age distribution of the population that would occur under Projection I. In Figure 7.2, compare the age distribution of the population in Projection I in the year 2000 and especially in the year 2035 with the actual age distribution in 1975. The population in 2035 would include twice as many people in the age decade of the 60s as people in any one age decade below 40. The social problems associated with such an age distribution would be serious. The age distribution in 2035 under Projection II appears more reasonable. The trends of Chinese population in the early 1980s might be closer to the assumptions made in Projection III, since the Chinese government was advocating one-child families but still allowing many families to have more than one child. Coale (1981, pp. 93–94) writes:

> These projections illustrate a well-known demographic principle—the principle of the "momentum" of population growth. Rapid growth in the past has created the kind of age distribution in 1975 shown in Figure [7.2]. Given such an age distribution, reduction of the rate of childbearing to a level where each couple on the average produces just two surviving children (long-run replacement fertility) does not immediately stop the growth of population. The large number of young people brought into being by

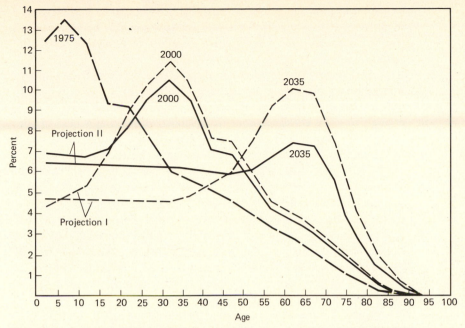

Figure 7.2 Coale's projected age distribution of Chinese population, 1975, 2000, 2035: percent in each five-year interval. (*Source:* Coale, 1981, p. 94. By permission.)

past high fertility will replace themselves—it is these large cohorts that set the size of the ultimate stationary population. Because fertility was not reduced in the 1950s and 1960s, the population of China must continue to grow. Realistically, positive growth must be accepted into the next century. Neither the extremely low fertility required to stop growth by 2000 nor the subsequent extremely unbalanced age distributions are acceptable as practical goals of policy.

7.5   LABOR SUPPLY AND LABOR POLICY

The size and age distribution of a country's population determine to a large extent its labor force. The potential supply of labor is limited by the number of persons of working age. However, the actual supply of labor depends on many economic factors that affect the willingness of the people of working age to work. In a society where people freely choose whether to work, where to work, and how much to work, the supply of labor depends on the monetary and nonmonetary returns of the job opportunities as compared with the returns from alternative uses of a person's time, mainly recreation, education, work in the household, and childbearing. The effects on choice of occupation of monetary and nonmonetary (or pecuniary and nonpecuniary) advantages and disadvantages of different occupations were aptly discussed in Chapter X of Book I of Adam Smith's *Wealth of Nations* (1776). People respond to economic incentives regarding not only how many hours to work but also whether to work. The latter decision affects a person's decisions to start working and to retire (so that the working age is itself a variable to be determined by economic forces) as well as whether he or she will seek employment during working age. By not working, a person can enjoy her leisure, go to school to improve her skills, engage in investment in human capital, or spend time in childbearing. In the United States, for example, during periods of economic depression or recession some people return to school or remain in school longer than otherwise.

In a society such as China in the 1980s, people also respond to the pecuniary and nonpecuniary rewards in supplying their labor, but the choices open to them are more limited. Starting from the educational stage, the small fraction of people fortunate enough to enter college cannot freely choose their major field of study. The number of students majoring in each field in each college or university is under the direction of the Ministry of Education. Once a major is chosen, it is very difficult, if not impossible, to change it. After a student graduates from college or from middle school, he or she is assigned a job by the Labor Bureau of city or county of residence. Once assigned to a job, the person would have difficulty changing to another job. Even under this rigid system, however, people try their best to choose the occupation of their own liking and to get assigned to a better or more suitable job by influencing the personnel in the Labor Bureau through the back door. If a person does not like his job, he will try to take sick leaves more often and put in fewer hours actually working. In short, the actual supply of labor in each occupation in China, as elsewhere, is affected by economic incentives, given the age distribution of the population.

Table 7.4 presents the total size of the labor force, its composition, and its ratio to total population in selected years. It is interesting to observe the rapid increase in the number of individually employed urban laborers since 1979, after economic policy was changed to allow greater freedom in establishing individual businesses. The last column of Table 7.4 shows a continually rising ratio of employed persons to total population. In Section 5.1 we pointed out that the increasing percentage of persons employed in urban areas was the major factor responsible for the increase in consumption per capita between 1957 and 1978, when the real wage rate showed no increase. This increase in labor participation is harder to explain. The age distribution of the population does not appear to be the answer, because the fraction of the population of working age was not continuously increasing. Why has a higher percentage of the Chinese people, and women in particular, become employed in more recent years?

Table 7.4   NUMBER OF EMPLOYED PERSONS IN CHINA

Year	Number of employed persons (10,000)				Ratio of employed to total population
	Total	Workers and staff	Individual urban laborers	Rural laborers	
1949	18,082	809	724	16,549	.3338
1952	20,729	1,603	883	18,243	.3606
1957	23,771	3,101	104	20,566	.3677
1965	28,670	4,965	171	23,534	.3952
1978	39,856	9,499	15	30,342	.4140
1979	40,581	9,967	32	30,582	.4160
1980	41,896	10,444	81	31,371	.4245
1981	43,280	10,940	113	32,227	.4325
1982	44,706	11,281	147	33,278	.4403

Source: Chinese Statistical Abstract, 1983, p. 18: the last column is the ratio of the first column to total population given in Table 7.1.

What economic conditions might have caused this increase? While a thorough study of this question remains to be undertaken, we can set forth the approach that an economist would take to answer it.

Like any other commodity or service, the quantity of labor employed depends on the demand for and the supply of labor. We will first present a theory of the supply of labor and then discuss the demand for labor, which in China is influenced to a large extent by government policy. The simplest theory of the supply of labor is based on the individual laborer's choice between working hours and leisure hours, given the total number of hours available to the individual, net of the hours required to sleep and perform other necessary tasks for survival (see Problem 8 of Chapter 1). Using the indifference curve analysis of Figure 1.2, we present in Figure 7.3 an individual's choice between the consumption of leisure time and of market goods. The horizontal axis measures the consumption of leisure time. Assume that the worker has a maximum of 100 hours (per week) to sell. The difference between 100 and the individual's leisure time is the number of working hours, which is measured along the horizontal axis from the point (100,0). The vertical axis measures the quantity of other consumption goods. By a theorem of Hicks (1946) on group demand, provided that the relative prices of a group of commodities remain unchanged, the group can be treated as a single commodity from the viewpoint of demand theory in the sense that the Slutsky equation (5.33) applies to the group as a whole. This theorem justifies the measurement of the consumption of all other commodities than leisure time along the vertical axis.

Denote the quantities of leisure time and of the group of other consumption goods respectively by x_1 and x_2. Let the wage rate be \$.40 per hour and the price per unit of the other commodities be \$2.00. By giving up all leisure time, or by working 100 hours, the worker can earn \$40, which is sufficient to purchase 20 units of consumption goods. By not working at all, the individual consumes 100 hours of leisure time but has no income to buy any consumption goods. His budget constraint is

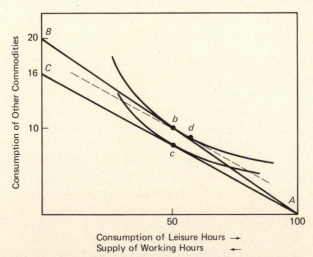

Figure 7.3 Deriving the supply of working hours from indifference curves.

$$\$.40\ x_1 + \$2.00\ x_2 = \$40 \tag{7.1}$$

which is depicted by the budget line AB in Figure 7.3. The wage rate of $.40 per hour can be interpreted as the price of consuming one hour of leisure time. The cost of this consumption is the forgone earning. The equilibrium point, given the budget line AB, is the point b at which the budget line is tangential to an indifference curve. This point shows the purchase of 50 hours of leisure time, or $100 - 50 = 50$ working hours, and the consumption of 10 units of other commodities.

The reader should review the discussion of Figure 1.2 in Section 1.3 for the choice of a consumer between rice and cloth. The theory expounded there is entirely applicable here for the choice between leisure time (and thus working time) and other consumption goods. In fact, Figure 7.3 is identical with Figure 1.2 except for the labeling of the axes. If the wage rate decreases from $.40 to $.32 per hour, the budget constraint will be changed from that shown in equation 7.1 to

$$\$.32\ x_1 + \$2.00\ x_2 = \$32 \tag{7.2}$$

and the budget line changed from AB to AC. By working 100 hours, or having no leisure time, the worker-consumer will have an income of $32, which permits him to buy 16 units of the other commodities. His new equilibrium point will be point c in Figure 7.3.

As before, the change from point b to point c can be broken down into a substitution effect and an income effect. The substitution effect is the change from point b to point d. It indicates that the worker will choose to consume more leisure, or to work less, when the wage rate is reduced relative to the price of the other commodities, or when the relative price of consuming leisure is reduced, provided that his real income is held fixed. Holding real income fixed, by Slutsky's definition, means having the new budget line pass the old equilibrium point b but changing its slope to that of the budget line AC. Holding real income fixed, according to Hicks's text (1946), means making the new budget line parallel to AC but tangential to the same indifference curve as before. The difference between the two definitions is minor when the change in price is small. For both definitions the substitution effect is always negative, as we explained in Sections 1.3 and 5.3. In the case of labor supply, this means that reducing the wage rate will always increase the consumption of leisure or decrease the supply of labor if real income is held fixed.

The income effect is the change from point d to point c. A reduction in the wage rate means a reduction in income if the price index of the other commodities is unchanged. This will ordinarily reduce the consumption of leisure or increase the supply of working hours, provided that leisure is not an inferior good. The income effect of a reduction in the wage rate is ordinarily to increase the supply of labor hours, as shown in Figure 7.3. Conversely, the income effect of an increase in the wage rate is ordinarily to reduce the supply of labor hours. The substitution effect of an increase in the wage rate is always to increase the number of working hours. When wages increase, the combined income and substitution effect is ordinarily an increase in the supply of working hours, because the substitution effect ordinarily dominates the income effect. However, it is possible that in certain ranges of the wage rate, especially when the wages are high, the income effect may dominate the substitution effect. In this case an increase in wage will call forth fewer working hours. Such a possibility can give rise to a *backward-bending* supply curve. This supply curve shows that when the wage rate increases from a low level, the supply of labor increases, but when the wage rate increases much further, the supply of labor is eventually reduced. In spite of this possibility, the response to a wage increase is ordinarily an increase in the supply of labor hours.

This theory of labor supply is confined to the decision of a single individual making his or her decision independently. While it is useful, it fails to account for the interdependence of the decisions of different members of the same family. A richer theory to explain the consumption, labor supply, and in fact the number of births of a family can be formulated by considering the joint decisions of a family as an economic unit. A family is assumed to maximize a utility function that may have as its arguments the consumption of physical commodities and services, the leisure times (and thus working hours) of its adult members, and perhaps the number of children. Leaving the number of children aside until Section 7.8, we briefly indicate how a theory based on family decisions can explain such phenomena as the decisions of housewives to work as well as the number of working hours each family member is willing to supply.

The potential income of the household includes its nonlabor income plus the hours available to the adult family members for work times their wage rates. By "work" is meant both market work (as part of the labor force) and work in the household. Married women not in the labor force spend most of their working hours doing household work. Albert Rees (1979, p. 4) explains the behavior of such a household as follows.

> Decisions about the allocation of time will reflect the total resources of the household, of which the most important are the time of household members of working age and the household's income from sources other than work. These decisions also reflect the opportunities for market work available to members of the household, including their potential market wage, their comparative advantages in nonmarket activities, and the amount and nature of household work that needs to be performed. An increase in the family's resources, unaccompanied by any other change in opportunities—such as an inheritance that substantially increases nonlabor income—should reduce total labor supply. Thus it might lead the family to decide that a teenage son should stay in school longer, that the elderly grandfather should retire earlier, or that the working wife should become a full-time homemaker. . . .
>
> A rise in the wage for the market work open to some members of the household may induce more participation by these members. Thus a rise in the salaries of school-teachers (relative to other wages and prices) should induce some women who have left work to care for their families to return to teaching. They could use some combination of hired domestic help, purchased services, and the reallocation of household duties to other members of the family to make up for the loss of some of their time in the home, or the family could consume somewhat less of the "goods" produced by work in the home, such as a tidy kitchen, home cooking, or a well-kept garden, and instead could consume more market goods.

This discussion merely sketches some essential features of a theory of labor supply based on family decision making and is far from being a presentation of the theory itself.

For a more thorough discussion, the reader may refer to Rees (1979, Chapters 1 and 2) and Becker (1981, Chapters 1 and 2). A more formal presentation, using the approach in the context of explaining the number of children in a family, will be given in Section 7.8.

Turning to the demand for labor, we will first comment on the marginal productivity theory of demand in the case of competitive markets and then discuss the demand for labor in China. In Section 1.5, especially following equation 1.25, we explained the demand for labor by a competitive firm that tries to maximize profits. Labor will be hired by the firm until the value of its marginal product equals or just covers its cost. If the firm has monopoly power, so that its demand curve is not infinitely elastic (or horizontal) but is negatively sloping, as illustrated in Figure 1.7, it will hire labor until its *marginal revenue product* equals its cost. Marginal revenue product is the extra revenue that the firm receives by selling the extra output produced by the additional unit of labor. If the demand curve is horizontal, or the price of the product remains the same when more is sold, marginal revenue product equals the value of the marginal product, which is equal to the marginal product times the price of the product. When the firm is facing a negatively sloping demand curve, the extra revenue from selling the marginal product will be somewhat less because the price of the product has to be reduced. The extra revenue equals the marginal product times the marginal revenue obtained by selling the extra product, and is called the marginal revenue product. This refinement aside, the essence of the marginal productivity theory of demand for labor is that labor will be hired if it produces more than or at least as much as its cost, implying that when its price is reduced, more will be hired.

Does the marginal productivity theory of demand for labor have relevance in China, where government policy affects the demand for labor in a significant way? The answer is yes if the government plans efficiently. Government policy affects the demand for labor at two levels. First, to the extent that government economic planning affects the development of agriculture and industry in China, it affects the demand for labor. Some factual information on the relation between economic development and employment in China is presented by Rawski (1979). Just as in a market economy, technology and the stock of capital in China affect the demand for labor through the production function. Government policy influences the stock of capital and technology, and therefore indirectly influences the demand for labor. Second, given the capital stock and technology, government labor policy may affect the number of laborers hired in various activities.

If the government guarantees a job to every person of working age and the labor bureaus assign jobs to all physically able adults, one might think that this will affect the demand for labor and assure full employment of the labor force. The Chinese experience, however, has shown otherwise. In the late 1970s and early 1980s, the government labor bureaus could not find jobs for many youths in urban areas. These people were in the state of waiting for job assignment or, in other words, in the state of unemployment. In addition, many people holding a job were not fully employed. Just assigning a job to a person is not equivalent to creating a demand for the person's labor services. Just keeping a laborer working in some job does not imply that she or he is productive if the products are of little economic value as a result of mistakes in economic planning. Many organizations were overstaffed and people on the payroll had very little to do. Chinese universities, for example, often had more teachers, administrators, and maintenance workers than students. Each Chinese worker was guaranteed job security—the "iron rice bowl" that could not be broken—no matter whether his or her work contributed to the productivity of the employing organization. Thus, government labor policy affects the number of jobs assigned more than the demand for labor.

Since economic reforms were initiated in 1979–1980, market forces have been allowed to influence the demand for labor and the marginal productivity theory of demand has become more relevant. First, agricultural reforms now permit many individual farm households to operate as independent economic units. Such profit-maximizing units will hire additional laborers according to the value of their marginal product as compared with the cost of hiring. Second, unemployed youths and other people in urban areas are encouraged to start small individually or collectively operated businesses. If these businesses are profit maximizing, the marginal productivity theory becomes relevant. Third, government industrial enterprises now have some autonomy in their production, pricing, and hiring decisions and are encouraged to operate as independent economic units. Although the degree of autonomy remains limited, the tendency to use profit-maximizing calculations makes the hiring decisions of these firms, to the extent that they have authority, dependent on marginal productivity considerations. Finally, even an enterprise operating under the direction and for the interest of the central government should be instructed to hire laborers up to the point where the marginal product just covers the wage, for this is simply a principle of economic efficiency. How can an enterprise be operating efficiently if it has to take care of extra laborers who are not productive, in the sense that their marginal product has less value than the wage cost? Yet the Chinese government in the early 1980s has not extended to the state-owned enterprises complete freedom to hire and discharge workers for the purpose of achieving economic efficiency. To that extent, the marginal productivity theory fails to explain the actual hiring behavior of these enterprises.

By encouraging private individuals to establish their own businesses and find their own employment, the Chinese government is recognizing the insufficiency of the employment opportunities that it can provide and the need to supplement them with opportunities provided by individual or collective businesses. Some economists point to the increase in employment during the three decades after 1949 as evidence of the success of the Chinese government's employment program. However, this view overlooks the fact that by being a monopoly in the supply of jobs until the recent economic reforms, the government probably prevented millions of useful jobs from being created by individual initiatives and thus deprived millions of Chinese people of job opportunities. The government might deserve some credit in creating certain jobs if the work involved is economically productive, but one has to consider what jobs could have been created by private individuals using the resources controlled by the government. In any case, even if government job creation is economically beneficial in many instances, government monopoly of the job market cannot be optimal, for the optimality would imply that no individuals have the ability to employ human resources efficiently.

In this section we have described certain important elements in the theory of the supply of and the demand for labor. The theoretical framework that we have presented might serve as the starting point for an empirical study of the demand and supply of labor in China. Such a study would be interesting and awaits the attention of labor economists interested in China.

7.6 INVESTMENT IN HUMAN CAPITAL

The productivity of a human being may be likened to the productivity of a piece of barren land. It can be increased by investment through education, training, and health care. The value of human resources far exceeds that of physical resources in the form of capital goods. In the United States, for example, the total payment to labor has accounted for approximately 75 percent of national income, the remaining 25 percent being derived from payments to capital in the form of rent, profit, and interest (even profit is sometimes attributed to the return to entrepreneurship, a form of earning from human management skills). Investment in human capital is therefore very important in economic development. It has been suggested that the reason why the United States is rich is that it has an abundance of human capital, relatively more so than physical capital which is plentiful in absolute terms when compared with that of many other countries. We noted in Section 1.1 that Germany and Japan recovered rapidly after the Second World War because both were heavily endowed with human capital.

The Chinese government has placed a strong emphasis on improving the educational level of the Chinese people since 1949, especially in spreading secondary education to the masses. Table 7.5 shows official data on Chinese student enrollment by level of school from 1949 to 1981. Total school enrollment increased from 54.4 million in 1952 to 194.75 million in 1981, or by somewhat less than fourfold, while population increased by less than twofold (see Table 7.2). During the same period, enrollment in institutions of higher learning increased more than sixfold; enrollment in secondary schools increased more than sixteenfold; and enrollment in primary schools increased somewhat less than threefold. The number of students per 1000 population increased from 109.4 (71,805/656.63) in 1957 to 191.8 (194,753/1,015.41) in 1981. An important element of education in China is political indoctrination. In the early 1950s, Communist party and Youth League organizations were founded in schools to carry out political and ideological work among Chinese youths. For a description of the educational system and educational policy in China, see the report by Ji Hua (1982).

It is noteworthy from Table 7.5 that during the economic collapse in 1961–1962 following the Great Leap Forward, total student enrollment declined, the secondary specialized schools being most seriously affected. Also noteworthy is the reduction in enrollment in institutions of higher learning during the Cultural Revolution from 1966 to 1976, with enrollment dropping from 674,000 in 1965 to a low of 48,000 in 1970. The Cultural Revolution, as people in China know, was engineered by Mao Zhedong, who had lost political power in the early 1960s as a result of the failure of the Great Leap Forward. To regain political power from the more pragmatic leadership of the Communist party, including President Liu Shaoqi, Mao rallied Chinese youth in the name of a cultural revolution. The youths attacked local party administrative personnel and organizations and interrupted the functioning of colleges and universities. Besides the party leadership that had taken over political control of China from Mao in the early 1960s, a main target was the Chinese intellectuals, whom Mao also distrusted. Many intellectuals were sympathetic with Mao's revolutionary cause during a period of war and political disorder in the 1940s, and Mao had no hesitation in using them because without their support the Communist movement might not have succeeded.

Table 7.5   STUDENT ENROLLMENT BY LEVEL OF SCHOOL, 1949 to 1981[a]
(10,000 Persons)

| Year | Total | Institutions of higher learning | Secondary schools[b] | | Primary schools |
			Secondary specialized schools	Regular secondary schools	
1949	2,577.6	11.7	22.9	103.9	2,439.1
1950	3,062.7	13.7	25.7	130.5	2,892.4
1951	4,527.1	15.3	38.3	156.8	4,315.4
1952	5,443.6	19.1	63.6	249.0	5,110.0
1953	5,550.5	21.2	66.8	293.3	5,166.4
1954	5,571.7	25.3	60.8	358.7	5,121.8
1955	5,788.7	28.8	53.7	390.0	5,312.6
1956	6,987.8	40.3	81.2	516.5	6,346.6
1957	7,180.5	44.1	77.8	628.1	6,428.3
1958	9,906.1	66.0	147.0	852.0	8,640.3
1959	10,489.4	81.2	149.5	917.8	9,117.9
1960	10,962.6	96.2	221.6	1,026.0	9,379.1
1961	8,707.7	94.7	120.3	851.8	7,578.6
1962	7,840.4	83.0	53.5	752.8	6,923.9
1963	8,070.1	75.0	45.2	761.6	7,157.5
1964	10,382.5	68.5	53.1	854.1	9,294.5
1965	13,120.1	67.4	54.7	933.8	11,620.9
1966	11,691.9	53.4	47.0	1,249.8	10,341.7
1967	11,539.7	40.9	30.8	1,223.7	10,244.3
1968	11,467.3	25.9	12.8	1,392.3	10,036.3
1969	12,103.0	10.9	3.8	2,021.5	10,066.8
1970	13,181.1	4.8	6.4	2,641.9	10,528.0
1971	14,368.9	8.3	21.8	3,127.6	11,211.2
1972	16,185.3	19.4	34.2	3,582.5	12,549.2
1973	17,096.5	31.4	48.2	3,446.5	13,570.4
1974	18,238.1	43.0	63.4	3,650.3	14,481.4
1975	19,681.0	50.1	70.7	4,466.1	15,094.1
1976	20,967.5	56.5	69.0	5,836.5	15,005.5
1977	21,528.9	62.5	68.9	6,779.9	14,617.6
1978	21,346.8	85.6	88.9	6,548.3	14,624.0
1979	20,789.8	102.0	119.9	5,905.0	14,662.9
1980	20,419.2	114.4	124.3	5,508.1	14,627.0
1981	19,475.3	127.9	106.9	4,859.6	14,332.8

[a]Excludes spare-time schools.
[b]Excludes workers' training schools.
Source: Statistical Yearbook of China, 1981, p. 451.

In 1957 Mao advocated the free expression of diverse ideas and opinions, saying "Let 100 flowers bloom," but when some intellectuals expressed opinions highly critical of Mao's regime, they were imprisoned, sent into internal exile, removed from their jobs, or otherwise silenced. The Cultural Revolution was another occasion in which the intellectuals were victimized. Certain elements in society, including those having capitalist or feudal ideas, were identified as targets for attack. Each unit, or organization, was required to identify a certain number of these undesirable elements, and the required number were usually found. Professors and other individuals so identified were paraded on the streets carrying signs of their classification. They also had to confess their guilt in public. Such humiliations drove a large number of intellectuals to commit suicide.

From September 1966 to February 1972, all universities were closed in China. From February 1972 to the autumn of 1976, universities were open again, but admission was decided by political considerations rather than by scholastic qualifications. Youths from workers' and peasants' families having insufficient academic qualifications were assigned by their units to go to universities. The quality of instruction was below standard, and the preparation of the students was generally inadequate. Therefore, for 10 years from September 1966 to September 1976, college education in China practically stopped. The disruptive effect on the formation of human capital was tremendous. From Table 7.5 we can estimate roughly that at least 700,000 to 800,000 students of college age did not receive a college education for 10 years, noting that the enrollment in institutions of higher learning was as high as 947,000 in 1961, a figure regained only after 1979. In the meantime, most of the teaching staff in colleges and universities could not continue their research and learning. In addition, more than 100 million primary and middle-school students were receiving low-quality education as the Cultural Revolution interrupted the education at the lower levels as well.

To get a rough estimate of the economic loss caused by this interruption of the educational process, note that the value of one year of education would include not only the direct cost of providing the education (tuition, subsidies to the school, and the like) but also the forgone earning of one year's work by the individual, for these are the costs of education. For example, in choosing to spend one year in college rather than working, an individual must figure that the present value of that year's education, in terms of the increase in future earnings, should at least equal the wage that he or she could earn plus the tuition and other direct costs of education during that year. From the social point of view, the Chinese government, by putting a person through college for one year rather than assigning him or her to work, must figure that the present value of that year's education as measured by the increase in the individual's future productivity should at least equal his or her forgone product plus the direct cost of education during that year. In fact, the value of education often turns out to be larger than given by the above calculation, because investment in education has been found to yield higher returns than investment in physical assets. Estimates of the rate of return to college and high school education in the United States can be found in Becker (1964, Chapters IV and VI). Using this calculation, we can conclude that the economic loss to China is at least equal to that of putting some 700,000 to 800,000 persons with college education and a large fraction of 100 million persons with primary or secondary education out of work for 10 years, plus the waste in teachers' times and the physical and other human resources tied up with the educational institutions for 10 years. China will not recover from this loss for many decades to come.

After 1977 the Chinese educational system returned fairly rapidly to a normal state, granted the loss of qualified teachers due to the Cultural Revolution. How efficient is the Chinese system in promoting investment in human capital? Let us consider both the demand for and the supply of educational services. In a market economy individuals choose to get educated because the monetary and psychic returns to education at least cover the costs of education, including the forgone earnings and the direct costs paid while in school. As Gary Becker (1964, p. 1) writes:

Some activities primarily affect future well-being; the main impact of others is in the present. Some affect money income and others psychic income, that is, consumption. Sailing primarily affects consumption, on-the-job training primarily affects money income, and a college education could affect both. These effects may operate either through physical resources or through human resources. This study is concerned with activities that influence future monetary and psychic income by increasing the resources in people. These activities are called investments in human capital.

The many forms of such investments include schooling, on-the-job training, medical care, migration, and searching for information about prices and incomes. They differ in their effects on earnings and consumption, in the amounts typically invested, in the size of returns, and in the extent to which the connection between investment and return is perceived. But all these investments improve skills, knowledge, or health, and thereby raise money or psychic incomes.

Recent years have witnessed intensive concern with and research on investment in human capital, much of it contributed or stimulated by T. W. Schultz. The main motivating factor has probably been a realization that the growth of physical capital, at least as conventionally measured, explains a relatively small part of the growth of income in most countries. The search for better explanations has led to improved measures of physical capital and to an interest in less tangible entities, such as technological change and human capital. . . .

From the economic point of view, an individual decides to invest in himself or herself according to the same principle that he or she uses to invest in physical assets. Recall from the discussion in Section 1.9 that in investing in physical assets, an individual estimates the extra future revenues to be derived from this asset and discounts them by the rate of interest to calculate their present value. If the present value is larger than the present cost of the investment, the investment will be undertaken. Equivalently, the rate of return to the investment is the rate of interest that would make the present value of the extra income stream equal to the present cost of the investment. When the rate of return so calculated is higher than the market rate of interest used to compute the present value, it means that the present value is larger than the cost of the investment. In the case of investment in human capital through education and training, the individual also compares the present value of the extra future monetary and psychic incomes to be derived from the education with the cost of education. The total cost of education includes the direct costs (tuition, fees, and so on) and the earnings forgone by not working while receiving the education, which is the opportunity cost of the individual's time. Again, the rate of return to education is that rate of discount that would equate the cost of education with the present value of the extra monetary and psychic income resulting from education. When the future returns are raised, people will invest more in education, just as in the case of investing in physical assets. An interesting topic is the social return to education. In our rough estimate of the value of the loss of human capital during the Cultural Revolution earlier in this section, we assumed that the increase in the value of human capital to society due to education is at least equal to its total cost. To estimate the social value of education empirically is not an easy task. However, the study of the private return to education is important because the return affects the demand for education by private citizens.

In China the incentive to invest in human capital—that is, the demand for education—is affected by the limited opportunities available to individuals after receiving the education. As reported previously, the choice of one's major field of concentration, employment opportunities (including the nature of the work and the location of the job), and the possibilities of advancement and of receiving a high income are all limited by government policy, which attempts to restrict, control, and direct individual actions. Such restrictive policies and practices dampen the individual's incentives to get an education. As a farmer is unwilling to invest in physical capital for his farm unless he can earn a healthy return by such an investment, a young person is unwilling to expend energy to get educated unless the education will enable him or her to earn additional monetary and psychic incomes in the future. By limiting the individual's economic opportunities, the government in effect discourages him or her from getting educated. This partly explains why so many young people in China had low morale and drifted aimlessly. On the positive side, since 1979 some Chinese students and scholars have been allowed to study or to receive additional training abroad. Some 8000 of them were in the United States in the early 1980s. By and large, they were well motivated, and their performance has been extremely impressive. One explanation is that these people were carefully selected for their past achievements and high motivation. Another explanation is that these people realized that future opportunities would be open to them at home to utilize the additional education and training received abroad. Large investments in human capital are crucial for rapid economic development. The demand for such investments will be limited if people are not given the opportunities to benefit freely from such investments.

To turn now to the supply of educational services: The Chinese government has succeeded in expanding educational facilities at all levels, as evidenced by the large increases in student enrollment shown in Table 7.5 and commented on earlier. Ji Hua (1982, pp. 743–744) of the Chinese Ministry of Education reports that soon after the Communist government gained control over China in 1949, it took over all public and private schools and merged them with missionary schools that had been financed by foreign subsidies, and established control over all schools.

After 1952, the institutes of higher learning and their departments were reorganized, teaching reforms were introduced and the unified college enrollment system and system of assigning college graduates were adopted. In this way, higher education was brought under the control of state planning. . . . Chinese schools at all levels formulated for each subject matter a set of teaching plans, a syllabus and textbooks —all of them geared basically to actual conditions in China.

In 1961, . . . we worked out three sets of basic rules for schools: the "Draft Provisional Regulations Concerning the Work in Institutes of Higher Learning Directly under the Ministry of Education" (which became "Sixty Regulations for Institutes of Higher Learning"); the "Draft Provisional Regulations Concerning the Work in Full-time Middle Schools" (which became the "Fifty Regulations for Middle Schools"); and the "Draft Provisional Regulations Concerning the Work in Full-time Primary Schools" (which became the "Fifty Regulations for Primary Schools"). . . .

The most important characteristic of the supply of education in China is that practically all educational services (outside the family) are provided and controlled by the government. Before 1949 many primary and middle schools were private, as were some of the best colleges and universities. It is difficult for an educator associated with a successful private university to appreciate a government's policy of monopolizing the supply of education. To say the least, the failure to allow the establishment of private universities and educational institutions at lower levels must have deprived the Chinese of a large supply of educational services that would have been forthcoming from private resources. In 1980 a Hong Kong alumnus of Ling Nan University previously located in Canton offered a contribution of $10 million U.S. if that university could be reopened. This gift has not yet been accepted. On an encouraging note, by 1982 private individuals had already begun to establish vocational schools on a limited scale in some cities in China. The private Tianjin United University was founded by a group of alumni of United, Beijing, Qinghua, Zhejiang, and Yenjing universities and opened in September 1983 with an enrollment of approximately 1200 part-time students, who were staff and workers in Chinese enterprises. It offers 14 concentrations in the humanities, natural sciences, law, engineering, medicine, and economics. Government monopoly of education may be gradually abandoned in the future for the sake of economic development.

Since the establishment of formal diplomatic relations with the United States in January 1979, the government of the People's Republic of China has sent students and visiting scholars to the United States and other Western countries to study and to receive additional training. Even allowing for the possibility that some students might not return to China, this investment will contribute significantly to increasing the stock of human capital in China. Perhaps the increase will eventually outweigh the tremendous loss of human capital that occurred when the large majority of Chinese students and scholars visiting the United States and other Western countries in 1949, when the new regime was established, decided not to return home. Emigration, like the reluctance to get educated, is a loss in human capital to society resulting from restrictive government policies. In spite of strong measures to prevent emigration, millions of Chinese did escape to Hong Kong, where the Chinese population increased from about 1 million in 1948 to over 5 million in the late 1970s, with many having migrated from Hong Kong to the rest of the world. Before 1949, when movement of the Chinese population between Hong Kong and mainland China was completely free, there had been no large influx of population to Hong Kong. Migration is considered by economists as a form of investment in human capital because it increases the present value of the future earnings of individuals involved. Emigration from China helps raise the personal earnings of the emigrants. Migration within China by individuals seeking better job opportunities would raise both the earnings of the individuals and Chinese national income, as explained in Section 1.7. Thus the restriction of labor mobility within China could be considered an obstruction to investment in human capital.

Besides schooling, another form of investment in human capital is on-the-job training. In a market economy such as that of the United States, on-the-job training is provided by private enterprises. General training improves the skills that are useful to many other firms besides the employer-firm providing it, and its cost is mostly borne by the employee-trainees. Specific training improves the skills that are useful only to the firm providing it, and its cost is mostly borne by the employer. Becker (1963,

Chapter II) provides a theoretical discussion of both types of on-the-job training and other forms of investment in human capital. In China, on-the-job training is provided in many state-owned enterprises. The Chinese government has an extensive program to improve the skills of workers, as reported in an article by Zheng Ji (1982) of the Policy Research Department of the State Bureau of Labor.

According to Zheng (1982, pp. 699–700), the labor departments and some large factories and mines have set up many vocational training schools. Between 1949 and 1980 some 1.43 million students were trained in these schools. The government also established a new apprenticeship system, which was a modification of the old system under which the majority of China's skilled workers were trained. The system of vocational training was interrupted during the Cultural Revolution of 1966–1976. Vocational schools were restored afterward, with enrollment rising to 680,000 in 1980.

> The students spend half of their time in school workshops or in productive enterprises to receive on-the-job training and the other half in classes for general and technical education. . . . In recent years, more than one million apprentices have been enrolled each year in industrial enterprises owned by the state. The duration varies from trade to trade and from profession to profession. In general, it lasts three years; at a minimum, no less than two years.

> Vocational training of on-the-job workers is mainly provided by the enterprises, which will draw up plans and train workers systematically in accordance with their own production needs and with the workers' technical competence. Enterprises generally set up a special office to deal with this matter. On-the-job training is provided in various forms. Different forms are used for different trades and workers, and training may be full-time, part-time or spare-time. Workers are paid basic wages during the period of training, and receive rewards for exemplary results (p. 700).

7.7 HEALTH SERVICES

Another form of investment in human capital is the improvement of health. Since 1949 the Chinese government has had an extensive program to improve the health of the Chinese people. One indicator of the improvement achieved is the decline in the annual death rate from 17 per 1000 in 1952 to 6.6 per 1000 in 1982, as shown in Table 7.3. Wei Zhi (1982) of the Ministry of Public Health reports that such infectious diseases as plague, smallpox, venereal diseases, kala-azar, recurrent fever, and typhus have been successively eradicated or brought under control. While schistosomiasis was once prevalent in 347 counties of 12 provinces and more than 10 million people suffered from this disease in an area of 13,000 square miles infested with snails, in the past 31 years snails have been wiped out in two-thirds of the affected areas and two-thirds of the sufferers have been cured. The incidence of malaria has been greatly reduced. Keshan disease, Kaschin-Beck disease, and endemic flourosis have been partly controlled. The incidence of acute infectious diseases such as poliomyelitis, measles, diphtheria, pertussis, and tetanus in newborn infants has decreased considerably. Mortality caused by respiratory diseases, digestive diseases, and acute infectious diseases has dropped, and chronic, noninfectious conditions—heart and cerebrovascular diseases and malignant tumors—have become the leading causes of death. Wei writes:

Much has been done with regard to environmental, industrial, food, and school hygiene, as well as health protection from radiation. Since 1971, systematic tests and surveys have been carried out on the water quality of five big water systems, including 177 rivers, five lakes and six bays, and on the air quality in 75 cities, producing 730,000 items of scientific data. We have organized several nationwide campaigns for screening and treating occupational diseases. . . .

In the past 31 years, 406,000 students have graduated from higher medical colleges. . . . From 1949 to 1980, the number of medical and health institutions rose from 3,600 to 181,000, an increase of 49.2 times; hospital beds from 80,000 to 1,982,000, an increase of 24.8 times; and professional medical and health workers from 541,000 to 3,535,000, an increase of 6.5 times. Among the latter, health technicians increased from 505,000 to 2,798,000, an increase of 5.5 times; and physicians from 360,000 to 1,153,000, an increase of 3.2 times. From 1949 to 1980, based on the average number for every thousand persons, hospital beds increased from 0.15 to 2.02, health technicians from 0.93 to 2.85, and physicians from 0.67 to 1.17 (pp. 753–754).

The *Statistical Yearbook of China, 1981* (p. 477), shows that of the 3.535 million health workers in health institutions in 1980, 2.798 million were classified as medical personnel, among whom 1.153 million were physicians, .466 million were nurses, and 1.179 million were other medical personnel. The medical personnel here listed excluded part-time health workers in urban and rural areas. Among the physicians, 262,000 were doctors of traditional Chinese medicine, 447,000 were senior doctors of Western medicine, and 444,000 were junior doctors of Western medicine who had received two to three years of training after high school. In 1980 there were also 1.463 million rural "barefoot doctors" among the part-time health workers in rural areas. The main difference between medical services in China and in the United States is the low cost and the associated lower quality of medical services in China. Concerning the training of physicians and other health workers, China is willing to use a large number of physicians, some with much less training than physicians in the United States receive. As a result, many people in China are able to obtain fairly inexpensive medical service. In the United States doctors are often too well trained for the common illnesses they treat. The quality of other medical services, including services provided in hospitals, is also much higher in the United States. Much of the new equipment for health examinations and health care is very expensive. It is very costly to provide the best care with a minimum risk to all patients. The cost of medical care can be reduced tremendously by lowering the quality and increasing the risk to the patients slightly, as is done in China.

William Hsiao (1983) points out that China provides health care through a three-tier system that is managed and financed locally. In the first tier, the part-time barefoot doctors provide preventive and primary care. For more serious illnesses, they refer patients to the second tier: commune health centers, which may have 10 to 30 beds and an outpatient clinic serving a population of 10,000 to 25,000 and which are staffed by junior doctors. The most seriously ill patients are referred by the commune health centers to the third tier: county hospitals staffed with senior doctors. The cooperative medical system that organizes the barefoot doctors and provides other medical services to the rural population is part of the commune system and is financed by the communes' welfare funds.

The system of medical care, as Hsiao reports, is seriously affected by the economic reforms in agriculture discussed in Section 3.8, in three major respects. First, the supply of medical care from the cooperative medical system declines as barefoot doctors find it more profitable to work full-time in farming or to set up private practices outside the system, and as the funding from communes is reduced with more farm incomes accruing to individual farm families. Second, the demand for better-quality medical care increases as incomes of farmers increase, part of the demand being satisfied by private services outside the system. Third, the cooperative medical system itself is in danger of collapsing as its financing becomes difficult, as the barefoot doctors leave, and as its administrative personnel are lured away by the higher income of farming. In the 1980s China needs to find a new medical system in a new economic environment.

*7.8 ECONOMIC EXPLANATIONS OF THE BIRTH RATE

In Section 7.2 we pointed out that as per capita income increases in the process of economic development, the birth rate usually goes down. This phenomenon was observed in China before the drastic family planning measures introduced by the government in 1980. Table 7.1 shows the great drop in the birth rate that occurred after the economic collapse of the Great Leap Forward and the rapid rise that followed the economic recovery. Thus, economic factors appear to influence the birth rate. In Section 7.5 we sketched a theory of family decisions concerning the supply of labor by both husbands and wives and the way labor supply is affected by economic forces. Economists recognize that educated couples in developed countries plan the number and timing of their children, together with their other economic activities, including particularly the wife's education and professional development. Economic decisions of the family thus encompass not only the demand for market commodities and the supply of labor but also the demand for children in the family. Some people may be reluctant to accept the idea that having children is an economic decision, just like the purchase of an automobile. The term "demand for children" may convey a lack of love for children. In fact, accepting an economic explanation of family planning does not mean believing that children are equivalent to automobiles. It means only accepting the idea that economic factors affect both the ability to buy a car and the ability to have an additional child.

The basic theory of the demand for children includes the cost of having children in the expenditures that are subject to the budget constraint. Therefore, the consumer unit has to make a choice between having children and having consumer goods. This theory is expounded in Becker (1981, pp. 95–102). Let the utility function of a family be written as

$$u = u(n,Z) \tag{7.3}$$

where n denotes the number of children and Z denotes the quantity of consumption goods. The budget constraint is

$$p_n n + \pi_z Z = I \tag{7.4}$$

where p_n denotes the cost per child, π_z denotes the unit price of consumption goods, and I denotes full income, which includes nonlabor income plus the maximum labor income that can be earned by using all the time available to the adult family members. The cost of having a child includes the market goods consumed by a child and the cost of the time the parents spend in rearing the child. A simple analysis ignores the dynamic aspects of the problem, as does the traditional theory of consumer behavior presented in Section 5.3.

As in the traditional theory, the consumer unit is assumed to maximize the utility function (equation 7.3) subject to the budget constraint (equation 7.4). The demand for children depends on the relative price of children and full income. An increase in the relative price of children, or in the ratio of p_n to π_z, will reduce the demand for children relative to consumption goods if real income is held constant. This is the substitution effect of a change in p_n. Under normal circumstances, an increase in income will increase the demand for children.

Becker (1981, pp. 86–97) cites evidence that over the last several hundred years farm families have been larger than urban families—in the city of Florence and its surrounding countryside in 1427, in large Italian *communi* in 1901, and in the United States in 1800. Part of the explanation, according to Becker, is the low cost of rearing children on farms, including the costs of food and housing. Furthermore, the net cost of children is reduced if they contribute to family income by working in the household or in the marketplace. Insofar as children have been more productive on farms than in cities, the net cost of having children is lower for farm families. As an economy develops and agriculture becomes more mechanized and complex, the cost advantage of raising children on farms is reduced. This may explain why urban–rural fertility differentials have narrowed in developed countries during the twentieth century. Because the value of the mother's time is an important part of the cost of having children, Becker points out that the increase in the earning power of women during the past 100 years in developed countries is a major cause of both the increase in the participation of married women in the labor force and the decline in fertility rates. It would be of interest to find out whether this observation is relevant for China in the two decades since the mid-1960s. For example, in China do married women having higher earning power tend to have fewer children, holding the husbands' incomes and other relevant factors constant?

Besides economic calculations, the availability of birth control methods also affects the fertility rate. It is not easy to measure the effect of improvement in birth control methods on the birth rate, and scholars differ on this subject. To cite one opinion, Becker (1981, pp. 99–102) believes that the effect is small and presents three arguments. First, by some calculations, the simple birth control methods of increasing the marriage age, reducing the frequency of coition during marriage, and prolonging breastfeeding can be shown to be effective in significantly reducing the fertility rate. Other such primitive birth control methods have been known for centuries. Second, improved birth control methods are not sufficient to reduce fertility, as evidenced, for example, by the high birth rate of poor Indian families that were informed of and encouraged to use these methods. Third, modern birth control methods are not necessary to reduce fertility, as evidenced by the large reductions in fertility in many societies before these methods were developed.

Concerning the income effect on the demand for children, Becker (1981, p. 102) cites cross-section evidence of the positive relation between family income and number of children. However, there are also instances of negative relations between income and fertility. One possible explanation is that the cost of children increases with income because the wives of men with higher incomes tend to have higher potential earnings, as suggested by Mincer (1963), or to have higher values on their time, as suggested by Willis (1973). Another explanation is offered by Becker and Lewis (1973) and further expounded by Tomes (1978). They argue that one effect of increasing income is to increase the quality of children rather than the quantity. This argument is developed by assuming that the family maximizes the utility function

$$u = u(n,q,Z) \tag{7.5}$$

where q denotes the quality of each of the n children in a family. Let p_c denote the constant cost of one unit of quality. The total amount spent on n children is $p_c q n$. The budget constraint is therefore

$$p_c q n + \pi_z Z = I \tag{7.6}$$

where π_z and I denote respectively the price per unit of consumer goods and full income, as in the constraint shown in equation 7.4.

Maximization of the utility function 7.5 subject to the constraint 7.6 gives the first-order conditions for equilibrium

$$\frac{\partial u}{\partial n} = \lambda p_c q = \lambda \pi_n$$

$$\frac{\partial u}{\partial q} = \lambda p_c n = \lambda \pi_q$$

$$\frac{\partial u}{\partial Z} = \lambda \pi_z \tag{7.7}$$

where λ is the Lagrange multiplier, or the marginal utility of income, and $\pi_n = p_c q$ and $\pi_q = p_c n$ are respectively the shadow prices per child and per unit of quality. These shadow prices depend on the price per unit of quality p_c. Note that the shadow price π_n is a function of q and that the shadow price π_q is a function of n. The shadow price π_n of having each child increases with q because increasing q will raise the amount spent on each child. The shadow price π_q of a unit of quality increases with n because increasing n will raise the cost of improving the quality of each and every child, as more children will be affected.

When p_c, π_z, and I are held constant, an increase in n will raise the shadow price $\pi_q = n p_c$ of quality and thus will reduce the demand for q. The reduction in q lowers the shadow price $\pi_n = p_c q$ of each child, which in turn increases the demand for n. The process continues until a new equilibrium is reached. A small increase in n would result in a large reduction in q. Similarly, a small increase in q would result in a large reduction in n.

To explain the large reductions in fertility rates observed in many countries—including the United States between 1960 and 1972, Japan between 1950 and 1960, Taiwan between 1960 and 1975, and England and Wales between 1871 and 1901—Becker (1981, pp. 107–109) refines the above theory by adding a fixed cost p_n of each child and a fixed cost p_q of quality. The fixed cost p_n includes the time, money, and discomfort associated with pregnancy and delivery, the costs of avoiding pregnancy and childbirth, and other monetary and psychic costs that are independent of quality. The fixed cost p_q of quality is independent of the number of children because of joint consumption by different children; it includes the cost of clothing and other items shared by them. When these fixed costs are incorporated, the budget constraint becomes

$$p_n n + p_q q + p_c qn + \pi_z Z = I \tag{7.8}$$

Maximization of the utility function 7.5 subject to the constraint 7.8 gives the first-order conditions

$$\frac{\partial u}{\partial n} = \lambda(p_n + p_c q) = \lambda p_c q(1 + r_n) = \lambda \pi_n$$

$$\frac{\partial u}{\partial q} = \lambda(p_q + p_c n + \frac{\partial p_c}{\partial q} nq) = \lambda p_c n(1 + r_q + \epsilon_{pq}) = \lambda \pi_q$$

$$\frac{\partial u}{\partial Z} = \lambda \pi_z \tag{7.9}$$

where $r_n = p_n/p_c q$ and $r_q = p_q/p_c n$ are the ratios of fixed to variable costs of quantity and quality respectively, and $1 + \epsilon_{pq}$ is the ratio of marginal variable cost to average variable costs of quality. The definition of the shadow prices π_n and π_q given in 7.9 imply

$$\frac{\pi_n}{\pi_q} = \frac{q}{n} \frac{(1 + r_n)}{(1 + r_q + \epsilon_{pq})} \tag{7.10}$$

The ratio of π_n to π_q depends not only on the ratio of q to n as in the condition 7.7, but also on the ratios r_n and r_q of fixed to variable costs of quantity and quality, and on the ratio $1 + \epsilon_{pq}$ of marginal to average variable cost of quality.

An increase in the fixed cost p_n would raise the shadow price of children π_n and would induce a substitution of q and Z for the number n of children. Because of the interaction between n and q, the increase in q would raise π_n further, as π_n is a function of q. The reduction in n would lower π_q further, and so forth until a new equilibrium is reached. Becker presents some illustrative calculations to show that a large reduction in n and a large increase in q could result from a moderate increase in the fixed cost of children or a moderate decrease in the ratio $1 + \epsilon_{pq}$ of marginal to average costs of quality that raises the ratio π_n/π_q by only 10 to 20 percent initially. Thus, moderate initial increase in the relative price of having children could explain both the large reductions in fertility and the large increases in quality of children that have been observed in the United States, Japan, Taiwan, and Great Britain during the periods mentioned.

The theoretical framework based on the utility function 7.5 has been applied to explain both the number and timing of children as well as their average quality, usually measured by expenditure per child. The reader may refer to Becker and Tomes (1976), Razin (1980), and Nerlove and Razin (1981). The approach appears to be interesting and promising, but it is controversial, and important unresolved problems remain. Chinese data are likely to become sufficient for statistical testing of this theoretical framework. Such testing could lead to improvement of the theory as well as a better understanding of the factors affecting fertility in China.

PROBLEMS

1. Comment on the interpolation of population figures in column 1 of Table 7.1. Are you satisfied with the interpolation? Can you suggest a better way to interpolate? Explain.
2. Coale (1981, p. 89) quotes Liu Zheng's data as showing an average death rate in China of 17 per 1000 for 1958–1961, the period of the Great Leap Forward and the associated food crisis. Using the death rates given in Table 7.1 for the adjacent years 1957 and 1962 as a guide, what is your estimate of the number of deaths in excess of the trend during the four years 1958–1961?
3. What are the major changes in the birth rate in China between 1952 and 1981? How do you explain these changes?
4. Describe the population policy of the Chinese government from 1949 to 1982. Provide a brief evaluation of this policy.
5. Explain how an increase in the marriage age of women from 25 to 28 would affect the birth rate in the 10 years after the change. State your assumptions.
6. Using an aggregate production function, provide an estimate of per capita national income in China in 1980 assuming that beginning with the actual population in 1957, population had increased more slowly than the historical record to only 700 million in 1980. Present and justify a hypothetical population growth path from 1957 to 1980. State the assumptions used in your estimate of per capita income.
7. What explains the increase in employment in China from 1952 to 1980? What factors might explain the increase in the labor participation rate?
8. What is the marginal productivity theory of demand for labor? Why is this theory relevant or not relevant to China?
9. Explain the concept of investment in human capital. In what ways is it similar to and different from investment in physical capital?
10. It has been said that investment in human capital is more important than investment in physical capital in the process of economic development. What does this statement mean? Do you agree? Explain.
11. Describe the provision of educational services in China from 1952 to 1982. In particular, what have educational conditions been during the Cultural Revolution and during the past 10 years? Evaluate the current government policy toward education.
12. What affects the choice between the consumption of goods and of leisure by an individual? When the individual's wages increase, will he or she work more or less? Explain.
13. What factors affect the labor participation rate of married women? In particular, discuss the effects of an increase in family nonlabor income, an increase in the husband's wages, an increase in the wife's own wages, an increase in the wages of a housemaid, and a reduction in the tuition of the school to which the wife may go.
14. Using a family utility function that has consumption goods and the number of children as two arguments, explain how an increase in family income would affect the number of children. How could one explain the cross-section observations showing that families with higher incomes tend to have fewer children?
15. Using a family utility function that has consumption goods, the number of children, and the quality of children as three arguments, define the shadow price of having each child and explain how an increase in the quality of children would affect this shadow price and the number of children.

16. What is your explanation of the reductions in birth rate observed in many countries in the course of their economic development?

17. Assuming that data are available, specify one regression equation concerning one aspect of population figures for China that you would like to estimate. State your hypothesis. Specify the dependent variable and each explanatory variable. Do you require time-series or cross-section data? What can you learn from the regression analysis, and how?

REFERENCES

Becker, G. S. 1964. *Human capital.* New York: Columbia University Press.

————. 1981. *A treatise on the family.* Cambridge, Mass.: Harvard University Press.

Becker, G. S., and H. G. Lewis. 1973. On the interaction between the quantity and quality of children. *Journal of Political Economy* 81:S279–S288.

Becker, G. S., and N. Tomes. 1976. Child endowments and quantity and quality of children. *Journal of Political Economy* 84:S143–S162.

Butz, W. P., and M. P. Ward. 1979. The emergency of countercyclical U.S. fertility. *American Economic Review* 69:318–328.

Chinese State Statistics Bureau. 1982. *Statistical yearbook of China, 1981.* Hong Kong: Hong Kong Economics Review Publishing House.

Coale, A. J. 1981. Population trends, population policy, and population studies in China. *Population and Development Review* 7:85–97.

————. 1983. Population trends in China and India (a review). *Proceedings of the National Academy of Sciences U.S.A.* 80:1757–1763.

Family Planning Office, State Council. 1982. Family planning in China. In Economic Research Center, State Council of the People's Republic of China, *Almanac of China's economy, 1981.* Hong Kong: Modern Cultural Company Limited. Pp. 761–765.

Hicks, J. R. 1946. *Value and capital.* 2d ed. London: Oxford University Press.

Hsiao, W. 1983. Transformation of health care for 800 millions. Mimeographed. Boston: School of Public Health, Harvard University.

Ji Hua. 1982. Education in China. In Economic Research Center, State Council of the People's Republic of China, *Almanac of China's economy, 1981.* Hong Kong: Modern Cultural Company Limited. Pp. 743–752.

Mao Zedong. 1949. Weisin lishi guan de pochan [The bankruptcy of the idealistic view of history], 12–13. In *Mao Zedong xuanji,* [*Selected works of Mao Zedong*], 1960. Beijing: People's Publishing Society, Vol. IV, p. 1515.

Mincer, J. 1963. Market prices, opportunity costs, and income effects. In *Measurement in economics,* Carl F. Christ et al., eds. Stanford, Calif.: Stanford University Press.

Nerlove, M. 1974. Economic growth and population perspectives of the "new home economics." Reprint of the Agricultural Development Council, New York.

Nerlove, M., and A. Razin. 1981. Child spacing and numbers: An empirical analysis. In *Essays in the theory and measurement of consumer behavior in honour of Sir Richard Stone,* A. Deaton, ed. New York: Cambridge University Press.

Razin, A. 1980. Number, birth spacing and quality of children: A microeconomic view. in *Research in population economics, II,* J. Simon and J. Da Vanzo, eds. Greenwich, Conn.: JAI Press.

Rees, A. 1979. *The economics of work and pay.* New York: Harper & Row.

Schultz, T. P. 1981. *The economics of population.* Reading, Mass.: Addison-Wesley.

Tomes, N. 1978. A model of child endowments, and the quality and quantity of children. Ph.D. dissertation, University of Chicago.

Wei Zhi. 1982. China's health services. In Economic Research Center, State Council of the People's Republic of China, *Almanac of China's economy, 1981.* Hong Kong: Modern Cultural Company Limited. Pp. 753–760.

Willis, R. J. 1973. A new approach to the economic theory of fertility behavior. *Journal of Political Economy* 81:S14–S64.

Zheng Ji. 1982. Employment, wages, workers' welfare and labor protection in China. In Economic Research Center, State Council of the People's Republic of China, *Almanac of China's economy, 1981.* Hong Kong: Modern Cultural Company Limited. Pp. 698–706.

chapter 8

Foreign Trade and Investment

8.1 TRENDS IN CHINA'S FOREIGN TRADE

In 1952 and in 1978 the total value of China's foreign trade, or the sum of the values of exports and imports, was approximately 11 percent of national income. Economic policies and political changes have affected the ratio of the total value of foreign trade to national income. The ratio increased somewhat in the middle 1950s with the import of Soviet technology during the first Five-Year Plan. It declined during the Cultural Revolution of the late 1960s and early 1970s, when China pursued a policy of self-sufficiency, reaching the lowest value of 5.8 percent of national income in 1970 and 1971. The ratio climbed back to 11.8 percent in 1978 and then increased rapidly to 18.7 percent in 1981, when China was beginning to pursue an outward-looking policy for the four modernizations. Table 8.1 shows the value of China's exports and imports, their total, and the ratio of the total to national income.

Besides the swings in the ratio of the value of foreign trade to national income, changes also occurred concerning China's trading partners. Data on China's foreign trade with selected countries and regions are given on pp. 359–371 of *Statistical Yearbook of China, 1981* (Chinese State Statistics Bureau, 1982). In particular, the value of trade with the United States (p. 370) dropped from $238 million U.S. in 1950 to practically zero in 1952, remained at zero until 1972, and increased to $476 million in 1974, $992 million in 1978 (after a decline to $294 million in 1977), and to $4,813 million in 1980. These figures demonstrate the rapid responses of foreign trade to changing circumstances. The value of trade with the Soviet Union (p. 363) rose from $338 million U.S. in 1950 to $1.064 billion in 1952, to the peak of $2.097 billion in 1959, declined to the lowest point of $47 million in 1970, and increased to $492 million in 1980. Japan was China's leading trading partner in 1980, accounting for $9.201 billion U.S. (p. 359) out of the total value of $37.82 billion in trade.

Table 8.1   VALUE OF CHINA'S IMPORTS AND EXPORTS

Year	(RMB 100 million)			Total in U.S. dollars (100 million)	Ratio of total to national income
	Exports	**Imports**	**Total**		
1950	20.2	21.4	41.6	11.3	
1951	24.2	35.3	59.5	19.6	
1952	27.1	37.5	64.6	19.4	.110
1953	34.8	46.1	80.9	23.7	.120
1954	40.0	44.7	84.7	24.4	.119
1955	48.7	61.1	109.8	31.4	.146
1956	55.7	53.0	108.7	32.1	.128
1957	54.5	50.0	104.5	31.1	.115
1958	67.1	61.7	128.8	38.7	.115
1959	78.1	71.2	149.3	43.8	.122
1960	63.3	65.2	128.5	38.1	.105
1961	47.8	43.0	90.8	29.4	.091
1962	47.1	33.8	80.9	26.6	.088
1963	50.0	35.7	85.7	29.2	.086
1964	55.4	42.1	97.5	34.7	.084
1965	63.1	55.3	118.4	42.5	.085
1966	66.0	61.1	127.1	46.2	.080
1967	58.8	53.4	112.2	41.6	.075
1968	57.6	50.9	108.5	40.5	.077
1969	59.8	47.2	107.0	40.3	.066
1970	56.8	56.1	112.9	45.9	.058
1971	68.5	52.4	120.9	48.5	.058
1972	82.9	64.0	146.9	63.0	.069
1973	116.9	103.6	220.5	109.8	.095
1974	139.4	152.8	292.2	145.7	.124
1975	143.0	147.4	290.4	147.5	.116
1976	134.8	129.3	264.1	134.4	.108
1977	139.7	132.8	272.5	148.0	.102
1978	167.7	187.4	355.1	206.4	.118
1979	211.7	242.9	454.6	293.3	.135
1980	272.4	291.4	563.8	378.2	.154
1981	371.2	346.2	717.4	403.7	.182
1982	420.0	329.5	749.5	389.4	.176

Source: Statistical Yearbook of China, 1981, p. 357; for 1981 and 1982, *China's Statistical Abstract, 1983,* p. 74. The last column relies on the national income figures in column 1 of Table 6.1 and, for 1981 and 1982, national incomes of 394.0 and 424.7 billion given in *China's Statistical Abstract, 1983,* p. 3.

Another important aspect of China's foreign trade, the commodity composition of imports and exports, has also changed since the 1950s. As Table 8.2 shows, the export of agricultural products accounted for 59.3 percent of total exports in 1952 but fell to only 18.7 percent in 1980. At the same time, the export of industrial and mineral products increased from 17.9 percent to 51.8 percent. This change in the ratio of agricultural to industrial exports reflects the process of industrialization in China. As far as imports are concerned, producer goods accounted for almost 90 percent of the total in 1952 and for almost 79 percent in 1980, the remaining percentage being classified as imports of consumer goods. The moderate increase in the fraction of consumer-good imports reflects the recent emphasis on consumption as compared with

Table 8.2 PERCENTAGE COMPOSITION OF CHINA'S IMPORTS AND EXPORTS

Year	Industrial and mineral products[a]	Processed farm and side line products[b]	Farm and sideline products[c]	Producer goods	Consumption goods
1950	9.3	33.2	57.5	83.4	16.6
1951	14.0	31.4	54.6	81.3	18.7
1952	17.9	22.8	59.3	89.4	10.6
1953	18.4	25.9	55.7	92.1	7.9
1954	24.0	27.7	48.3	92.3	7.7
1955	25.5	28.4	46.1	93.8	6.2
1956	26.1	31.3	42.6	91.5	8.5
1957	28.4	31.5	40.1	92.0	8.0
1958	27.5	37.0	35.5	93.1	6.9
1959	23.7	38.7	37.6	95.7	4.3
1960	26.7	42.3	31.0	95.4	4.6
1961	33.4	45.9	20.7	61.9	38.1
1962	34.7	45.9	19.4	55.2	44.8
1963	32.9	42.9	24.2	56.0	44.0
1964	32.9	39.1	28.0	55.5	44.5
1965	30.9	36.0	33.1	66.5	33.5
1966	26.6	37.5	35.9	72.2	27.8
1967	24.4	36.3	39.3	76.0	24.0
1968	21.8	38.2	40.0	77.2	22.8
1969	23.5	39.1	37.4	82.4	17.6
1970	25.6	37.7	36.7	82.7	17.3
1971	28.9	34.9	36.2	83.9	16.1
1972	27.7	41.0	31.3	79.4	20.6
1973	24.7	39.5	35.8	76.4	23.6
1974	33.8	29.8	36.4	75.7	24.3
1975	39.3	31.1	29.6	85.4	14.6
1976	38.9	32.7	28.4	86.8	13.2
1977	38.5	33.9	27.6	76.1	23.9
1978	37.4	35.0	27.6	81.4	18.6
1979	44.0	32.9	23.1	81.3	18.7
1980	51.8	29.5	18.7	78.9	21.1

[a]Including metals and mineral products, machinery and instruments, chemicals, Western medicine, chinaware, chemical fibers, and chemical fiber products.
[b]Including processed grain and edible oil food, textiles, native and animal products, and handicrafts.
[c]Including grain, cotton, edible oil, eggs, livestock and poultry, aquatic products, vegetables and dried fruits, raw lacquer, and crude Chinese drugs.
Source: Statistical Yearbook of China, 1981, p. 358.

capital accumulation. Note from Table 8.2 that during the period of rapid industrialization beginning with the first Five-Year Plan in 1953–1957 and terminating in the middle of the second Five-Year Plan in 1958–1962, the import of consumption goods was reduced to 8 percent or below of total imports, only to rise rapidly to about 40 percent or above during the economic adjustment of 1961–1964. At the height of the Cultural Revolution of the late 1960s and early 1970s, the fraction of total imports devoted to consumption goods was reduced to below 20 percent.

In Section 8.2 we will discuss the economic gain from international trade as advanced in Ricardo's theory of comparative advantage. Section 8.3 presents the Heckscher-Ohlin theory of international trade, which explains how the supply of inputs or factors of production affects the pattern of trade. Section 8.4 is concerned with the determination of foreign exchange rates in the market. With the above theoretical tools, we will go on to study foreign trade policy and practices in China in Section 8.5, and the problems arising in China's foreign trade in Section 8.6. Section 8.7 deals with foreign investment in China. Section 8.8 attempts to incorporate foreign trade and investment in macroeconomic model 6.37 presented in Chapter 6.

8.2 RICARDO'S THEORY OF COMPARATIVE ADVANTAGE

In Section 1.2 we presented the Edgeworth diagram of Figure 1.1 to show that two persons can both gain by trading. Both a farmer and a textile worker gain when the farmer trades the rice he has produced for the cloth produced by the worker. Because of diminishing marginal rates of substitution of rice for cloth, as reflected in the convex indifference curves for rice and cloth, when the farmer has plenty of rice relative to cloth, the extra rice has little value to the farmer as compared to the value of cloth. At the same time, when the textile worker has plenty of cloth relative to rice, she is willing to trade her cloth for the farmer's rice. Trading takes place until neither person can gain by trading. The same analysis applies to trade between two countries. If country A has plenty of rice relative to cloth and country B has plenty of cloth relative to rice, the people in both countries will gain by trading for the same reason that both the farmer and the worker gain in the example of Figure 1.1.

However, the analysis of Figure 1.1 does not explain which country should sell rice and buy cloth or why one country has plenty of rice or cloth to start with. It deals only with consumer preferences as summarized by the indifference curves, not with the production of rice and cloth. In other words, it is concerned with the demand for rice and cloth but not with their supply. The theory of David Ricardo, as expounded in his *On the Principles of Political Economy and Taxation* (1821), does concern itself with the production side of international trade. In the terminology of our Figure 1.6 in Section 1.7, Ricardo's theory is concerned with the production transformation curve of each country. The slope of the production transformation curve measures (the negative of) the marginal rate of substitution in production between two commodities. If the marginal rate of substitution of rice for cloth is 3, for example, then 3 more kilograms of rice can be produced by reducing the production of cloth by 1 meter. Thus the slope of the production transformation curve shows how easy it is to produce one commodity relative to another, or how plentiful the supply of one commodity is relative to another. When the supply of one commodity in a country is plentiful relative to another commodity, that country can gain by exporting the first commodity and importing the second.

The last proposition can be demonstrated by using Figure 8.1, where the output of rice is measured along the horizontal axis and the output of cloth along the vertical axis. Let *A* and *B* be the production transformation curves of countries A and B, respectively. Country A can produce 100 units (million metric tons) of rice or 10 units (billion meters) of cloth by devoting all its resources to either. By producing 1 less unit of cloth, it can produce 10 more units of rice. Country B can produce 50 units of rice or 20 units of cloth if it devotes all its resources to either. By producing one less unit of cloth, it can produce 2.5 more units of rice. Without trade, points *a* and *b* are the

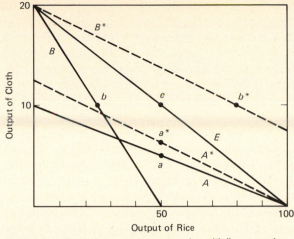

Figure 8.1 Trade between two countries with linear production transformation curves.

equilibrium points of countries A and B, respectively. The former shows a combination of 50 units of rice and 5 units of cloth. The latter is a combination of 25 units of rice and 10 units of cloth. These points are obtained by maximizing a utility function $u = x_1 x_2$ (with x_1 and x_2 denoting the quantities of rice and cloth respectively) subject to the respective production transformation constraints, but the particular utility function is chosen for illustrative purpose only. Here we are bypassing the theoretical problems of defining indifference curves and utility functions for a society by assuming that all individuals have the same utility function and that all income and outputs are divided equally, so that a diagram drawn for the society is simply a magnification of the diagram for each individual (see Problem 1 at the end of this chapter). In this example, country A produces and consumes 50 units of rice and 5 units of cloth, while country B produces and consumes 25 units of rice and 10 units of cloth.

The total output of rice from both countries is 75 units, and the total output of cloth from both countries is 15 units. If country A specializes in the production of rice and country B in the production of cloth, together they can produce 100 units of rice and 20 units of cloth. If country A then trades 40 units of its rice for 8 units of cloth, as compared with 50 units of rice and 8 units of cloth without specialization and trade, country B will have 40 units of rice and 12 units of cloth, more than the 25 units of rice and 10 units of cloth it had before. Therefore, there is a gain from specialization and trade. Such a gain exists also from specialization and trade between two provinces in a country (see Problem 12 at the end of Chapter 3).

After specialization, exactly how much of each commodity will be traded and at what relative price depends on the demand conditions in the two countries, as summarized by their respective indifference curves. Given the indifference curves of each country and its output of rice or cloth, the relative price of rice to cloth determines the amount of rice or cloth each country is willing to trade, according to the theory of demand as expounded in Section 1.3 and Figure 1.2. For example, having produced 100 units of rice and given the relative price of rice to cloth of .1, country A faces the trade transformation curve (or budget line) A in Figure 8.1. It will choose the point a at which an indifference curve is tangential to the transformation curve. If the relative price of rice to cloth is raised to .125, country A will face the transformation curve indicated by the broken line $A*$ in Figure 8.1, and its equilibrium point will be $a*$, at which another indifference curve is tangential to the transformation curve $A*$. At point $a*$ country A demands 50 units of rice and 6.25 units of cloth. It will therefore export 50 units of rice and import 6.25 units of cloth at a price ratio of .125 of rice to cloth. Similarly, having produced 20 units of cloth, country B will change its demand for rice and cloth from point b to a new point $b*$ when the relative price of rice to cloth is .125. At the relative price .125, country B's transformation curve is the broken line $B*$ in Figure 8.1, which is parallel to the $A*$. The equilibrium point $b*$ is tangential to an indifference curve indicating country B's demands for rice and cloth of 80 and 10 units, respectively. Thus, at the relative price of .125, country B wants to export 10 units of cloth and import 80 units of rice, while country A is willing to export only 50 units of rice and import 6.25 units of cloth. There is an excess demand for rice and an excess supply of cloth. The relative price of rice will increase until country A's supply of rice equals country B's demand and country B's supply of cloth equals country A's demand. In our example, where a utility function of $u = x_1 x_2$ is assumed for both countries, the equilibrium will be reached when the relative price of rice to cloth is increased to .20. At the relative price .20, both countries A and B will face the transformation curve E in Figure 8.1 and will have the equilibrium point e. Country A will export 50 units of rice to country B and will import 10 units of cloth from country B. In general, at equilibrium the transformation curves of the two countries need not be identical, but have to be parallel, showing that they are facing the same relative price (see Problem 2). A simplifying assumption in the analyses of this and the following section is zero transportation costs. This assumption will be relaxed at the end of Section 8.4.

In the above example, we have assumed linear production transformation curves. The gain from trade remains when this assumption is dropped. As long as the slopes of the production transformation curves or the marginal rates of substitution in production are different in two countries *at their current levels of production,* both can gain by trade. The marginal rate of substitution shows the number of units of the first commodity (rice) that can be obtained by producing one less unit of the second commodity (cloth). For example, if the marginal rates are 10 and 2.5 respectively for countries A and B, country A is relatively more efficient in producing the first commodity (rice) than country B. By producing one less unit of the second commodity (cloth), country A can produce 10 more units of rice. But country B can recover the one unit of cloth that country A sacrifices by giving up only 2.5 units of rice. Therefore, between the two countries willing to trade, there will be an extra $10 - 2.5 = 7.5$ units of rice left over to share. In other words, there is a gain from trade. A country should produce more of the commodity for which it has a *comparative advantage.* Between two countries A and B, country A has a comparative advantage in producing rice if by giving up one unit of cloth, it can produce more rice than country B—that is, if the marginal rate of substitution of rice for cloth is higher in country A. Here the marginal rates of substitution are measured at the current production levels for both countries. If the production transformation curves are nonlinear, the marginal rates of substitution will change. In the case of nonlinear production transformation curves, when country A produces more rice, the marginal rate of substitution of rice for cloth will decrease. When country B produces less rice, the marginal rate will increase.

Figure 8.2 illustrates the trading between two countries with nonlinear production transformation curves indicated by A and B, respectively. Without trade, country A's equilibrium is shown by point a, at which its transformation curve is tangential to an indifference curve. Country B's equilibrium is shown by point b. Country A has a comparative advantage in producing rice and country B has a comparative advantage in producing cloth. Figure 8.2 is intentionally drawn in such a way that country A will produce 100 units of rice, country B will produce 20 units of cloth, and after trading, the equilibrium point e is the same as in Figure 8.1. If the production transformation curve of country A were to cross the line E, as shown by the broken curve above A, at the relative price given by the slope of line E country A would not produce 100 units of rice but would produce less rice and some cloth, as given by the point p. With trading at the above relative price, country A's transformation curve is shown by E^*, which passes the point p and on its left is a straight line parallel to E. Another possibility is that country B is a small country, with its production transformation curve completely below that of country A and the maximum output of cloth below 10 units. In these cases, country A may end up producing both cloth and rice at the equilibrium point with trade. However, as long as the marginal rates of substitution are different in the two countries before trading takes place, there is gain from trading, as explained in the preceding paragraph.

The same point concerning the gain from trade applies when there are many commodities and many countries trading with one another. Any country can gain by trading if the marginal rate of substitution in domestic production of any two commodities is different from their relative price in the world market. The reason for the gain is the same as stated above. If the marginal rate of substitution of rice for cloth is 10 in country A and the relative price of cloth to rice in the world market is 2.5, cloth is relatively cheap and rice is relatively expensive in the world market. Country A

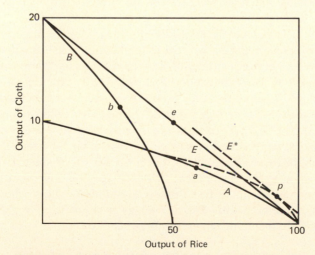

Figure 8.2 Trade between two countries with nonlinear production transformation curves.

should produce more rice for export and use the revenue to import cloth. By producing one less unit of cloth, A can produce 10 more units of rice, which can be traded for 10/2.5, or 4, units of cloth in the world market. In a competitive economy, as we explained in Chapter 1, the relative price of rice to cloth at home is equal to their marginal rate of substitution in production. Therefore, whenever domestic price ratios are different from world price ratios, there is gain from trade. This gain is realized if the citizens of a country are allowed to export and import freely for profit, thus taking advantage of any differences between domestic price ratios and world price ratios. This is the essence of the argument in favor of free trade.

8.3 THE HECKSCHER-OHLIN THEORY OF TRADE

In the preceding section we explained how different production transformation curves in different countries can lead to gain from international trade. In this section we ask why the production transformation curves in different countries are different and explore how the factors contributing to their differences affect trade. There are two main reasons for the differences in the production transformation curves. They are differences in technology and in the amounts of inputs available. A production transformation curve is derived from the production functions of the outputs (which summarize the state of technology) given the total quantities of the inputs available. Recall how the production transformation curve of Figure 1.6 was derived using the production functions

$$x_1 = \sqrt{x_5 x_6} \text{ and } x_2 = \sqrt{x_3 x_4} \tag{8.1}$$

where x_1 and x_2 are the outputs of rice and cloth, x_5 and x_3 are the labor inputs in producing rice and cloth respectively, x_6 is the quantity of land and x_4 is the quantity of machines. Assuming the quantities x_6 and x_4 to be fixed and the total quantity of labor to be given, we can derive the combinations of outputs (x_1, x_2) that can be produced by allocating different quantities of labor in the production of the two commodities, thus tracing out the production transformation curve.

In the theory of Heckscher (1919) and Ohlin (1933), the technology is assumed to be identical in different countries, so that differences in transformation curves are attributed to differences in the quantities of inputs available. Furthermore, in contrast with the Cobb-Douglas production function as exemplified by equation 8.1, the production function employed assumes that each production process—or each activity, in the language of Koopmans (1951)—requires fixed amounts of different inputs for the production of one unit of output. To illustrate, assume that there are two production processes or activities, one for producing rice and the other for producing cloth. In general, there could be two or more production processes for producing cloth, but we simplify our discussion in this illustration. Process 1 requires 2 units of labor and .5 units of capital to produce 1 unit of rice. Process 2 requires 5 units of labor and 5 units of capital to produce 1 unit of cloth. The technology is summarized by the coefficients in Table 8.3, which are the input requirements per unit of output in each of the two processes.

Let there be 100 units of labor and 50 units of capital available in an economy. Let x_1 and x_2 denote the outputs of rice and cloth, respectively. To produce the outputs

Table 8.3 ILLUSTRATIVE INPUT COEFFICIENTS FOR TWO PRODUCTION PROCESSES

Input	Process 1 Rice production	Process 2 Cloth production	Quantity of input available
Labor	2	5	100
Capital	.5	5	50

(x_1,x_2), $2x_1 + 5x_2$ units of labor and $.5x_1 + 5x_2$ units of capital are required, according to the input coefficients of Table 8.3. Since these input requirements cannot exceed the inputs available, we have the following two inequality restrictions on the outputs:

$$2x_1 + 5x_2 \leq 100 \qquad (8.2)$$

$$.5x_1 + 5x_2 \leq 50 \qquad (8.3)$$

Geometrically, the output combinations (x_1,x_2) that satisfy the inequality constraint 8.2 are all the points on or below line B of Figure 8.1. The output combinations (x_1,x_2) that satisfy the inequality constraint 8.3 are all the points on or below line A of Figure 8.1. The economy's production transformation curve is given by two line segments. The first segment is taken from the left portion of line A before it intersects with line B. The second segment is taken from the right portion of line B after it intersects with line A. For the points (x_1,x_2) on the first segment, all 50 units of capital are used up and there are units of labor unused (since these points are below the restriction B specified by the inequality 8.2). For the points (x_1,x_2) on the second segment, all 100 units of labor are used up and there are units of capital unused (since these points are below the restriction A specified by the inequality 8.3). Thus, we have derived the production transformation curve for an economy from its technology, as summarized by the input coefficients of each production process and its supply of inputs (see Problem 3).

Assume that the same technology is available in countries A and B. However, let country A have only 50 units of capital but more than 200 units of labor. Its production transformation curve will be line A in Figure 8.1 because the constraint 8.2 is not binding. Let country B have only 100 units of labor but more than 100 units of capital. Its production transformation curve will be line B in Figure 8.1 because the constraint 8.3 is not binding. Thus, we have derived the linear production transformation curves A and B for the two countries A and B, as shown in Figure 8.1, from the technology of Table 8.3 by assuming different supplies of the two inputs for the two countries. Country A is assumed to have plenty of labor and country B plenty of capital. According to Table 8.3, the production of rice requires relatively more labor and less capital as compared with the production of cloth. In the production of rice the ratio of labor requirement to capital requirement is 2/.5, or 4. In the production of cloth the ratio is 5/5, or 1. In other words, the production of rice is relatively labor-intensive while the production of cloth is relatively capital-intensive. Since country A has more labor than country B (200 units as compared with 100 units) and country B has more capital than country A (100 units as compared with 50 units), country A will specialize in the production of the labor-intensive commodity (rice) and country B will specialize in the production of the capital-intensive commodity (cloth). Such a specialization was discussed in the preceding section, but in this section we have traced the source of the specialization in the relative supplies of the inputs or factors of production.

This example illustrates a basic theorem of Heckscher-Ohlin in international trade. A country with plenty of labor (or capital) will tend to specialize in producing labor-intensive (or capital-intensive) commodities and will export these commodities in exchange for the capital-intensive (or labor-intensive) commodities. This theorem holds true when the production transformation curves of the countries concerned are nonlinear. To illustrate, let us modify the above example by assuming country A to have 180 units of labor and 50 units of capital and country B to have 100 units of labor and 80 units of capital. The production transformation curve of each country will consist of two line segments, but the main part of country A's is given by line *A* and country B's by line *B* in Figure 8.1. Country A will still produce rice for export and country B will still produce cloth for export. The demonstration of this result is left as an exercise (see Problem 4).

By completing this exercise, the reader will find that the same tools that were used in the preceding section to determine the quantities of exports and imports of each country and the relative prices of the commodities traded are applicable here. What we have added in this section is the relation between the production transformation curve, which defines comparative advantage, and the relative supplies of the factors. In the preceding section we said that country A exports rice because it has a comparative advantage in producing rice as revealed by a comparison of the slope of its production transformation curve with the slope of the production transformation curve of country B. In this section we say that country A exports rice because the production of rice is labor-intensive and country A has plenty of labor as compared with country B.

In the preceding section we also pointed out that if country A exports rice, it means that in country A the marginal rate of substitution of rice for cloth is large as compared with country B, or the price of rice relative to cloth is small (if a competitive market is allowed to function) as compared with country B or the world market. After country A exports rice and imports cloth, the price of rice relative to cloth will increase in country A because the supply of rice decreases and the supply of cloth increases in country A. The relative price of rice to cloth will continue to increase until it equals the relative price in the world market and there is no further gain by an additional export of rice, under the assumption of zero transportation cost. In the meantime, after the opening of the world market and the increases in the demand for domestic rice and in the price of rice in country A, the demand for labor also increases, since labor is used intensively in the production of rice. Similarly, the import of cloth lowers the demand for domestic cloth as well as the price of cloth. The demand for capital also decreases, since capital is used intensively in the production of cloth. With the increase in demand for labor and the decrease in demand for capital, the price of labor will go up and the price of capital goods will go down. An exposition of the effects of international trade on the prices of inputs based on the Heckscher-Ohlin theory can be found in Kenen (1984, Chapter 4).

It might be suggested that the Heckscher-Ohlin theory as presented here has limited applicability because of its assumption that the same technology is available to each country. This criticism becomes less forceful when it is recognized that there is much flexibility in using the supply of inputs in specifying the technology available to each country. To illustrate, let country A have the technology given by Table 8.3. Let country C have a better process for producing rice, one that requires only 1 unit of labor and .5 units of capital. The technology of country C can be summarized by the input coefficients of two processes, the first (called process 3) having coefficients 1 and .5 for labor and capital respectively, and the second having coefficients 5 and 5 as in Table 8.3. One may say that country C has a different technology from that of country A. However, on closer examination it might turn out that the reason process 3 uses less labor than process 1 in the production of rice is that it employs a special hybrid seed that is not available to country A. This particular seed, let us say, cannot simply be imported because it has to be developed locally to fit the climate and soil conditions of country A. There are two ways to model the technologies of countries A and C. One is to use two different tables of input coefficients, as suggested above. The alternative is to use the same table for both countries, as given in Table 8.4. This table consists of input coefficients for three processes, each employing up to three inputs. The technology of Table 8.4 is assumed to be available to both countries A and C, but country A has no supply of the third input.

The use of a special input in the last paragraph to get around the difference in technology in two countries might appear to be artificial. To make the specification of technology more appealing, let us change the third factor from hybrid seed to scientific and technical personnel who are capable of developing a hybrid seed in country A. Instead of saying that country A lacks the technology incorporated in process 3, which requires 1 and .5 units of labor and capital respectively to produce one unit of rice, one can say that country A has all the technology given by Table 8.4 but lacks scientific and technical personnel (which replaces hybrid seed as the third input). After all, most of the modern technology used in production in the developed countries is public knowledge. Any country can use it, provided that technical and managerial personnel are available. One can say that the same, or almost the same, technology is available to every country, but some countries have larger supplies of technical and managerial personnel than others.

The option to model a difference in technology as a difference in the supply of technical personnel is also open when we discuss foreign investment, the second topic of this chapter. Foreign investment can be viewed as import of capital goods, import of technology, import of technical and managerial personnel, or a combination of these, all of which can help to improve the production transformation curve of the importing country. International trade of final products also improves the transformation curve facing a trading country, as shown in Figure 8.1, though not the *production* transformation curve.

Table 8.4   ILLUSTRATIVE INPUT COEFFICIENTS FOR THREE PRODUCTION PROCESSES

Input	Process 1 Rice production	Process 2 Cloth production	Process 3 Rice production
Labor	2	5	1
Capital	.5	5	.5
Hybrid seed	0	0	1

8.4 DETERMINATION OF FOREIGN EXCHANGE RATES

In Sections 8.2 and 8.3 we have explained why and how a country gains from international trade and the relation between trade and the country's production transformation curve that is determined by technology and the supply of inputs. We have not dealt with the financial aspect of trade. The theories of Sections 8.2 and 8.3 apply even when there is no paper money in each country and trade takes place through barter. These theories, like the theories of demand and supply in a competitive economy set forth in Chapter 1, deal with the quantities of different commodities traded or consumed and their relative prices, but not their absolute prices in money terms.

To understand how exchange rates between currencies in different countries are determined by market forces, consider the factors affecting the demand for and supply of these currencies. To begin with, consider the trading of two goods, rice and cloth, between two countries, A and B. Given the production transformation curves of these two countries and their demand conditions, production and trading of the two commodities by the two countries are determined by the analysis set forth in Sections 8.2 and 8.3. For example, in the situation depicted in Figure 8.1, country A produces 100 units of rice and exports 50 units to country B; country B produces 20 units of cloth and exports 10 units to country A. The relative price of rice to cloth is .20 in both countries. Let country A's monetary unit be the dollar and country B's be the yuan. Let the prices of rice and cloth in country A be .20 and 1 dollar, respectively. Let the prices of rice and cloth in country B be .40 and 2 yuan, respectively. Common sense tells us that in this situation one dollar must be worth two yuan, or the exchange rate of the yuan is .5 dollar.

The commonsense conclusion can be justified in the following way. If the exchange rate were otherwise, there would be an excess demand for one currency to alter the exchange rate to the above level. For example, assume that the exchange rate of the yuan is .6 dollar. Traders can exchange one yuan for .6 dollar to buy 3 units of rice in country A. That amount of rice can be sold in country B for $3 \times .4$, or 1.2, yuan for a profit. Such traders will be selling yuan and buying dollars. This increases the demand for dollars relative to the demand for yuan, thus increasing the price of the dollar relative to the yuan or lowering the exchange rate of yuan in dollars. The exchange rate will cease to change when one yuan can buy exactly as much in country B as it can in country A after conversion to dollars.

This analysis suggests that the exchange rate of yuan in terms of dollars equals the ratio of the dollar prices in country A to the yuan prices in country B for the same commodities. In our example, the dollar prices are half the yuan prices for rice and cloth. Therefore, each yuan should be worth half a dollar. This explanation of the exchange rate is known as the *purchasing power parity theory*. According to this theory, the exchange rate between two currencies should equal the ratio of the prices in the two countries. Each currency should be capable of buying the same bundle of commodities domestically as it can buy in a foreign country after conversion to the latter's currency.

If the exchange rate depends on the ratio of monetary or absolute prices in the two countries concerned and if, as a first approximation, absolute prices in each country depend on its money supply, then, as a first approximation, the exchange rate is affected by the relative money supplies in the two countries. Recall that when we study a competitive market economy in Chapter 1, we use the demand and supply conditions to determine the relative prices of different commodities, but not their absolute prices in money terms. In Section 6.6 we point out that as a first approximation, the absolute prices are determined by the supply of money in relation to the total output of an economy. As a first approximation, if the supply of money in country A increases by 20 percent, its absolute prices will increase by 20 percent and its foreign exchange rate will be reduced by 20 percent. This analysis is independent of the analysis of the production transformation curves that determine comparative advantage and trading patterns between countries. A finer theory than a first approximation will be concerned with the interactions between monetary forces and the production and trading of commodities. For example, as we pointed out in Section 6.6, money supply can affect the rate of interest, which in turn affects investment and thus the production of producer goods relative to consumer goods. We will not be concerned with such refinements here.

Even without such refinements, the purchasing power parity theory of exchange rates should be modified or extended in several ways. First, the absolute prices in the two countries that determine the exchange rate should refer to the prices of internationally traded goods only. Prices of goods and services that are consumed only at home should not be included in the purchasing power parity calculation. For example, the price of labor services may be very low in China when converted to U.S. dollars at the prevailing exchange rate, but China may not be able to export these services directly to the United States. It can export labor services indirectly by using them to produce labor-intensive products for exports. As we pointed out in Section 8.3, such exports would tend to raise the wage rate in China if the wage rate were determined by the forces of demand and supply in the market.

Second, besides the trading of goods and services, other factors affect the demand for and supply of currencies of different countries. Besides the export of goods, one important source of supply of foreign currencies is the inflow of foreign capital. Foreign investment is one source of capital inflow. If corporations in the United States want to invest in China, they have to sell U.S. dollars for Chinese RMB to pay for the cost of the investments in China. This will increase the supply of U.S. dollars in China and, other things being equal, raise the exchange rate of RMB in terms of dollars. In the future, if the investments turn out to be successful, the investing corporations will receive Chinese RMB, which they can trade for dollars. The supply of RMB will increase, thus lowering the exchange rate of RMB in terms of dollars. Foreign aid is another source of supply of a foreign currency. It tends to reduce the exchange rate of the currency of the country extending aid.

There are other sources of capital inflow than foreign investment. For example, foreign currencies will flow into a country to earn a high return if the interest rate in that country is high. Such flows will decrease the exchange rates of the foreign currencies. Thus, because of banking regulations favorable to depositors, Switzerland receives large quantities of foreign currencies for deposit in banks. This tends to raise the exchange rate of the Swiss franc and to lower the interest rate paid by Swiss banks.

Third, the purchasing power parity theory, after the above two modifications are incorporated, can be applied to explain the exchange rates of many countries by considering the trading and capital flows between any one country and the rest of the world. The exchange rate of any country depends on the absolute prices of internationally traded goods in that country as compared with world market prices, in whatever international currency. It also depends on the inflow of foreign capital as compared with the outflow of its own capital abroad.

Fourth, because of the existence of transportation costs, which we have assumed to be zero in the above analysis, the purchasing power of one currency, measured in domestically produced goods, may be somewhat different from that measured in foreign goods. Concerning the analysis of Sections 8.2 and 8.3, when transportation costs exist, trade will take place to a lesser extent than predicted by the theory and relative prices between commodities may not be completely equalized in different countries.

Fifth, the theories of trade and exchange rate determination set forth above are based on free trade and free capital flows among countries. In reality, many trade restrictions exist, such as import quotas and tariffs. Furthermore, the governments of many countries, including China, set their exchange rates rather than letting them be determined by the forces of demand and supply. The analysis of Sections 8.2 and 8.3 can assist the reader in evaluating the economic consequences of trade restrictions. The analysis of this section sets bounds to the exchange rate that a government can enforce and reveals the economic effects of enforcing an exchange rate different from a market equilibrium rate.

As the tools of demand and supply are useful in explaining market prices and in studying the effects of government price regulation, the theory of exchange rate determination in this section is useful in explaining exchange rates in free markets and in studying the effects of government control of exchange rates. When the exchange rate of the home currency is set above the market rate as determined by the forces of demand and supply set forth above, people will try to sell home currency to buy more foreign currencies than the supply offered in the market. Further controls to limit the purchase of foreign currencies will be required. In China, for example, RMB cannot be freely used to purchase foreign currencies.

8.5   FOREIGN TRADE POLICY IN CHINA

Perhaps the most significant aspect of China's foreign trade policy in the 1980s is the drastic reversal from self-sufficiency to trade expansion. As can be observed in the last column of Table 8.2, the ratio of the total value of foreign trade to national income increased from a low of .058 in 1970 to a high of .182 in 1981. According to Zhang (1982, p. 621), as of 1980 China had established trade relations with more than 170 countries and regions and had signed bilateral government trade agreements or protocols with more than 80 of them. One can only interpret the change as resulting from the realization among Chinese leaders of the gain to be achieved from international trade, as we discussed in Sections 8.2 and 8.3.

China is largely a planned economy. Foreign trade is directed by central planning. When construction projects are included in a five-year plan, some require the imports of foreign capital goods and materials. Certain consumption goods in the plan have to be imported, including food grain when the domestic supply is insufficient. All these projected imports require the use of foreign exchanges, which have to be earned by the planned exports of domestically produced goods. Thus, exports, imports, and the supply of and demand for foreign exchange have to be incorporated in any central economic planning. Foreign trade plans are parts of China's economic plans. In the State Council, as described in Section 2.6, the Ministry of Foreign Trade directs the affairs of foreign trade. It incorporates the Bureau of Import-Export Control and the General Administration of Customs, and is assisted by the General Administration of Travel and Tourism and the State Administration of Exchange Control (now part of the People's Bank).

In June 1979 the People's Congress adopted a policy for the modernization of China, which included a policy of foreign trade expansion. The ratio of the total value of foreign trade to national income increased immediately, from .118 in 1978 to .135 in 1979, .154 in 1980, and .182 in 1981. Following the shift in policy from an emphasis on developing heavy industry to an emphasis on developing light industry and agriculture, the composition of imports changed. The imports of machinery and raw materials for heavy industry were reduced, and imports of food grains, cooking oils, materials for agricultural use, and raw materials for textiles and light industry increased. As reported in the article on foreign trade by Zhang (1982, p. 622), in 1980 imports of grains, animal fats and vegetable oils, cotton, synthetic fibers, chemical fertilizers, industrial chemicals, and wood pulp were 51 percent higher than in 1979. Their combined share in the total value of imports rose to 52.8 percent in 1980 from 41.7 percent in 1979. Imports of steel, nonferrous metals, machinery, and instruments decreased by 3.5 percent from 1979 and together accounted for 47.2 percent of the total value of imports, as compared with 58.3 percent in 1979.

As for the composition of exports, in 1980 the proportion of exports of heavy industrial products went up, while that of agricultural and sideline products, textiles, and light industrial products declined. As Table 8.2 shows, agricultural and sideline products decreased from 23.1 percent to 18.7 percent, while industrial and mineral products increased from 44.0 percent to 51.8 percent. In particular, the value of exported machine tools increased from 65.56 million RMB in 1979 to 77.88 million in 1980, and the export of tools and instruments increased from 112.19 million RMB to 147.30 million. Although China increased the value of its exports of machinery and transport equipment by 44.6 percent between 1979 and 1980, its imports of machinery and transport equipment still far exceeded its exports in 1981, being 9.798 billion RMB as compared with 1.815 billion (*Statistical Yearbook of China, 1981,* p. 390). The quantities of major exported commodities from 1950 to 1980 are given on pages 372–384 of the *Statistical Yearbook of China, 1981;* the quantities of major imported commodities are given on pages 385–389.

China's foreign trade policy has three main characteristics. First, imports are controlled by the government so that essential consumer goods and capital goods from abroad can be acquired in the process of modernization. Second, to obtain the foreign exchange to pay for the necessary imports, the Chinese government tries to direct and encourage the expansion of exports. New government units were set up in the early 1980s for the purpose of increasing exports. Besides directing selected centrally run enterprises to expand their exports, the government encourages provincially run and collective enterprises to obtain export licenses to compete in the world market. Third, to ensure that the foreign exchange obtained from exports is used to pay for essential imports, the government controls foreign exchange by setting the exchange rate and monopolizing and regulating the trading of foreign exchange. Foreign exchanges are not allowed to be traded freely in the marketplace. To obtain foreign exchange for a purpose approved by the government, an importer, an enterprise, or a tourist has to apply to the Administration of Exchange Control, which is a part of the People's Bank. Furthermore, a system of multiple exchange rates is practiced. To encourage certain exporters, the government pays them more RMB per U.S. dollar earned than according to the standard official exchange.

Concerning import policy in the early 1980s, Zhang (1982, p. 623) writes:

> During the period of economic readjustment, imports of agricultural and industrial materials needed for maintaining economic stability and developing the textile and light industries must be timely and orderly. Imports of technology and equipment needed for upgrading existing industries, for expanding energy production, communications and transportation facilities and for advancing science, education and culture must be organized in a planned way. . . . In drawing up foreign trade plans, we must take into consideration our actual export capabilities. . . . From the short-term as well as the long-term point of view, import controls will be necessary. . . .

> We shall not import those items that can be produced domestically in sufficient quantity and with satisfactory quality. Items that we can make at home but are still importing now will eventually be supplied mainly by domestic production. In this way, we can save our limited foreign exchange for the most essential items and make the composition of our imports more reasonable.

To promote exports, the Chinese government has taken the following actions since 1979 (Yen, 1982). First, exports have been decentralized. While commodities of the first categories (defined in Section 2.2), including coal, oil, food grain, steel, and others, are still exported by enterprises under the direct control of the Ministry of Foreign Trade, commodities of the second category can be exported by enterprises under other ministries, subject to the approval of the State Council. Other commodities can be exported by trading companies established under the jurisdiction of provincial governments. Export licenses are issued by provincial bureaus of foreign trade authorized by the Ministry of Foreign Trade, rather than directly by the ministry, as used to be the case.

Second, trading companies have been formed in cooperation with manufacturing enterprises as well as industrial enterprises specializing in the production of export products. These enterprises are responsible for their own profits and losses. Many provinces and cities have set up areas specializing in the production of agricultural and related products for export.

Third, special treatment is given to exporting companies and enterprises to encourage them to export, including allowing them to retain part of the foreign exchange they earn and extending to them special loans in RMB or in foreign exchange for short-term financing or long-term capital expansion. Since 1981 a more favorable exchange rate has been granted to exporters in exchanging the foreign currency earned for RMB. For example, in 1981, while the official exchange rate was 1 U.S. dollar for 1.6 RMB, the more favorable rate was 1 to 2.8 RMB.

Fourth, several coastal provinces, including Guangdong and Fujian, have established export-processing zones. Foreign investors are encouraged to set up factories in these zones, independently or jointly with Chinese enterprises, to process imported or locally produced materials for export. No import duties are levied on materials processed for exports. A main purpose is to absorb Chinese labor while using the capital and technical knowledge of the foreign investors. The use of export-processing zones to promote exports was found to be successful in Taiwan, which established the Kaohsiung Export-Processing Zone in December 1966 (see Li, 1976, pp. 352–358). Also, joint ventures with foreign investors outside the export-processing zones have been established. These developments are relevant not only to China's foreign trade but also to foreign investment in China, a topic to be treated in Section 8.7.

8.6 PROBLEMS WITH CHINA'S FOREIGN TRADE

While China's foreign trade has expanded greatly since 1979, there are several problems associated with it which have been discussed in the Chinese literature, an example being the articles on pages 1–2 of the August 22, 1983, issue of the *World Economic Herald,* a weekly journal in Chinese published in Shanghai and edited jointly by the Chinese World Economic Association and the Institute of World Economics of the Shanghai Academy of Social Science.

The first problem is how to decide what to import and what to export. In China, where imports and exports are subject to government direction to a large extent, by what means does the government decide what and how much to import and to export? In the preceding section we quoted from an article by Zhang Peiji (1982) of the Ministry of Foreign Trade indicating that imports are a part of the overall planning of production and investment. Foreign consumer and producer goods are depended upon to satisfy the needs of consumption and capital accumulation. The principles of planning are discussed in Sections 2.1 and 2.2, and we have nothing to add here.

A difficult question concerns the choice of the kinds and quantities of exports to pay for the imports. Chinese government officials have some awareness of the principle of comparative advantage, as evidenced by their choice of labor-intensive products for export, such as handicraft products. Further study is required to establish whether officials violate this principle by increasing the export of certain machinery and machine tools produced by skilled labor and technicians in China. One guideline that they sometimes use in choosing a commodity for export is the ratio of the cost of the product in RMB to the net revenue from the product in a foreign currency, typically U.S. dollars. If this "RMB cost per dollar" is 2.2, for example, it takes 2.2 yuan to earn a dollar of foreign exchange. If the exchange rate is 2.0, for example, this product is considered a poor candidate for export because it takes more RMB to exchange one dollar by exporting than by currency exchanging. Of course, whether the official exchange rate should serve as the cutoff point for the use of this ratio depends on whether the rate truly reflects the purchasing power of one dollar relative to that of one yuan RMB. If the purchasing power (in terms of internationally traded goods) of one dollar is in fact 3 times that of one RMB, while the official exchange rate is only 2, it would be worthwhile to export a commodity with a ratio 2.2 for the "RMB cost per dollar." However, the most serious problem with using this ratio arises from the fact that the relative cost figures often do not reflect the relative tradeoff possibilities or the marginal rates of substitution in production because of government regulation of prices. Prices of certain agricultural products, cost of labor, and cost of using land are set too low. This would affect the numerator in the above ratio. In practice, the ratio is used merely as a guide and not as the sole determinant of a commodity for export, but no better criteria are available.

The second problem is that many exporting enterprises continue to expand their exports even when they are operating at a loss. They often compete with other Chinese exporting firms by lowering their prices or giving special commissions or kickbacks to foreign agents for handling their products, resulting in high ratios of RMB cost per dollar earned or in actual losses in their operations. While the Chinese government sets official export prices and guidelines for commission rates to foreign agents, the provincial exporting companies have charged lower prices and have given higher commission rates as well as other kickbacks. The losses incurred in exports amount to selling products below cost to benefit foreign consumers.

The third problem is how to determine an appropriate exchange rate or set of exchange rates. The official exchange rate of RMB in terms of U.S. dollars has declined since 1980, or the exchange rate of one U.S. dollar in terms of RMB has gone up. The latter rate was approximately 1.5 in 1980, 1.7 in 1981, 1.9 in 1982, and 1.97 in 1983. Thus, from 1980 to 1983 the RMB was steadily devalued relative to the U.S. dollar. Ordinarily, the devaluation of a country's currency has the effect of increasing its exports and decreasing its imports, because it makes that country's products cheaper to foreigners and makes foreign goods more expensive to its own citizens. If the elasticity of demand in the world market for that country's exports is larger than one, as is ordinarily the case because there are close substitutes for these products in the world market, increasing the quantity of exports (at a lower price in foreign exchange) will lead to a larger total revenue in foreign exchange. Whatever the elasticity of demand in the domestic market for imports is, increasing the domestic prices of imports due to devaluation (given constant prices of these products in the world market) will lead to a reduction in the total quantities purchased at home and thus in the total expenditures for exports in foreign exchange. Therefore, a devaluation of a country's currency will tend to increase a trade surplus or to reduce a trade deficit.

In the case of China, the steady devaluation between 1980 and 1983 was in terms of U.S. dollars, while the U.S. dollar was itself appreciating in terms of some other major currencies. The Chinese RMB was not necessarily devalued in terms of these currencies. Be that as it may, it is interesting to note that China ran a trade deficit (with the dollar value of its imports higher than that of its exports) of $1.14 billion U.S. in 1978, $2.01 billion in 1979, $1.28 billion in 1980, a trade surplus of $1.41 billion in 1981, $4.7 billion in 1982 (*Chinese Statistical Abstract, 1983,* p. 74), and a likely trade deficit in 1983. The devaluation of the RMB in 1981 and 1982 contributed to the trade surpluses in these two years. The Chinese government probably devalued the RMB to correct the trade deficits from 1978 to 1980. (Not only the official exchange rate of the Chinese currency was devalued. Since 1981 some exporters have been able to get 2.8 yuan for 1 U.S. dollar under the dual exchange rate system, which further encourages exports.) Trade surpluses and deficits are signs used by the government to adjust the official exchange rate of its currency. However, even when foreign trade is nearly balanced and the official exchange rate remains unchanged, with government control of imports and regulation of exports, there is no guarantee that at the official exchange rate one Chinese RMB has the same purchasing power in the world market as in China. For example, in 1983 800 RMB when exchanged for $400 was sufficient to buy a good color television set in the world market, but not sufficient to buy one in China. After overvaluing the RMB in terms of U.S. dollars, the Chinese government avoids a trade deficit by restricting imports. In so doing, it prevents Chinese consumers from enjoying the foreign consumer goods and Chinese producers from using the foreign producer goods by trading their own products according to the principle of comparative advantage.

Readers of Sections 8.2 to 8.4 understand how these problems are solved by market economies practicing free trade. First, the government has no difficulty in deciding what to import and what to export. As long as the marginal rate of substitution in production or the relative prices of two commodities at home are different from the relative prices in the world market (after transportation costs are absorbed), there is economic gain from trade and traders will automatically engage in trade to equalize the price ratios. Trade will stop when there will be no further gain. Government planning will require certain state enterprises to import foreign producer goods. However, to allow the state enterprises to purchase these goods cheaply by supplying them with undervalued foreign currencies, the government encourages inefficiency of these enterprises.

Second, in a market economy one need not be concerned with enterprises engaged in export expansion when the operations are unprofitable. They automatically stop producing for export if such operations become unprofitable. The reason Chinese enterprises allegedly continued to export their products at a loss must be that there were economic incentives for them to do so. These incentives may include the foreign exchange that the enterprises are allowed to retain and the special loans extended to exporting enterprises. If foreign exchange is actually worth more than its RMB equivalent obtained at the official exchange rate, a loss of the operation on paper may actually mean a profit if measured by the actual purchasing power of the foreign exchange retained. All special favorable treatments to exporters encourage the expansion of exports when the operations are apparently unprofitable on the accounting books. Furthermore, competition among Chinese exporters in the world market is not necessarily a bad thing if they produce in competitive conditions. American computer manufacturers compete with one another in the world market, as do Japanese automobile manufacturers. Competition in the world market ensures that domestic enterprises operate efficiently and that inefficient manufacturers cannot enter the world market, or even survive in the domestic market when world trade is free.

Third, as we have pointed out, the exchange rate is automatically determined in the market by the demand for and the supply of the currency in question, like the price of any commodity. We have witnessed how the exchange rate of a freely traded currency such as the Hong Kong dollar is determined daily or even hourly by the forces of demand and supply. Living in a free-trade area, the people of Hong Kong enjoy all the consumer goods produced in different parts of the world and pay for them by exporting products and performing services according to the principle of comparative advantage. Almost no government control of imports and exports is involved. There is no shortage of foreign exchange, and the Hong Kong government does not have to control the supply of foreign exchange. In fact, levying taxes at low rates is sufficient for the government of Hong Kong to earn substantial foreign exchanges for remittance to the British government. More funds, including foreign exchange, can be obtained by taxing a rich economy at low rates than by controlling a small amount of foreign exchanges earned by an unproductive economy.

This summary of how the problems of foreign trade are solved by market economies practicing free trade is intended to highlight the difficulties facing the Chinese or any economic planners who control imports, regulate exports, set official exchange rates differing from market rates, and set the prices of labor, land, capital, materials, and consumer goods to suit special planning purposes. Just as an understanding of the functioning of a market economy as set forth in Chapter 1 increases one's appreciation of the working of a centrally planned economy as described in Chapter 2, an understanding of the functioning of international trade as set forth in Sections 8.2 to 8.4 increases one's appreciation of the three problems of foreign trade facing the Chinese government. The problems associated with administrative decisions on economic affairs, as compared with decisions by market forces, are as real in the sphere of international trade as in domestic production and trade. Once resources are not priced by the competitive forces of demand and supply, it is difficult for any planner to make economically correct decisions concerning what to produce, how much to produce, and what and how much to export and import, not to speak of the need to provide proper incentives to the economic agents to carry out their tasks. The Chinese government has come to appreciate the usefulness of market forces in the regulation of the economy. It has instituted reforms to decentralize production for the domestic as well as the foreign market. As of 1984 it did not decontrol the prices of labor, land, many important products and materials, and the price of U.S. dollars (namely, the exchange rate). Accordingly, rational economic calculations could not be successfully carried out by enterprises engaged in production for domestic consumption, capital accumulation, and exports. This was the main hindrance to the achievement of economic efficiency in China.

One argument often advanced to justify import restrictions is the protection of infant domestic industries. The theory of comparative advantage discussed in Section 8.2 is based on a given technology. Comparative advantage changes as technology changes, as we pointed out in Section 8.3, through the import either of new technology or of some scarce factors required to use the technology. In the process of economic development and technological change, a country's comparative advantage changes. For example, Japan did not have a comparative advantage in producing automobiles in the 1960s but it did have such an advantage in the 1970s. While infant industries are being developed, some argue, they should be protected from foreign competition by tariffs or other restrictions on competing imports. This argument was advanced in Taiwan in the 1960s to protect a domestic automobile manufacturer from foreign competition. The cost of producing an automobile by the manufacturer was about two and a half times the world price. Such protection lasted for 15 years, and the production cost of this manufacturer was still about two times the world price. In the meantime, consumers in Taiwan incurred a great loss by paying more than two times the world price for their automobiles. The resources that they used up to pay for these expensive automobiles could have been used to purchase more than twice as many automobiles from abroad. In other words, the economy of Taiwan was using a very inefficient way of producing or acquiring its automobiles. By allowing free trade, it could have acquired twice as many automobiles, or it could have paid only half as much for the automobiles it actually acquired. In many developed countries, import restrictions have been imposed to protect not infant industries, but declining industries that no longer produce at a comparative advantage. Such restrictions may be good for the owners and workers of those industries, but they are bad in general for the consumers of the countries concerned. See Baldwin (1969) for a criticism of the infant-industry argument.

In mainland China, importation of many consumer products such as cameras, television sets, stereos, and video equipment is restricted. Consumers lose by not being able to buy these products. To protect domestic infant industries is not the only argument justifying this policy. The government may decide which products consumers should consume and which products are luxury items consumers should not consume. Furthermore, the purchase of foreign consumer goods uses up valuable foreign exchanges, which should be saved for more important consumer items and for capital accumulation. The last argument is not easy to justify if the principle of comparative advantage is understood. If a consumer decides to buy a foreign-made color television set (assuming it can be imported freely) for $380, he has to give up the consumption of $380 worth of other resources to acquire it. Under free trade, the latter resources could be traded in the world market for $380 U.S. and there should be no problem of the shortage of foreign exchanges. One might imagine that the resources the consumer gives up consist of two domestic black-and-white television sets that could not be exchanged for $380 in the world market. In that case, given the exchange rate of RMB to be market-determined, the conclusion must be that the two domestic television sets are overpriced at home and China should not produce them. Under free trade and market-determined exchange rates, there should be no shortage of U.S. dollars in China. Any (internationally traded) good in China selling for 1 RMB must be worth approximately its U.S. dollar equivalent in the world market. Trade is determined by comparative advantages. The exchange rates will adjust so that the relative supply of and demand for U.S. dollars and Chinese RMB will be equal.

The main reason it is difficult to develop infant industries by import restrictions is the lack of competition. Without foreign competition, the protected domestic producers have no incentive to improve their products or change their technology. In the meantime, the consumers are forced to buy inferior products at higher prices than necessary. To develop an infant industry, if such an industry can be identified, a better method than import restriction is to provide the enterprises of that industry with subsidies of fixed and declining amounts during a specified period—of, say, 5 years. This alternative method has several advantages over imposing import restrictions. First, consumers would not be deprived of the better and cheaper foreign products. Second, domestic producers would have incentives to improve because of foreign competition. The availability of good-quality foreign products in the home market would also have a demonstration effect, stimulating domestic manufacturers to produce better products. One reason the opening of China in the late 1970s is beneficial to China's economic development is that it enables Chinese planners and managers to see what goes on in the outside world. Third, through the subsidies the government knows exactly the cost involved in helping to develop the industry concerned. By imposing import restrictions, the government does not know this cost and therefore may not care about the economic loss involved; only the consumers suffer. Knowing the cost involved and having to pay for it from its own budget would enable the government to choose a sound policy for developing infant industry and would help to prevent an inefficient industry from being protected for an extended period.

To say that subsidies of fixed amounts and durations are better than import restrictions for the purpose of developing infant industries is not to say that it is easy for the government to identify a promising industry to develop. A well-trained staff is required to identify such industries and to devise appropriate means of continually upgrading their technologies. The development of new industries and the upgrading of existing industries are related to the subject of foreign investment, to be discussed in the next section. One important principle in carrying out these tasks is that the central government should not set up and run monopolies in these industries. The central government can promote the development of an industry by various means, including providing subsidies and technical assistance in the form of training programs to its managerial, technical, and production staff. It can even set up new enterprises in the industry, but to prevent enterprises at the provincial and local levels and those established under collective ownership to compete would be harmful to the development of the industry. Most important of all, in the process of industrial development, prices should be unregulated, so that accurate cost and benefit calculations can be performed by state-owned and collectively owned enterprises and by consumers and workers to ensure economic efficiency.

8.7 FOREIGN INVESTMENT IN CHINA

Figures 8.1 and 8.2 show that through foreign trade a country can obtain its combinations of outputs beyond the boundary of its production transformation curve. Section 8.3 explained that by importing capital and new technology, a country can extend the production transformation curve itself. In physical terms, foreign investment takes the form of import of capital goods and technology to China. In money terms, foreign exchanges flow to China to pay for the associated imported goods and services from the foreign personnel. The history of capital inflows to China since 1949 has been summarized in an article by the Research Department of China's Foreign Investment Commission, "China's Absorption of Foreign Investment" (1982).

This history began in February 1950, when the governments of the People's Republic of China and the Soviet Union signed an agreement for the latter to provide the former with a long-term loan of 7.4 billion old rubles (equivalent to $1.9 billion U.S.) at a 2.5 percent annual interest rate. The loan helped finance some major projects in the first Five-Year Plan. In the early 1960s, Soviet aid ceased, and China paid back the principal and interest of the loan by 1965. Beginning in the early 1960s, China turned to Japan and some Western countries for capital equipment and technology, paying for them partly by deferred payment. In 1979 China adopted an open-door economic policy. The Foreign Investment Control Commission was established in the State Council and was given the responsibility of working out, in consultation with other relevant departments, the policy and law on foreign investment, formulating regulations on joint ventures, organizing departments to review and approve the agreements, contracts, and rules governing joint ventures, and coordinating the use of foreign funds by various departments and localities.

The article by the Foreign Investment Commission (1982, pp. 627–630) lists and describes six forms of foreign investment. The first is foreign loans. By the end of 1979, foreign loan agreements signed between the Bank of China and foreign countries totaled $27.6 billion U.S., of which $11.8 billion was in the form of export credits extended by Britain, France, Italy, Canada, Sweden, Australia, and Belgium. Most of the export credits were not used. In 1980 China reached agreements on loans with the governments of Japan and Belgium. The former was to finance six projects for the construction of three railroads, two ports, and a hydroelectric power station. The latter was an interest-free 30-year loan of $31.5 million U.S. to purchase power-generating equipment.

The second form of foreign investment is joint ventures. By the end of 1980, 20 joint-venture enterprises had been approved by the Chinese government, with investments totaling $210 million U.S. and some $170 million from overseas Chinese. They include 13 industrial enterprises, 3 hotels, 1 catering company, 2 service enterprises, and 1 pig farm. In 1980, 12 such enterprises went into operation. Chang (1982) describes the rules governing joint ventures and more facts concerning them.

The third area is compensatory trade and cooperative management. The purpose is to process imported materials and assemble imported parts for the purpose of exports. The imported materials and parts are exempt from tariffs, and the operations are exempt from industrial and commercial taxes. In 1980, 205 compensatory trade items were transacted and some 300 cooperative management projects had been approved.

The fourth area is joint exploration and exploitation of offshore oil. In 1980 China signed nine agreements for maritime geophysical surveys in the South China Sea, the southern Yellow Sea, and Bohai Bay with over 40 oil companies from the United States, Britain, France, and Italy. By the end of 1980, four contracts had been signed for joint prospecting and exploitation of offshore oil.

The fifth form of foreign investment is special economic zones, a subject alluded to in Section 8.5. In these zones foreign enterprises and individuals and overseas Chinese are encouraged to invest in or to establish joint-venture enterprises in the fields of industry, agriculture, commerce, tourism, housing construction, and other services. In August 1980 the Standing Committee of the Fifth National People's Congress approved the "Regulations on Special Economic Zones in Guangdong Province." A Special Zone Administration was established.

The sixth area is investment through the China International Trust and Investment Corporation (CITIC), established in 1979 to channel, absorb, and use foreign capital, to import advanced technology and equipment, and to run joint ventures with foreign firms. By the end of 1980, four projects financed by CITIC with foreign capital accounted for a total investment of $16 million U.S.

The article by the Foreign Investment Commission (1982, p. 630) states the priorities of using foreign capital as follows:

> During the early 1980's, we will give priority to use of foreign funds in the following sectors: (1) development of crude oil, coal and electricity; (2) construction of railways,

harbours, telecommunications and infrastructure in urban areas and industrial zones; (3) small and medium-sized projects (which require small investments, yield rapid economic results and help expand exports) in textile and light industries, building-materials, chemical, metallurgical, machine-building and electronic industries and tourism; and (4) technical transformation of existing enterprises.

The priorities in using foreign investment should be understood in the context of China's planned economy. Economic planning affects the industries, the sectors, and the parts of the economic infrastructure to which capital formation by domestic or foreign sources will be directed.

How rapidly foreign investment will expand in China depends on the demand for and supply of foreign investment. The demand is affected by the rate of capital formation in China and the ability of China to absorb foreign capital. Foreign investment is a part of capital formation. Even though the capital is provided by foreign sources, a foreign loan has to be repaid eventually by domestic savings, and a foreign investment creates future flows of goods from China through its earnings. China's ability to absorb foreign capital depends on the availability of resources in China that are complementary to the imported capital goods in production. A new machine may require technicians and certain skilled workers to operate. Operation of a computer requires skilled maintenance personnel, programmers, and users. It takes time to acquire these complementary inputs. The import of foreign capital goods at a higher rate than can be supported by the available complementary goods would not be economically efficient.

On the supply side, foreign investors have to consider the profitability of their investments. Up to the early 1980s, there were several problems with which foreigners had to contend when considering investing in China. First, the legal system in China had yet to be modified and made known to foreign investors to give them sufficient familiarity with and confidence in the system to consider investing. Second, business practices in China had to be improved. Some of the problematical practices were those of the Chinese government bureaucrats, who ran industrial enterprises inefficiently and were difficult to work with. Third, there was the Chinese government bureaucracy itself, which had to approve all contracts related to joint ventures, compensatory trade, and cooperative managements. It was not unusual for a government bureaucrat to violate a contract. For example, a foreign investor operating a hotel in Peking was promised a given percentage of earnings in foreign exchange to be remitted abroad; when the hotel turned out to be extremely profitable, the percentage was reduced. Fourth, without a free market for many important materials, it was difficult to operate an industrial enterprise in China using domestic or foreign capital. Sixth, the authority of the management, foreign or domestic, over the employees was limited. Wage rates were fixed by the government. There were regulations concerning job security, making it difficult for the management to discharge workers.

When the policy of expanding foreign investments was announced in 1979, many potential investors were enthusiastic and had high hopes of doing a lot of business in China. In the two to three years following, some of them were disappointed by the problems just mentioned, but foreign investment continued to take place in China at a moderate rate. The rate of foreign investment in China in the 1980s depends partly on how fast these problems can be overcome.

8.8   FOREIGN TRADE AND INVESTMENT IN A MACROECONOMIC MODEL

In this chapter so far, we have discussed foreign trade and investment mainly from the microeconomic point of view. The macroeconomic effects of foreign trade can be briefly indicated by amending the macroeconomic model of equations 6.75 to incorporate additional variables and equations related to foreign trade in the following way.

First, equation 1 of 6.75 defining national income is changed to read

$$y_t = c_t + j_{1t} + j_{2t} + ex_t - im_t \tag{8.4}$$

where ex_t and im_t denoted exports and imports in physical terms, respectively. Second, the demand for imports can be explained approximately by real national income itself. Since imports consist of consumer goods and different investment goods, it may be more accurate to assume im_t to be a function of c_t, j_{1t}, and j_{2t} separately. Thus we add a new import equation.

$$im_t = \beta_0 + \beta_1 c_t + \beta_2 j_{1t} + \beta_3 j_{2t} \tag{8.5}$$

This assumption is not in conflict with the fact that Chinese imports were determined by government planning. It merely says that in calculating the import requirement for the economy, the economic planners had to consider the amounts of total consumption and total investments.

Third, exports can be assumed to be a function of the total real income of the countries importing from China and the relative price of Chinese goods to other goods available in the world market. Let the total real income of the countries buying Chinese goods be denoted by z_t. The relative price of Chinese exports in the world market is measured by

$$px_t = \frac{P_t}{Q_t} f_t$$

where P_t is the Chinese price index (more accurately, of Chinese exports only), Q_t is a world price index in U.S. dollars, and f_t is the exchange rate of RMB in terms of U.S. dollars. If P_t and Q_t were fixed, an increase in f_t would make Chinese exports more expensive in the world market. If f_t were fixed, an increase in the ratio P_t/Q_t would make Chinese exports more expensive. The export equation is

$$ex_t = \rho_o + \rho_1 z_t + \rho_2 px_t \tag{8.6}$$

Any exogenous change, such as a change in the world income z_t, would affect the export variable ex_t through equation 8.6. This in turn will have a multiplier effect on Chinese national income, as explained in Sections 6.3 and 6.5, following equations 6.22 and 6.68. (See Problem 15.) We have added two equations, 8.5 and 8.6, to explain the two new endogenous variables im_t and ex_t. We assume f_t to be determined by the Chinese government, and z_t and Q_t are exogenously given.

To incorporate foreign investment into our model, consider the case of a foreign company establishing itself in a special economic zone. It brings in its own machinery, buys tax-free imported materials, and processes them with Chinese labor to manufacture certain products for export. If the capital stock and investment variables in our model refer to capital stock and investment belonging to the Chinese, the variables

k_t and j_t will not be affected by this foreign investment. The investment will increase the demand for labor in China and will accordingly raise the wage rate if the latter is allowed to be influenced by market forces—government regulation of the wage rate notwithstanding, since the government determines wages partly according to market conditions. However, our model is not detailed enough to have a demand-for-labor equation. One way to incorporate the above investment project into our model is to treat the output of the Chinese laborers employed by this foreign company and other outputs of this nature as an additional component of y_t. This component can be assumed to be a linear function of the stock of foreign capital in China, and the stock of foreign capital accumulates by additional foreign investment according to an equation similar to equation 6.4.

Alternatively, if we choose to specify a model to explain Chinese gross or net *domestic product* rather than national income, the output and capital stock variables should include what is produced or installed in China even when owned by foreigners. We can include foreign investment as additional variables to be added to the right-hand sides of investment equations 4 and 6 of 6.75. Additional equations are required to explain these two components of foreign investment. Of course, foreign investment has other effects, such as improving the skills of Chinese management personnel and laborers, but the incorporation of such effects requires a different type of model from the one constructed in Chapter 6 to study certain basic macroeconomic relations.

The model 6.75 was presented to explain a few major macroeconomic variables, including aggregate consumption, aggregate investment, national income, and the price level, to which we have now added imports and exports. Different economic models are constructed to serve different purposes. For example, an econometric model different from 6.75 can be constructed to help solve the basic allocative problems facing the Chinese economic planners. These problems include the determination of what fractions of total national output are to be devoted to current consumption and investment, how total investment is to be distributed among the major industries in the state sector, and how much each industry is to produce in order to satisfy the needs of consumption and investment. In Chow (1982), I have outlined such a model, which consists of four parts, a dynamic input-output model, a set of final demand equations, a set of equations to determine income and prices, and a set of equations to determine government revenues and expenditures. I have also explained how optimal control methods as expounded in Chow (1975, 1981) can be used in conjunction with such a model to solve the basic allocative problems facing the Chinese economic planners. Econometric modeling and optimal control methods are technical subjects dealing with how economic planning should be done. They are beyond the scope of the present book, which is concerned mainly with explaining how the Chinese economy actually works.

In this chapter we have studied only a few selected aspects of China's foreign trade and investment. The theory of foreign trade is extensive and is beyond the scope of this book. The history of foreign investment in China before the Second World War has not been touched upon at all. Interested readers are referred to Remer (1933). For a study of the effects of exports on economic growth with reference to Taiwan, see Kuo (1983, Chapter 7). Reynolds (1983) employs a simple model to study the relationship between foreign trade and China's domestic economy from 1978 to 1981 and the role of technology acquisition. Articles by the Export and Import Affairs Administration

Commission (1982) and by Wei (1982) appearing in the *Almanac of China's Economy, 1981,* deal with China's importation of technology and with China's aid to other developing countries, respectively.

PROBLEMS

1. Let A in Figure 8.1 be the production transformation curve of a country and let its social welfare function be $u = x_1 x_2$, where x_1 and x_2 represent the quantities of rice and cloth, respectively. Show that the point $a = (50,5)$ is obtained by maximizing u subject to the production constraint A.

2. In place of Figure 8.1, use an Edgeworth diagram as given in Figure 1.1 to show the equilibrium points of countries A and B with and without international trade. Let the origin (0,0) for country B be the point at the upper right corner of the diagram. Show the contract curve as defined at the end of Section 1.2, assuming the utility function for both countries to be $u = x_1 x_2$. Without assuming this utility function, show graphically how the final equilibrium with international trade may be at a point different from the center of the diagram.

3. Modify the technology given in Table 8.3 by assuming that in addition to the labor and capital inputs specified, processes 1 and 2 require 1 and 5 units of managerial personnel, respectively. Assume that there are 60 units of managerial personnel available. Specify mathematically and draw the production transformation curve. Draw the production transformation curve assuming the supply of managerial personnel to be 40 units instead.

4. Assume the technology of Table 8.3 for both countries A and B. Let the supplies of labor and capital, respectively, be 180 and 50 for country A and 100 and 80 for country B. Draw the production transformation curves for countries A and B. Assuming the relative price of rice to cloth in the world market to be 12, draw the transformation curves for countries A and B, allowing for the possibility of trade. Using an Edgeworth diagram and a utility function $u = x_1 x_2$ for each country, show graphically the equilibrium relative price of rice to cloth, the outputs of rice and cloth in each country, and the quantities of country A's export of rice to and import of cloth from country B.

5. What are the main differences between the Cobb-Douglas production function and the input coefficient matrix as exemplified in Table 8.4 as alternative means to specify a technology?

6. How is a production transformation curve derived from a Cobb-Douglas production function, and from a coefficient matrix as given in Table 2.4?

7. What is meant by comparative advantage? Why does a country gain by international trade?

8. It has been suggested that the Chinese government should restrict the import of consumer goods such as color television sets in order to save the valuable foreign exchanges for more important uses. Do you agree? Explain.

9. Explain the infant-industry argument for the restriction of imports. Is it justified? Why?

10. By what principles does the Chinese government select its exports? Can you suggest better ways to determine China's exports?

11. How would the foreign exchange rate of RMB in terms of U.S. dollars be determined in a free market? Explain the market mechanism that determines it.

12. In 1981 and 1982 China devalued the exchange rate of RMB in terms of U.S. dollars. In these two years China ran a trade surplus. Is there a relation between these two facts? Explain.

13. Explain the role of foreign investment in the economic development of China.

14. Appraise China's policy toward foreign investment, including the steps it takes to encourage foreign investment. What other steps would you suggest?

15. How would you analyze the effects of exports on national income using a macroeconomic model? Show how the multiplier effect can be calculated using the revised version of model 6.75 suggested in Section 8.8.

16. Can you suggest ways to incorporate foreign investment in a macroeconomic model in addition to those suggested in Section 8.8?

REFERENCES

Baldwin, R. E. 1969. The case against infant-industry tariff protection. *Journal of Political Economy* 77:295–305.

Chang, Jung-Feng. 1982. The joint venture system in Communist China: Problems and prospects. Economic Paper No. 2. Taipei: Chung-Hua Institution for Economic Research.

Chinese State Statistics Bureau. 1982. *Statistical yearbook of China, 1981.* Hong Kong: Hong Kong Economic Review Publishing House.

Chow, G. C. 1975. *Analysis and control of dynamic economic systems.* New York: Wiley.

———. 1981. *Econometric analysis by control methods.* New York: Wiley.

———. 1982. Outline of an econometric model for Chinese economic planning. *Journal of Economic Dynamics and Control* 4:171–190.

Customs General Administration. 1982. China's customs service. In Economic Research Center, State Council of the People's Republic of China, *Almanac of China's economy, 1981.* Hong Kong: Modern Cultural Company Limited. Pp. 635–642.

Export and Import Affairs Administrative Commission. 1982. China's importation of technology. In Economic Research Center, *Almanac of China's economy, 1981,* pp. 625–626.

Foreign Investment Commission. 1982. China's absorption of foreign investment. In Economic Research Center, *Almanac of China's economy, 1981,* pp. 627–630.

Heckscher, E. 1919. The effect of foreign trade on the distribution of income. *Economisk Tidskrift* 21. Reprinted as Chapter 13 of *Readings in the theory of international trade,* American Economic Association ed. Philadelphia: Blakiston, 1949.

Kenen, P. B. 1984. *The international economy.* Englewood Cliffs, N. J.: Prentice-Hall.

Koopmans, T. C. ed. 1951. *Activity analysis of production and allocation.* New York: Wiley.

Kuo, Shirley W. Y. 1983. *The Taiwan economy in transition.* Boulder, Colo.: Westview Press.

Li, K. T. 1976. A report on the establishment of the Kaohsiung export processing zone. Chapter 20 of *The experience of dynamic economic growth on Taiwan.* Taipei: Mei Ya Publications.

Ohlin, B. 1933. *Interregional and international trade.* Cambridge, Mass.: Harvard University Press.

Remer, C. F. 1933. *Foreign investment in China.* New York: Macmillan.

Reynolds, B. L. 1983. Economic reforms and external imbalance in China, 1978–81. *American Economic Review* 73, No. 2:325–328.

Wei, Jing. 1982. China's aid in development projects to other countries. In Economic Research Center, *Almanac of China's economy, 1981,* pp. 631–634.

Yen, Tzung-Ta. 1982. A study of export performance in mainland China (in Chinese). Economic Paper No. 3. Taipei: Chung-Hua Institution for Economic Research.

Zhang Peiji. 1982. Growth of China's foreign trade. In Economic Research Center, *Almanac of China's economy, 1981,* pp. 621–624.

INDEX